A SELECTED EDITION OF W. D. HOWELLS

Volume 32

Literary Friends and Acquaintance

W. D. HOWELLS

Literary Friends and Acquaintance

A Personal Retrospect of American Authorship

Edited by

David F. Hiatt and Edwin H. Cady

EDWIN H. CADY, GENERAL EDITOR
RONALD GOTTESMAN, TEXTUAL EDITOR
DAVID J. NORDLOH AND THOMAS WORTHAM
ASSOCIATE TEXTUAL EDITORS

INDIANA UNIVERSITY PRESS

Bloomington and London

1968

Acknowledgments

For indispensable support in money and morale the editors of this volume and the Howells Edition Center gladly express their gratitude to Barnaby C. Keeney and the National Endowment for the Humanities; to William M. Gibson and the Center for Editions of American Authors, Modern Language Association of America; to Elvis J. Stahr, President, and Joseph L. Sutton, Dean of Faculties, Indiana University; to Herman B Wells and the Indiana University Foundation; and to William White Howells and the Heirs of W. D. Howells.

David Tobin, Ann Hofstra, and Jane C. Scarola contributed substantially to the completion of the volume. Eleanor Hiatt and Norma Cady deserve the usual wifely tributes and much more: they worked hard and effectively.

Our thanks are also extended, for special help, to:

George Arms, University of New Mexico
William H. Bond, Houghton Library, Harvard University
Cecil K. Byrd, Indiana University Library
William Cagle, Lilly Library, Indiana University
Charles E. Feinberg, Detroit, Michigan
Judith Hahn, Carroll College Library
Carolyn Jakeman, Houghton Library, Harvard University
Watt P. Marchman, Rutherford B. Hayes Memorial Library
James B. Meriwether, University of South Carolina
Mark Musa, Indiana University
Walter T. K. Nugent, Indiana University
David Randall, Lilly Library, Indiana University
Anthony Shipps, Indiana University Library
Paul Starr, Carroll College Library
Bergliot Stephenson, Carroll College Library
Alene Lowe White, Western Reserve Historical Society

Contents

Illustrations

Introduction

AT the age of nine, with almost no schooling except in his father's pioneer print shop, Howells undertook to teach himself Spanish and prepare a biography of Cervantes. On his deathbed, in 1920, he was writing of "The American James." The lives of writers perpetually engaged his curiosity—both the great dead and the "literary friends and acquaintance" he cultivated all his life. Throughout his career he edited, introduced, reviewed, and criticized literary memoirs. The genre fascinated him.

Given his interest in the literary memoir, Howells acquired extraordinary materials for writing it from his extraordinary capacity for friendship with other authors. Summing up at seventy-five, he said:

> ... if I missed the personal acquaintance of Cooper and Irving and Poe and Prescott I was personally acquainted with all the others in whom the story of American literature sums itself. I knew Hawthorne and Emerson and Walt Whitman; I knew Longfellow and Holmes and Whittier and Lowell; I knew Bryant and Bancroft and Motley; I knew Harriet Beecher Stowe and Julia Ward Howe; I knew Artemus Ward and Stockton and Mark Twain; I knew Parkman and Fiske.[1]

The list is startling but it was too modest, intended to be symbolic, not exhaustive, and retrospective, not modern.

Whether Howells missed Melville or not, he knew Thoreau, Jewett, Freeman, William and Henry James, De Forest, Cable, Garland, Wister, Crane, Norris, Fuller, Tarkington, Herrick, Whitlock, Frost—American authors of both sexes, every region, and each generation from 1860 to 1920. He published, edited,

---

1. In "A Tribute to William Dean Howells," *Harper's Weekly*, LVI (9 March 1912), 28.

advised, joked and confided with, defended, recruited, reviewed, read manuscript and proofs for, corresponded with and saw scores of writers. There was every reason he should ask, rhetorically yet seriously, of Charles Eliot Norton in 1892: "Why, in fact, should not I make a Personal History of American Literature for the thirty years since I have been a part of it?"[2]

I

Howells himself never quite liked the title of what became *Literary Friends and Acquaintance*, wishing, as he said, "long too late" that he had called it *Literary Friends and Neighbors*.[3] If one prefers the idea more emphasized in the full title of the book— "A Personal Retrospect of American Authorship"—and nicely put in the title implied to Norton, that is finally to regret that Howells did not in fact finish writing a "Personal History of American Literature." He was writing too much else in his best memoiristic period: "half a dozen novels, as many more novelettes and shorter stories, with essays and criticisms and verses...."[4] In two senses he left the work incomplete, beginning with a series of papers sporadically produced between 1894 and 1900.

The provenience of these literary memoirs of the nineties was complex. The years 1888–1890 had been black for Howells. His involvement in the fate of the Haymarket Anarchists and then the death of his daughter Winifred harrowed his psyche. A deepening creativity brought him to the tragic vision of *A Hazard of New Fortunes*, *The Shadow of a Dream*, and *Stops of Various Quills*. And something about those developments opened an autobiographical vein in his imagination. Among other things, he published *A Boy's Town* (1890), *My Year in a Log Cabin* (1893), and *My Literary Passions* (1895).

The sources of this autobiographical impulse were, however,

2. *Life in Letters of William Dean Howells*, ed. Mildred Howells (Garden City, N.Y., 1928), II, 27.
3. "Bibliographical," *Literary Friends and Acquaintance*, p. 4.
4. *Idem.*

not only psychic. Howells in 1891 terminated his contract with the Harpers and vacated his magazine column, "The Editor's Study." Probing for ways to lure him back, H. M. Alden dickered with him about placing literary reminiscences in the "Study" or, later, in a new "department" to be called, "say, Editor's Table-Talk."[5] After Howells declined to resume the yoke of a department and contract, Alden proposed to negotiate a "general plan of your Personal Studies of American Literary History."[6] Howells at first intended, as he confided to Norton, "reminiscences of literary life in Cambridge and Boston, just as I wish. The papers will be separable and will follow each other irregularly, beginning some time next year; and they will form a sort of conspect of twenty-five years of our literature, tale quale fu."[7]

As they worked out, the papers became a mixed set. "My First Visit to New England" appeared in *Harper's Monthly*, May–August 1894; "First Impressions of Literary New York," June 1895; "Roundabout to Boston," August 1895; "Literary Boston Thirty Years Ago," November 1895. In 1896 came the separate pieces on Holmes and Longfellow. Then there was a hiatus until 1900 and the difficult piece on Lowell, which Alden finally declined and *Scribner's* published, September 1900. Finally, "Some Literary Memories of Cambridge," *Harper's*, November 1900, appeared more or less simultaneously with the book.

Though the scenes and insights of Howells' memoir have become famous, his mere gathering of magazine pieces could not be the same as shaping out a well-realized book. It was not the fashion of that decenter day to publish concerning one's living friends. As a long career stretched into its fourth and fifth decades, however, friends died and it was natural for Howells to celebrate them. When the second edition of *Literary Friends and Acquaintance* was published in 1910, it had been enriched by the addition of

5. Alden to WDH, 1 September 1891; 26 September 1892. MSS at Houghton Library, Harvard University. Quoted by permission of the Harvard College Library.
6. Alden to WDH, 31 January 1893. MS at Houghton Library.
7. WDH to Norton, 26 February 1893. MS at Houghton Library.

an essay on Bret Harte and by that jewel of its genre, *My Mark Twain*.

The added 117 pages did not, however, begin to constitute the entirety of what Howells wrote but never collected towards his potential personal history of American literature. Not only did he write a number of other, or further, and very interesting accounts of his experiences with American writers, he made clear in various reviews, columns, and essays the fact that he possessed insights into the problems and processes of American literary history, insights still valid, still suggestive. But there is authority in the argument that the book we have is in fact the only book of its kind which Howells chose to make. Aladdin's palace, lacking far more than a casement, unfinished must remain.

II

In June of 1900, the strain of finishing *Literary Friends and Acquaintance* wearied Howells out. He wrote to Aldrich:

> In these days I seem to be all autobiography; but thank heaven I have done my reminiscences of literary Cambridge and Boston, and they are to be booked for oblivion next fall. How gladly I would never speak of myself again! But it's somehow always being tormented out of me, in spite of the small pleasure and pride the past gives me. "It's so damned humiliating," as Mark Twain once said of *his* past.[8]

His "pleasure and pride" in the book were not to be "small," however; it won private and public acclaim from the start. Norton, before the printing of the Lowell material, wrote that it gave him "extraordinary pleasure," that "the paper on Lowell as it now stands is altogether as it should be, and the summing up at the end forms a beautiful close." He was delighted with the account of himself in "Cambridge Neighbors":

> Your kind words incline me to sing *Nunc dimittis*. Sweeter, kinder, more idealizing words were never written, and they are dear to me because of the affection which inspires them, and which,

---

8. *Life in Letters*, II, 129.

I trust, may be to others their justification. It is not the praise, but the love from which it springs that I care for, and by and by when you and I are only memories, I want no other record than "He was loved by some of the best of men."[9]

The work brought warm letters from Aldrich, Sylvester Baxter, Clarence Darrow, Annie Fields, Mrs. Francis J. Child, and others less well known. A note from William James, upon reading "Cambridge Neighbors," characterized both the writer and the general private praise:

Over and over again this year I have been wondering how & where it was with you and yours, and wishing to send you a word of affectionate greeting, but after reading your article on Cambridge people in the 70s in a recent Harper's monthly, the cup runneth over. It is exquisitely felt & done, and the photografs bring back the dead. Nothing could be better than your characterization of my lamented Sire, and what you write of Boyesen, whom I barely saw, makes me wish now that I had known him better. You haven't laid it on thick enough on Child, though: That man's entity is my strongest reason for believing in an immortal soul. The whole article shows your inimitable way of apprehending, feeling and reproducing the realities you meet with, earnest and tender, yet also playful and free.[10]

Public reception of *Literary Friends and Acquaintance*, save for some Anglo-American stress in an unsigned *Athenaeum* review (No. 3840, 1 June 1901, pp. 686–687), proved essentially favorable, often enthusiastic. Reviving the old Realism War, the *Athenaeum* sneered that Howells was always a "hero-worshipper of great writers, provided they were his fellow-countrymen" and complained that Howells "seems to go out of his way to write unpleasantly about us."

E. C. Stedman (*Book Buyer*, XXI, 1900, 549–556) shared the *Athenaeum*'s concern about the absence of an index, but otherwise generally rejoiced:

9. Norton to WDH, 13 February, 8 March, 13 March 1900. MSS at Houghton Library.
10. William James to WDH, 16 November 1900. MS at Houghton Library.

I recall his estimate of Longfellow's genius, written not so long ago, which some of us thought too high. Yet it would be hard to impugn the closing statement of the beautiful chapter on "The White Mr. Longfellow,"—a chapter that, with those on Holmes and Lowell, belongs to the culminative portion of this retrospect. The pupil had lived to be one of the judges of the fragmentary reliquiæ of the dead poet, and so gave his voice for the publication of all that had any completeness, since "in every one there was a touch of his exquisite art, the grace of his most exquisite spirit." One felt that "the art of Longfellow held out to the end with no touch of decay in it, and that it equalled the art of any other poet of his time. It knew when to give itself, and more and more it knew when to withhold itself." Howells still is "sure that with Tennyson and Browning Longfellow shared in the expression of an age which more completely than any former age got itself said by its poets."

Somewhat defensive regarding New York, Stedman suggested that young Howells had arrived there at a bad time, which accounted for the ironies of "My Impressions of Literary New York." The review was richly illustrated, reproducing twelve of the illustrations from the book. Stedman's own literary faith echoed quietly from the concluding paragraph:

Mr. Howells' unswerving fidelity to truth is his master-trait, and this quality affords a clue to the determination of his own career. Though a member in full standing of the most attractive group, exemplifying culture and the labor poets delight in, which this country has known,—that of Longfellow and his Dante circle,—his natural evolution, unstayed by the exquisite Academic influences, made him a realist in imaginative fiction, and the head of our native school. That young D'Artagnan of the pen,—who must forgive this reversion to the dearest hero of the romanticists—well and fairly won his marshal's baton, and to our good fortune has lived, unlike the King's Musketeer, to regild it on successive fields.

Perhaps the most perceptive of the periodical reviews was John White Chadwick's (*Nation*, LXXI, 13 December 1900, 474–475). He was at once warm,

Nowhere has Mr. Howells written more delightfully. The subtile but not too obvious rhythm of his sentences is a perpetual charm. But the spirit of these recollections is, if possible, more admirable than their form.

and generally perceptive,

Famed and unfamed are treated with such kindness as one must go far to equal—say, to Grant's memoirs. Yet there is ample firmness and discrimination. The result is not reached by a judicious balancing of praise and blame, but by a geniality which suffuses the most depreciatory judgments with a kindly warmth and light. There is something delightful in the fearless-ness of Mr. Howells's admirations. Some of them sound a chal-lenge to the depreciations of our English friends, but here and there to their excessive praise, as in the case of Poe, whose damnation, however, by Emerson as "the jingle-man" Mr. Howells would not accept as a complete characterization.

Chadwick charged the book with certain errors—such as the comment that Curtis was at one time a communist and the "inevitable mistake" of confusing William Henry with William Ellery Channing—but ended with praise:

It would be a congenial task to follow Mr. Howells into the details of his last chapter, in which his Cambridge neighbors are commented on in terms of warm affection and intelligent discrimination. In the account of Mr. Boyesen we cannot but admire the loyalty that exaggerates the importance of his friend. The elder James will be a discovery to many who have known him hitherto only in that fine audacity of his style which has survived in some degree in the writing of his son William. It is very good to have some of the other "unknown heroes equal to the greatest heroes known" set in a light which makes their virtues plain. It is a lofty privilege to be introduced into such vital contact with so many noble spirits, few if any of them more engaging than the writer who is never for a moment absent from the pleasant scene.

Possibly Howells was most gratified by the praise of Richard Le Gallienne, which appeared in the Boston *Evening Transcript* (18 December 1900):

Whatever the future may think of Mr. W. D. Howells's novels, and plays, and the poetry about which he is too modest, there can be no doubt that in his "Literary Friends and Acquaintances" [*sic*] he has produced one of the most delightful books of reminiscence ever written, a book which, alike for its subject matter and its personal charm of presentation, must always keep its place, not merely as an important document toward the writing of the history of American literature, but on that charmed shelf which holds the American essayist—or shelves, I ought to have said, for American literature is perhaps richer in essay than in any other literary product. It is the best book of its kind written by an Anglo-Saxon writer for years. I wish we had any impressions so good, and so admirably woven into a complete impression, of the English literary figures contemporary with the American literary figures whom Mr. Howells depicts. If we have, the book has escaped me. And, of course, Mr. Howells's book is one in which, if Americans have a patriotic first right of rejoicing, Englishmen have certainly a second—a second very close to that first; for surely the writers whom Mr. Howells celebrates have meant no less to English readers than to American.

Le Gallienne worked with the book in considerable detail, calling attention to the nuances of Howells' opinions; he closed with Howells' tribute to Norton, commenting,

These are brave words and said with the dignity which becomes the spirit that animates them. For one more good book at a time when there are none too many, thank you, Mr. Howells.

III

The beginnings of "My Memories of Mark Twain" were simpler than those of *Literary Friends and Acquaintance*.[11] Howells had regularly, even deliberately, written favorable criticism of

---

11. For another account of the provenience of *My Mark Twain*, which appeared after this was completed, see William Dean Howells, *My Mark Twain: Reminiscences and Criticisms*, edited and with an introduction by Marilyn Austin Baldwin (Baton Rouge, La., 1967).

Twain over the years. When Clemens was on his deathbed, the enterprising F. A. Duneka of Harper solicited a memoir from Howells. On 20 April 1910, the day before Clemens' death, Howells replied:

> You know I would *like* to write about Clemens; and if I did, it would be something unique, for I should tell him as I have known him for forty years: the most truthful man I *ever* knew. But don't make me—don't *let* me—promise till I get my head out of this cloud in which I have been living with the anxieties of the last two months.—It wrings my heart to think of Clemens dying.[12]

Howells was deep in clouds of anxiety at the time. Mary Noyes Mead, Mrs. Howells' sister, had died in March. Elinor Howells herself, who had been declining for at least five years, was confined to bed; she would die on 6 May 1910. Perhaps to escape from these troubles, Howells worked with alacrity and success on his Twain memoir. He sent the first material to Duneka by 27 April, within a week. Duneka, apparently hoping to hurry into print, wrote twice on 28 April, enclosing proofs in his second letter and commenting,

> I wonder whether one dares say in print that a man has been drunk. One may say that he has been a thief, a defaulter, dishonest in every way, worthless, a murderer perhaps, and the public will accept that, but to say a man has been drunk is to say a thing from which the reader instinctively recoils.

He added that in itself the fact of Twain's having once been drunk was unimportant but that it would make headlines all over the country. Prohibition, after all, loomed in the near historical offing. The next day, 29 April, Howells replied, accepting Duneka's suggestions: "You're right about that passage. I've cut it out. I hope you will like the rest of my paper still better. It's working out splendidly."

On 1 May, Howells sent more copy to Duneka and promised him another installment. The next day he wrote again, enclosing

---

12. WDH to Duneka, 20 April 1910. MS at American Antiquarian Society. Quoted by permission.

a letter from Clara Clemens Gabrilowitsch and asking to see a "*revise*" of the first installment.[13] During the sad, hectic two weeks which followed there appears to have been no correspondence. On 13 May, however, Duneka sent an extra payment ($1,500) for "My Memories of Mark Twain," which Howells acknowledged the same day. On 16 May Howells urged Duneka to hurry with the "Clemens proof" to be forwarded to Clara.[14] By 23 May, the work was done, and Howells wrote to Albert Bigelow Paine:

> I thank [you] for your kind words, which I am so helpless to reply to.
> I have finished the "memories," and now that they are done they do not record Clemens [as] I had hoped. But they record my affection for him.
> If I can help in any way with the Life, you know I will gladly do so.[15]

"My Memories of Mark Twain" was published in the July, August, and September issues of *Harper's Monthly*.

Howells experienced some uneasiness about the shape of his memoir, writing to Duneka thrice more in late May and early June relative to changes in galley proofs. By 15 June, however, he had gone to work on the book. On 9 September he wrote to Duneka:

> I get letters by every mail about the Mark Twain papers. I hope for the sake of Franklin Square as well [as] my own that the book will be acceptable. If it were to do again I could do it twice as well. But all life is a belated conception of imperfection.[16]

On 10 September, *My Mark Twain: Reminiscences and Criticisms*—a title selected in May—was issued.

---

13. Duneka to WDH, 28 April; WDH to Duneka, 29 April, 1, 2 May. MSS at American Antiquarian Society.

14. WDH to Duneka, 13, 16 May. MSS at American Antiquarian Society.

15. WDH to Paine, 23 May 1910. MS at Huntington Library. Quoted by permission.

16. WDH to Duneka, 9 September 1910. MS at American Antiquarian Society.

The reviews of the book were few and brief, which may attest more to the popularity of *Harper's* than to the reception of the book. *The Dial* and *Literary Digest* printed positive notices, though short; *Review of Reviews* (XLII, October 1910, 510) gave the book eleven lines, saying, "It is Mr. Howells at his best," and reprinting the Lakewood picture (1908) of Howells and Twain seated. The *Nation* (XCI, 27 October 1910, 395) published nearly a column of generous praise, tucked among notices of other books:

> The genial spirit of the immortal fun-maker himself has touched the hundred pages of reminiscence with characteristic gayety, and it is a vivid picture one gets, not simply of "the Lincoln of our literature," but of a rare friendship between two richly endowed natures.

D. F. H.
E. H. C.

The Heirs of W. D. Howells

W. D. Howells

Literary Friends and Acquaintance

BIBLIOGRAPHICAL

LONG BEFORE I began the papers which make up this volume, I had meant to write of literary history in New England as I had known it in the lives of its great exemplars during the twenty-five years I lived near them. In fact, I had meant to do this from the time I came among them; but I let the days in which I almost constantly saw them go by without record save such as I carried in a memory retentive, indeed, beyond the common, but not so full as I could have wished when I began to invoke it for my work. Still, upon insistent appeal, it responded in sufficient abundance; and, though I now wish I could have remembered more instances, I think my impressions were accurate enough. I am sure of having tried honestly to impart them in the ten years or more when I was desultorily endeavoring to share them with the reader.

The papers were written pretty much in the order they have here, beginning with *My First Visit to New England,* which dates from the earliest eighteen-nineties, if I may trust my recollection of reading it from the manuscript to the editor of *Harper's Magazine,* where we lay under the willows of Magnolia one pleasant summer morning in the first years of that decade. It was printed no great while after in that periodical; but I was so long in finishing the study of Lowell that it had been anticipated in *Harper's* by other reminiscences of him, and it was therefore first printed in *Scribner's Magazine.* It was the paper with which I took the most pains, and when it was completed I still felt it so incomplete that I referred it to his closest and my best friend,

3

the late Charles Eliot Norton, for his criticism. He thought it wanting in unity; it was a group of studies instead of one study, he said; I must do something to draw the different sketches together in a single effect of portraiture; and this I did my best to do.

It was the latest written of the three articles which give the volume substance, and it represents more finally and fully than the others my sense of the literary importance of the men whose like we shall not look upon again. Longfellow was easily the greatest poet of the three, Holmes often the most brilliant and felicitous, but Lowell, in spite of his forays in politics, was the finest scholar and the most profoundly literary, as he was above the others most deeply and thoroughly New England in quality.

While I was doing these sketches, sometimes slighter and sometimes less slight, of all those poets and essayists and novelists I had known in Cambridge and Boston and Concord and New York, I was doing many other things: half a dozen novels, as many more novelettes and shorter stories, with essays and criticisms and verses; so that in January, 1900, I had not yet done the paper on Lowell, which, with another, was to complete my reminiscences of American literary life as I had witnessed it. When they were all done at last they were republished in a volume which found instant favor beyond my deserts if not its own.

There was a good deal of trouble with the name, but *Literary Friends and Acquaintance* was an endeavor for modest accuracy with which I remained satisfied until I thought, long too late, of *Literary Friends and Neighbors*. Then I perceived that this would have been still more accurate and quite as modest, and I gladly give any reader leave to call the book by that name who likes.

Since the collection was first made, I have written little else quite of the kind, except the paper on Bret Harte, which was first printed shortly after his death; and the study of Mark Twain, which I had been preparing to make for forty years and more, and wrote in two weeks of the spring of 1910. Others of my time and place have now passed whither there is neither time nor place, and there are moments when I feel that I must try to call them back and pay them such honor as my sense of their worth may give; but the impulse has as yet failed to effect itself, and I do not know how long I shall spare myself the supreme pleasure-pain, the "*höchst angenehmer Schmerz*," of seeking to live here with those who live here no more.

W. D. H.

_____

Part First

MY FIRST VISIT TO NEW ENGLAND

I

IF THERE WAS any one in the world who had his being more wholly in literature than I had in 1860, I am sure I should not have known where to find him, and I doubt if he could have been found nearer the centres of literary activity than I then was, or among those more purely devoted to literature than myself. I had been for three years a writer of news paragraphs, book notices, and political leaders on a daily paper in an inland city, and I do not know that my life differed outwardly from that of any other young journalist, who had begun as I had in a country printing-office, and might be supposed to be looking forward to advancement in his profession, or in public affairs. But inwardly it was altogether different with me. Inwardly I was a poet, with no wish to be anything else, unless in a moment of careless affluence I might so far forget myself as to be a novelist. I was, with my friend J. J. Piatt, the half-author of a little volume of very unknown verse, and Mr. Lowell had lately accepted and had begun to print in the Atlantic Monthly five or six poems of mine. Besides this I had written poems, and sketches, and criticisms for the Saturday Press of New York, a long-forgotten but once very lively expression of literary intention in an extinct bohemia of that city; and I was always writing poems, and sketches, and criticisms in our own paper. These, as well as my feats in the renowned periodicals of the East, met with kindness, if not honor, in my own city which ought to have given me grave doubts whether I was any real prophet. But it only intensified my literary ambition, already so strong that my veins might well have run ink rather than blood, and gave me a higher opinion of my fellow-citizens, if such a thing could be. They were indeed very charming people, and such of them as I mostly saw were readers and lovers of books. Society in Columbus at that day had a pleasant refinement which I think I do not exaggerate in the fond retrospect. It had the finality which it seems to have had nowhere since the war; it had certain fixed ideals, which were none the less graceful and becoming because they were the simple old American ideals, now vanished, or fast vanishing, before the knowledge of good and evil as they have it in Europe, and as it has imparted itself to American travel and sojourn. There was a mixture of many strains in the capital of Ohio, as there was throughout the State. Virginia, Kentucky, Pennsylvania, New York, and New England all joined to characterize the manners and customs. I suppose it was the South which gave the social tone; the intellectual taste among the elders was the Southern taste for the classic and the standard in literature; but we who were younger preferred the modern authors: we read Thackeray, and George Eliot, and Hawthorne, and Charles Reade, and De Quincey, and Tennyson, and Browning, and Emerson, and Longfellow; and I, I read Heine, and evermore Heine, when there was not some new thing from the others. Now and then an immediate French book penetrated to us: we read Michelet and About, I remember. We looked to England and the East largely for our literary opinions; we accepted the Saturday Review as law if we could not quite receive it as gospel. One of us took the Cornhill Magazine, because Thackeray was the editor; the Atlantic Monthly counted many readers among us; and a visiting young lady from New England, who screamed at sight of the periodical in one of our houses, "Why, have you got the Atlantic Monthly *out here?*" could be answered, with cold superiority, "There are several *contributors* to the Atlantic in Columbus." There were in fact two: my roommate, who wrote Browning for it, while I wrote Heine and Longfellow. But I suppose two are as rightfully several as twenty are.

II

That was the heyday of lecturing, and now and then a literary light from the East swam into our skies. I heard and saw Emerson, and I once met Bayard Taylor socially, at the hospitable house where he was a guest after his lecture. Heaven knows how I got through the evening. I do not think I opened my mouth to address him a word; it was as much as I could do to sit and look at him, while he tranquilly smoked, and chatted with our host, and quaffed the beer which we had very good in the West. All the while I did him homage as the first author by calling whom I had met. I longed to tell him how much I liked his poems, which we used to get by heart in those days, and I longed (how much more I longed!) to have him know that—

"Auch ich war in Arkadien geboren,"

that I had printed poems in the Atlantic Monthly and the Saturday Press, and was the potential author of things destined to eclipse all literature hitherto attempted. But I could not tell him; and there was no one else who thought to tell him. Perhaps it was as well so; I might have perished of his recognition; for my modesty was equal to my merit.

In fact I think we were all rather modest young fellows, we who formed the group wont to spend some part of every evening at that house, where there was always music, or whist, or gay talk, or all three. We had our opinions of literary matters, but (perhaps because we had mostly accepted them from England or New England, as I have said) we were not vain of them; and we would by no means have urged them before a living literary man like that. I believe none of us ventured to speak, except the poet, my roommate, who said, He believed so and so was the original of so and so; and was promptly told, He had no right to say such a thing. Naturally, we came away rather critical of our host's guest, whom I afterwards knew as the kindliest heart in the world. But we had not shone in his presence, and that galled us; and we chose to think that he had not shone in ours.

III

At that time he was filling a large space in the thoughts of the young people who had any thoughts about literature. He had come to his full repute as an agreeable and intelligent traveller, and he still wore the halo of his early adventures afoot in foreign lands when they were yet really foreign. He had not written his novels of American life, once so welcomed, and now so forgotten; it was very long before he had achieved that incomparable translation of Faust, which must always remain the finest and best, and which would keep his name alive with Goethe's, if he had done nothing else worthy of remembrance. But what then most commended him to the regard of us star-eyed youth (now blinking sadly toward our seventies) was the poetry which he printed in the magazines from time to time: in the first Putnam's (where there was a dashing picture of him in an Arab burnoose and a turban), and in Harper's, and in the Atlantic. It was often very lovely poetry, I thought, and I still think so; and it was rightfully his, though it paid the inevitable allegiance to the manner of the great masters of the day. It was graced for us by the pathetic romance of his early love, which some of its sweetest and saddest numbers confessed, for the young girl he married almost in her death hour; and we who were hoping to have our hearts broken, or already had them so, would have been glad of something more of the obvious poet in the popular lecturer we had seen refreshing himself after his hour on the platform.

He remained for nearly a year the only author I had seen, and I met him once again before I saw any other. Our second meeting was far from Columbus, as far as remote Quebec, when I was on my way to New England by way of Niagara and the Canadian rivers and cities. I stopped in Toronto, and realized myself abroad without any signal adventures; but at Montreal something very pretty happened to me. I came into the hotel office, the evening of a first day's lonely sight-seeing, and vainly explored the register for the name of some acquaintance; as I turned from it two smartly dressed young fellows embraced it, and I heard one of them say, to my great amaze and happiness, "Hello, here's Howells!"

"Oh," I broke out upon him, "I was just looking for some one *I* knew. I hope you are some one who knows *me !*"

"Only through your contributions to the Saturday Press," said the young fellow, and with these golden words, the precious first personal recognition of my authorship I had ever received from a stranger, and the rich reward of all my literary endeavor, he introduced himself and his friend. I do not know what became of this friend, or where or how he eliminated himself; but we two others were inseparable from that moment. He was a young lawyer from New York, and when I came back from Italy, four or five years later, I used to see his sign in Wall Street, with a never-fulfilled intention of going in to see him. In whatever world he happens now to be, I should like to send him my greetings, and confess to him that my art has never since brought me so sweet a recompense, and nothing a thousandth part so much like Fame, as that outcry of his over the hotel register in Montreal. We were comrades for four or five rich days, and shared our pleasures and expenses in viewing the monuments of those ancient Canadian capitals, which I think we valued at all their picturesque worth. We made jokes to mask our emotions; we giggled and made giggle, in the right way; we fell in and out of love with all the pretty faces and dresses we saw; and we talked evermore about literature and literary people. He had more acquaintance with the one, and more passion for the other, but he could tell me of Pfaff's lager-beer cellar on Broadway, where the Saturday Press fellows and the other bohemians met; and this, for the time, was enough: I resolved to visit it as soon as I reached New York, in spite of the tobacco and beer (which I was given to understand were *de rigueur*), though they both, so far as I had known them, were apt to make me sick.

I was very desolate after I parted from this good fellow, who returned to Montreal on his way to New York, while I remained in Quebec to continue later on mine to New England. When I came in from seeing him off in a calash for the boat, I discovered

Bayard Taylor in the reading-room, where he sat sunken in what seemed a somewhat weary muse. He did not know me, or even notice me, though I made several errands in and out of the reading-room in the vain hope that he might do so: doubly vain, for I am aware now that I was still flown with the pride of that pretty experience in Montreal, and trusted in a repetition of something like it. At last, as no chance volunteered to help me, I mustered courage to go up to him and name myself, and say I had once had the pleasure of meeting him at Doctor ——'s in Columbus. The poet gave no sign of consciousness at the sound of a name which I had fondly begun to think might not be so all unknown. He looked up with an unkindling eye, and asked, Ah, how was the Doctor? and when I had reported favorably of the Doctor, our conversation ended.

He was probably as tired as he looked, and he must have classed me with that multitude all over the country who had shared the pleasure I professed in meeting him before; it was surely my fault that I did not speak my name loud enough to be recognized, if I spoke it at all; but the courage I had mustered did not quite suffice for that. In after-years he assured me, first by letter and then by word, of his grief for an incident which I can only recall now as the untoward beginning of a cordial friendship. It was often my privilege, in those days, as reviewer and editor, to testify my sense of the beautiful things he did in so many kinds of literature, but I never liked any of them better than I liked him. He had a fervent devotion to his art, and he was always going to do the greatest things in it, with an expectation of effect that never failed him. The things he actually did were none of them mean, or wanting in quality, and some of them are of a lasting charm that any one may feel who will turn to his poems; but no doubt many of them fell short of his hopes of them with the reader. It was fine to meet him when he was full of a new scheme; he talked of it with a single-hearted joy, and tried to make you see it of the same colors and proportions it wore to his eyes. He spared no toil to make it the perfect thing he dreamed it, and he was not discouraged by any disappointment he suffered with the critic or the public.

He was a tireless worker, and at last his health failed under his labors at the newspaper desk, beneath the midnight gas, when he should long have rested from such labors. I believe he was obliged to do them through one of those business fortuities which deform and embitter all our lives; but he was not the man to spare himself in any case. He was always attempting new things, and he never ceased endeavoring to make his scholarship reparation for the want of earlier opportunity and training. I remember that I met him once in a Cambridge street with a book in his hand which he let me take in mine. It was a Greek author, and he said he was just beginning to read the language at fifty: a patriarchal age to me of the early thirties! I suppose I intimated the surprise I felt at his taking it up so late in the day, for he said, with charming seriousness, "Oh, but you know, I expect to use it in the other world." Yes, that made it worth while, I consented; but was he sure of the other world? "As sure as I am of this," he said; and I have always kept the impression of the young faith which spoke in his voice, and was more than his words.

I saw him last in the hour of those tremendous adieux which were paid him in New York before he sailed to be Minister in Germany. It was one of the most graceful things done by President Hayes, who, most of all our Presidents after Lincoln, honored himself in honoring literature by his appointments, to give that place to Bayard Taylor. There was no one more fit for it, and it was peculiarly fit that he should be so distinguished to a people who knew and valued his scholarship, and the service he had done German letters. He was as happy in it, apparently, as a man could be in anything here below, and he enjoyed to the last drop the many cups of kindness pressed to his lips in parting; though I believe these farewells, at a time when he was already fagged with work and excitement, were notably harmful to him, and helped to hasten his end. Some of us who were near of friendship went down to see him off when he sailed, as the dismal and futile wont of friends is; and I recall the kind, great fellow standing in the cabin, amid those sad flowers that heaped the tables, saying good-by to one after another, and smiling fondly, smiling wearily, upon all. There was champagne, of course, and an odious hilarity, without meaning, and without remission, till the warning bell chased us ashore, and our brave poet escaped with what was left of his life.

IV

I have followed him far from the moment of our first meeting; but even on my way to venerate those New England luminaries, which chiefly drew my eyes, I could not pay a less devoir to an author who, if Curtis was not, was chief of the New York group of authors in that day. I distinguished between the New-Englanders and the New-Yorkers, and I suppose there is no question but our literary centre was then in Boston, wherever it is, or is not, at present. But I thought Taylor then, and I think him now, one of the first in our whole American province of the republic of letters, in a day when it was in a recognizably flourishing state, whether we regard quantity or quality in the names that gave it lustre. Lowell was then in perfect command of those varied forces which will long, if not lastingly, keep him in memory as first among our literary men, and master in more kinds than any other American. Longfellow was in the fulness of his world-wide fame, and in the ripeness of the beautiful genius which was not to know decay while life endured. Emerson had emerged from the popular darkness which had so long held him a hopeless mystic, and was shining a lambent star of poesy and prophecy at the zenith. Hawthorne, the exquisite artist, the unrivalled dreamer, whom we still always liken this one and that one to, whenever this one or that one promises greatly to please us, and still leave without a rival, without a companion, had lately returned from his long sojourn abroad, and had given us the last of the incomparable romances which the world was to have perfect from his hand. Doctor Holmes had surpassed all expectations in those who most admired his brilliant humor and charming poetry by the invention of a new attitude if not a new sort in literature. The turn that civic affairs had taken was favorable to the widest recognition of Whittier's splendid lyrical gift; and that heart of fire, doubly snow-bound by Quaker tradition and Puritan environment, was penetrating every generous breast with its flamy impulses, and fusing all wills in its noble purpose. Mrs. Stowe, who far outfamed the rest as the author of the most renowned novel ever written, was proving it no accident or miracle by the fiction she was still writing.

This great New England group might be enlarged perhaps without loss of quality by the inclusion of Thoreau, who came somewhat before his time, and whose drastic criticism of our expediential and mainly futile civilization would find more intelligent acceptance now than it did then, when all resentment of its defects was specialized in enmity to Southern slavery. Dr. Edward Everett Hale belonged in this group too, by virtue of that humor the most inventive and the most fantastic, the sanest, the sweetest, the truest, which had begun to find expression in the Atlantic Monthly; and there a wonderful young girl had written a series of vivid sketches and taken the heart of youth everywhere with amaze and joy, so that I thought it would be no less an event to meet Harriet Prescott than to meet any of those I have named.

I expected somehow to meet them all, and I imagined them all easily accessible in the office of the Atlantic Monthly, which had lately adventured in the fine air of high literature where so many other periodicals had gasped and died before it. The best of these, hitherto, and better even than the Atlantic for some reasons, the lamented Putnam's Magazine, had perished of inanition at New York, and the claim of the commercial capital to the literary primacy had passed with that brilliant venture. New York had nothing distinctive to show for American literature but the decrepit and doting Knickerbocker Magazine. Harper's New Monthly, though Curtis had already come to it from the wreck of Putnam's, and it had long ceased to be eclectic in material, and had begun to stand for native work in the allied arts which it has since so magnificently advanced, was not distinctively literary, and the Weekly had just begun to make itself known. The Century, Scribner's, the Cosmopolitan, McClure's, and I know not what others, were still unimagined by five, and ten, and twenty years, and the Galaxy was to flash and fade before any of them should kindle its more effectual fires. The Nation, which was destined to chastise rather than nurture our young literature, had still six years of dreamless potentiality before it; and the Nation was always more Bostonian than New-Yorkish by nature, whatever it was by nativity.

Philadelphia had long counted for nothing in the literary field. Graham's Magazine at one time showed a certain critical force, but it seemed to perish of this expression of vitality; and there remained Godey's Lady's Book and Peterson's Magazine, publications really incredible in their insipidity. In the South there was nothing but a mistaken social ideal, with the moral principles all standing on their heads in defence of slavery; and in the West there was a feeble and foolish notion that Western talent was repressed by Eastern jealousy. At Boston chiefly, if not at Boston alone, was there a vigorous intellectual life among such authors as I have named. Every young writer was ambitious to join his name with theirs in the Atlantic Monthly, and in the lists of Ticknor and Fields, who were literary publishers in a sense such as the business world has known nowhere else before or since. Their imprint was a warrant of quality to the reader and of immortality to the author, so that if I could have had a book issued by them at that day I should now be in the full enjoyment of an undying fame.

v

Such was the literary situation as the passionate pilgrim from the West approached his holy land at Boston, by way of the Grand Trunk Railway from Quebec to Portland. I have no recollection of a sleeping-car, and I suppose I waked and watched during the whole of that long, rough journey; but I should hardly have slept if there had been a car for the purpose. I was too eager to see what New England was like, and too anxious not to lose the least glimpse of it, to close my eyes after I crossed the border at Island Pond. I found that in the elm-dotted levels of Maine it was very like the Western Reserve in northern Ohio, which is, indeed, a portion of New England transferred with all its characteristic features, and flattened out along the lake shore. It was not till I began to run southward into the older regions of the country that it lost this look, and became gratefully strange to me. It never had the effect of hoary antiquity which I had expected of a country settled more than two centuries; with its wood-built farms and villages it looked newer than the coal-smoked brick of southern Ohio. I had prefigured the New England landscape bare of forests, relieved here and there with the trees of orchards or plantations; but I found apparently as much woodland as at home.

At Portland I first saw the ocean, and this was a sort of disappointment. Tides and salt water I had already had at Quebec, so that I was no longer on the alert for them; but the color and the vastness of the sea I was still to try upon my vision. When I stood on the Promenade at Portland with the kind young Unitarian minister whom I had brought a letter to, and who led me there for a most impressive first view of the ocean, I could not make more of it than there was of Lake Erie; and I have never thought the color of the sea comparable to the tender blue of the lake. I did not hint my disappointment to my friend; I had too much regard for the feelings of an Eastern man to decry his ocean to his face, and I felt besides that it would be vulgar and provincial to make comparisons. I am glad now that I held my tongue, for that kind soul is no longer in this world, and I should not like to think he knew how far short of my expectations the sea he was so proud of had fallen. I went up with him into a tower or belvedere there was at hand; and when he pointed to the eastern horizon and said, Now there was nothing but sea between us and Africa, I pretended to expand with the thought, and began to sound myself for the emotions which I ought to have felt at such a sight. But in my heart I was empty, and heaven knows whether I saw the steamer which the ancient mariner in charge of that tower invited me to look at through his telescope. I never could see anything but a vitreous glare through a telescope, which has a vicious habit of dodging about through space, and failing to bring down anything of less than planetary magnitude.

But there was something at Portland vastly more to me than seas or continents, and that was the house where Longfellow was born. I believe, now, I did not get the right house, but only the house he went to live in later; but it served, and I rejoiced in it with a rapture that could not have been more genuine if it had been the real birthplace of the poet. I got my friend to show me

> "the breezy dome of groves,
> The shadows of Deering's woods,"

because they were in one of Longfellow's loveliest and tenderest poems; and I made an errand to the docks, for the sake of the

> "black wharves and the slips,
> And the sea-tides tossing free,
> And Spanish sailors with bearded lips,
> And the beauty and mystery of the ships,
> And the magic of the sea,"

mainly for the reason that these were colors and shapes of the fond vision of the poet's past. I am in doubt whether it was at this time or a later time that I went to revere

> "the dead captains as they lay
> In their graves o'erlooking the tranquil bay,
> Where they in battle died,"

but I am quite sure it was now that I wandered under

> "the trees which shadow each well-known street,
> As they balance up and down,"

for when I was next in Portland the great fire had swept the city avenues bare of most of those beautiful elms, whose Gothic arches and traceries I well remember.

The fact is that in those days I was bursting with the most romantic expectations of life in every way, and I looked at the whole world as material that might be turned into literature, or that might be associated with it somehow. I do not know how I managed to keep these preposterous hopes within me, but perhaps the trick of satirizing them, which I had early learnt, helped me to do it. I was at that particular moment resolved above all things to see things as Heinrich Heine saw them, or at least to report them as he did, no matter how I saw them; and I went about framing phrases to this end, and trying to match the objects of interest to them whenever there was the least chance of getting them together.

VI

I do not know how I first arrived in Boston, or whether it was before or after I had passed a day or two in Salem. As Salem is on the way from Portland, I will suppose that I stopped there first, and explored the quaint old town (quainter then than now, but still quaint enough) for the memorials of Hawthorne and of the witches which united to form the Salem I cared for. I went and looked up the House of Seven Gables, and suffered an unreasonable disappointment that it had not a great many more of them; but there was no loss in the death-warrant of Bridget Bishop, with the sheriff's return of execution upon it, which I found at the Court-house; if anything, the pathos of that witness of one of the cruelest delusions in the world was rather in excess of my needs; I could have got on with less. I saw the pins which the witches were sworn to have thrust into the afflicted children, and I saw Gallows Hill, where the hapless victims of the perjury were hanged. But that death-warrant remained the most vivid color of my experience of the tragedy; I had no need to invite myself to a sense of it, and it is still like a stain of red in my memory.

The kind old ship's captain whose guest I was, and who was transfigured to poetry in my sense by the fact that he used to voyage to the African coast for palm-oil in former days, led me all about the town, and showed me the Custom-house, which I desired to see because it was in the preface to the Scarlet Letter. But I perceived that he did not share my enthusiasm for the author, and I became more and more sensible that in Salem air there was a cool undercurrent of feeling about him. No doubt the place was not altogether grateful for the celebrity his romance had given it, and would have valued more the uninterrupted quiet of its own flattering thoughts of itself; but when it came to hearing a young lady say she knew a girl who said she would like to poison Hawthorne, it seemed to the devout young pilgrim from the West that something more of love for the great romancer would not have been too much for him. Hawthorne had already had his say, however, and he had not used his native town with any great tenderness. Indeed, the advantages to any place of having a great genius born and reared in its midst are so doubtful that it might be well for localities designing to become the birthplaces of distinguished authors to think twice about it. Perhaps only the largest capitals, like London and Paris, and New York and Chicago, ought to risk it. But the authors have an unaccountable perversity, and will seldom come into the world in the large cities, which are alone without the sense of neighborhood, and the personal susceptibilities so unfavorable to the practice of the literary art.

I dare say that it was owing to the local indifference to her greatest name, or her reluctance from it, that I got a clearer impression of Salem in some other respects than I should have had if I had been invited there to devote myself solely to the associations of Hawthorne. For the first time I saw an old New England town, I do not know but the most characteristic, and took into my young Western consciousness the fact of a more complex civilization than I had yet known. My whole life had been passed in a region where men were just beginning ancestors, and the conception of family was very imperfect. Literature of course was full of it, and it was not for a devotee of Thackeray to be theoretically ignorant of its manifestations; but I had hitherto carelessly supposed that family was nowhere regarded seriously in America except in Virginia, where it furnished a joke for the rest of the nation. But now I found myself confronted with it in its ancient houses, and heard its names pronounced with a certain consideration, which I dare say was as much their due in

Salem as it could be anywhere. The names were all strange, and all indifferent to me, but those fine square wooden mansions, of a tasteful architecture, and a pale buff-color, withdrawing themselves in quiet reserve from the quiet street, gave me an impression of family as an actuality and a force which I had never had before, but which no Westerner can yet understand the East without taking into account. I do not suppose that I conceived of family as a fact of vital import then; I think I rather regarded it as a color to be used in any æsthetic study of the local conditions. I am not sure that I valued it more even for literary purposes, than the steeple which the captain pointed out as the first and last thing he saw when he came and went on his long voyages, or than the great palm-oil casks, which he showed me, and which I related to the tree that stood

"Auf brennender Felsenwand."

Whether that was the kind of palm that gives the oil, or was a sort only suitable to be the dream of a lonely fir-tree in the North on a cold height, I am in doubt to this day.

I heard, not without concern, that the neighboring industry of Lynn was penetrating Salem, and that the ancient haunt of the witches and the birthplace of our subtlest and somberest wizard was becoming a great shoe-town; but my concern was less for its memories and sensibilities than for an odious duty which I owed that industry, together with all the others in New England. Before I left home I had promised my earliest publisher that I would undertake to edit, or compile, or do something literary to, a work on the operation of the more distinctive mechanical inventions of our country, which he had conceived the notion of publishing by subscription. He had furnished me, the most immechanical of humankind, with a letter addressed generally to the great mills and factories of the East, entreating their managers to unfold their mysteries to me for the purposes of this volume. His letter had the effect of shutting up some of them like clams, and others it put upon their guard against my researches, lest I should seize the secret of their special inventions and publish it to the world. I could not tell the managers that I was both morally and mentally incapable of this; that they might have explained and demonstrated the properties and functions of their most recondite machinery, and upon examination afterwards found me guiltless of having anything but a few verses of Heine or Tennyson or Longfellow in my head. So I had to suffer in several places from their unjust anxieties, and from my own weariness of their ingenious engines, or else endure the pangs of a bad conscience from ignoring them. As long as I was in Canada I was happy, for there was no industry in Canada that I saw, except that of the peasant girls, in their Evangeline hats and kirtles, tossing the hay in the way-side fields; but when I reached Portland my troubles began. I went with that young minister of whom I have spoken to a large foundry, where they were casting some sort of ironmongery, and inspected the process from a distance beyond any chance spurt of the molten metal, and came away sadly uncertain of putting the rather fine spectacle to any practical use. A manufactory where they did something with coal-oil (which I now heard for the first time called kerosene) refused itself to me, and I said to myself that probably all the other industries of Portland were as reserved, and I would not seek to explore them; but when I got to Salem, my conscience stirred again. If I knew that there were shoe-shops in Salem, ought not I to go and inspect their processes? This was a question which would not answer itself to my satisfaction, and I had no peace till I learned that I could see shoe-making much better at Lynn, and that Lynn was such a little way from Boston that I could readily run up there, if I did not wish to examine the shoe machinery at once. I promised myself that I would run up from Boston, but in order to do this I must first go to Boston.

VII

I am supposing still that I saw Salem before I saw Boston, but however the fact may be, I am sure that I decided it would be better to see shoe-making in Lynn, where I really did see it, thirty years later. For the purposes of the present visit, I contented myself with looking at a machine in Haverhill, which chewed a shoe sole full of pegs, and dropped it out of its iron jaws with an indifference as great as my own, and probably as little sense of how it had done its work. I may be unjust to that machine; heaven knows I would not wrong it; and I must confess that my head had no room in it for the conception of any machinery but the mythological, which also I despised, in my revulsion from the eighteenth-century poets to those of my own day.

I cannot quite make out after the lapse of so many years just how or when I got to Haverhill, or whether it was before or after I had been in Salem. There is an apparitional quality in my presences, at this point or that, in the dim past; but I hope that, for the credit of their order, ghosts are not commonly taken with such trivial things as I was. For instance, in Haverhill I was much interested by the sight of a young man, coming gayly down the steps of the hotel where I lodged, in peg-top trousers so much more peg-top than my own that I seemed to be wearing mere spring-bottoms in comparison; and in a day when every one who respected himself had a necktie as narrow as he could get, this youth had one no wider than a shoestring, and red at that, while mine measured almost an inch, and was black. To be sure, he was one of a band of negro minstrels, who were to give a concert that night, and he had a right to excel in fashion.

I will suppose, for convenience' sake, that I visited Haverhill, too, before I reached Boston: somehow that shoe-pegging machine must come in, and it may as well come in here. When I actually found myself in Boston, there were perhaps industries which it would have been well for me to celebrate, but I either made believe there were none, or else I honestly forgot all about them. In either case I released myself altogether to the literary and historical associations of the place. I need not say that I gave myself first to the first, and it rather surprised me to find that the literary associations of Boston referred so largely to Cambridge. I did not know much about Cambridge, except that it was the seat of the university where Lowell was, and Longfellow had been, professor; and somehow I had not realized it as the home of these poets. That was rather stupid of me, but it is best to own the truth, and afterward I came to know the place so well that I may safely confess my earlier ignorance.

I had stopped in Boston at the Tremont House, which was still one of the first hostelries of the country, and I must have inquired my way to Cambridge there; but I was sceptical of the direction the Cambridge horse-car took when I found it, and I hinted to the driver my anxieties as to why he should be starting east when I had been told that Cambridge was west of Boston. He reassured me in the laconic and sarcastic manner of his kind, and we really reached Cambridge by the route he had taken.

The beautiful elms that shaded great part of the way massed themselves in the "groves of academe" at the Square, and showed pleasant glimpses of "Old Harvard's scholar factories red," then far fewer than now. It must have been in vacation, for I met no one as I wandered through the college yard, trying to make up my mind as to how I should learn where Lowell lived; for it was he whom I had come to find. He had not only taken the poems I sent him, but he had printed two of them in a single number of the Atlantic, and had even written me a little note about them, which I wore next my heart in my breast pocket till I almost wore it out; and so I thought I might fitly report myself to him. But I have always been helpless in finding my way, and I was still depressed by my failure to convince the horse-car driver that he had taken the wrong road. I let several people go by without questioning them, and those I did ask abashed me farther by not knowing what I wanted to know. When I had remitted my search for the moment, an ancient man, with an open mouth and an inquiring eye, whom I never afterwards made out in Cambridge, addressed me with a hospitable offer to show me the Washington Elm. I thought this would give me time to embolden myself for the meeting with the editor of the Atlantic if I should ever find him, and I went with that kind old man, who when he had shown me the tree, and the spot where Washington stood when he took command of the con-

Nathaniel Hawthorne

tinental forces, said that he had a branch of it, and that if I
would come to his house with him he would give me a piece. In
the end, I meant merely to flatter him into telling me where I
could find Lowell, but I dissembled my purpose and pretended
a passion for a piece of the historic elm, and the old man led me
not only to his house but his wood-house, where he sawed me
off a block so generous that I could not get it into my pocket. I
feigned the gratitude which I could see that he expected, and
then I took courage to put my question to him. Perhaps that
patriarch lived only in the past, and cared for history and not
literature. He confessed that he could not tell me where to find
Lowell; but he did not forsake me; he set forth with me upon the
street again, and let no man pass without asking him. In the
end we met one who was able to say where Mr. Lowell was, and
I found him at last in a little study at the rear of a pleasant, old-
fashioned house near the Delta.

Lowell was not then at the height of his fame; he had just
reached this thirty years after, when he died; but I doubt if he
was ever after a greater power in his own country, or more completely embodied the literary aspiration which would not and
could not part itself from the love of freedom and the hope of
justice. For the sake of these he had been willing to suffer the
reproach which followed their friends in the earlier days of the
antislavery struggle. He had outlived the reproach long before;
but the fear of his strength remained with those who had felt it,
and he had not made himself more generally loved by the Fable
for Critics than by the Biglow Papers, probably. But in the Vision
of Sir Launfal and the Legend of Brittany he had won a liking
if not a listening far wider than his humor and his wit had got
him; and in his lectures on the English poets, given not many
years before he came to the charge of the Atlantic, he had proved
himself easily the wisest and finest critic in our language. He was
already, more than any American poet,

> "Dowered with the hate of hate, the scorn of scorn,
>   The love of love,"

and he held a place in the public sense which no other author
among us has held. I had myself never been a great reader of his
poetry, when I met him, though when I was a boy of ten years I
had heard my father repeat passages from the Biglow Papers
against war and slavery and the war for slavery upon Mexico,
and later I had read those criticisms of English poetry, and I
knew Sir Launfal must be Lowell in some sort; but my love for
him as a poet was chiefly centred in my love for his tender
rhyme, Auf Wiedersehen, which I cannot yet read without something of the young pathos it first stirred in me. I knew and felt
his greatness somehow apart from the literary proofs of it; he
ruled my fancy and held my allegiance as a character, as a man;
and I am neither sorry nor ashamed that I was abashed when I
first came into his presence; and that in spite of his words of
welcome I sat inwardly quaking before him. He was then forty-
one years old, and nineteen my senior, and if there had been
nothing else to awe me, I might well have been quelled by the
disparity of our ages. But I have always been willing and even
eager to do homage to men who have done something, and
notably to men who have done something in the sort I wished
to do something in, myself. I could never recognize any other
sort of superiority; but that I am proud to recognize; and I had
before Lowell some such feeling as an obscure subaltern might
have before his general. He was by nature a bit of a disciplinar-
ian, and the effect was from him as well as in me; I dare say he
let me feel whatever difference there was, as helplessly as I felt it.
At the first encounter with people he always was apt to have a
certain frosty shyness, a smiling cold, as from the long, high-
sunned winters of his Puritan race; he was not quite himself till
he had made you aware of his quality: then no one could be
sweeter, tenderer, warmer than he; then he made you free of his
whole heart; but you must be his captive before he could do that.
His whole personality had now an instant charm for me; I could
not keep my eyes from those beautiful eyes of his, which had a
certain starry serenity, and looked out so purely from under his
white forehead, shadowed with auburn hair untouched by age;

or from the smile that shaped the auburn beard, and gave the face in its form and color the Christ-look which Page's portrait has flattered in it.

His voice had as great a fascination for me as his face. The vibrant tenderness and the crisp clearness of the tones, the perfect modulation, the clear enunciation, the exquisite accent, the elect diction—I did not know enough then to know that these were the gifts, these were the graces, of one from whose tongue our rough English came music such as I should never hear from any other. In this speech there was nothing of our slipshod American slovenliness, but a truly Italian conscience and an artistic sense of beauty in the instrument.

I saw, before he sat down across his writing-table from me, that he was not far from the medium height; but his erect carriage made the most of his five feet and odd inches. He had been smoking the pipe he loved, and he put it back in his mouth, presently, as if he found himself at greater ease with it, when he began to chat, or rather to let me show what manner of young man I was by giving me the first word. I told him of the trouble I had in finding him, and I could not help dragging in something about Heine's search for Börne, when he went to see him in Frankfort; but I felt at once this was a false start, for Lowell was such an impassioned lover of Cambridge, which was truly his *patria*, in the Italian sense, that it must have hurt him to be unknown to any one in it; he said, a little dryly, that he should not have thought I would have so much difficulty; but he added, forgivingly, that this was not his own house, which he was out of for the time. Then he spoke to me of Heine, and when I showed my ardor for him, he sought to temper it with some judicious criticisms, and told me that he had kept the first poem I sent him, for the long time it had been unacknowledged, to make sure that it was not a translation. He asked me about myself, and my name, and its Welsh origin, and seemed to find the vanity I had in this harmless enough. When I said I had tried hard to believe that I was at least the literary descendant of Sir James Howels, he corrected me gently with "James Howel," and took down a volume of the Familiar Letters from the shelves behind him to prove me wrong. This was always his habit, as I found afterwards: when he quoted anything from a book he liked to get it and read the passage over, as if he tasted a kind of hoarded sweetness in the words. It visibly vexed him if they showed him in the least mistaken; but

"The love he bore to learning was at fault"

for this foible, and that other of setting people right if he thought them wrong. I could not assert myself against his version of Howel's name, for my edition of his letters was far away in Ohio, and I was obliged to own that the name was spelt in several different ways in it. He perceived, no doubt, why I had chosen the form likest my own, with the title which the pleasant old turn-coat ought to have had from the many masters he served according to their many minds, but never had except from that erring edition. He did not afflict me for it, though; probably it amused him too much; he asked me about the West, and when he found that I was as proud of the West as I was of Wales, he seemed even better pleased, and said he had always fancied that human nature was laid out on rather a larger scale there than in the East, but he had seen very little of the West. In my heart I did not think this then, and I do not think it now; human nature has had more ground to spread over in the West; that is all; but "it was not for me to bandy words with my sovereign." He said he liked to hear of the differences between the different sections, for what we had most to fear in our country was a wearisome sameness of type.

He did not say now, or at any other time during the many years I knew him, any of those slighting things of the West which I had so often to suffer from Eastern people, but suffered me to praise it all I would. He asked me what way I had taken in coming to New England, and when I told him, and began to rave of the beauty and quaintness of French Canada, and to pour out my joy in Quebec, he said, with a smile that had now lost all its frost, Yes, Quebec was a bit of the seventeenth century; it was in many ways more French than France, and its people spoke the language of Voltaire, with the accent of Voltaire's time.

I do not remember what else he talked of, though once I remembered it with what I believed an ineffaceable distinctness. I set nothing of it down at the time; I was too busy with the letters I was writing for a Cincinnati paper; and I was severely bent upon keeping all personalities out of them. This was very well, but I could wish now that I had transgressed at least so far as to report some of the things that Lowell said; for the paper did not print my letters, and it would have been perfectly safe, and very useful for the present purpose. But perhaps he did not say anything very memorable; to do that you must have something positive in your listener; and I was the mere response, the hollow echo, that youth must be in like circumstances. I was all the time afraid of wearing my welcome out, and I hurried to go when I would so gladly have staid. I do not remember where I meant to go, or why he should have undertaken to show me the way across-lots, but this was what he did; and when we came to a fence, which I clambered gracelessly over, he put his hands on the top, and tried to take it at a bound. He tried twice, and then laughed at his failure, but not with any great pleasure, and he was not content till a third trial carried him across. Then he said, "I commonly do that the first time," as if it were a frequent habit with him, while I remained discreetly silent, and for that moment at least felt myself the elder of the man who had so much of the boy in him. He had, indeed, much of the boy in him to the last, and he parted with each hour of his youth reluctantly, pathetically.

VIII

We walked across what must have been Jarvis Field to what must have been North Avenue, and there he left me. But before he let me go he held my hand while he could say that he wished me to dine with him; only, he was not in his own house, and he would ask me to dine with him at the Parker House in Boston, and would send me word of the time later.

I suppose I may have spent part of the intervening time in viewing the wonders of Boston, and visiting the historic scenes and places in it and about it. I certainly went over to Charlestown, and ascended Bunker Hill Monument, and explored the navy-yard, where the immemorial man-of-war begun in Jackson's time was then silently stretching itself under its long shed in a poetic arrest, as if the failure of the appropriation for its completion had been some kind of enchantment. In Boston, I early presented my letter of credit to the publisher it was drawn upon, not that I needed money at the moment, but from a young eagerness to see if it would be honored; and a literary attaché of the house kindly went about with me, and showed me the life of the city. A great city it seemed to me then, and a seething vortex of business as well as a whirl of gayety, as I saw it in Washington Street, and in a promenade concert at Copeland's restaurant in Tremont Row. Probably I brought some idealizing force to bear upon it, for I was not all so strange to the world as I must seem; perhaps I accounted for quality as well as quantity in my impressions of the New England metropolis, and aggrandized it in the ratio of its literary importance. It seemed to me old, even after Quebec, and very likely I credited the actual town with all the dead and gone Bostonians in my sentimental census. If I did not it was no fault of my cicerone, who thought even more of the city he showed me than I did. I do not know now who he was, and I never saw him after I came to live there, with any certainty that it was he, though I was often tormented with the vision of a spectacled face like his, but not like enough to warrant me in addressing him.

He became part of that ghostly Boston of my first visit, which would sometimes return and possess again the city I came to know so familiarly in later years, and to be so passionately interested in. Some color of my prime impressions has tinged the fictitious experiences of people in my books, but I find very little of it in my memory. This is like a web of frayed old lace, which I have to take carefully into my hold for fear of its fragility, and make out as best I can the figure once so distinct in it. There are the narrow streets, stretching saltwards to the docks, which I haunted for their quaintness, and there is Faneuil Hall, which I cared to see so much more because Wendell Phillips had spoken in it than because Otis and Adams had. There is the old Colonial House, and there is the State House, which I dare say I explored, with the Common sloping before it. There is Beacon Street, with the Hancock House where it is incredibly no more, and there are the beginnings of Commonwealth Avenue, and the other streets of the Back Bay, laid out with their basements left hollowed in the made land, which the gravel trains were yet making out of the westward hills. There is the Public Garden, newly planned and planted, but without the massive bridge destined to make so ungratefully little of the lake that occasioned it. But it is all very vague, and I could easily believe now that it was some one else who saw it then in my place.

I think that I did not try to see Cambridge the same day that I saw Lowell, but wisely came back to my hotel in Boston, and tried to realize the fact. I went out another day, with an acquaintance from Ohio, whom I ran upon in the street. We went to Mount Auburn together, and I viewed its monuments with a reverence which I dare say their artistic quality did not merit. But I am not sorry for this, for perhaps they are not quite so bad as some people pretend. The gothic chapel of the cemetery, unstoried as it was, gave me, with its half-dozen statues standing or sitting about, an emotion such as I am afraid I could not receive now from the Acropolis, Westminster Abbey, and Santa Croce in one. I tried hard for some æsthetic sense of it, and I made believe that I thought this thing and that thing in the place moved me with its fitness or beauty; but the truth is that I had no taste in anything but literature, and did not feel the effect I would so willingly have experienced.

I did genuinely love the elmy quiet of the dear old Cambridge streets, though, and I had a real and instant pleasure in the yellow colonial houses, with their white corners and casements and their green blinds, that lurked behind the shrubbery of the avenue I passed through to Mount Auburn. The most beautiful among them was the most interesting for me, for it was the house of Longfellow; my companion, who had seen it before, pointed it out to me with an air of custom, and I would not let him see that I valued the first sight of it as I did. I had hoped that somehow I might be so favored as to see Longfellow himself, but when I asked about him of those who knew, they said, "Oh, he is at Nahant," and I thought that Nahant must be a great way off, and at any rate I did not feel authorized to go to him there. Neither did I go to see the author of the Amber Gods, who lived at Newburyport, I was told, as if I should know where Newburyport was; I did not know, and I hated to ask. Besides, it did not seem so simple as it had seemed in Ohio, to go and see a young lady simply because I was infatuated with her literature; even as the envoy of all the infatuated young people of Columbus, I could not quite do this; and when I got home, I had to account for my failure as best I could. Another failure of mine was the sight of Whittier, which I then very much longed to have. They said, "Oh, Whittier lives at Amesbury," but that put him at an indefinite distance, and without the introduction I never would ask for, I found it impossible to set out in quest of him. In the end, I saw no one in New England whom I was not presented to in the regular way, except Lowell, whom I thought I had a right to call upon in my quality of contributor, and from the acquaintance I had with him by letter. I neither praise nor blame myself for this; it was my shyness that withheld me rather than my merit. There is really no harm in seeking the presence of a famous man, and I doubt if the famous man resents the wish of people to look upon him without some measure, great or little, of affectation. There are bores everywhere, but he is likelier to find them in the wonted figures of society than in those young people, or old people, who come to him in the love of what he has done. I am well aware how furiously Tennyson sometimes met his worshippers, and how insolently Carlyle, but I think these facts are little specks in their sincerity. Our own gentler and honester celebrities did not forbid approach, and I have known some of them caress adorers who seemed hardly worthy of their kindness; but that was better than to have hurt any sensitive spirit who had ventured too far, by the rules that govern us with common men.

IX

My business relations were with the house that so promptly honored my letter of credit. This house had published in the East the campaign life of Lincoln which I had lately written, and I dare say would have published the volume of poems I had written earlier with my friend Piatt, if there had been any public for it; at least, I saw large numbers of the book on the counters. But all my literary affiliations were with Ticknor & Fields, and it was the Old Corner Book-Store on Washington Street that drew my heart as soon as I had replenished my pocket in Cornhill. After verifying the editor of the Atlantic Monthly I wished to verify its publishers, and it very fitly happened that when I was shown into Mr. Fields's little room at the back of the store, with its window looking upon School Street, and its scholarly keeping in books and prints, he had just got the magazine sheets of a poem of mine from the Cambridge printers. He was then lately from abroad, and he had the zest for American things which a foreign sojourn is apt to renew in us, though I did not know this then, and could not account for it in the kindness he expressed for my poem. He introduced me to Mr. Ticknor, who I fancied had not read my poem; but he seemed to know what it was from the junior partner, and he asked me whether I had been paid for it. I confessed that I had not, and then he got out a chamois-leather bag, and took from it five half-eagles in gold and laid them on the green cloth top of the desk, in much the shape and of much the size of the Great Bear. I have never since felt myself paid so lavishly for any literary work, though I have had more for a single piece than the twenty-five dollars that dazzled me in this constellation. The publisher seemed aware of the poetic character of the transaction; he let the pieces lie a moment, before he gathered them up and put them into my hand, and said, "I always think it is pleasant to have it in gold."

But a terrible experience with the poem awaited me, and

quenched for the moment all my pleasure and pride. It was The Pilot's Story, which I suppose has had as much acceptance as anything of mine in verse (I do not boast of a vast acceptance for it), and I had attempted to treat in it a phase of the national tragedy of slavery, as I had imagined it on a Mississippi steamboat. A young planter has gambled away the slave-girl who is the mother of his child, and when he tells her, she breaks out upon him with the demand:

"What will you say to our boy when he cries for me, there in Saint Louis?"

I had thought this very well, and natural and simple, but a fatal proof-reader had not thought it well enough, or simple and natural enough, and he had made the line read:

"What will you say to our boy when he cries for '*Ma*,' there in Saint Louis?"

He had even had the inspiration to quote the word he preferred to the one I had written, so that there was no merciful possibility of mistaking it for a misprint, and my blood froze in my veins at sight of it. Mr. Fields had given me the sheets to read while he looked over some letters, and he either felt the chill of my horror, or I made some sign or sound of dismay that caught his notice, for he looked round at me. I could only show him the passage with a gasp. I dare say he might have liked to laugh, for it was cruelly funny, but he did not; he was concerned for the magazine as well as for me. He declared that when he first read the line he had thought I could not have written it so, and he agreed with me that it would kill the poem if it came out in that shape. He instantly set about repairing the mischief, so far as could be. He found that the whole edition of that sheet had been printed, and the air blackened round me again, lighted up here and there with baleful flashes of the newspaper wit at my cost, which I previsioned in my misery; I knew what I should have said of such a thing myself, if it had been another's. But the publisher at once decided that the sheet must be reprinted, and I went away weak as if in the escape from some deadly peril.

Afterwards it appeared that the line had passed the first proof-reader as I wrote it, but that the final reader had entered so sympathetically into the realistic intention of my poem as to contribute the modification which had nearly been my end.

x

As it fell out, I lived without farther difficulty to the day and hour of the dinner Lowell made for me; and I really think, looking at myself impersonally, and remembering the sort of young fellow I was, that it would have been a great pity if I had not. The dinner was at the old-fashioned Boston hour of two, and the table was laid for four people in some little upper room at Parker's, which I was never afterwards able to make sure of. Lowell was already there when I came, and he presented me, to my inexpressible delight and surprise, to Dr. Holmes, who was there with him.

Holmes was in the most brilliant hour of that wonderful second youth which his fame flowered into long after the world thought he had completed the cycle of his literary life. He had already received full recognition as a poet of delicate wit, nimble humor, airy imagination, and exquisite grace, when the Autocrat papers advanced his name indefinitely beyond the bounds which most immortals would have found range enough. The marvel of his invention was still fresh in the minds of men, and time had not dulled in any measure the sense of its novelty. His readers all fondly identified him with his work; and I fully expected to find myself in the Autocrat's presence when I met Dr. Holmes. But the fascination was none the less for that reason; and the winning smile, the wise and humorous glance, the whole genial manner was as important to me as if I had foreboded something altogether different. I found him physically of the Napoleonic height which spiritually overtops the Alps, and I could look into his face without that unpleasant effort which giants of inferior mind so often cost the man of five feet four.

A little while after, Fields came in, and then our number and my pleasure were complete.

Nothing else so richly satisfactory, indeed, as the whole affair could have happened to a like youth at such a point in his career; and when I sat down with Dr. Holmes and Mr. Fields, on Lowell's right, I felt through and through the dramatic perfection of the event. The kindly Autocrat recognized some such quality of it in terms which were not the less precious and gracious for their humorous excess. I have no reason to think that he had yet read any of my poor verses, or had me otherwise than wholly on trust from Lowell; but he leaned over toward his host, and said, with a laughing look at me, "Well, James, this is something like the apostolic succession; this is the laying on of hands." I took his sweet and caressing irony as he meant it; but the charm of it went to my head long before any drop of wine, together with the charm of hearing him and Lowell calling each other James and Wendell, and of finding them still cordially boys together.

I would gladly have glimmered before those great lights in the talk that followed, if I could have thought of anything brilliant to say, but I could not, and so I let them shine without a ray of reflected splendor from me. It was such talk as I had, of course, never heard before, and it is not saying enough to say that I have never heard such talk since except from these two men. It was as light and kind as it was deep and true, and it ranged over a hundred things, with a perpetual sparkle of Dr. Holmes's wit, and the constant glow of Lowell's incandescent sense. From time to time Fields came in with one of his delightful stories (sketches of character they were, which he sometimes did not mind caricaturing), or with some criticism of the literary situation from his stand-point of both lover and publisher of books. I heard fames that I had accepted as proofs of power treated as factitious, and witnessed a frankness concerning authorship, far and near, that I had not dreamed of authors using. When Dr. Holmes understood that I wrote for the Saturday Press, which was running amuck among some Bostonian immortalities of the day, he seemed willing that I should know they were not thought so very undying in Boston, and that I should not take the notion of a Mutual Admiration Society too seriously, or accept the New York bohemian view of Boston as true. For the most part the talk did not address itself to me, but became an exchange of thoughts and fancies between himself and Lowell. They touched, I remember, on certain matters of technique, and the doctor confessed that he had a prejudice against some words that he could not overcome; for instance, he said, nothing could induce him to use *'neath* for *beneath,* no exigency of versification or stress of rhyme. Lowell contended that he would use any word that carried his meaning; and I think he did this to the hurt of some of his earlier things. He was then probably in the revolt against too much literature in literature, which every one is destined sooner or later to share; there was a certain roughness, very like crudeness, which he indulged before his thought and phrase mellowed to one music in his later work. I tacitly agreed rather with the doctor, though I did not swerve from my allegiance to Lowell, and if I had spoken I should have sided with him: I would have given that or any other proof of my devotion. Fields casually mentioned that he thought The Dandelion was the most popularly liked of Lowell's briefer poems, and I made haste to say that I thought so too, though I did not really think anything about it; and then I was sorry, for I could see that the poet did not like it, quite; and I felt that I was duly punished for my dishonesty.

Hawthorne was named among other authors, probably by Fields, whose house had just published his Marble Faun, and who had recently come home on the same steamer with him. Dr. Holmes asked if I had met Hawthorne yet, and when I confessed that I had hardly yet even hoped for such a thing, he smiled his winning smile, and said: "Ah, well! I don't know that you will ever feel you have really met him. He is like a dim room with a little taper of personality burning on the corner of the mantel."

They all spoke of Hawthorne, and with the same affection, but the same sense of something mystical and remote in him; and every word was priceless to me. But these masters of the craft I was prentice to probably could not have said anything that I should not have found wise and well, and I am sure now I should have been the loser if the talk had shunned any of the phases of human nature which it touched. It is best to find that all men are of the same make, and that there are certain universal things which interest them as much as the supernal things, and amuse them even more. There was a saying of Lowell's which he was fond of repeating at the menace of any form of the transcendental, and he liked to warn himself and others with his homely, "Remember the dinner-bell." What I recall of the whole effect of a time so happy for me is that in all that was said, however high, however fine, we were never out of hearing of the dinner-bell; and perhaps this is the best effect I can leave with the reader. It was the first dinner served in courses that I had sat down to, and I felt that this service gave it a romantic importance which the older fashion of the West still wanted. Even at Governor Chase's table in Columbus the Governor carved; I knew of the dinner *à la Russe*, as it was then called, only from books; and it was a sort of literary flavor that I tasted in the successive dishes. When it came to the black coffee, and then to the *petits verres* of cognac, with lumps of sugar set fire to atop, it was something that so far transcended my home-kept experience that it began to seem altogether visionary.

Neither Fields nor Dr. Holmes smoked, and I had to confess that I did not; but Lowell smoked enough for all three, and the spark of his cigar began to show in the waning light before we rose from the table. The time that never had, nor can ever have, its fellow for me, had to come to an end, as all times must, and when I shook hands with Lowell in parting, he overwhelmed me by saying that if I thought of going to Concord he would send me a letter to Hawthorne. I was not to see Lowell again during my stay in Boston; but Dr. Holmes asked me to tea for the next evening, and Fields said I must come to breakfast with him in the morning.

XI

I recall with the affection due to his friendly nature, and to the kindness afterwards to pass between us for many years, the whole aspect of the publisher when I first saw him. His abundant hair, and his full "beard as broad as ony spade," that flowed from his throat in Homeric curls, were touched with the first frost. He had a fine color, and his eyes, as keen as they were kind, twinkled restlessly above the wholesome russet-red of his cheeks. His portly frame was clad in those Scotch tweeds which had not yet displaced the traditional broadcloth with us in the West, though I had sent to New York for a rough suit, and so felt myself not quite unworthy to meet a man fresh from the hands of the London tailor.

Otherwise I stood as much in awe of him as his jovial soul would let me; and if I might I should like to suggest to the literary youth of this day some notion of the importance of his name to the literary youth of my day. He gave æsthetic character to the house of Ticknor & Fields, but he was by no means a silent partner on the economic side. No one can forecast the fortune of a new book, but he knew as well as any publisher can know not only whether a book was good, but whether the reader would think so; and I suppose that his house made as few bad guesses, along with their good ones, as any house that ever tried the uncertain temper of the public with its ventures. In the minds of all who loved the plain brown cloth and tasteful print of its issues he was more or less intimately associated with their literature; and those who were not mistaken in thinking De Quincey one of the delightfulest authors in the world, were especially grateful to the man who first edited his writings in book form, and proud that this edition was the effect of American sympathy with them. At that day, I believed authorship the noblest calling in the world, and I should still be at a loss to name any nobler. The great authors I had met were to me the sum of greatness, and if I could not rank their publisher with them by virtue of equal achievement, I handsomely brevetted him worthy of their friendship, and honored him in the visible measure of it.

In his house beside the Charles, and in the close neighborhood

of Dr. Holmes, I found an odor and an air of books such as I
fancied might belong to the famous literary houses of London.
It is still there, that friendly home of lettered refinement, and
the gracious spirit which knew how to welcome me, and make
the least of my shyness and strangeness, and the most of the little
else there was in me, illumines it still, though my host of that
rapturous moment has many years been of those who are only
with us unseen and unheard. I remember his burlesque pretence
that morning of an inextinguishable grief when I owned that I
had never eaten blueberry cake before, and how he kept returning to the pathos of the fact that there should be a region of the
earth where blueberry cake was unknown. We breakfasted in
the pretty room whose windows look out through leaves and
flowers upon the river's coming and going tides, and whose walls
were covered with the faces and the autographs of all the contemporary poets and novelists. The Fieldses had spent some days
with Tennyson in their recent English sojourn, and Mrs. Fields
had much to tell of him, how he looked, how he smoked, how
he read aloud, and how he said, when he asked her to go with
him to the tower of his house, "Come up and see the sad English
sunset!" which had an instant value to me such as some rich
verse of his might have had. I was very new to it all, how new I
could not very well say, but I flattered myself that I breathed in
that atmosphere as if in the return from life-long exile. Still I
patriotically bragged of the West a little, and I told them proudly
that in Columbus no book since Uncle Tom's Cabin had sold so
well as The Marble Faun. This made the effect that I wished,
but whether it was true or not, heaven knows; I only know that
I heard it from our leading bookseller, and I made no question
of it myself.

After breakfast, Fields went away to the office, and I lingered,
while Mrs. Fields showed me from shelf to shelf in the library,
and dazzled me with the sight of authors' copies, and volumes
invaluable with the autographs and the pencilled notes of the
men whose names were dear to me from my love of their work.
Everywhere was some souvenir of the living celebrities my hosts

Ralph Waldo Emerson

had met; and whom had they not met in that English sojourn in days before England embittered herself to us during our Civil War? Not Tennyson only, but Thackeray, but Dickens, but Charles Reade, but Carlyle, but many a minor fame was in my ears from converse so recent with them that it was as if I heard their voices in their echoed words.

I do not remember how long I staid; I remember I was afraid of staying too long, and so I am sure I did not stay as long as I should have liked. But I have not the least notion how I got away, and I am not certain where I spent the rest of a day that began in the clouds, but had to be ended on the common earth. I suppose I gave it mostly to wandering about the city, and partly to recording my impressions of it for that newspaper which never published them. The summer weather in Boston, with its sunny heat struck through and through with the coolness of the sea, and its clear air untainted with a breath of smoke, I have always loved, but it had then a zest unknown before; and I should have thought it enough simply to be alive in it. But everywhere I came upon something that fed my famine for the old, the quaint, the picturesque, and however the day passed it was a banquet, a festival. I can only recall my breathless first sight of the Public Library and of the Athenæum Gallery: great sights then, which the Vatican and the Pitti hardly afterwards eclipsed for mere emotion. In fact I did not see these elder treasuries of literature and art between breakfasting with the Autocrat's publisher in the morning, and taking tea with the Autocrat himself in the evening, and that made a whole world's difference.

XII

The tea of that simpler time is wholly inconceivable to this generation, which knows the thing only as a mild form of afternoon reception; but I suppose that in 1860 very few dined late in our whole pastoral republic. Tea was the meal people asked people to when they wished to sit at long leisure and large ease; it came at the end of the day, at six o'clock, or seven; and one went to it in morning dress. It had an unceremonied domesticity in the abundance of its light dishes, and I fancy these did not vary much from East to West, except that we had a Southern touch in our fried chicken and corn bread; but at the Autocrat's tea table the cheering cup had a flavor unknown to me before that day. He asked me if I knew it, and I said it was English breakfast tea; for I had drunk it at the publisher's in the morning, and was willing not to seem strange to it. "Ah, yes," he said; "but this is the flower of the souchong; it is the blossom, the poetry of tea," and then he told me how it had been given him by a friend, a merchant in the China trade, which used to flourish in Boston, and was the poetry of commerce, as this delicate beverage was of tea. That commerce is long past, and I fancy that the plant ceased to bloom when the traffic fell into decay.

The Autocrat's windows had the same outlook upon the Charles as the publisher's, and after tea we went up into a back parlor of the same orientation, and saw the sunset die over the water, and the westering flats and hills. Nowhere else in the world has the day a lovelier close, and our talk took something of the mystic coloring that the heavens gave those mantling expanses. It was chiefly his talk, but I have always found the best talkers are willing that you should talk if you like, and a quick sympathy and a subtle sense met all that I had to say from him and from the unbroken circle of kindred intelligences about him. I saw him then in the midst of his family, and perhaps never afterwards to better advantage, or in a finer mood. We spoke of the things that people perhaps once liked to deal with more than they do now; of the intimations of immortality, of the experiences of morbid youth, and of all those messages from the tremulous nerves which we take for prophecies. I was not ashamed, before his tolerant wisdom, to acknowledge the effects that had lingered so long with me in fancy and even in conduct, from a time of broken health and troubled spirit; and I remember the exquisite tact in him which recognized them as things common to all, however peculiar in each, which left them mine for whatever obscure vanity I might have in them, and yet gave me the companionship of the whole race in their experience. We spoke of forebodings and presentiments; we approached the mystic confines of the world from which no traveller has yet returned with a passport *en règle* and properly *visé*; and he held his light course through these filmy impalpabilities with a charming sincerity, with the scientific conscience that refuses either to deny the substance of things unseen, or to affirm it. In the gathering dusk, so weird did my fortune of being there and listening to him seem, that I might well have been a blessed ghost, for all the reality I felt in myself.

I tried to tell him how much I had read him from my boyhood, and with what joy and gain; and he was patient of these futilities, and I have no doubt imagined the love that inspired them, and accepted that instead of the poor praise. When the sunset passed, and the lamps were lighted, and we all came back to our dear little firm-set earth, he began to question me about my native region of it. From many forgotten inquiries I recall his asking me what was the fashionable religion in Columbus, or the Church that socially corresponded to the Unitarian Church in Boston. He had first to clarify my intelligence as to what Unitarianism was; we had Universalists but not Unitarians; but when I understood, I answered from such vantage as my own wholly outside Swedenborgianism gave me, that I thought most of the most respectable people with us were of the Presbyterian Church; some were certainly Episcopalians, but upon the whole the largest number were Presbyterians. He found that very strange indeed; and said that he did not believe there was a Presbyterian Church in Boston; that the New England Calvinists were all of the Orthodox Church. He had to explain Orthodoxy to me, and then I could confess to one Congregational Church in Columbus.

Probably I failed to give the Autocrat any very clear image of our social frame in the West, but the fault was altogether mine, if I did. Such lecturing tours as he had made had not taken him among us, as those of Emerson and other New-Englanders had, and my report was positive rather than comparative. I was full of pride in journalism at that day, and I dare say that I vaunted the brilliancy and power of our newspapers more than they merited; I should not have been likely to wrong them otherwise. It is strange that in all the talk I had with him and Lowell, or rather heard from them, I can recall nothing said of political affairs, though Lincoln had then been nominated by the Republicans, and the Civil War had practically begun. But we did not imagine such a thing in the North; we rested secure in the belief that if Lincoln were elected the South would eat all its fiery words, perhaps from the mere love and inveterate habit of fire-eating.

I rent myself away from the Autocrat's presence as early as I could, and as my evening had been too full of happiness to sleep upon at once, I spent the rest of the night till two in the morning wandering about the streets and in the Common with a Harvard Senior whom I had met. He was a youth of like literary passions with myself, but of such different traditions in every possible way that his deeply schooled and definitely regulated life seemed as anomalous to me as my own desultory and self-found way must have seemed to him. We passed the time in the delight of trying to make ourselves known to each other, and in a promise to continue by letter the effort, which duly lapsed into silent patience with the necessarily insoluble problem.

XIII

I must have lingered in Boston for the introduction to Hawthorne which Lowell had offered me, for when it came, with a little note of kindness and counsel for myself such as only Lowell had the gift of writing, it was already so near Sunday that I staid over till Monday before I started. I do not recall what I did with the time, except keep myself from making it a burden to the people I knew, and wandering about the city alone. Nothing of it remains to me except the fortune that favored me that Sunday night with a view of the old Granary Burying-ground on Tremont Street. I found the gates open, and I explored every path in the place, wreaking myself in such meagre emotion as I could get from the tomb of the Franklin family, and rejoicing with the whole soul of my Western modernity in the evidence of a remote antiquity which so many of the dim inscriptions afforded. I do not think that I have ever known anything practically older than these monuments, though I have since supped so full of classic and mediæval ruin. I am sure that I was more deeply touched by the epitaph of a poor little Puritan maiden who died at sixteen in the early sixteen-thirties than afterwards by the tomb of Cæcilia Metella, and that the heart-ache which I tried to put into verse when I got back to my room in the hotel was none the less genuine because it would not lend itself to my literary purpose, and remains nothing but pathos to this day.

I am not able to say how I reached the town of Lowell, where I went before going to Concord, that I might ease the unhappy conscience I had about those factories which I hated so much to see, and have it clean for the pleasure of meeting the fabricator of visions whom I was authorized to molest in any air-castle where I might find him. I only know that I went to Lowell, and visited one of the great mills, which with their whirring spools, the ceaseless flight of their shuttles, and the bewildering sight and sound of all their mechanism have since seemed to me the death of the joy that ought to come from work, if not the captivity of those who tended them. But then I thought it right and well for me to be standing by,

"With sick and scornful looks averse,"

while these others toiled; I did not see the tragedy in it, and I got my pitiful literary antipathy away as soon as I could, no wiser for the sight of the ingenious contrivances I inspected, and I am sorry to say no sadder. In the cool of the evening I sat at the door of my hotel, and watched the long files of the work-worn factory-girls stream by, with no concern for them but to see which was pretty and which was plain, and with no dream of a truer order than that which gave them ten hours' work a day in those hideous mills and lodged them in the barracks where they rested from their toil.

XIV

I wonder if there is a stage that still runs between Lowell and Concord, past meadow walls, and under the caressing boughs of way-side elms, and through the bird-haunted gloom of woodland roads, in the freshness of the summer morning? By a blessed chance I found that there was such a stage in 1860, and I took it from my hotel, instead of going back to Boston and up to Concord as I must have had to do by train. The journey gave me the intimacy of the New England country as I could have had it in no other fashion, and for the first time I saw it in all the summer sweetness which I have often steeped my soul in since. The meadows were newly mown, and the air was fragrant with the grass, stretching in long winrows among the brown bowlders, or capped with canvas in the little haycocks it had been gathered into the day before. I was fresh from the affluent farms of the Western Reserve, and this care of the grass touched me with a rude pity, which I also bestowed on the meagre fields of corn and wheat; but still the land was lovelier than any I had ever seen, with its old farm-houses, and brambled gray stone walls, its stony hill-sides, its staggering orchards, its wooded tops, and its thick-brackened valleys. From West to East the difference was as great as I afterwards found it from America to Europe, and my impression of something quaint and strange was no keener when I saw Old England the next year than when I saw New England now. I had imagined the landscape bare of trees, and I was astonished to find it almost as full of them as at home, though they all looked very little, as they well might to eyes used to the primeval forests of Ohio. The road ran through them from time to time, and took their coolness on its smooth hard reaches, and then issued again in the glisten of the open fields.

I made phrases to myself about the scenery as we drove along; and yes, I suppose I made phrases about the young girl who was one of the inside passengers, and who, when the common strangeness had somewhat worn off, began to sing, and sang most of the way to Concord. Perhaps she was not very sage, and I am sure she was not of the caste of Vere de Vere, but she was pretty enough, and she had a voice of a birdlike tunableness, so that I would not have her out of the memory of that pleasant journey if I could. She was long ago an elderly woman, if she lives, and I suppose she would not now point out her fellow-passenger if he strolled in the evening by the house where she had dismounted, upon her arrival in Concord, and laugh and pull another girl away from the window, in the high excitement of the prodigious adventure.

XV

Her fellow-passenger was in far other excitement; he was to see Hawthorne, and in a manner to meet Priscilla and Zenobia, and Hester Prynne and little Pearl, and Miriam and Hilda, and Hollingsworth and Coverdale, and Chillingworth and Dimmesdale, and Donatello and Kenyon; and he had no heart for any such poor little reality as that, who could not have been got into any story that one could respect, and must have been difficult even in a Heinesque poem.

I wasted that whole evening and the next morning in fond delaying, and it was not until after the indifferent dinner I got at the tavern where I stopped, that I found courage to go and present Lowell's letter to Hawthorne. I would almost have foregone meeting the weird genius only to have kept that letter, for it said certain infinitely precious things of me with such a sweetness, such a grace as Lowell alone could give his praise. Years afterwards, when Hawthorne was dead, I met Mrs. Hawthorne, and told her of the pang I had in parting with it, and she sent it me, doubly enriched by Hawthorne's keeping. But now if I were to see him at all I must give up my letter, and I carried it in my hand to the door of the cottage he called The Wayside. It was never otherwise than a very modest place, but the modesty was greater then than to-day, and there was already some preliminary carpentry at one end of the cottage, which I saw was to result in an addition to it. I recall pleasant fields across the road before it; behind rose a hill wooded with low pines, such as is made in Septimius Felton the scene of the involuntary duel between Septimius and the young British officer. I have a sense of the woods coming quite down to the house, but if this was so I do not know what to do with a grassy slope which seems to have stretched part way up the hill. As I approached, I looked for the tower which the author was fabled to climb into at sight of the coming guest, and pull the ladder up after him; and I wondered whether he would fly before me in that sort, or imagine some easier means of escaping me.

The door was opened to my ring by a tall handsome boy whom I suppose to have been Mr. Julian Hawthorne; and the next moment I found myself in the presence of the romancer, who entered from some room beyond. He advanced carrying his head with a heavy forward droop, and with a pace for which I decided that the word would be *pondering*. It was the pace of a bulky man of fifty, and his head was that beautiful head we all know from the many pictures of it. But Hawthorne's *look* was different from that of any picture of him that I have seen. It was sombre and brooding, as the look of such a poet should have been; it was the look of a man who had dealt faithfully and therefore sorrowfully with that problem of evil which forever attracted, forever evaded Hawthorne. It was by no means troubled; it was full of a dark repose. Others who knew him better and saw him oftener were familiar with other aspects, and I remember that one night at Longfellow's table, when one of the guests happened to speak of the photograph of Hawthorne which hung in a corner of the room, Lowell said, after a glance at it, "Yes, it's good; but it hasn't his fine *accipitral* look."

In the face that confronted me, however, there was nothing of keen alertness; but only a sort of quiet, patient intelligence, for which I seek the right word in vain. It was a very regular face, with beautiful eyes; the mustache, still entirely dark, was dense over the fine mouth. Hawthorne was dressed in black, and he had a certain effect which I remember, of seeming to have on a black cravat with no visible collar. He was such a man that if I had ignorantly met him anywhere I should have instantly felt him to be a personage.

I must have given him the letter myself, for I have no recol-

lection of parting with it before, but I only remember his offering
me his hand, and making me shyly and tentatively welcome.
After a few moments of the demoralization which followed his
hospitable attempts in me, he asked if I would not like to go up
on his hill with him and sit there, where he smoked in the afternoon. He offered me a cigar, and when I said that I did not
smoke, he lighted it for himself, and we climbed the hill together.
At the top, where there was an outlook in the pines over the
Concord meadows, we found a log, and he invited me to a place
on it beside him, and at intervals of a minute or so he talked
while he smoked. Heaven preserved me from the folly of trying
to tell him how much his books had been to me, and though we
got on rapidly at no time, I think we got on better for this inter-
position. He asked me about Lowell, I dare say, for I told him of
my joy in meeting him and Dr. Holmes, and this seemed greatly
to interest him. Perhaps because he was so lately from Europe,
where our great men are always seen through the wrong end of
the telescope, he appeared surprised at my devotion, and asked
me whether I cared as much for meeting them as I should care
for meeting the famous English authors. I professed that I cared
much more, though whether this was true, I now have my
doubts, and I think Hawthorne doubted it at the time. But he
said nothing in comment, and went on to speak generally of
Europe and America. He was curious about the West, which he
seemed to fancy much more purely American, and said he
would like to see some part of the country on which the shadow,
or, if I must be precise, the damned shadow, of Europe had not
fallen. I told him I thought the West must finally be characterized
by the Germans, whom we had in great numbers, and, purely
from my zeal for German poetry, I tried to allege some proofs
of their present influence, though I could think of none outside
of politics, which I thought they affected wholesomely. I knew
Hawthorne was a Democrat, and I felt it well to touch politics
lightly, but he had no more to say about the fateful election then
pending than Holmes or Lowell had.

With the abrupt transition of his talk throughout, he began

somehow to speak of women, and said he had never seen a woman whom he thought quite beautiful. In the same way he spoke of the New England temperament, and suggested that the apparent coldness in it was also real, and that the suppression of emotion for generations would extinguish it at last. Then he questioned me as to my knowledge of Concord, and whether I had seen any of the notable people. I answered that I had met no one but himself, as yet, but I very much wished to see Emerson and Thoreau. I did not think it needful to say that I wished to see Thoreau quite as much because he had suffered in the cause of John Brown as because he had written the books which had taken me; and when he said that Thoreau prided himself on coming nearer the heart of a pine-tree than any other human being, I could say honestly enough that I would rather come near the heart of a man. This visibly pleased him, and I saw that it did not displease him, when he asked whether I was not going to see his next neighbor Mr. Alcott, and I confessed that I had never heard of him. That surprised as well as pleased him; he remarked, with whatever intention, that there was nothing like recognition to make a man modest; and he entered into some account of the philosopher, whom I suppose I need not be much ashamed of not knowing then, since his influence was of the immediate sort that makes a man important to his townsmen while he is still strange to his countrymen.

Hawthorne descanted a little upon the landscape, and said certain of the pleasant fields below us belonged to him; but he preferred his hill-top, and if he could have his way those arable fields should be grown up to pines too. He smoked fitfully, and slowly, and in the hour that we spent together, his whiffs were of the desultory and unfinal character of his words. When we went down, he asked me into his house again, and would have me stay to tea, for which we found the table laid. But there was a great deal of silence in it all, and at times, in spite of his shadowy kindness, I felt my spirits sink. After tea, he showed me a bookcase, where there were a few books toppling about on the half-filled shelves, and said, coldly, "This is my library." I knew that men

were his books, and though I myself cared for books so much, I
found it fit and fine that he should care so little, or seem to care
so little. Some of his own romances were among the volumes on
these shelves, and when I put my finger on the Blithedale
Romance and said that I preferred that to the others, his face
lighted up, and he said that he believed the Germans liked that
best too.

Upon the whole we parted such good friends that when I
offered to take leave he asked me how long I was to be in Concord,
and not only bade me come to see him again, but said he would
give me a card to Emerson, if I liked. I answered, of course, that
I should like it beyond all things; and he wrote on the back of
his card something which I found, when I got away, to be, "I find
this young man worthy." The quaintness, the little stiffness of it,
if one pleases to call it so, was amusing to one who was not without his sense of humor, but the kindness filled me to the throat
with joy. In fact, I entirely liked Hawthorne. He had been as
cordial as so shy a man could show himself; and I perceived, with
the repose that nothing else can give, the entire sincerity of his
soul.

Nothing could have been farther from the behavior of this
very great man than any sort of posing, apparently, or a wish to
affect me with a sense of his greatness. I saw that he was as much
abashed by our encounter as I was; he was visibly shy to the
point of discomfort, but in no ignoble sense was he conscious,
and as nearly as he could with one so much his younger he made
an absolute equality between us. My memory of him is without
alloy one of the finest pleasures of my life. In my heart I paid
him the same glad homage that I paid Lowell and Holmes, and
he did nothing to make me think that I had overpaid him. This
seems perhaps very little to say in his praise, but to my mind it is
saying everything, for I have known but few great men, especially
of those I met in early life, when I wished to lavish my admiration
upon them, whom I have not the impression of having left in my
debt. Then, a defect of the Puritan quality, which I have found
in many New-Englanders, is that, wittingly or unwittingly, they

propose themselves to you as an example, or if not quite this, that they surround themselves with a subtle ether of potential disapprobation, in which, at the first sign of unworthiness in you, they helplessly suffer you to gasp and perish; they have good hearts, and they would probably come to your succor out of humanity, if they knew how, but they do not know how. Hawthorne had nothing of this about him; he was no more tacitly than he was explicitly didactic. I thought him as thoroughly in keeping with his romances as Dr. Holmes had seemed with his essays and poems, and I met him as I had met the Autocrat in the supreme hour of his fame. He had just given the world the last of those incomparable works which it was to have finished from his hand; the Marble Faun had worthily followed, at a somewhat longer interval than usual, the Blithedale Romance, and the House of Seven Gables, and the Scarlet Letter, and had perhaps carried his name higher than all the rest, and certainly farther. Everybody was reading it, and more or less bewailing its indefinite close, but yielding him that full honor and praise which a writer can hope for but once in his life. Nobody dreamed that thereafter only precious fragments, sketches more or less faltering, though all with the divine touch in them, were further to enrich a legacy which in its kind is the finest the race has received from any mind. As I have said, we are always finding new Hawthornes, but the illusion soon wears away, and then we perceive that they were not Hawthornes at all; that he had some peculiar difference from them, which, by-and-by, we shall no doubt consent must be his difference from all men evermore.

I am painfully aware that I have not summoned before the reader the image of the man as it has always stood in my memory, and I feel a sort of shame for my failure. He was so altogether simple that it seems as if it would be easy to do so; but perhaps a spirit from the other world would be simple too, and yet would no more stand at parle, or consent to be sketched, than Hawthorne. In fact, he was always more or less merging into the shadow, which was in a few years wholly to close over him; there was nothing uncanny in his presence, there was nothing even unwilling, but he had that apparitional quality of some great minds which kept Shakespeare largely unknown to those who thought themselves his intimates, and has at last left him a sort of doubt. There was nothing teasing or wilfully elusive in Hawthorne's impalpability, such as I afterward felt in Thoreau; if he was not there to your touch, it was no fault of his; it was because your touch was dull, and wanted the use of contact with such natures. The hand passes through the veridical phantom without a sense of its presence, but the phantom is none the less veridical for all that.

XVI

I kept the evening of the day I met Hawthorne wholly for the thoughts of him, or rather for that reverberation which continues in the young sensibilities after some important encounter. It must have been the next morning that I went to find Thoreau, and I am dimly aware of making one or two failures to find him, if I ever really found him at all.

He is an author who has fallen into that abeyance, awaiting all authors, great or small, at some time or another; but I think that with him, at least in regard to his most important book, it can be only transitory. I have not read the story of his hermitage beside Walden Pond since the year 1858, but I have a fancy that if I should take it up now, I should think it a wiser and truer conception of the world than I thought it then. It is no solution of the problem; men are not going to answer the riddle of the painful earth by building themselves shanties and living upon beans and watching ant-fights; but I do not believe Tolstoy himself has more clearly shown the hollowness, the hopelessness, the unworthiness of the life of the world than Thoreau did in that book. If it were newly written it could not fail of a far vaster acceptance than it had then, when to those who thought and felt seriously it seemed that if slavery could only be controlled, all things else would come right of themselves with us. Slavery has not only been controlled, but it has been destroyed, and yet things have not begun to come right with us; but it was in the order of Providence that chattel slavery should cease before industrial slavery, and the infinitely crueler and stupider vanity and luxury bred of it, should be attacked. If there was then any prevision of the struggle now at hand, the seers averted their eyes, and strove only to cope with the less evil. Thoreau himself, who had so clear a vision of the falsity and folly of society as we still have it, threw himself into the tide that was already, in Kansas and Virginia, reddened with war; he aided and abetted the John Brown raid, I do not recall how much or in what sort; and he had suffered in prison for his opinions and actions. It was this inevitable heroism of his that, more than his literature even, made me wish to see him and revere him; and I do not believe that I should have found the veneration difficult, when at last I met him in his insufficient person, if he had otherwise been present to my glowing expectation. He came into the room a quaint, stump figure of a man, whose effect of long trunk and short limbs was heightened by his fashionless trousers being let down too low. He had a noble face, with tossed hair, a distraught eye, and a fine aquilinity of profile, which made me think at once of Don Quixote and of Cervantes; but his nose failed to add that foot to his stature which Lamb says a nose of that shape will always give a man. He tried to place me geographically after he had given me a chair not quite so far off as Ohio, though still across the whole room, for he sat against one wall, and I against the other; but apparently he failed to pull himself out of his revery by the effort, for he remained in a dreamy muse, which all my attempts to say something fit about John Brown and Walden Pond seemed only to deepen upon him. I have not the least doubt that I was needless and valueless about both, and that what I said could not well have prompted an important response; but I did my poor best, and I was terribly disappointed in the result. The truth is that in those days I was a helplessly concrete young person, and all forms of the abstract, the airdrawn, afflicted me like physical discomforts. I do not remember that Thoreau spoke of his books or of himself at all, and when he began to speak of John Brown, it was not the warm, palpable, loving, fearful old man of my conception, but a sort of John Brown type, a John Brown ideal, a John Brown principle, which we were somehow (with long pauses between the vague, orphic phrases) to cherish, and to nourish ourselves upon.

It was not merely a defeat of my hopes, it was a rout, and I felt myself so scattered over the field of thought that I could hardly bring my forces together for retreat. I must have made some effort, vain and foolish enough, to rematerialize my old demigod, but when I came away it was with the feeling that there was very little more left of John Brown than there was of me. His body was not mouldering in the grave, neither was his soul marching on; his ideal, his type, his principle alone existed, and I did not know what to do with it. I am not blaming Thoreau; his words were addressed to a far other understanding than mine, and it was my misfortune if I could not profit by them. I think, or I venture to hope, that I could profit better by them now; but in this record I am trying honestly to report their effect with the sort of youth I was then.

XVII

Such as I was, I rather wonder that I had the courage, after this experiment of Thoreau, to present the card Hawthorne had given me to Emerson. I must have gone to him at once, however, for I cannot make out any interval of time between my visit to the disciple and my visit to the master. I think it was Emerson himself who opened his door to me, for I have a vision of the fine old man standing tall on his threshold, with the card in his hand, and looking from it to me with a vague serenity, while I waited a moment on the door-step below him. He must then have been about sixty, but I remember nothing of age in his aspect, though I have called him an old man. His hair, I am sure, was still entirely dark, and his face had a kind of marble youthfulness, chiselled to a delicate intelligence by the highest and noblest thinking that any man has done. There was a strange charm in Emerson's eyes, which I felt then and always, something like that

I saw in Lincoln's, but shyer, but sweeter and less sad. His smile was the very sweetest I have ever beheld, and the contour of the mask and the line of the profile were in keeping with this incomparable sweetness of the mouth, at once grave and quaint, though quaint is not quite the word for it either, but subtly, not unkindly arch, which again is not the word.

It was his great fortune to have been mostly misunderstood, and to have reached the dense intelligence of his fellow-men after a whole lifetime of perfectly simple and lucid appeal, and his countenance expressed the patience and forbearance of a wise man content to bide his time. It would be hard to persuade people now that Emerson once represented to the popular mind all that was most hopelessly impossible, and that in a certain sort he was a national joke, the type of the incomprehensible, the byword of the poor paragrapher. He had perhaps disabused the community somewhat by presenting himself here and there as a lecturer, and talking face to face with men in terms which they could not refuse to find as clear as they were wise; he was more and more read, by certain persons, here and there; but we are still so far behind him in the reach of his far-thinking that it need not be matter of wonder that twenty years before his death he was the most misunderstood man in America. Yet in that twilight where he dwelt he loomed large upon the imagination; the minds that could not conceive him were still aware of his greatness. I myself had not read much of him, but I knew the essays he was printing in the Atlantic, and I knew certain of his poems, though by no means many; yet I had this sense of him, that he was somehow, beyond and above my ken, a presence of force and beauty and wisdom, uncompanioned in our literature. He had lately stooped from his ethereal heights to take part in the battle of humanity, and I suppose that if the truth were told he was more to my young fervor because he had said that John Brown had made the gallows glorious like the cross, than because he had uttered all those truer and wiser things which will still a hundred years hence be leading the thought of the world.

I do not know in just what sort he made me welcome, but I am aware of sitting with him in his study or library, and of his presently speaking of Hawthorne, whom I probably celebrated as I best could, and whom he praised for his personal excellence, and for his fine qualities as a neighbor. "But his last book," he added, reflectively, "is a mere mush," and I perceived that this great man was no better equipped to judge an artistic fiction than the groundlings who were then crying out upon the indefinite close of the Marble Faun. Apparently he had read it, as they had, for the story, but it seems to me now, if it did not seem to me then, that as far as the problem of evil was involved, the book must leave it where it found it. That is forever insoluble, and it was rather with that than with his more or less shadowy people that the romancer was concerned. Emerson had, in fact, a defective sense as to specific pieces of literature; he praised extravagantly, and in the wrong place, especially among the new things, and he failed to see the worth of much that was fine and precious beside the line of his fancy.

He began to ask me about the West, and about some unknown man in Michigan, who had been sending him poems, and whom he seemed to think very promising, though he has not apparently kept his word to do great things. I did not find what Emerson had to say of my section very accurate or important, though it was kindly enough, and just enough as to what the West ought to do in literature. He thought it a pity that a literary periodical which had lately been started in Cincinnati should be appealing to the East for contributions, instead of relying upon the writers nearer home; and he listened with what patience he could to my modest opinion that we had not the writers nearer home. I never was of those Westerners who believed that the West was kept out of literature by the jealousy of the East, and I tried to explain why we had not the men to write that magazine full in Ohio. He alleged the man in Michigan as one who alone could do much to fill it worthily, and again I had to say that I had never heard of him.

I felt rather guilty in my ignorance, and I had a notion that it did not commend me, but happily at this moment Mr. Emerson was called to dinner, and he asked me to come with him. After dinner we walked about in his "pleached garden" a little, and then we came again into his library, where I meant to linger only till I could fitly get away. He questioned me about what I had seen of Concord, and whom besides Hawthorne I had met, and when I told him only Thoreau, he asked me if I knew the poems of Mr. William Ellery Channing. I have known them since, and felt their quality, which I have gladly owned a genuine and original poetry; but I answered then truly that I knew them only from Poe's criticisms: cruel and spiteful things which I should be ashamed of enjoying as I once did.

"Whose criticisms?" asked Emerson.

"Poe's," I said again.

"Oh," he cried out, after a moment, as if he had returned from a far search for my meaning, *"you mean the jingle-man !"*

I do not know why this should have put me to such confusion, but if I had written the criticisms myself I do not think I could have been more abashed. Perhaps I felt an edge of reproof, of admonition, in a characterization of Poe which the world will hardly agree with; though I do not agree with the world about him, myself, in its admiration. At any rate, it made an end of me for the time, and I remained as if already absent, while Emerson questioned me as to what I had written in the Atlantic Monthly. He had evidently read none of my contributions, for he looked at them, in the bound volume of the magazine which he got down, with the effect of being wholly strange to them, and then gravely affixed my initials to each. He followed me to the door, still speaking of poetry, and as he took a kindly enough leave of me, he said one might very well give a pleasant hour to it now and then.

A pleasant hour to poetry! I was meaning to give all time and all eternity to poetry, and I should by no means have wished to find pleasure in it; I should have thought that a proof of inferior quality in the work; I should have preferred anxiety, anguish even, to pleasure. But if Emerson thought from the glance he gave my verses that I had better not lavish myself upon that kind of thing, unless there was a great deal more of me than I could have made apparent in our meeting, no doubt he was right. I was only too painfully aware of my shortcoming, but I felt that it was shorter-coming than it need have been. I had somehow not prospered in my visit to Emerson as I had with Hawthorne, and I came away wondering in what sort I had gone wrong. I was not a forth-putting youth, and I could not blame myself for anything in my approaches that merited withholding; indeed, I made no approaches; but as I must needs blame myself for something, I fell upon the fact that in my confused retreat from Emerson's presence I had failed in a certain slight point of ceremony, and I magnified this into an offence of capital importance. I went home to my hotel, and passed the afternoon in pure misery. I had moments of wild question when I debated whether it would be better to go back and own my error, or whether it would be better to write him a note, and try to set myself right in that way. But in the end I did neither, and I have since survived my mortal shame some forty years or more. But at the time it did not seem possible that I should live through the day with it, and I thought that I ought at least to go and confess it to Hawthorne, and let him disown the wretch who had so poorly repaid the kindness of his introduction by such misbehavior. I did indeed walk down by the Wayside, in the cool of the evening, and there I saw Hawthorne for the last time. He was sitting on one of the timbers beside his cottage, and smoking with an air of friendly calm. I had got on very well with him, and I longed to go in, and tell him how ill I had got on with Emerson; I believed that though he cast me off, he would understand me, and would perhaps see some hope for me in another world, though there could be none in this.

But I had not the courage to speak of the affair to any one but Fields, to whom I unpacked my heart when I got back to Boston, and he asked me about my adventures in Concord. By this time I could see it in a humorous light, and I did not much mind his lying back in his chair and laughing and laughing, till I thought he would roll out of it. He perfectly conceived the situation, and got an amusement from it that I could get only through sympathy with him. But I thought it a favorable moment to propose myself as the assistant editor of the Atlantic Monthly, which I had the belief I could very well become, with advantage to myself if not to the magazine. He seemed to think so too; he said that if the place had not just been filled, I should certainly have had it; and it was to his recollection of this prompt ambition of mine that I suppose I may have owed my succession to a like vacancy some four years later. He was charmingly kind; he entered with the sweetest interest into the story of my economic life, which had been full of changes and chances already. But when I said very seriously that now I was tired of these fortuities, and would like to be settled in something, he asked, with dancing eyes,

"Why, how old are you?"

"I am twenty-three," I answered, and then the laughing fit took him again.

"Well," he said, "you begin young, out there!"

In my heart I did not think that twenty-three was so very young, but perhaps it was; and if any one were to say that I had been portraying here a youth whose aims were certainly beyond his achievements, who was morbidly sensitive, and if not conceited was intolerably conscious, who had met with incredible kindness, and had suffered no more than was good for him, though he might not have merited his pain any more than his joy, I do not know that I should gainsay him, for I am not at all sure that I was not just that kind of youth when I paid my first visit to New England.

Part Second

FIRST IMPRESSIONS OF LITERARY NEW YORK

I T WAS by boat that I arrived from Boston, on an August morning of 1860, which was probably of the same quality as an August morning of 1900. I used not to mind the weather much in those days; it was hot or it was cold, it was wet or it was dry, but it was not my affair; and I suppose that I sweltered about the strange city, with no sense of anything very personal in the temperature, until nightfall. What I remember is being high up in a hotel long since laid low, listening in the summer dark, after the long day was done, to the Niagara roar of the omnibuses whose tide then swept Broadway from curb to curb, for all the miles of its length. At that hour the other city noises were stilled, or lost in this vaster volume of sound, which seemed to fill the whole night. It had a solemnity which the modern comer to New York will hardly imagine, for that tide of omnibuses has long since ebbed away, and has left the air to the strident discords of the elevated trains and the irregular alarum of the grip-car gongs, which blend to no such harmonious thunder as rose from the procession of those ponderous and innumerable vans. There was a sort of inner quiet in the sound, and when I chose I slept off to it, and woke to it in the morning refreshed and strengthened to explore the literary situation in the metropolis.

I

Not that I think I left this to the second day. Very probably I lost no time in going to the office of the Saturday Press, as soon as I had my breakfast after arriving, and I have a dim impression of anticipating the earliest of the Bohemians, whose gay theory of life obliged them to a good many hardships in lying down early in the morning, and rising up late in the day. If it was the office-boy who bore me company during the first hour of my visit, by-and-by the editors and contributors actually began to come in. I would not be very specific about them if I could, for since that Bohemia has faded from the map of the republic of letters, it has grown more and more difficult to trace its citizenship to any certain writer. There are some living who knew the Bohemians and even loved them, but there are increasingly few who were of them, even in the fond retrospect of youthful follies and errors. It was in fact but a sickly colony, transplanted from the mother asphalt of Paris, and never really striking root in the pavements of New York; it was a colony of ideas, of theories, which had perhaps never had any deep root anywhere. What these ideas, these theories, were in art and in life, it would not be very easy to say; but in the Saturday Press they came to violent expression, not to say explosion, against all existing forms of respectability. If respectability was your *bête noire*, then you were a Bohemian; and if you were in the habit of rendering yourself in prose, then you necessarily shredded your prose into very fine paragraphs of a sentence each, or of a very few words, or even of one word. I believe this fashion prevailed till very lately with some of the dramatic critics, who thought that it gave a quality of epigram to the style; and I suppose it was borrowed from the more spasmodic moments of Victor Hugo, by the editor of the Press. He brought it back with him when he came home from one of those sojourns in Paris which possess one of the French accent rather than the French language; I long desired to write in that fashion myself, but I had not the courage.

This editor was a man of such open and avowed cynicism that he may have been, for all I know, a kindly optimist at heart; some say, however, that he had really talked himself into being what he seemed. I only know that his talk, the first day I saw him, was of such a sort that if he was half as bad, he would have been too bad to be. He walked up and down his room saying what

lurid things he would directly do if any one accused him of respectability, so that he might disabuse the minds of all witnesses.
There were four or five of his assistants and contributors listening
to the dreadful threats, which did not deceive even so great innocence as mine, but I do not know whether they found it the
sorry farce that I did. They probably felt the fascination for him
which I could not disown, in spite of my inner disgust; and were
watchful at the same time for the effect of his words with one who
was confessedly fresh from Boston, and was full of delight in the
people he had seen there. It appeared, with him, to be proof of
the inferiority of Boston that if you passed down Washington
Street, half a dozen men in the crowd would know you were
Holmes, or Lowell, or Longfellow, or Wendell Phillips; but in
Broadway no one would know who you were, or care to the
measure of his smallest blasphemy. I have since heard this more
than once urged as a signal advantage of New York for the
æsthetic inhabitant, but I am not sure, yet, that it is so. The un-
recognized celebrity probably has his mind quite as much upon
himself as if some one pointed him out, and otherwise I cannot
think that the sense of neighborhood is such a bad thing for the
artist in any sort. It involves the sense of responsibility, which
cannot be too constant or too keen. If it narrows, it deepens; and
this may be the secret of Boston.

II

It would not be easy to say just why the Bohemian group
represented New York literature to my imagination, for I certainly associated other names with its best work, but perhaps it
was because I had written for the Saturday Press myself, and
had my pride in it, and perhaps it was because that paper really
embodied the new literary life of the city. It was clever, and full
of the wit that tries its teeth upon everything. It attacked all
literary shams but its own, and it made itself felt and feared. The
young writers throughout the country were ambitious to be seen
in it, and they gave their best to it; they gave literally, for the
Saturday Press never paid in anything but hopes of paying,

vaguer even than promises. It is not too much to say that it was very nearly as well for one to be accepted by the Press as to be accepted by the Atlantic, and for the time there was no other literary comparison. To be in it was to be in the company of Fitz James O'Brien, Fitzhugh Ludlow, Mr. Aldrich, Mr. Stedman, and whoever else was liveliest in prose or loveliest in verse at that day in New York. It was a power, and although it is true that, as Henry Giles said of it, "Man cannot live by snapping-turtle alone," the Press was very good snapping-turtle. Or, it seemed so then; I should be almost afraid to test it now, for I do not like snapping-turtle so much as I once did, and I have grown nicer in my taste, and want my snapping-turtle of the very best. What is certain is that I went to the office of the Saturday Press in New York with much the same sort of feeling I had in going to the office of the Atlantic Monthly in Boston, but I came away with a very different feeling. I had found there a bitterness against Boston as great as the bitterness against respectability, and as Boston was then rapidly becoming my second country, I could not join in the scorn thought of her and said of her by the Bohemians. I fancied a conspiracy among them to shock the literary pilgrim, and to minify the precious emotions he had experienced in visiting other shrines; but I found no harm in that, for I knew just how much to be shocked, and I thought I knew better how to value certain things of the soul than they. Yet when their chief asked me how I got on with Hawthorne, and I began to say that he was very shy and I was rather shy, and the king of Bohemia took his pipe out to break in upon me with "Oh, a couple of shysters!" and the rest laughed, I was abashed all they could have wished, and was not restored to myself till one of them said that the thought of Boston made him as ugly as sin: then I began to hope again that men who took themselves so seriously as that need not be taken very seriously by me.

In fact I had heard things almost as desperately cynical in other newspaper offices before that, and I could not see what was so distinctively Bohemian in these *anime prave*, these souls so baleful by their own showing. But apparently Bohemia was not a state that you could well imagine from one encounter, and since my stay in New York was to be very short, I lost no time in acquainting myself farther with it. That very night I went to the beer-cellar, once very far up Broadway, where I was given to know that the Bohemian nights were smoked and quaffed away. It was said, so far West as Ohio, that the queen of Bohemia sometimes came to Pfaff's: a young girl of a sprightly gift in letters, whose name or pseudonym had made itself pretty well known at that day, and whose fate, pathetic at all times, out-tragedies almost any other in the history of letters. She was seized with hydrophobia from the bite of her dog, on a railroad train; and made a long journey home in the paroxysms of that agonizing disease, which ended in her death after she reached New York. But this was after her reign had ended, and no such black shadow was cast forward upon Pfaff's, whose name often figured in the verse and the epigrammatically paragraphed prose of the Saturday Press. I felt that as a contributor and at least a brevet Bohemian I ought not to go home without visiting the famous place, and witnessing if I could not share the revels of my comrades. As I neither drank beer nor smoked, my part in the carousal was limited to a German pancake, which I found they had very good at Pfaff's, and to listening to the whirling words of my commensals, at the long board spread for the Bohemians in a cavernous space under the pavement. There were writers for the Saturday Press and for Vanity Fair (a hopefully comic paper of that day), and some of the artists who drew for the illustrated periodicals. Nothing of their talk remains with me, but the impression remains that it was not so good talk as I had heard in Boston. At one moment of the orgy, which went but slowly for an orgy, we were joined by some belated Bohemians whom the others made a great clamor over; I was given to understand they were just recovered from a fearful debauch; their locks were still damp from the wet towels used to restore them, and their eyes were very frenzied. I was presented to these types, who neither said nor did anything worthy of their awful appearance, but dropped into seats at the table, and ate of the supper with an appetite that seemed poor. I staid hoping vainly for worse things till eleven o'clock, and then I rose and took my leave of a literary condition that had distinctly disappointed me. I do not say that it may not have been wickeder and wittier than I found it; I only report what I saw and heard in Bohemia on my first visit to New York, and I know that my acquaintance with it was not exhaustive. When I came the next year the Saturday Press was no more, and the editor and his contributors had no longer a common centre. The best of the young fellows whom I met there confessed, in a pleasant exchange of letters which we had afterwards, that he thought the pose a vain and unprofitable one; and when the Press was revived, after the war, it was without any of the old Bohemian characteristics except that of not paying for material. It could not last long upon these terms, and again it passed away, and still waits its second palingenesis.

The editor passed away too, not long after, and the thing that he had inspired altogether ceased to be. He was a man of a certain sardonic power, and used it rather fiercely and freely, with a joy probably more apparent than real in the pain it gave. In my last knowledge of him he was much milder than when I first knew him, and I have the feeling that he too came to own before he died that man cannot live by snapping-turtle alone. He was kind to some neglected talents, and befriended them with a vigor and a zeal which he would have been the last to let you call generous. The chief of these was Walt Whitman, who, when the Saturday Press took it up, had as hopeless a cause with the critics on either side of the ocean as any man could have. It was not till long afterward that his English admirers began to discover him, and to make his countrymen some noisy reproaches for ignoring him; they were wholly in the dark concerning him when the Saturday Press, which first stood his friend, and the young men whom the Press gathered about it, made him their cult. No doubt he was more valued because he was so offensive in some ways than he would have been if he had been in no way offensive, but it remains a fact that they celebrated him quite as much as was good for them. He was often at Pfaff's with them, and the night of my visit he was the chief fact of my experience. I did not know he was there till I was on my way out, for he did not sit at the table under the pavement, but at the head of one further into the room. There, as I passed, some friendly fellow stopped me and named me to him, and I remember how he leaned back in his chair, and reached out his great hand to me, as if he were going to give it me for good and all. He had a fine head, with a cloud of Jovian hair upon it, and a branching beard and mustache, and gentle eyes that looked most kindly into mine, and seemed to wish the liking which I instantly gave him, though we hardly passed a word, and our acquaintance was summed up in that glance and the grasp of his mighty fist upon my hand. I doubt if he had any notion who or what I was beyond the fact that I was a young poet of some sort, but he may possibly have remembered seeing my name printed after some very Heinesque verses in the Press. I did not meet him again for twenty years, and then I had only a moment with him when he was reading the proofs of his poems in Boston. Some years later I saw him for the last time, one day after his lecture on Lincoln, in that city, when he came down from the platform to speak with some hand-shaking friends who gathered about him. Then and always he gave me the sense of a sweet and true soul, and I felt in him a spiritual dignity which I will not try to reconcile with his printing in the forefront of his book a passage from a private letter of Emerson's, though I believe he would not have seen such a thing as most other men would, or thought ill of it in another. The spiritual purity which I felt in him no less than the dignity is something that I will no more try to reconcile with what denies it in his page; but such things we may well leave to the adjustment of finer balances than we have at hand. I will make sure only of the greatest benignity in the presence of the man. The apostle of the rough, the uncouth, was the gentlest person; his barbaric yawp, translated into the terms of social encounter, was an address of singular quiet, delivered in a voice of winning and endearing friendliness.

As to his work itself, I suppose that I do not think it so valuable in effect as in intention. He was a liberating force, a very "imperial anarch" in literature; but liberty is never anything but a means, and what Whitman achieved was a means and not an end, in what must be called his verse. I like his prose, if there is a difference, much better; there he is of a genial and comforting quality, very rich and cordial, such as I felt him to be when I met him in person. His verse seems to me not poetry, but the materials of poetry, like one's emotions; yet I would not misprize it, and I am glad to own that I have had moments of great pleasure in it. Some French critic quoted in the Saturday Press (I cannot think of his name) said the best thing of him when he said that he made you a partner of the enterprise, for that is precisely what he does, and that is what alienates and what endears in him, as you like or dislike the partnership. It is still something neighborly, brotherly, fatherly, and so I felt him to be when the benign old man looked on me and spoke to me.

III

That night at Pfaff's must have been the last of the Bohemians for me, and it was the last of New York authorship too, for the time. I do not know why I should not have imagined trying to see Curtis, whom I knew so much by heart, and whom I adored, but I may not have had the courage, or I may have heard that he was out of town; Bryant, I believe, was then out of the country; but at any rate I did not attempt him either. The Bohemians were the beginning and the end of the story for me, and to tell the truth I did not like the story. I remember that as I sat at that table under the pavement, in Pfaff's beer-cellar, and listened to the wit that did not seem very funny, I thought of the dinner with Lowell, the breakfast with Fields, the supper at the Autocrat's, and felt that I had fallen very far. In fact it can do no harm at this distance of time to confess that it seemed to me then, and for a good while afterward, that a person who had seen the men and had the things said before him that I had in Boston, could not keep himself too carefully in cotton; and this was what I did all the following winter, though of course it was a secret between me and me. I dare say it was not the worst thing I could have done, in some respects.

My sojourn in New York could not have been very long, and the rest of it was mainly given to viewing the monuments of the city from the windows of omnibuses and the platforms of horse-cars. The world was so simple then that there were perhaps only a half-dozen cities that had horse-cars in them, and I travelled in those conveyances at New York with an unfaded zest, even after my journeys back and forth between Boston and Cambridge. I have not the least notion where I went or what I saw, but I suppose that it was up and down the ugly east and west avenues, then lying open to the eye in all the hideousness now partly concealed by the elevated roads, and that I found them very stately and handsome. Indeed, New York was really handsomer then than it is now, when it has so many more pieces of beautiful architecture, for at that day the sky-scrapers were not yet, and there was a fine regularity in the streets that these brute bulks have robbed of all shapeliness. Dirt and squalor there were aplenty, but there was infinitely more comfort. The long succession of cross streets was yet mostly secure from business, after you passed Clinton Place; commerce was just beginning to show itself in Union Square, and Madison Square was still the home of the McFlimsies, whose kin and kind dwelt unmolested in the brownstone stretches of Fifth Avenue. I tried hard to imagine them from the acquaintance Mr. Butler's poem had given me, and from the knowledge the gentle satire of the Potiphar Papers had spread broadcast through a community shocked by the excesses of our best society; it was not half so bad then as the best now, probably. But I do not think I made very much of it, perhaps because most of the people who ought to have been in those fine mansions were away at the sea-side and the mountains.

The mountains I had seen on my way down from Canada, but the sea-side not, and it would never do to go home without visiting some famous summer resort. I must have fixed upon Long Branch because I must have heard of it as then the most fashionable; and one afternoon I took the boat for that place. By this means I not only saw sea-bathing for the first time, but I saw a storm at sea: a squall struck us so suddenly that it blew away all the camp-stools of the forward promenade; it was very exciting, and I long meant to use in literature the black wall of cloud that settled on the water before us like a sort of portable midnight; I now throw it away upon the reader, as it were; it never would come in anywhere. I staid all night at Long Branch, and I had a bath the next morning before breakfast: an extremely cold one, with a life-line to keep me against the undertow. In this rite I had the company of a young New-Yorker, whom I had met on the boat coming down, and who was of the light, hopeful, adventurous business type which seems peculiar to the city, and which has always attracted me. He told me much about his life, and how he lived, and what it cost him to live. He had a large room at a fashionable boarding-house, and he paid fourteen dollars a week. In Columbus I had such a room at such a house, and paid three and a half, and I thought it a good deal. But those were the days before the war, when America was the cheapest country in the world, and the West was incredibly inexpensive.

After a day of lonely splendor at this scene of fashion and gayety, I went back to New York, and took the boat for Albany on my way home. I noted that I had no longer the vivid interest in nature and human nature which I had felt in setting out upon my travels, and I said to myself that this was from having a mind so crowded with experiences and impressions that it could receive no more; and I really suppose that if the happiest phrase had offered itself to me at some moments, I should scarcely have looked about me for a landscape or a figure to fit it to. I was very glad to get back to my dear little city in the West (I found it seething in an August sun that was hot enough to have calcined the limestone State House), and to all the friends I was so fond of.

IV

I did what I could to prove myself unworthy of them by refusing their invitations, and giving myself wholly to literature, during the early part of the winter that followed; and I did not realize my error till the invitations ceased to come, and I found myself in an unbroken intellectual solitude. The worst of it was that an ungrateful Muse did little in return for the sacrifices I made her, and the things I now wrote were not liked by the editors I sent them to. The editorial taste is not always the test of merit, but it is the only one we have, and I am not saying the editors were wrong in my case. There were then such a very few places where you could market your work: the Atlantic in Boston and Harper's in New York were the magazines that paid, though the Independent newspaper bought literary material; the Saturday Press printed it without buying, and so did the old Knickerbocker Magazine, though there was pecuniary good-will in both these cases. I toiled much that winter over a story I had long been writing, and at last sent it to the Atlantic, which had published five poems for me the year before. After some weeks, or it may have been months, I got it back with a note saying that the editors had the less regret in returning it because they saw that in the May number of the Knickerbocker the first chapter of the story had appeared. Then I remembered that, years before, I had sent this chapter to that magazine, as a sketch to be printed by itself, and afterwards had continued the story from it. I had never heard of its acceptance, and supposed of course that it was rejected; but on my second visit to New York I called at the Knickerbocker office, and a new editor, of those that the magazine was always having in the days of its failing fortunes, told me that he had found my sketch in rummaging about in a barrel of his predecessors' manuscripts, and had liked it, and printed it. He said that there were fifteen dollars coming to me for that sketch, and might he send the money to me? I said that he might, though I do not see, to this day, why he did not give it me on the spot; and he made a very small minute in a very large sheet of paper (really like Dick Swiveller), and promised I should have it that night; but I sailed the next day for Liverpool without it. I sailed without the money for some verses that Vanity Fair bought of me, but I hardly expected that, for the editor, who

was then Artemus Ward, had frankly told me in taking my address that ducats were few at that moment with Vanity Fair.

I was then on my way to be consul at Venice, where I spent
the next four years in a vigilance for Confederate privateers
which none of them ever surprised. I had asked for the consulate
at Munich, where I hoped to steep myself yet longer in German
poetry, but when my appointment came, I found it was for
Rome. I was very glad to get Rome even; but the income of the
office was in fees, and I thought I had better go on to Washington
and find out how much the fees amounted to. People in Columbus who had been abroad said that on five hundred dollars you
could live in Rome like a prince, but I doubted this; and when I
learned at the State Department that the fees of the Roman consulate came to only three hundred, I perceived that I could not
live better than a baron, probably, and I despaired. The kindly
chief of the consular bureau said that the President's secretaries,
Mr. John Nicolay and Mr. John Hay, were interested in my appointment, and he advised my going over to the White House
and seeing them. I lost no time in doing that, and I learned that
as young Western men they were interested in me because I was
a young Western man who had done something in literature, and
they were willing to help me for that reason, and for no other
that I ever knew. They proposed my going to Venice; the salary
was then seven hundred and fifty, but they thought they could
get it put up to a thousand. In the end they got it put up to fifteen
hundred, and so I went to Venice, where if I did not live like a
prince on that income, I lived a good deal more like a prince
than I could have done at Rome on a fifth of it.

If the appointment was not present fortune, it was the beginning of the best luck I have had in the world, and I am glad to
owe it all to those friends of my verse, who could have been no
otherwise friends of me. They were then beginning very early
careers of distinction which have not been wholly divided. Mr.
Nicolay could have been about twenty-five, and Mr. Hay nineteen or twenty. No one dreamed as yet of the opportunity opening to them in being so constantly near the man whose life they

Walt Whitman

have written, and with whose fame they have imperishably inter-wrought their names. I remember the sobered dignity of the one, and the humorous gayety of the other, and how we had some young men's joking and laughing together, in the anteroom where they received me, with the great soul entering upon its travail beyond the closed door. They asked me if I had ever seen the President, and I said that I had seen him at Columbus, the year before; but I could not say how much I should like to see him again, and thank him for the favor which I had no claim to at his hands, except such as the slight campaign biography I had written could be thought to have given me. That day or another, as I left my friends, I met him in the corridor without, and he looked at the space I was part of with his ineffably melancholy eyes, without knowing that I was the indistinguish-able person in whose "integrity and abilities he had reposed such special confidence" as to have appointed him consul for Venice and the ports of the Lombardo-Venetian Kingdom, though he might have recognized the terms of my commission if I had re-minded him of them. I faltered a moment in my longing to ad-dress him, and then I decided that every one who forebore to speak needlessly to him, or to shake his hand, did him a kindness; and I wish I could be as sure of the wisdom of all my past behavior as I am of that piece of it. He walked up to the water-cooler that stood in the corner, and drew himself a full goblet from it, which he poured down his throat with a backward tilt of his head, and then went wearily within doors. The whole affair, so simple, has always remained one of a certain pathos in my memory, and I would rather have seen Lincoln in that unconscious moment than on some statelier occasion.

v

I went home to Ohio, and sent on the bond I was to file in the Treasury Department; but it was mislaid there, and to prevent another chance of that kind I carried on the duplicate myself. It was on my second visit that I met the generous young Irish-man William D. O'Connor, at the house of my friend Piatt, and heard his ardent talk. He was one of the promising men of that day, and he had written an antislavery novel in the heroic mood of Victor Hugo, which greatly took my fancy; and I believe he wrote poems too. He had not yet risen to be the chief of Walt Whitman's champions outside of the Saturday Press, but he had already espoused the theory of Bacon's authorship of Shakespeare, then newly exploited by the poor lady of Bacon's name, who died constant to it in an insane asylum. He used to speak of the reputed dramatist as "the fat peasant of Stratford," and he was otherwise picturesque of speech in a measure that consoled, if it did not convince. The great war was then full upon us, and when in the silences of our literary talk its awful breath was heard, and its shadow fell upon the hearth where we gathered round the first fires of autumn, O'Connor would lift his beautiful head with a fine effect of prophecy, and say, "Friends, I feel a sense of victory in the air." He was not wrong; only the victory was for the other side.

Who beside O'Connor shared in these saddened symposiums I cannot tell now; but probably other young journalists and office-holders, intending littérateurs, since more or less extinct. I make certain only of the young Boston publisher who issued a very handsome edition of Leaves of Grass, and then failed promptly if not consequently. But I had already met, in my first sojourn at the capital, a young journalist who had given hostages to poetry, and whom I was very glad to see and proud to know. Mr. Stedman and I were talking over that meeting the other day, and I can be surer than I might have been without his memory, that I found him at a friend's house, where he was nursing himself for some slight sickness, and that I sat by his bed while our souls launched together into the joyful realms of hope and praise. In him I found the quality of Boston, the honor and passion of literature, and not a mere pose of the literary life; and the world knows without my telling how true he has been to his ideal of it. His earthly mission then was to write letters from Washington for the New York World, which started in life as a good young evening paper, with a decided religious tone, so that the Saturday

Press could call it the Night-blooming Serious. I think Mr. Stedman wrote for its editorial page at times, and his relation to it as a Washington correspondent had an authority which is wanting to the function in these days of perfected telegraphing. He had not yet achieved that seat in the Stock Exchange whose possession has justified his recourse to business, and has helped him to mean something more single in literature than many more singly devoted to it. I used sometimes to speak about that with another eager young author in certain middle years when we were chafing in editorial harness, and we always decided that Stedman had the best of it in being able to earn his living in a sort so alien to literature that he could come to it unjaded, and with a gust unspoiled by kindred savors. But no man shapes his own life, and I dare say that Stedman may have been all the time envying us our tripods from his high place in the Stock Exchange. What is certain is that he has come to stand for literature and to embody New York in it as no one else does. In a community which seems never to have had a conscious relation to letters, he has kept the faith with dignity and fought the fight with constant courage. Scholar and poet at once, he has spoken to his generation with authority which we can forget only in the charm which makes us forget everything else.

But his fame was still before him when we met, and I could bring to him an admiration for work which had not yet made itself known to so many but any admirer was welcome. We talked of what we had done, and each said how much he liked certain things of the other's; I even seized my advantage of his helplessness to read him a poem of mine which I had in my pocket; he advised me where to place it; and if the reader will not think it an unfair digression, I will tell here what became of that poem, for I think its varied fortunes were amusing, and I hope my own sufferings and final triumph with it will not be without encouragement to the young literary endeavorer. It was a poem called, with no prophetic sense of fitness, Forlorn, and I tried it first with the Atlantic Monthly, which would not have it. Then I offered it in person to a former editor of Harper's

Monthly, but he could not see his advantage in it, and I carried it overseas to Venice with me. From that point I sent it to all the English magazines as steadily as the post could carry it away and bring it back. On my way home, four years later, I took it to London with me, where a friend who knew Lewes, then just beginning with the Fortnightly Review, sent it to him for me. It was promptly returned, with a letter wholly reserved as to its quality, but full of a poetic gratitude for my wish to contribute to the Fortnightly. Then I heard that a certain Mr. Lucas was about to start a magazine, and I offered the poem to him. The kindest letter of acceptance followed me to America, and I counted upon fame and fortune as usual, when the news of Mr. Lucas's death came. I will not poorly joke an effect from my poem in the fact; but the fact remains. By this time I was a writer in the office of the Nation newspaper, and after I left this place to be Mr. Fields's assistant on the Atlantic, I sent my poem to the Nation, where it was printed at last. In such scant measure as my verses have pleased it has found rather unusual favor, and I need not say that its misfortunes endeared it to its author.

But all this is rather far away from my first meeting with Stedman in Washington. Of course I liked him, and I thought him very handsome and fine, with a full beard cut in the fashion he has always worn it, and with poet's eyes lighting an aquiline profile. Afterwards, when I saw him afoot, I found him of a worldly splendor in dress, and envied him, as much as I could envy him anything, the New York tailor whose art had clothed him: I had a New York tailor too, but with a difference. He had a worldly dash along with his supermundane gifts, which took me almost as much, and all the more because I could see that he valued himself nothing upon it. He was all for literature, and for literary men as the superiors of every one. I must have opened my heart to him a good deal, for when I told him how the newspaper I had written for from Canada and New England had ceased to print my letters, he said, "Think of a man like ——— sitting in judgment on a man like *you!*" I thought of it, and was avenged if not comforted; and at any rate I liked

Stedman's standing up so stiffly for the honor of a craft that is rather too limp in some of its votaries.

I suppose it was he who introduced me to the Stoddards, whom I met in New York just before I sailed, and who were then in the glow of their early fame as poets. They knew about my poor beginnings, and they were very, very good to me. Stoddard went with me to Franklin Square, and gave the sanction of his presence to the ineffectual offer of my poem there. But what I relished most was the long talks I had with them both about authorship in all its phases, and the exchange of delight in this poem and that, this novel and that, with gay, wilful runs away to make some wholly irrelevant joke, or fire puns into the air at no mark whatever. Stoddard had then a fame, with the sweetness of personal affection in it, from the lyrics and the odes that will perhaps best keep him known, and Mrs. Stoddard was beginning to make her distinct and special quality felt in the magazines, in verse and fiction. In both it seems to me that she has failed of the recognition which her work merits. Her tales and novels have in them a foretaste of realism, which was too strange for the palate of their day, and is now too familiar, perhaps. It is a peculiar fate, and would form the scheme of a pretty study in the history of literature. But in whatever she did she left the stamp of a talent like no other, and of a personality disdainful of literary environment. In a time when most of us had to write like Tennyson, or Longfellow, or Browning, she never would write like any one but herself.

I remember very well the lodging over a corner of Fourth Avenue and some downtown street where I visited these winning and gifted people, and tasted the pleasure of their racy talk, and the hospitality of their good-will toward all literature, which certainly did not leave me out. We sat before their grate in the chill of the last October days, and they set each other on to one wild flight of wit after another, and again I bathed my delighted spirit in the atmosphere of a realm where for the time at least no

"rumor of oppression or defeat,
Of unsuccessful or successful war,"

could penetrate. I liked the Stoddards because they were frankly not of that Bohemia which I disliked so much, and thought it of no promise or validity; and because I was fond of their poetry and found them in it. I liked the absolutely literary keeping of their lives. He had then, and for long after, a place in the Custom-house, but he was no more of that than Lamb was of India House. He belonged to that better world where there is no interest but letters, and which was as much like heaven for me as anything I could think of.

The meetings with the Stoddards repeated themselves when I came back to sail from New York, early in November. Mixed up with the cordial pleasure of them in my memory is a sense of the cold and wet outdoors, and the misery of being in those infamous New York streets, then as for long afterwards the squalidest in the world. The last night I saw my friends they told me of the tragedy which had just happened at the camp in the City Hall Park. Fitz James O'Brien, the brilliant young Irishman who had dazzled us with his story of The Diamond Lens, and frozen our blood with his ingenious tale of a ghost—What was It?—a ghost that could be felt and heard, but not seen—had enlisted for the war, and risen to be an officer with the swift process of the first days of it. In that camp he had just then shot and killed a man for some infraction of discipline, and it was uncertain what the end would be. He was acquitted, however, and it is known how he afterwards died of lockjaw from a wound received in battle.

VI

Before this last visit in New York there was a second visit to Boston, which I need not dwell upon, because it was chiefly a revival of the impressions of the first. Again I saw the Fieldses in their home; again the Autocrat in his, and Lowell now beneath his own roof, beside the study fire where I was so often to sit with him in coming years. At dinner (which we had at two o'clock) the talk turned upon my appointment, and he said of me to his wife: "Think of his having got Stillman's place! We ought to put poison in his wine," and he told me of the wish the painter had to go to Venice and follow up Ruskin's work there in a book of his own. But he would not let me feel very guilty, and I will not pretend that I had any personal regret for my good fortune.

The place was given me perhaps because I had not nearly so many other gifts as he who lost it, and who was at once artist, critic, journalist, traveller, and eminently each. I met him afterwards in Rome, which the powers bestowed upon him instead of Venice, and he forgave me, though I do not know whether he forgave the powers. We walked far and long over the Campagna, and I felt the charm of a most uncommon mind in talk which came out richest and fullest in the presence of the wild nature which he loved and knew so much better than most other men. I think that the book he would have written about Venice is forever to be regretted, and I do not at all console myself for its loss with the book I have written myself.

At Lowell's table that day they spoke of what sort of winter I should find in Venice, and he inclined to the belief that I should want a fire there. On his study hearth a very brisk one burned when we went back to it, and kept out the chill of a cold easterly storm. We looked through one of the windows at the rain, and he said he could remember standing and looking out of that window at such a storm when he was a child; for he was born in that house, and his life had kept coming back to it. He died in it, at last.

In a lifting of the rain he walked with me down to the village, as he always called the denser part of the town about Harvard Square, and saw me aboard a horse-car for Boston. Before we parted he gave me two charges: to open my mouth when I began to speak Italian, and to think well of women. He said that our race spoke its own tongue with its teeth shut, and so failed to master the languages that wanted freer utterance. As to women, he said there were unworthy ones, but a good woman was the best thing in the world, and a man was always the better for honoring women.

Part Third

ROUNDABOUT TO BOSTON

DURING the four years of my life in Venice the literary intention was present with me at all times and in all places. I wrote many things in verse, which I sent to the magazines in every part of the English-speaking world, but they came unerringly back to me, except in three instances only, when they were kept by the editors who finally printed them. One of these pieces was published in the Atlantic Monthly; another in Harper's Magazine; the third was got into the New York Ledger through the kindness of Dr. Edward Everett Hale, who used I know not what mighty magic to that end. I had not yet met him; but he interested himself in my ballad as if it had been his own. His brother, Charles Hale, later Consul-General for Egypt, whom I saw almost every moment of the two visits he paid Venice in my time, had sent it to him, after copying it in his own large, fair hand, so that it could be read. He was not quite of that literary Boston which I so fondly remembered my glimpses of; he was rather of a journalistic and literary Boston which I had never known; but he was of Boston, after all. He had been in Lowell's classes at Harvard; he had often met Longfellow in Cambridge; he knew Doctor Holmes, of course; and he let me talk of my idols to my heart's content. I think he must have been amused by my raptures; most people would have been; but he was kind and patient, and he listened to me with a sweet intelligence which I shall always gratefully remember. He died too young, with his life's possibilities mainly unfulfilled; but none who knew him could fail to imagine them, or to love him for what he was.

I

Besides those few pitiful successes, I had nothing but defeats in the sort of literature which I supposed was to be my calling, and the defeats threw me upon prose; for some sort of literary thing, if not one, then another, I must do if I lived; and I began to write those studies of Venetian life which afterwards became a book, and which I contributed as letters to the Boston Advertiser, after vainly offering them to more æsthetic periodicals. However, I do not imagine that it was a very smiling time for any literary endeavorer at home in the life-and-death civil war then waging. Some few young men arose who made themselves heard amid the din of arms even as far as Venice, but most of these were hushed long ago. I fancy Theodore Winthrop, who began to speak, as it were, from his soldier's grave, so soon did his death follow the earliest recognition by the public, and so many were his posthumous works, was chief of these; but there were others whom the present readers must make greater effort to remember. Forceythe Willson, who wrote The Old Sergeant, became known for the rare quality of his poetry; and now and then there came a poem from Aldrich, or Stedman, or Stoddard. The great new series of the Biglow Papers gathered volume with the force they had from the beginning. The Autocrat was often in the pages of the Atlantic, where one often found Whittier and Emerson, with many a fresh name now faded. In Washington the Piatts were writing some of the most beautiful verse of the war, and Brownell was sounding his battle lyrics like so many trumpet blasts. The fiction which followed the war was yet all to come. Whatever was done in any kind had some hint of the war in it, inevitably; though in the very heart of it Longfellow was setting about his great version of Dante, peacefully, prayerfully, as he has told in the noble sonnets which register the mood of his undertaking.

At Venice, if I was beyond the range of literary recognition I was in direct relations with one of our greatest literary men, who was again of that literary Boston which mainly represented

American literature to me. The official chief of the consul at Venice was the United States Minister at Vienna, and in my time this minister was John Lothrop Motley, the historian. He was removed, later, by that Johnson administration which followed Lincoln's so forgottenly that I name it with a sense of something almost prehistoric. Among its worst errors was the attempted discredit of a man who had given lustre to our name by his work, and who was an ardent patriot as well as accomplished scholar. He visited Venice during my first year, which was the darkest period of the civil war, and I remember with what instant security, not to say severity, he rebuked my scarcely whispered misgivings of the end, when I ventured to ask him what he thought it would be. Austria had never recognized the Secessionists as belligerents, and in the complications with France and England there was little for our minister but to share the home indignation at the sympathy of those powers with the South. In Motley this was heightened by that feeling of astonishment, of wounded faith, which all Americans with English friendships experienced in those days, and which he, whose English friendships were many, experienced in peculiar degree.

I drifted about with him in his gondola, and refreshed myself, long a-hungered for such talk, with his talk of literary life in London. Through some acquaintance I had made in Venice I was able to be of use to him in getting documents copied for him in the Venetian Archives, especially the Relations of the Venetian Ambassadors at different courts during the period and events he was studying. All such papers passed through my hands in transmission to the historian, though now I do not quite know why they need have done so; but perhaps he was willing to give me the pleasure of being a partner, however humble, in the enterprise. My recollection of him is of courtesy to a far younger man unqualified by patronage, and of a presence of singular dignity and grace. He was one of the handsomest men I ever saw, with beautiful eyes, a fine blond beard of modish cut, and a sensitive nose, straight and fine. He was altogether a figure of worldly splendor; and I had reason to know that he did not let the credit of our nation suffer at the most aristocratic court in Europe for want of a fit diplomatic costume, when some of our ministers were trying to make their office do its full effect upon all occasions in "the dress of an American gentleman." The morning after his arrival Mr. Motley came to me with a handful of newspapers which, according to the Austrian custom at that day, had been opened in the Venetian post-office. He wished me to protest against this on his behalf as an infringement of his diplomatic extra-territoriality, and I proposed to go at once to the director of the post: I had myself suffered in the same way, and though I knew that a mere consul was helpless, I was willing to see the double-headed eagle trodden under foot by a Minister Pleni-potentiary. Mr. Motley said that he would go with me, and we put off in his gondola to the post-office. The director received us with the utmost deference. He admitted the irregularity which the minister complained of, and declared that he had no choice but to open every foreign newspaper, to whomsoever addressed. He suggested, however, that if the minister made his appeal to the Lieutenant-Governor of Venice, Count Toggenburg would no doubt instantly order the exemption of his newspapers from the general rule.

Mr. Motley said he would give himself the pleasure of calling upon the Lieutenant-Governor, and "How fortunate," he added, when we were got back into the gondola, "that I should have happened to bring my court dress with me!" I did not see the encounter of the high contending powers, but I know that it ended in a complete victory for our minister.

I had no farther active relations of an official kind with Mr. Motley, except in the case of a naturalized American citizen, whose property was slowly but surely wasting away in the keeping of the Venetian courts. An order had at last been given for the surrender of the remnant to the owner; but the Lombardo-Venetian authorities insisted that this should be done through the United States Minister at Vienna, and Mr. Motley held as firmly that it must be done through the United States Consul at Venice. I could only report to him from time to time the unyielding attitude of the Civil Tribunal, and at last he consented, as he wrote, "to act officiously, not officially, in the matter," and the hapless claimant got what was left of his estate.

I had a glimpse of the historian afterwards in Boston, but it was only for a moment, just before his appointment to England, where he was made to suffer for Sumner in his quarrel with Grant. That injustice crowned the injuries his country had done a most faithful patriot and high-spirited gentleman, whose fame as a historian once filled the ear of the English-speaking world. His books seemed to have been written in a spirit already no longer modern; and I did not find the greatest of them so moving as I expected when I came to it with all the ardor of my admiration for the historian. William the Silent seemed to me, by his worshipper's own showing, scarcely level with the popular movement which he did not so much direct as follow; but it is a good deal for a prince to be able even to follow his people; and it cannot be said that Motley does not fully recognize the greatness of the Dutch people, though he may see the Prince of Orange too large. The study of their character made at least a theoretical democrat of a scholar whose instincts were not perhaps democratic, and his sympathy with that brave little republic between the dikes strengthened him in his fealty to the great commonwealth between the oceans. I believe that so far as he was of any political tradition, he was of the old Boston Whig tradition; but when I met him at Venice he was in the glow of a generous pride in our war as a war against slavery. He spoke of the negroes and their simple-hearted, single-minded devotion to the Union cause in terms that an original abolitionist might have used, at a time when original abolitionists were not so many as they have since become.

For the rest, I fancy it was very well for us to be represented at Vienna in those days by an ideal democrat who was also a real swell, and who was not likely to discredit us socially when we so much needed to be well thought of in every way. At a court where the family of Count Schmerling, the Prime Minister, could not be received for want of the requisite descents, it was well to have a minister who would not commit the mistake of inviting the First Society to meet the Second Society, as a former Envoy Extraordinary had done, with the effect of finding himself left entirely to the Second Society during the rest of his stay in Vienna.

II

One of my consular colleagues under Motley was another historian, of no such popularity, indeed, nor even of such success, but perhaps not of inferior powers. This was Richard Hildreth, at Trieste, the author of one of the sincerest if not the truest histories of the United States, according to the testimony both of his liking and his misliking critics. I have never read his history, and I speak of it only at second hand; but I had read, before I met him, his novel of Archy Moore, or The White Slave, which left an indelible impression of his imaginative verity upon me. The impression is still so deep that after the lapse of nearly forty years since I saw the book, I have no misgiving in speaking of it as a powerful piece of realism. It treated passionately, intensely, though with a superficial coldness, of wrongs now so remote from us in the abolition of slavery that it is useless to hope it will ever be generally read hereafter, but it can safely be praised to any one who wishes to study that bygone condition, and the literature which grew out of it. I fancy it did not lack recognition in its time, altogether, for I used to see it in Italian and French translations on the bookstalls. I believe neither his history nor his novel brought the author more gain than fame. He had worn himself out on a newspaper when he got his appointment at Trieste, and I saw him in the shadow of the cloud that was wholly to darken him before he died. He was a tall thin man, absent, silent: already a phantom of himself, but with a scholarly serenity and dignity amidst the ruin, when the worst came.

I first saw him at the pretty villa where he lived in the suburbs of Trieste, and where I passed several days, and I remember him always reading, reading, reading. He could with difficulty be roused from his book by some strenuous appeal from his family to his conscience as a host. The last night he sat with Paradise Lost in his hand, and nothing could win him from it till he had finished it. Then he rose to go to bed. Would not he bid his parting guest good-by? The idea of farewell perhaps dimly penetrated to him. He responded, without looking round,

> "They, hand in hand, with wandering steps and slow,
> Through Eden took their solitary way,"

and so left the room.

I had earlier had some dealings with him as a fellow-consul concerning a deserter from an American ship whom I inherited from my predecessor at Venice. The man had already been four or five months in prison, and he was in a fair way to end his life there; for it is our law that a deserting sailor must be kept in the consul's custody till some vessel of our flag arrives, when the consul can oblige the master to take the deserter and let him work his passage home. Such a vessel rarely came to Venice even in times of peace, and in times of war there was no hope of any. So I got leave of the consul at Trieste to transfer my captive to that port, where now and then an American ship did touch. The flag determines the nationality of the sailor, and this unhappy wretch was theoretically our fellow-citizen; but when he got to Trieste he made a clean breast of it to the consul. He confessed that when he shipped under our flag he was a deserter from a British regiment at Malta; and he begged piteously not to be sent home to America, where he had never been in his life, nor ever wished to be. He wished to be sent back to his regiment at Malta, and to whatever fate awaited him there. The case certainly had its embarrassments; but the American consul contrived to let our presumptive compatriot slip into the keeping of the British consul, who promptly shipped him to Malta. In view of the strained relations between England and America at that time this was a piece of masterly diplomacy.

Besides my old Ohio-time friend Moncure D. Conway, who paid us a visit, and in his immediate relations with literary Boston seemed to bring the mountain to Mahomet, I saw no one else more literary than Henry Ward Beecher. He was passing through Venice on his way to those efforts in England in behalf of the Union which had a certain great effect at the time; and in the tiny parlor of our apartment on the Grand Canal, I can still see him sitting athletic, almost pugilistic, of presence, with his strong face, but kind, framed in long hair that swept above his massive forehead, and fell to the level of his humorously smiling mouth. His eyes quaintly gleamed at the things we told him of our life in the strange place; but he only partly relaxed from his strenuous pose, and the hands that lay upon his knees were clinched. Afterwards, as he passed our balcony in a gondola, he lifted the brave red fez he was wearing (many people wore the fez for one caprice or another) and saluted our eagle and us: we were often on the balcony behind the shield to attest the authenticity of the American eagle.

III

Before I left Venice, however, there came a turn in my literary luck, and from the hand I could most have wished to reverse the adverse wheel of fortune. I had labored out with great pains a paper on recent Italian comedy, which I sent to Lowell, then with his friend Professor Norton jointly editor of the North American Review; and he took it and wrote me one of his loveliest letters about it, consoling me in an instant for all the defeat I had undergone, and making it sweet and worthy to have lived through that misery. It is one of the hard conditions of this state that while we can mostly make out to let people taste the last drop of bitterness and ill-will that is in us, our love and gratitude are only semi-articulate at the best, and usually altogether tongue-tied. As often as I tried afterwards to tell Lowell of the benediction, the salvation, his letter was to me, I failed. But perhaps he would not have understood, if I had spoken out all that was in me with the fulness I could have given a resentment. His message came after years of thwarted endeavor, and reinstated me in the belief that I could still do something in literature.

To be sure, the letters in the Advertiser had begun to make their impression; among the first great pleasures they brought me was a recognition from my diplomatic chief at Vienna; but I valued my admission to the North American peculiarly because it was Lowell let me in, and because I felt that in his charge it must be the place of highest honor. He spoke of the pay for my article, in his letter, and asked me where he should send it, and I answered, to my father-in-law, who put it in his savings-bank, where he lived, in Brattleboro, Vermont. There it remained, and I forgot all about it, so that when his affairs were settled some years later and I was notified that there was a sum to my credit in the bank, I said, with the confidence I have nearly always felt when wrong, that I had no money there. The proof of my error was sent me in a check, and then I bethought me of the pay for Recent Italian Comedy.

It was not a day when I could really afford to forget money due me, but then it was not a great deal of money. The Review was as poor as it was proud, and I had two dollars a printed page for my paper. But this was more than I got from the Advertiser, which gave me five dollars a column for my letters, printed in a type so fine that the money, when translated from greenbacks into gold at a discount of 2.80, must have been about a dollar a thousand words. However, I was richly content with that, and would gladly have let them have the letters for nothing.

Before I left Venice I had made my sketches into a book, which I sent on to Messrs. Trübner & Co., in London. They had consented to look at it to oblige my friend Conway, who during his sojourn with us in Venice, before his settlement in London, had been forced to listen to some of it. They answered me in due time that they would publish an edition of a thousand, at half profits, if I could get some American house to take five hundred copies. When I stopped in London I had so little hope of being able to do this that I asked the Trübners if I might, without losing their offer, try to get some other London house to publish my book. They said Yes, almost joyously; and I began to take my manuscript about. At most places they would not look at me or it, and they nowhere consented to read it. The house promptest in refusing to consider it afterwards pirated one of my novels, and with some expressions of good intention in that direction, never paid me anything for it; though I believe the English still think that this sort of behavior was peculiar to the American publisher in the old buccaneering times. I was glad to go back to the Trübners with my book, and on my way across the Atlantic I met a publisher who finally agreed to take those five hundred copies. This was Mr. M. M. Hurd, of Hurd & Houghton, a house then newly established in New York and Cambridge. We played ring-toss and shuffleboard together, and became of a friendship which lasts to this day. But it was not till some months later, when I saw him in New York, that he consented to publish my book. I remember how he said, with an air of vague misgiving, and an effect of trying to justify himself in an imprudence, that it was not a great matter anyway. I perceived that he had no faith in it, and to tell the truth I had not much myself. But the book had an instant success, and it has gone on from edition to edition ever since. There was just then the interest of a not wholly generous surprise at American things among the English. Our success in putting down the great Confederate rebellion had caught the fancy of our cousins, and I think it was to this mood of theirs that I owed largely the kindness they showed my book. There were long and cordial reviews in all the great London journals, which I used to carry about with me like love-letters; when I tried to show them to other people, I could not understand their coldness concerning them.

At Boston, where we landed on our return home, there was a moment when it seemed as if my small destiny might be linked at once with that of the city which later became my home. I ran into the office of the Advertiser to ask what had become of some sketches of Italian travel I had sent the paper, and the managing editor made me promise not to take a place anywhere before I had heard from him. I gladly promised, but I did not hear from him, and when I returned to Boston a fortnight later, I found that a fatal partner had refused to agree with him in engaging

me upon the paper. They even gave me back half a dozen unprinted letters of mine, and I published them in the Nation, of
New York, and afterwards in the book called Italian Journeys.

But after I had encountered fortune in this frowning disguise,
I had a most joyful little visit with Lowell, which made me forget there was anything in the world but the delight and glory of
sitting with him in his study at Elmwood and hearing him talk.
It must have been my freshness from Italy which made him talk
chiefly of his own happy days in the land which so sympathetically
brevets all her lovers fellow-citizens. At any rate he would talk
of hardly anything else, and he talked late into the night, and
early into the morning. About two o'clock, when all the house
was still, he lighted a candle, and went down into the cellar, and
came back with certain bottles under his arms. I had not a very
learned palate in those days (or in these, for that matter), but I
knew enough of wine to understand that these bottles had been
chosen upon that principle which Longfellow put in verse, and
used to repeat with a humorous lifting of the eyebrows and
hollowing of the voice:

> "If you have a friend to dine,
>   Give him your best wine;
> If you have two,
>   The second-best will do."

As we sat in their mellow after-glow, Lowell spoke to me of my
own life and prospects, wisely and truly, as he always spoke. He
said that it was enough for a man who had stuff in him to be
known to two or three people, for they would not suffer him to
be forgotten, and it would rest with himself to get on. I told him
that though I had not given up my place at Venice, I was not
going back, if I could find anything to do at home, and I was
now on my way to Ohio, where I should try my best to find something; at the worst, I could turn to my trade of printer. He did
not think it need ever come to that; and he said that he believed
I should have an advantage with readers, if not with editors, in
hailing from the West; I should be more of a novelty. I knew

very well that even in my own West I should not have this advantage unless I appeared there with an Eastern imprint, but I
could not wish to urge my misgiving against his faith. Was I not
already richly successful? What better thing personally could
befall me, if I lived forever after on milk and honey, than to be
sitting there with my hero, my master, and having him talk to
me as if we were equal in deed and in fame?

The cat-bird called in the syringa thicket at his door, before
we said the good-night which was good-morning, using the sweet
Italian words, and bidding each other the *Dorma bene* which
has the quality of a benediction. He held my hand, and looked
into my eyes with the sunny kindness which never failed me,
worthy or unworthy; and I went away to bed. But not to sleep;
only to dream such dreams as fill the heart of youth when the
recognition of its endeavor has come from the achievement it
holds highest and best.

IV

I found nothing to do in Ohio; some places that I heard of
proved impossible one way or another, in Columbus and Cleveland, and Cincinnati; there was always the fatal partner; and
after three weeks I was again in the East. I came to New York,
resolved to fight my way in, somewhere, and I did not rest a
moment before I began the fight.

My notion was that which afterwards became Bartley Hubbard's. "Get a basis," said the softening cynic of the Saturday
Press, when I advised with him, among other acquaintances.
"Get a salaried place, something regular on some paper, and
then you can easily make up the rest." But it was a month before
I achieved this vantage, and then I got it in a quarter where I
had not looked for it. I wrote editorials on European and literary topics for different papers, but mostly for the Times, and
they paid me well and more than well; but I was nowhere offered
a basis, though once I got so far towards it as to secure a personal
interview with the editor-in-chief, who made me feel that I had
seldom met so busy a man. He praised some work of mine that

he had read in his paper, but I was never recalled to his presence; and now I think he judged rightly that I should not be a lastingly good journalist. My point of view was artistic; I wanted time to prepare my effects.

There was another and clearer prospect opened to me on a literary paper, then newly come to the light, but long since gone out in the dark. Here again my work was taken, and liked so much that I was offered the basis (at twenty dollars a week) that I desired; I was even assigned to a desk where I should write in the office; and the next morning I came joyfully down to Spruce Street to occupy it. But I was met at the door by one of the editors, who said lightly, as if it were a trifling affair, "Well, we've concluded to *waive* the idea of an engagement," and once more my bright hopes of a basis dispersed themselves. I said, with what calm I could, that they must do what they thought best, and I went on skirmishing baselessly about for this and the other papers which had been buying my material.

I had begun printing in the Nation those letters about my Italian journeys left over from the Boston Advertiser; they had been liked in the office, and one day the editor astonished and delighted me by asking how I would fancy giving up outside work to come there and write only for the Nation. We averaged my gains from all sources at forty dollars a week, and I had my basis as unexpectedly as if I had dropped upon it from the skies.

This must have been some time in November, and the next three or four months were as happy a time for me as I have ever known. I kept on printing my Italian material in the Nation; I wrote criticisms for it (not very good criticisms, I think now), and I amused myself very much with the treatment of social phases and events in a department which grew up under my hand. My associations personally were of the most agreeable kind. I worked with joy, with ardor, and I liked so much to be there, in that place and in that company, that I hated to have each day come to an end.

I believed that my lines were cast in New York for good and all; and I renewed my relations with the literary friends I had made before going abroad. I often stopped, on my way up town, at an apartment the Stoddards had in Lafayette Place, or near it; I saw Stedman, and reasoned high, to my heart's content, of literary things with them and him.

With the winter Bayard Taylor came on from his home in Kennett and took an apartment in East Twelfth Street, and once a week Mrs. Taylor and he received all their friends there, with a simple and charming hospitality. There was another house which we much resorted to—the house of James Lorrimer Graham, afterwards Consul-General at Florence, where he died. I had made his acquaintance at Venice three years before, and I came in for my share of that love for literary men which all their perversities could not extinguish in him. It was a veritable passion, which I used to think he could not have felt so deeply if he had been a literary man himself. There were delightful dinners at his house, where the wit of the Stoddards shone, and Taylor beamed with joyous good-fellowship and overflowed with invention; and Huntington, long Paris correspondent of the Tribune, humorously tried to talk himself into the resolution of spending the rest of his life in his own country. There was one evening when C. P. Cranch, always of a most pensive presence and aspect, sang the most killingly comic songs; and there was another evening when, after we all went into the library, something tragical happened. Edwin Booth was of our number, a gentle, rather silent person in company, or with at least little social initiative, who, as his fate would, went up to the cast of a huge hand that lay upon one of the shelves. "Whose hand is this, Lorry?" he asked our host, as he took it up and turned it over in both his own hands. Graham feigned not to hear, and Booth asked again, "Whose hand is this?" Then there was nothing for Graham but to say, "It's Lincoln's hand," and the man for whom it meant such unspeakable things put it softly down without a word.

v

It was one of the disappointments of a time which was nearly all joy that I did not then meet a man who meant hardly less than Lowell himself for me. George William Curtis was during my first winter in New York away on one of the long lecturing rounds to which he gave so many of his winters, and I did not see him till seven years afterwards, at Mr. Norton's in Cambridge. He then characteristically spent most of the evening in discussing an obscure point in Browning's poem of My Last Duchess. I have long forgotten what the point was, but not the charm of Curtis's personality, his fine presence, his benign politeness, his almost deferential tolerance of difference in opinion. Afterwards I saw him again and again in Boston and New York, but always with a sense of something elusive in his graciousness, for which something in me must have been to blame. Cold, he was not, even to the youth that in those days was apt to shiver in any but the higher temperatures, and yet I felt that I made no advance in his kindness towards anything like the friendship I knew in the Cambridge men. Perhaps I was so thoroughly attuned to their mood that I could not be put in unison with another; and perhaps in Curtis there was really not the material of much intimacy.

He had the potentiality of publicity in the sort of welcome he gave equally to all men; and if I asked more I was not reasonable. Yet he was never far from any man of good-will, and he was the intimate of multitudes whose several existence he never dreamt of. In this sort he had become my friend when he made his first great speech on the Kansas question in 1855, which will seem as remote to the young men of this day as the Thermopylæ question to which he likened it. I was his admirer, his lover, his worshipper before that for the things he had done in literature, for the Howadji books, and for the lovely fantasies of Prue and I, and for the sound-hearted satire of the Potiphar Papers, and now suddenly I learnt that this brilliant and graceful talent, this travelled and accomplished gentleman, this star of society who had dazzled me with his splendor far off in my Western village obscurity, was a man with the heart to feel the wrongs of men so little friended then as to be denied all the rights of men. I do not remember any passage of the speech, or any word of it, but I remember the joy, the pride with which the soul of youth recognizes in the greatness it has honored the goodness it may love. Mere politicians might be pro-slavery or antislavery without touching me very much, but here was the citizen of a world far greater than theirs, a light of the universal republic of letters, who was willing and eager to stand or fall with the just cause, and that was all in all to me. His country was my country, and his kindred my kindred, and nothing could have kept me from following after him.

His whole life taught the lesson that the world is well lost whenever the world is wrong; but never, I think, did any life teach this so sweetly, so winningly. The wrong world itself might have been entreated by him to be right, for he was one of the few reformers who have not in some measure mixed their love of man with hate of men; his quarrel was with error, and not with the persons who were in it. He was so gently steadfast in his opinions that no one ever thought of him as a fanatic, though many who held his opinions were assailed as fanatics, and suffered the shame if they did not win the palm of martyrdom. In early life he was a communist, and then when he came out of Brook Farm into the world which he was so well fitted to adorn, and which would so gladly have kept him all its own, he became an abolitionist in the very teeth of the world which abhorred abolitionists. He was a believer in the cause of women's rights, which has no picturesqueness, and which chiefly appeals to the sense of humor in the men who never dreamt of laughing at him. The man who was in the last degree amiable was to the last degree unyielding where conscience was concerned; the soul which was so tender had no weakness in it; his lenity was the divination of a finer justice. His honesty made all men trust him when they doubted his opinions; his good sense made them doubt their own opinions, when they had as little question of their own honesty.

I should not find it easy to speak of him as a man of letters only, for humanity was above the humanities with him, and we all know how he turned from the fairest career in literature to tread the thorny path of politics because he believed that duty led the way, and that good citizens were needed more than good romancers. No doubt they are, and yet it must always be a keen regret with the men of my generation who witnessed with such rapture the early proofs of his talent, that he could not have devoted it wholly to the beautiful, and let others look after the true. Now that I have said this I am half ashamed of it, for I know well enough that what he did was best; but if my regret is mean, I will let it remain, for it is faithful to the mood which many have been in concerning him.

There can be no dispute, I am sure, as to the value of some of the results he achieved in that other path. He did indeed create anew for us the type of good-citizenship, well-nigh effaced in a sordid and selfish time, and of an honest politician and a pure-minded journalist. He never really forsook literature, and the world of actual interests and experiences afforded him outlooks and perspectives, without which æsthetic endeavor is self-limited and purblind. He was a great man of letters, he was a great orator, he was a great political journalist, he was a great citizen, he was a great philanthropist. But that last word with its conventional application scarcely describes the brave and gentle friend of men that he was. He was one that helped others by all that he did, and said, and was, and the circle of his use was as wide as his fame. There are other great men, plenty of them, common great men, whom we know as names and powers, and whom we willingly let the ages have when they die, for, living or dead, they are alike remote from us. They have never been with us where we live; but this great man was the neighbor, the contemporary, and the friend of all who read him or heard him; and even in the swift forgetting of this electrical age the stamp of his personality will not be effaced from their minds or hearts.

VI

Of those evenings at the Taylors' in New York, I can recall best the one which was most significant for me, and even fatefully significant. Mr. and Mrs. Fields were there, from Boston, and I renewed all the pleasure of my earlier meetings with them. At the end Fields said, mockingly, "Don't despise Boston!" and I answered, as we shook hands, "Few are worthy to live in Boston." It was New-Year's eve, and that night it came on to snow so heavily that my horse-car could hardly plough its way up to Forty-seventh Street through the drifts. The next day and the next, I wrote at home, because it was so hard to get down town. The third day I reached the office and found a letter on my desk from Fields, asking how I should like to come to Boston and be his assistant on the Atlantic Monthly. I submitted the matter at once to my chief on the Nation, and with his frank good-will I talked it over with Mr. Osgood, of Ticknor & Fields, who was to see me further about it if I wished, when he came to New York; and then I went to Boston to see Mr. Fields concerning details. I was to sift all the manuscripts and correspond with contributors; I was to do the literary proof-reading of the magazine; and I was to write the four or five pages of book-notices, which were then printed at the end of the periodical in finer type; and I was to have forty dollars a week. I said that I was getting that already for less work, and then Mr. Fields offered me ten dollars more. Upon these terms we closed, and on the first of March, which was my twenty-ninth birthday, I went to Boston and began my work. I had not decided to accept the place without advising with Lowell; he counselled the step, and gave me some shrewd and useful suggestions. The whole affair was conducted by Fields with his unfailing tact and kindness, but it could not be kept from me that the qualification I had as practical printer for the work was most valued, if not the most valued, and that as proof-reader I was expected to make it avail on the side of economy. Somewhere in life's feast the course of humble-pie must always come in; and if I did not wholly relish this bit of it, I dare say it was good for me, and I digested it perfectly.

Part Fourth

LITERARY BOSTON AS I KNEW IT

A<small>MONG</small> my fellow-passengers on the train from New York to Boston, when I went to begin my work there in 1866, as the assistant editor of the Atlantic Monthly, was the late Samuel Bowles, of the Springfield Republican, who created in a subordinate city a journal of metropolitan importance. I had met him in Venice several years earlier, when he was suffering from the cruel insomnia which had followed his overwork on that newspaper, and when he told me that he was sleeping scarcely more than one hour out of the twenty-four. His worn face attested the misery which this must have been, and which lasted in some measure while he lived, though I believe that rest and travel relieved him in his later years. He was always a man of cordial friendliness, and he now expressed a most gratifying interest when I told him what I was going to do in Boston. He gave himself the pleasure of descanting upon the dramatic quality of the fact that a young newspaper man from Ohio was about to share in the destinies of the great literary periodical of New England.

I

I do not think that such a fact would now move the fancy of the liveliest newspaper man, so much has the West since returned upon the East in a refluent wave of authorship. But then the West was almost an unknown quality in our literary problem; and in fact there was scarcely any literature outside of New

England. Even this was of New England origin, for it was almost wholly the work of New England men and women in the "splendid exile" of New York. The Atlantic Monthly, which was distinctively literary, was distinctively a New England magazine, though from the first it had been characterized by what was more national, what was more universal, in the New England temperament. Its chief contributors for nearly twenty years were Longfellow, Lowell, Holmes, Whittier, Emerson, Dr. Hale, Col. Higginson, Mrs. Stowe, Whipple, Rose Terry Cooke, Mrs. Julia Ward Howe, Mrs. Prescott Spofford, Mrs. Phelps Ward, and other New England writers who still lived in New England, and largely in the region of Boston. Occasionally there came a poem from Bryant, at New York, from Mr. Stedman, from Mr. Stoddard and Mrs. Stoddard, from Mr. Aldrich, and from Bayard Taylor. But all these, except the last, were not only of New England race, but of New England birth. I think there was no contributor from the South but Mr. M. D. Conway, and as yet the West scarcely counted, though four young poets from Ohio, who were not immediately or remotely of Puritan origin, had appeared in early numbers; Alice Cary, living with her sister in New York, had written now and then from the beginning. Mr. John Hay solely represented Illinois by a single paper, and he was of Rhode Island stock. It was after my settlement at Boston that Mark Twain, of Missouri, became a figure of world-wide fame at Hartford; and longer after, that Mr. Bret Harte made that progress Eastward from California which was telegraphed almost from hour to hour, as if it were the progress of a prince. Miss Constance F. Woolson had not yet begun to write. Mr. James Whitcomb Riley, Mr. Maurice Thompson, Miss Edith Thomas, Octave Thanet, Mr. Charles Warren Stoddard, Mr. H. B. Fuller, Mrs. Catherwood, Mr. Hamlin Garland, all whom I name at random among other Western writers, were then as unknown as Mr. Cable, Miss Murfree, Mrs. Rives Chanler, Miss Grace King, Mr. Joel Chandler Harris, Mr. Thomas Nelson Page, in the South, which they by no means fully represent.

The editors of the Atlantic had been eager from the beginning to discover any outlying literature; but, as I have said, there was in those days very little good writing done beyond the borders of New England. If the case is now different, and the best known among living American writers are no longer New-Englanders, still I do not think the South and West have yet trimmed the balance; and though perhaps the new writers now more commonly appear in those quarters, I should not be so very sure that they are not still characterized by New England ideals and examples. On the other hand, I am very sure that in my early day we were characterized by them, and wished to be so; we even felt that we failed in so far as we expressed something native quite in our own way. The literary theories we accepted were New England theories, the criticism we valued was New England criticism, or, more strictly speaking, Boston theories, Boston criticism.

II

Of those more constant contributors to the Atlantic whom I have mentioned, it is of course known that Longfellow and Lowell lived in Cambridge, Emerson at Concord, and Whittier at Amesbury. Colonel Higginson was still and for many years afterwards at Newport; Mrs. Stowe was then at Andover; Miss Prescott of Newburyport had become Mrs. Spofford, and was presently in Boston, where her husband was a member of the General Court; Mrs. Phelps Ward, as Miss Elizabeth Stuart Phelps, dwelt in her father's house at Andover. The chief of the Bostonians were Mrs. Julia Ward Howe, Dr. Holmes, and Dr. Hale. Yet Boston stood for the whole Massachusetts group, and Massachusetts, in the literary impulse, meant New England. I suppose we must all allow, whether we like to do so or not, that the impulse seems now to have pretty well spent itself. Certainly the city of Boston has distinctly waned in literature, though it has waxed in wealth and population. I do not think there are in Boston to-day even so many talents with a literary coloring in law, science, theology, and journalism as there were formerly;

though I have no belief that the Boston talents are fewer or feebler than before. I arrived in Boston, however, when all talents had more or less a literary coloring, and when the greatest talents were literary. These expressed with ripened fulness a civilization conceived in faith and brought forth in good works; but that moment of maturity was the beginning of a decadence which could only show itself much later. New England has ceased to be a nation in itself, and it will perhaps never again have anything like a national literature; but that was something like a national literature; and it will probably be centuries yet before the life of the whole country, the American life as distinguished from the New England life, shall have anything so like a national literature. It will be long before our larger life interprets itself in such imagination as Hawthorne's, such wisdom as Emerson's, such poetry as Longfellow's, such prophecy as Whittier's, such wit and grace as Holmes's, such humor and humanity as Lowell's.

The literature of those great men was, if I may suffer myself the figure, the Socinian graft of a Calvinist stock. Their faith, in its varied shades, was Unitarian, but their art was Puritan. So far as it was imperfect—and great and beautiful as it was, I think it had its imperfections—it was marred by the intense ethicism that pervaded the New England mind for two hundred years, and that still characterizes it. They or their fathers had broken away from orthodoxy in the great schism at the beginning of the century, but, as if their heterodoxy were conscience-stricken, they still helplessly pointed the moral in all they did; some pointed it more directly, some less directly; but they all pointed it. I should be far from blaming them for their ethical intention, though I think they felt their vocation as prophets too much for their good as poets. Sometimes they sacrificed the song to the sermon, though not always, nor nearly always. It was in poetry and in romance that they excelled; in the novel, so far as they attempted it, they failed. I say this with the names of all the Bostonian group, and those they influenced, in mind, and with a full sense of their greatness. It may be ungracious to say that they have left no heirs to their peculiar greatness; but it would be foolish to say that they left an estate where they had none to bequeath. One cannot take account of such a fantasy as Judd's Margaret. The only New-Englander who has attempted the novel on a scale proportioned to the work of the New-Englanders in philosophy, in poetry, in romance, is Mr. De Forest, who is of New Haven, and not of Boston. I do not forget the fictions of Dr. Holmes, or the vivid inventions of Dr. Hale, but I do not call them novels; and I do not forget the exquisitely realistic art of Miss Jewett or Miss Wilkins, which is free from the ethicism of the great New England group, but which has hardly the novelist's scope. New England, in Hawthorne's work, achieved supremacy in romance; but the romance is always an allegory, and the novel is a picture in which the truth to life is suffered to do its unsermonized office for conduct; and New England yet lacks her novelist, because it was her instinct and her conscience in fiction to be true to an ideal of life rather than to life itself.

Even when we come to the exception that proves the rule, even to such a signal exception as Uncle Tom's Cabin, I think that what I say holds true. That is almost the greatest work of imagination that we have produced in prose, and it is the work of a New England woman, writing from all the inspirations and traditions of New England. It is like begging the question to say that I do not call it a novel, however; but really, is it a novel, in the sense that War and Peace is a novel, or Madame Bovary, or L'Assommoir, or Phineas Finn, or Doña Perfecta, or Esther Waters, or Marta y María, or The Return of the Native, or Virgin Soil, or David Grieve? In a certain way it is greater than any of these except the first; but its chief virtue, or its prime virtue, is in its address to the conscience, and not its address to the taste; to the ethical sense, not the æsthetical sense.

This does not quite say the thing, but it suggests it, and I should be sorry if it conveyed to any reader a sense of slight; for I believe no one has felt more deeply than myself the value of New England in literature. The comparison of the literary situation at Boston to the literary situation at Edinburgh in the times of the reviewers has never seemed to me accurate or adequate, and it holds chiefly in the fact that both seem to be of the past. Certainly New York is yet no London in literature, and I think Boston was once vastly more than Edinburgh ever was, at least in quality. The Scotch literature of the palmy days was not wholly Scotch, and even when it was rooted in Scotch soil it flowered in the air of an alien speech. But the New England literature of the great day was the blossom of a New England root; and the language which the Bostonians wrote was the native English of scholars fitly the heirs of those who had brought the learning of the universities to Massachusetts Bay two hundred years before, and was of as pure a lineage as the English of the mother-country.

III

The literary situation which confronted me when I came to Boston was, then, as native as could well be; and whatever value I may be able to give a personal study of it will be from the effect it made upon me as one strange in everything but sympathy. I will not pretend that I saw it in its entirety, and I have no hope of presenting anything like a kinetoscopic impression of it. What I can do is to give here and there a glimpse of it; and I shall wish the reader to keep in mind the fact that it was in a "state of transition," as everything is always and everywhere. It was no sooner recognizably native than it ceased to be fully so; and I became a witness of it after the change had begun. The publishing house which so long embodied New England literature was already attempting enterprises out of the line of its traditions, and one of these had brought Mr. T. B. Aldrich from New York, a few weeks before I arrived upon the scene in that dramatic quality which I think never impressed any one but Mr. Bowles. Mr. Aldrich was the editor of Every Saturday when I came to be assistant editor of the Atlantic Monthly. We were of nearly the same age, but he had a distinct and distinguished priority of reputation, insomuch that in my Western remoteness I had always ranged him with such elders and betters of mine as

Holmes and Lowell, and never imagined him the blond, slight youth I found him, with every imaginable charm of contemporaneity. It is no part of the office which I have intended for these slight and sufficiently wandering glimpses of the past to show any writer in his final place; and above all I do not presume to assign any living man his rank or station. But I should be false to my own grateful sense of beauty in the work of this poet if I did not at all times recognize his constancy to an ideal which his name stands for. He is known in several kinds, but to my thinking he is best in a certain nobler kind of poetry; a serious sort in which the thought holds him above the scrupulosities of the art he loves and honors so much. Sometimes the file slips in his hold, as the file must and will; it is but an instrument at the best; but there is no mistouch in the hand that lays itself upon the reader's heart with the pulse of the poet's heart quick and true in it. There are sonnets of his, grave, and simple, and lofty, which I think of with the glow and thrill possible only from very beautiful poetry, and which impart such an emotion as we can feel only

> "When a great thought strikes along the brain
> And flushes all the cheek."

When I had the fortune to meet him first, I suppose that in the employ of the kindly house we were both so eager to serve, our dignities were about the same; for if the Atlantic Monthly was a somewhat prouder affair than an eclectic weekly like Every Saturday, he was supreme in his place, and I was subordinate in mine. The house was careful, in the attitude of its senior partner, not to distinguish between us, and we were not slow to perceive the tact used in managing us; we had our own joke of it; we compared notes to find whether we were equally used in this thing or that; and we promptly shared the fun of our discovery with Fields himself.

We had another impartial friend (no less a friend of joy in the life which seems to have been pretty nearly all joy, as I look back upon it) in the partner who became afterwards the head

John Greenleaf Whittier

of the house, and who forecast in his bold enterprises the change
from a New England to an American literary situation. In the
end James R. Osgood failed, though all his enterprises succeeded.
The anomaly is sad, but it is not infrequent. They were greater
than his powers and his means, and before they could reach their
full fruition, they had to be enlarged to men of longer purse and
longer patience. He was singularly fitted both by instinct and
by education to become a great publisher; and he early perceived
that if a leading American house were to continue at Boston, it
must be hospitable to the talents of the whole country. He found-
ed his future upon those generous lines; but he wanted the
qualities as well as the resources for rearing the superstructure.
Changes began to follow each other rapidly after he came into
control of the house. Misfortune reduced the size and number
of its periodicals. The Young Folks was sold outright, and the
North American Review (long before Mr. Rice bought it and
carried it to New York) was cut down one-half, so that Aldrich
said, It looked as if Destiny had sat upon it. His own periodical,
Every Saturday, was first enlarged to a stately quarto and illustrated; and then, under stress of the calamities following the
great Boston Fire, it collapsed to its former size. Then both the
Atlantic Monthly and Every Saturday were sold away from
their old ownership, and Every Saturday was suppressed altogether, and we two ceased to be of the same employ. There
was some sort of evening rite (more funereal than festive) the
day after they were sold, and we followed Osgood away from it,
under the lamps. We all knew that it was his necessity that had
caused him to part with the periodicals; but he professed that it
was his pleasure, and he said, He had not felt so light-hearted
since he was a boy. We asked him, How could he feel gay when
he was no longer paying us our salaries, and how could he
justify it to his conscience? He liked our mocking, and limped
away from us with a rheumatic easing of his weight from one foot
to another: a figure pathetic now that it has gone the way to
dusty death, and dear to memory through benefactions unalloyed by one unkindness.

IV

But when I came to Boston early in 1866, the Atlantic Monthly and Harper's then divided our magazine world between them; the North American Review, in the control of Lowell and Professor Norton, had entered upon a new life; Every Saturday was an instant success in the charge of Mr. Aldrich, who was by taste and training one of the best editors; and Our Young Folks had the field of juvenile periodical literature to itself.

It was under the direction of Miss Lucy Larcom and of Mr. J. T. Trowbridge, who had come from western New York, where he was born, and must be noted as one of the first returners from the setting to the rising sun. He naturalized himself in Boston in his later boyhood, and he still breathes Boston air, where he dwells in the street called Pleasant, on the shore of Spy Pond, at Arlington, and still weaves the magic web of his satisfying stories for boys. He merges in their popularity the fame of a poet which I do not think will always suffer that eclipse, for his poems show him to have looked deeply into the heart of common humanity with a true and tender sense of it.

Miss Larcom scarcely seemed to change from date to date in the generation that elapsed between the time I first saw her and the time I saw her last, a year or two before her death. A goodness looked out of her comely face, which made me think of the Madonna's in Titian's Assumption, and her whole aspect expressed a mild and friendly spirit which I find it hard to put in words. She was never of the fine world of literature; she dwelt where she was born, in that unfashionable Beverly which is not Beverly Farms, and was of a simple, sea-faring, God-fearing race, as she has told in one of the loveliest autobiographies I know, A New England Girlhood. She was the author of many poems, whose number she constantly enlarged, but she was chiefly, and will be most lastingly, famed for the one poem, Hannah Binding Shoes, which years before my days in Boston had made her so widely known. She never again struck so deep or so true a note; but if one has lodged such a note in the ear of time, it is enough;

and if we are to speak of eternity, one might very well hold up one's head in the fields of asphodel, if one could say to the great others there, "I wrote Hannah Binding Shoes." Her poem is very, very sad, as all who have read it will remember; but Miss Larcom herself was above everything cheerful, and she had a laugh of mellow richness which willingly made itself heard. She was not only of true New England stock, and a Boston author by right of race, but she came up to that city every winter from her native town.

By the same right and on the same terms, another New England poetess, whom I met those first days in Boston, was a Boston author. When I saw Celia Thaxter she was just beginning to make her effect with those poems and sketches which the sea sings and flashes through as it sings and flashes around the Isles of Shoals, her summer home, where her girlhood had been passed in a freedom as wild as the curlew's. She was a most beautiful creature, still very young, with a slender figure, and an exquisite perfection of feature; she was in presence what her work was: fine, frank, finished. I do not know whether other witnesses of our literary history feel that the public has failed to keep her as fully in mind as her work merited; but I do not think there can be any doubt but our literature would be sensibly the poorer without her work. It is interesting to remember how closely she kept to her native field, and it is wonderful to consider how richly she made those sea-beaten rocks to blossom. Something strangely full and bright came to her verse from the mystical environment of the ocean, like the luxury of leaf and tint that it gave the narrower flower-plots of her native isles. Her gift, indeed, could not satisfy itself with the terms of one art alone, however varied, and she learned to express in color the thoughts and feelings impatient of the pallor of words.

She remains in my memories of that far Boston a distinct and vivid personality; as the authoress of Amber Gods, and In a Cellar, and Circumstance, and those other wild romantic tales, remains the gentle and somewhat evanescent presence I found her. Miss Prescott was now Mrs. Spofford, and her husband was

a rising young politician of the day. It was his duties as member
of the General Court that had brought them up from Newburyport to Boston for that first winter; and I remember that the
evening when we met he was talking of their some time going to
Italy that she might study for imaginative literature certain
Italian cities he named. I have long since ceased to own those
cities, but at the moment I felt a pang of expropriation which I
concealed as well as I could; and now I heartily wish she could
have fulfilled that purpose if it was a purpose, or realized that
dream if it was only a dream. Perhaps, however, that sumptuous
and glowing fancy of hers, which had taken the fancy of the
young readers of that day, needed the cold New England background to bring out all its intensities of tint, all its splendors of
light. Its effects were such as could not last, or could not be
farther evolved; they were the expression of youth musing away
from its environment and smitten with the glories of a world afar
and beyond, the great world, the fine world, the impurpled
world of romantic motives and passions. But for what they were,
I can never think them other than what they appeared: the
emanations of a rarely gifted and singularly poetic mind. I feel
better than I can say how necessarily they were the emanations
of a New England mind, and how to the subtler sense they must
impart the pathos of revolt from the colorless rigidities which are
the long result of puritanism in the physiognomy of New England
life.

Their author afterwards gave herself to the stricter study of
this life in many tales and sketches which showed an increasing
mastery; but they could not have the flush, the surprise, the
delight of a young talent trying itself in a kind native and, so far
as I know, peculiar to it. From time to time I still come upon a
poem of hers which recalls that earlier strain of music, of color,
and I am content to trust it for my abiding faith in the charm of
things I have not read for thirty years.

v

I speak of this one and that, as it happens, and with no thought
of giving a complete prospect of literary Boston thirty years ago.

I am aware that it will seem sparsely peopled in the effect I impart, and I would have the reader always keep in mind the great fames at Cambridge and at Concord, which formed so large a part of the celebrity of Boston. I would also like him to think of it as still a great town, merely, where every one knew every one else, and whose metropolitan liberation from neighborhood was just begun.

Most distinctly of that yet uncitified Boston was the critic Edwin P. Whipple, whose sympathies were indefinitely wider than his traditions. He was a most generous lover of all that was excellent in literature; and though I suppose we should call him an old-fashioned critic now, I suspect it would be with no distinct sense of what is newer fashioned. He was certainly as friendly to what promised well in the younger men as he was to what was done well in their elders; and there was no one writing in his day whose virtues failed of his recognition, though it might happen that his foibles would escape Whipple's censure. He wrote strenuously and of course conscientiously; his point of view was solely and always that which enabled him best to discern qualities. I doubt if he had any theory of criticism except to find out what was good in an author and praise it; and he rather blamed what was ethically bad than what was æsthetically bad. In this he was strictly of New England, and he was of New England in a certain general intelligence, which constantly grew with an interrogative habit of mind.

He liked to talk to you of what he had found characteristic in your work, to analyze you to yourself; and the very modesty of the man, which made such a study impersonal as far as he was concerned, sometimes rendered him insensible to the sufferings of his subject. He had a keen perception of humor in others, but he had very little humor; he had a love of the beautiful in literature which was perhaps sometimes greater than his sense of it.

I write from a cursory acquaintance with his work, not recently renewed. Of the presence of the man I have a vivider remembrance: a slight, short, ecclesiasticized figure in black, with a white neckcloth and a silk hat of strict decorum, and between the two a square face with square features, intensified in their regard by a pair of very large glasses, and the prominent, myopic eyes staring through them. He was a type of out-dated New England scholarship in these aspects, but in the hospitable qualities of his mind and heart, the sort of man to be kept fondly in the memory of all who ever knew him.

Out of the vague of that far-off time another face and figure, as essentially New England as this, and yet so different, relieve themselves. Charles F. Browne, whose drollery wafted his pseudonym as far as the English speech could carry laughter, was a Westernized Yankee. He added an Ohio way of talking to the Maine way of thinking, and he so became a literary product of a rarer and stranger sort than our literature had otherwise known. He had gone from Cleveland to London, with intervals of New York and the lecture platform, four or five years before I saw him in Boston, shortly after I went there. We had met in Ohio, and he had personally explained to me the ducatless well-meaning of Vanity Fair in New York; but many men had since shaken the weary hand of Artemus Ward when I grasped it one day in front of the Tremont Temple. He did not recognize me, but he gave me at once a greeting of great impersonal cordiality, with "How do you do? When did you come?" and other questions that had no concern in them, till I began to dawn upon him through a cloud of other half-remembered faces. Then he seized my hand and wrung it all over again, and repeated his friendly demands with an intonation that was now "Why, *how* are you,—how *are* you?" for me alone. It was a bit of comedy, which had the fit pathetic relief of his impending doom: this was already stamped upon his wasted face, and his gay eyes had the death-look. His large, loose mouth was drawn, for all its laughter at the fact which he owned; his profile, which burlesqued an eagle's, was the profile of a drooping eagle; his lank length of limb trembled away with him when we parted. I did not see him again; I scarcely heard of him till I heard of his death, and this sad image remains with me of the humorist who first gave the world a taste of the humor which characterizes the whole American people.

VI

I was meeting all kinds of distinguished persons, in my relation to the magazine, and early that winter I met one who remains in my mind above all others a person of distinction. He was scarcely a celebrity, but he embodied certain social traits which were so characteristic of literary Boston that it could not be approached without their recognition. The Muses have often been acknowledged to be very nice young persons, but in Boston they were really ladies; in Boston literature was of good family and good society in a measure it has never been elsewhere. It might be said even that reform was of good family in Boston; and literature and reform equally shared the regard of Edmund Quincy, whose race was one of the most aristocratic in New England. I had known him by his novel of Wensley (it came so near being a first-ratc novcl), and by his Life of Josiah Quincy, then a new book, but still better by his Boston letters to the New York Tribune. These dealt frankly, in the old antislavery days between 1850 and 1860, with other persons of distinction in Boston, who did not see the right so clearly as Quincy did, or who at least let their interests darken them to the ugliness of slavery. Their fault was all the more comical because it was the error of men otherwise so correct, of characters so stainless, of natures so upright; and the Quincy letters got out of it all the fun there was in it. Quincy himself affected me as the finest patrician type I had ever met. He was charmingly handsome, with a nose of most fit aquilinity, smooth-shaven lips, "educated whiskers," and perfect glasses; his manner was beautiful, his voice delightful, when at our first meeting he made me his reproaches in terms of lovely kindness for having used in my Venetian Life, the Briticism *directly* for *as soon as.*

Lowell once told me that Quincy had never had any calling or profession, because when he found himself in the enjoyment of a moderate income on leaving college, he decided to be simply a gentleman. He was too much of a man to be merely that, and he was an abolitionist, a journalist, and for conscience' sake a satirist. Of that political mood of society which he satirized was an eminent man whom it was also my good fortune to meet in my early days in Boston; and if his great sweetness and kindness had not instantly won my liking, I should still have been glad of the glimpse of the older and statelier Boston which my slight acquaintance with George Ticknor gave me. The historian of Spanish literature, the friend and biographer of Prescott, and a leading figure of the intellectual society of an epoch already closed, dwelt in the fine old square brick mansion which yet stands at the corner of Park Street and Beacon, though sunk now to a variety of business uses, and lamentably changed in aspect. The interior was noble, and there was an air of scholarly quiet and of lettered elegance in the library, where the host received his guests, which seemed to pervade the whole house, and which made its appeal to the imagination of one of them most potently. It seemed to me that to be master of such circumstance and keeping would be enough of life in a certain way; and it all lingers in my memory yet, as if it were one with the gentle courtesy which welcomed me.

Among my fellow-guests one night was George S. Hillard, now a faded reputation, and even then a life defeated of the high expectation of its youth. I do not know whether his Six Months in Italy still keeps itself in print; but it was a book once very well known; and he was perhaps the more gracious to me, as our host was, because of our common Italian background. He was of the old Silver-gray Whig society too, and I suppose that order of things imparted its tone to what I felt and saw in that place. The civil war had come and gone, and that order accepted the result if not with faith, then with patience. There were two young English noblemen there that night, who had been travelling in the South, and whose stories of the wretched conditions they had seen moved our host to some open misgiving. But the Englishmen had no question; in spite of all, they defended the accomplished fact, and when I ventured to say that now at least there could be a hope of better things, while the old order was only the perpetuation of despair, he mildly assented, with a gesture of the hand that waived the point, and a deeply sighed, "Perhaps; perhaps."

He was a presence of great dignity, which seemed to recall the past with a steadfast allegiance, and yet to relax itself toward the present in the wisdom of the accumulated years. His whole life had been passed in devotion to polite literature and in the society of the polite world; and he was a type of scholar such as only the circumstances of Boston could form. Those circumstances could alone form such another type as Quincy; and I wish I could have felt then as I do now the advantage of meeting them so contemporaneously.

VII

The historian of Spanish literature was an old man nearer eighty than seventy when I saw him, and I recall of him personally his dark tint, and the scholarly refinement of his clean-shaven face, which seemed to me rather English than American in character. He was quite exterior to the Atlantic group of writers, and had no interest in me as one of it. Literary Boston of that day was not a solidarity, as I soon perceived; and I understood that it was only in my quality of stranger that I saw the different phases of it. I should not be just to a vivid phase if I failed to speak of Mrs. Julia Ward Howe and the impulse of reform which she personified. I did not sympathize with this then so much as I do now, but I could appreciate it on the intellectual side. Once, many years later, I heard Mrs. Howe speak in public, and it seemed to me that she made one of the best speeches I had ever heard. It gave me for the first time a notion of what women might do in that sort if they entered public life; but when we met in those earlier days I was interested in her as perhaps our chief poetess. I believe she did not care much to speak of literature; she was alert for other meanings in life, and I remember how she once brought to book a youthful matron who had perhaps unduly lamented the hardships of housekeeping, with the sharp demand, "Child, where is your *religion ?*" After the many years of an acquaintance which had not nearly so many meet-

ings as years, it was pleasant to find her, at the latest, as strenuous
as ever for the faith of works, and as eager to aid Stepniak as
John Brown. In her beautiful old age she survives a certain
literary impulse of Boston, but a still higher impulse of Boston
she will not survive, for that will last while the city endures.

VIII

The Cambridge men were curiously apart from others that
formed the great New England group, and with whom in my
earlier ignorance I had always fancied them mingling. Now and
then I met Doctor Holmes at Longfellow's table, but not oftener
than now and then, and I never saw Emerson in Cambridge at
all except at Longfellow's funeral. In my first years on the
Atlantic I sometimes saw him, when he would address me some
grave, rather retrorsive civilities, after I had been newly introduced to him, as I had always to be on these occasions. I formed
the belief that he did not care for me, either in my being or doing,
and I am far from blaming him for that: on such points there
might easily be two opinions, and I was myself often of the mind
I imagined in him.

If Emerson forgot me, it was perhaps because I was not of
those qualities of things which even then, it was said, he could
remember so much better than things themselves. In his later
years I sometimes saw him in the Boston streets with his beautiful
face dreamily set, as he moved like one to whose vision

> "Heaven opens inward, chasms yawn,
>   Vast images in glimmering dawn,
>   Half shown, are broken and withdrawn."

It is known how before the end the eclipse became total and
from moment to moment the record inscribed upon his mind
was erased. Some years before he died I sat between him and
Mrs. Rose Terry Cooke, at an Atlantic Breakfast where it was
part of my editorial function to preside. When he was not asking
me who she was, I could hear him asking her who I was. His
great soul worked so independently of memory as we conceive

it, and so powerfully and essentially, that one could not help wondering if, after all, our personal continuity, our identity hereafter, was necessarily trammeled up with our enduring knowledge of what happens here. His remembrance absolutely ceased with an event, and yet his character, his personality, his identity fully persisted.

I do not know whether the things that we printed for Emerson after his memory began to fail so utterly were the work of earlier years or not, but I know that they were of his best. There were certain poems which could not have been more electly, more exquisitely his, or fashioned with a keener and juster self-criticism. His vision transcended his time so far that some who have tired themselves out in trying to catch up with him have now begun to say that he was no seer at all; but I doubt if these form the last court of appeal in his case. In manner, he was very gentle, like all those great New England men, but he was cold, like many of them, to the new-comer, or to the old-comer who came newly. As I have elsewhere recorded, I once heard him speak critically of Hawthorne, and once he expressed his surprise at the late flowering brilliancy of Holmes's gift in the Autocrat papers after all his friends supposed it had borne its best fruit. But I recall no mention of Longfellow, or Lowell, or Whittier from him. At a dinner where the talk glanced upon Walt Whitman he turned to me as perhaps representing the interest posterity might take in the matter, and referred to Whitman's public use of his privately written praise as something altogether unexpected. He did not disown it or withdraw it, but seemed to feel (not indignantly) that there had been an abuse of it.

IX

The first time I saw Whittier was in Fields's room at the publishing office, where I had come upon some editorial errand to my chief. He introduced me to the poet: a tall, spare figure in black of Quaker cut, with a keen, clean-shaven face, black hair, and vivid black eyes. It was just after his poem, Snow Bound, had made its great success, in the modest fashion of those days, and had sold not two hundred thousand but twenty thousand, and I tried to make him my compliment. I contrived to say that I could not tell him how much I liked it; and he received the inadequate expression of my feeling with doubtless as much effusion as he would have met something more explicit and abundant. If he had judged fit to take my contract off my hands in any way, I think he would have been less able to do so than any of his New England contemporaries. In him, as I have suggested, the Quaker calm was bound by the frosty Puritanic air, and he was doubly cold to the touch of the stranger, though he would thaw out to old friends, and sparkle in laugh and joke. I myself never got so far with him as to experience this geniality, though afterwards we became such friends as an old man and a young man could be who rarely met. Our better acquaintance began with some talk, at a second meeting, about Bayard Taylor's Story of Kennett, which had then lately appeared, and which he praised for its fidelity to Quaker character in its less amiable aspects. No doubt I had made much of my own Quaker descent (which I felt was one of the few things I had to be proud of), and he therefore spoke the more frankly of those traits of brutality into which the primitive sincerity of the sect sometimes degenerated. He thought the habit of plain-speaking had to be jealously guarded to keep it from becoming rude-speaking, and he matched with stories of his own some things I had heard my father tell of Friends in the backwoods who were Foes to good manners.

Whittier was one of the most generous of men towards the work of others, especially the work of a new man, and if I did anything that he liked, I could count upon him for cordial recognition. In the quiet of his country home at Danvers he apparently read all the magazines, and kept himself fully abreast of the literary movement, but I doubt if he so fully appreciated the importance of the social movement. Like some others of the great anti-slavery men, he seemed to imagine that mankind had won itself a clear field by destroying chattel slavery, and he had no sympathy with those who think that the man who may any moment be out of work is industrially a slave. This is not strange; so few men last over from one reform to another that the wonder is that any should, not that one should not. Whittier was prophet for one great need of the divine to man, and he spoke his message with a fervor that at times was like the trembling of a flame, or the quivering of midsummer sunshine. It was hard to associate with the man as one saw him, still, shy, stiff, the passion of his verse. This imbued not only his anti-slavery utterances, but equally his ballads of the old witch and Quaker persecution, and flashed a far light into the dimness where his interrogations of Mystery pierced. Whatever doubt there can be of the fate of other New England poets in the great and final account, it seems to me that certain of these pieces make his place secure.

There is great inequality in his work, and I felt this so strongly that when I came to have full charge of the Magazine, I ventured once to distinguish. He sent me a poem, and I had the temerity to return it, and beg him for something else. He magnanimously refrained from all show of offence, and after a while, when he had printed the poem elsewhere, he gave me another. By this time, I perceived that I had been wrong, not as to the poem returned, but as to my function regarding him and such as he. I had made my reflections, and never again did I venture to pass upon what contributors of his quality sent me. I took it and printed it, and praised the gods; and even now I think that with such men it was not my duty to play the censor in the periodical which they had made what it was. They had set it in authority over American literature, and it was not for me to put myself in authority over them. Their fame was in their own keeping, and it was not my part to guard it against them.

After that experience I not only practised an eager acquiescence in their wish to reach the public through the Atlantic, but I used all the delicacy I was master of in bowing the way to them. Sometimes my utmost did not avail, or more strictly speaking it did not avail in one instance with Emerson. He had given me upon much entreaty a poem which was one of his greatest and best, but the proof-reader found a nominative at odds with its verb. We had some trouble in reconciling them, and some other delays, and meanwhile Doctor Holmes offered me a poem for the same number. I now doubted whether I should get Emerson's poem back in time for it, but unluckily the proof did come back in time, and then I had to choose between my poets, or acquaint them with the state of the case, and let them choose what I should do. I really felt that Doctor Holmes had the right to precedence, since Emerson had withheld his proof so long that I could not count upon it; but I wrote to Emerson, and asked (as nearly as I can remember) whether he would consent to let me put his poem over to the next number, or would prefer to have it appear in the same number with Doctor Holmes's; the subjects were cognate, and I had my misgivings. He wrote me back to "return the proofs and break up the forms." I could not go to this iconoclastic extreme with the electrotypes of the magazine, but I could return the proofs. I did so, feeling that I had done my possible, and silently grieving that there could be such ire in heavenly minds.

x

Emerson, as I say, I had once met in Cambridge, but Whittier never; and I have a feeling that poet as Cambridge felt him to be, she had her reservations concerning him. I cannot put these into words which would not oversay them, but they were akin to those she might have refined upon in regard to Mrs. Stowe. Neither of these great writers would have appeared to Cambridge of the last literary quality; their fame was with a world too vast to be the test that her own

"One entire and perfect chrysolite"

would have formed. Whittier in fact had not arrived at the clear splendor of his later work without some earlier turbidity; he was still from time to time capable of a false rhyme, like *morn* and *dawn*. As for the author of Uncle Tom's Cabin her syntax was such a snare to her that it sometimes needed the combined skill of all the proof-readers and the assistant editor to extricate her. Of course, nothing was ever written into her work, but in changes of diction, in correction of solecisms, in transposition of phrases, the text was largely rewritten on the margin of her proofs. The soul of her art was present, but the form was so often absent, that when it was clothed on anew, it would have been hard to say whose cut the garment was of in many places. In fact, the proof-reading of the Atlantic Monthly was something almost fearfully scrupulous and perfect. The proofs were first read by the under proof-reader in the printing-office; then the head reader passed them to me perfectly clean as to typography, with his own abundant and most intelligent comments on the literature; and then I read them, making what changes I chose, and verifying every quotation, every date, every geographical and biographical name, every foreign word to the last accent, every technical and scientific term. Where it was possible or at all desirable the proof was next submitted to the author. When it came back to me, I revised it, accepting or rejecting the author's judgment according as he was entitled by his ability and knowledge or not to have them. The proof now went to the printers for correction; they sent it again to the head reader, who carefully revised it and returned it again to me. I read it a second time, and it was again corrected. After this it was revised in the office and sent to the stereotyper, from whom it came to the head reader for a last revision in the plates.

It would not do to say how many of the first American writers owed their correctness in print to the zeal of our proof-reading, but I may say that there were very few who did not owe something. The wisest and ablest were the most patient and grateful, like Mrs. Stowe, under correction; it was only the beginners and the more ignorant who were angry; and almost always the proof-reading editor had his way on disputed points. I look back now, with respectful amazement at my proficiency in detecting the errors of the great as well as the little. I was able to discover mistakes even in the classical quotations of the deeply lettered Sumner, and I remember, in the earliest years of my service on the Atlantic, waiting in this statesman's study amidst the prints and engravings that attested his personal resemblance to Edmund Burke, with his proofs in my hand and my heart in my mouth, to submit my doubts of his latinity. I forget how he received them; but he was not a very gracious person.

Mrs. Stowe *was* a gracious person, and carried into age the inalienable charm of a woman who must have been very charming earlier. I met her only at the Fieldses' in Boston, where one night I witnessed a controversy between her and Doctor Holmes concerning homœopathy and allopathy which lasted well through dinner. After this lapse of time, I cannot tell how the affair ended, but I feel sure of the liking with which Mrs. Stowe inspired me. There was something very simple, very motherly in her, and something divinely sincere. She was quite the person to take *au grand sérieux* the monstrous imaginations of Lady Byron's jealousy and to feel it on her conscience to make public report of them when she conceived that the time had come to do so.

XI

In Francis Parkman I knew much later than in some others a differentiation of the New England type which was not less characteristic. He, like so many other Boston men of letters, was of patrician family, and of those easy fortunes which Clio prefers her sons to be of, but he paid for these advantages by the suffering in which he wrought at what is, I suppose, our greatest history. He wrought at it piecemeal, and sometimes only by moments, when the terrible headaches which tormented him, and the disorder of the heart which threatened his life, allowed him a brief respite for the task which was dear to him. He must have been more than a quarter of a century in completing it, and in this time, as he once told me, it had given him a day laborer's wages; but of course money was the least return he wished from it. I read the irregularly successive volumes of The Jesuits in North America, The Old Régime in Canada, the Montcalm and Wolfe, and the others that went to make up the whole history with a

Harriet Beecher Stowe

sufficiently noisy enthusiasm, and our acquaintance began by his expressing his gratification with the praises of them that I had put in print. We entered into relations as contributor and editor, and I know that he was pleased with my eagerness to get as many detachable chapters from the book in hand as he could give me for the magazine, but he was of too fine a politeness to make this the occasion of his first coming to see me. He had walked out to Cambridge, where I then lived, in pursuance of a regimen which, I believe, finally built up his health; that it was unsparing, I can testify from my own share in one of his constitutionals in Boston, many years later.

His experience in laying the ground work for his history, and his researches in making it thorough, were such as to have liberated him to the knowledge of other manners and ideals, but he remained strictly a Bostonian, and as immutably of the Boston social and literary faith as any I knew in that capital of accomplished facts. He had lived like an Indian among the wild Western tribes; he consorted with the Canadian archaeologists in their mousings among the colonial archives of their fallen state; every year he went to Quebec or Paris to study the history of New France in the original documents; European society was open to him everywhere; but he had those limitations which I nearly always found in the Boston men. I remember his talking to me of The Rise of Silas Lapham, in a somewhat troubled and uncertain strain, and interpreting his rise as the achievement of social recognition, without much or at all liking it or me for it. I did not think it my part to point out that I had supposed the rise to be a moral one; and later I fell under his condemnation for certain high crimes and misdemeanors I had been guilty of against a well known ideal in fiction. These in fact constituted lese-majesty of romanticism, which seemed to be disproportionately dear to a man who was in his own way trying to tell the truth of human nature as I was in mine. His displeasures passed, however, and my last meeting with our greatest historian, as I think him, was of unalloyed friendliness. He came to me during my final year in Boston for nothing apparently but to tell me of his liking for a book of mine describing boy-life in Southern Ohio a half century ago. He wished to talk about many points of this, which he found the same as his own boy life in the neighborhood of Boston; and we could agree that the life of the Anglosaxon boy was pretty much the same everywhere. He had helped himself into my apartment with a crutch, but I do not remember how he had fallen lame. It was the end of his long walks, I believe, and not long afterwards I had the grief to read of his death. I noticed that perhaps through his enforced quiet, he had put on weight; his fine face was full; whereas when I first knew him he was almost delicately thin of figure and feature. He was always of a distinguished presence, and his face had a great distinction.

It had not the appealing charm I found in the face of James Parton, another historian I knew earlier in my Boston days. I cannot say how much his books, once so worthily popular, are now known, but I have an abiding sense of their excellence. I have not read the life of Voltaire, which was the last, but all the rest, from the first, I have read, and if there are better American biographies than those of Franklin or of Jefferson, I could not say where to find them. The Greeley and the Burr were younger books, and so was the Jackson, and they were not nearly so good; but to all the author had imparted the valuable humanity in which he abounded. He was never of the fine world of literature, the world that sniffs and sneers, and abashes the simpler-hearted reader. But he was a true artist, and English born as he was, he divined American character as few Americans have done. He was a man of eminent courage, and in the days when to be an agnostic was to be almost an outcast, he had the heart to say of the Mysteries, that he did not know. He outlived the condemnation that this brought, and I think that no man ever came near him without in some measure loving him. To me he was of a most winning personality, which his strong, gentle face expressed, and a cast in the eye which he could not bring to bear directly upon his vis-a-vis, endeared. I never met him without wishing more of his company, for he seldom failed to say something to whatever was most humane and most modern in me. Our last meeting was at Newburyport, whither he had long before removed from New York, and where in the serene atmosphere of the ancient Puritan town he found leisure and inspiration for his work. He was not then engaged upon any considerable task, and he had aged and broken somewhat. But the old geniality, the old warmth glowed in him, and made a summer amidst the storm of snow that blinded the wintry air without. A new light had then lately come into my life, by which I saw all things that did not somehow tell for human brotherhood dwarfish and ugly, and he listened, as I imagined, to what I had to say with the tolerant sympathy of a man who has been a long time thinking those things, and views with a certain amusement the zeal of the fresh discoverer.

There was yet another historian in Boston, whose acquaintance I made later than either Parkman's or Parton's, and whose very recent death leaves me with the grief of a friend. No one, indeed, could meet John Codman Ropes without wishing to be his friend, or without finding a friend in him. He had his likes and his dislikes, but he could have had no enmities except for evil and meanness. I never knew a man of higher soul, of sweeter nature, and his whole life was a monument of character. It cannot wound him now to speak of the cruel deformity which came upon him in his boyhood, and haunted all his after days with suffering. His gentle face showed the pain which is always the part of the hunchback, but nothing else in him confessed a sense of his affliction, and the resolute activity of his mind denied it in every way. He was, as is well known, a very able lawyer, in full practice, while he was making his studies of military history, and winning recognition for almost unique insight and thoroughness in that direction, though I believe that when he came to embody the results in those extraordinary volumes recording the battles of our civil war, he retired from the law in some measure. He knew these battles more accurately than the generals who fought them, and he was of a like proficiency in the European wars from the time of Napoleon down to our own time. I have heard a story, which I cannot vouch for, that when foreknowledge of his affliction, at the outbreak of our civil war, forbade him to be a soldier, he became a student of soldiership, and wreaked in that sort the passion of his most gallant spirit. But whether this was true or not, it is certain that he pursued the study with a devotion which never blinded him to the atrocity of war. Some wars he could excuse and even justify, but for any war that seemed wanton or aggressive, he had only abhorrence.

The last summer of a score that I had known him, we sat on the veranda of his cottage at York Harbor, and looked out over the moonlit sea, and he talked of the high and true things, with the inextinguishable zest for the inquiry which I always found in him, though he was then feeling the approaches of the malady which was so soon to end all groping in these shadows for him. He must have faced the fact with the same courage and the same trust with which he faced all facts. From the first I found him a deeply religious man, not only in the ecclesiastical sense, but in the more mystical meanings of the word, and he kept his faith as he kept his youth to the last. Every one who knew him, knows how young he was in heart, and how he liked to have those that were young in years about him. He wished to have his house in Boston, as well as his cottage at York, full of young men and young girls, whose joy of life he made his own, and whose society he preferred to his contemporaries'. One could not blame him for that, or for seeking the sun, wherever he could, but it would be a false notion of him to suppose that his sympathies were solely or chiefly with the happy. In every sort, as I knew him, he was fine and good. The word is not worthy of him, after some of its uses and associations, but if it were unsmutched by these, and whitened to its primitive significance, I should say he was one of the most perfect gentlemen I ever knew.

Part Fifth

OLIVER WENDELL HOLMES

ELSEWHERE we literary folk are apt to be such a common lot, with tendencies here and there to be a shabby lot; we arrive from all sorts of unexpected holes and corners of the earth, remote, obscure; and at the best we do so often come up out of the ground; but at Boston we were of ascertained and noted origin, and good part of us dropped from the skies. Instead of holding horses before the doors of theatres; or capping verses at the plough-tail; or tramping over Europe with nothing but a flute in the pocket; or walking up to the metropolis with no luggage but the MS. of a tragedy; or sleeping in doorways or under the arches of bridges; or serving as apothecaries' 'prentices —we were good society from the beginning. I think this was none the worse for us, and it was vastly the better for good society.

I

Literature in Boston, indeed, was so respectable, and often of so high a lineage, that to be a poet was not only to be good society, but almost to be good family. If one names over the men who gave Boston her supremacy in literature during that Unitarian harvest-time of the old Puritanic seed-time which was her Augustan age, one names the people who were and who had been socially first in the city ever since the self-exile of the Tories at the time of the Revolution. To say Prescott, Motley, Parkman, Lowell, Norton, Higginson, Dana, Emerson, Channing, was to say patrician, in the truest and often the best sense, if not the largest. Boston was small, but these were of her first citizens, and their primacy, in its way, was of the same quality as that, say, of

125

the chief families of Venice. But these names can never have the effect for the stranger that they had for one to the manner born. I say had, for I doubt whether in Boston they still mean all that they once meant, and that their equivalents meant in science, in law, in politics. The most famous, if not the greatest of all the literary men of Boston, I have not mentioned with them, for Longfellow was not of the place, though by his sympathies and relations he became of it; and I have not mentioned Oliver Wendell Holmes, because I think his name would come first into the reader's thought with the suggestion of social quality in the humanities.

Holmes was of the brahminical caste which his humorous recognition invited from its subjectivity in the New England consciousness into the light where all could know it and own it, and like Longfellow he was allied to the patriciate of Boston by the most intimate ties of life. For a long time, for the whole first period of his work, he stood for that alone, its tastes, its prejudices, its foibles even, and when he came to stand in his second period, for vastly, for infinitely more, and to make friends with the whole race, as few men have ever done, it was always, I think, with a secret shiver of doubt, a backward look of longing, and an eye askance. He was himself perfectly aware of this at times, and would mark his several misgivings with a humorous sense of the situation. He was essentially too kind to be of a narrow world, too human to be finally of less than humanity, too gentle to be of the finest gentility. But such limitations as he had were in the direction I have hinted, or perhaps more than hinted; and I am by no means ready to make a mock of them, as it would be so easy to do for some reasons that he has himself suggested. To value aright the affection which the old Bostonian had for Boston one must conceive of something like the patriotism of men in the times when a man's city was a man's country, something Athenian, something Florentine. The war that nationalized us liberated this love to the whole country, but its first tenderness remained still for Boston, and I suppose a Bostonian still thinks of himself first as a Bostonian and then as an American, in a way that no New-Yorker could deal with himself. The rich historical background dignifies and ennobles the intense public spirit of the place, and gives it a kind of personality.

II

In literature Dr. Holmes survived all the Bostonians who had given the city her primacy in letters, but when I first knew him there was no apparent ground for questioning it. I do not mean now the time when I visited New England, but when I came to live near Boston, and to begin the many happy years which I spent in her fine intellectual air. I found time to run in upon him, while I was there arranging to take my place on the *Atlantic Monthly*, and I remember that in this brief moment with him he brought me to book about some vaunting paragraph in the *Nation* claiming the literary primacy for New York. He asked me if I knew who wrote it, and I was obliged to own that I had written it myself, when with the kindness he always showed me he protested against my position. To tell the truth I do not think now I had any very good reasons for it, and I certainly could urge none that would stand against his. I could only fall back upon the saving clause that this primacy was claimed mainly if not wholly for New York in the future. He was willing to leave me the connotations of prophecy, but I think he did even this out of politeness rather than conviction, and I believe he had always a sensitiveness where Boston was concerned, which could not seem ungenerous to any generous mind. Whatever lingering doubt of me he may have had, with reference to Boston, seemed to satisfy itself when several years afterwards he happened to speak of a certain character in an early novel of mine, who was not quite the kind of Bostonian one could wish to be. The thing came up in talk with another person, who had referred to my Bostonian, and the doctor had apparently made his acquaintance in the book, and not liked him. "I understood, of course," he said, "that he was *a* Bostonian, not *the* Bostonian," and I could truthfully answer that this was by all means my own understanding too.

His fondness for his city, which no one could appreciate better than myself, I hope, often found expression in a burlesque excess in his writings, and in his talk perhaps oftener still. Hard upon my return from Venice I had a half-hour with him in his old study on Charles Street, where he still lived in 1865, and while I was there a young man came in for the doctor's help as a physician, though he looked so very well, and was so lively and cheerful, that I have since had my doubts whether he had not made a pretext for a glimpse of him as the Autocrat. The doctor took him upon his word, however, and said he had been so long out of practice that he could not do anything for him, but he gave him the address of another physician, somewhere near Washington Street. "And if you don't know where Washington Street is," he said, with a gay burst at a certain vagueness which had come into the young man's face, "you don't know anything."

We had been talking of Venice, and what life was like there, and he made me tell him in some detail. He was especially interested in what I had to say of the minute subdivision and distribution of the necessaries, the small coins, and the small values adapted to their purchase, the intensely retail character, in fact, of household provisioning; and I could see how he pleased himself in formulating the theory that the higher a civilization the finer the apportionment of the demands and supplies. The ideal, he said, was a civilization in which you could buy two cents' worth of beef, and a divergence from this standard was towards barbarism.

The secret of the man who is universally interesting is that he is universally interested, and this was above all the secret of the charm that Doctor Holmes had for every one. No doubt he knew it, for what that most alert intelligence did not know of itself was scarcely worth knowing. This knowledge was one of his chief pleasures, I fancy; he rejoiced in the consciousness which is one of the highest attributes of the highly organized man, and he did not care for the consequences in your mind, if you were so stupid as not to take him aright. I remember the delight Henry James, the father of the novelist, had in reporting to me the frankness of

the doctor, when he had said to him, "Holmes, you are intellectually the most alive man I ever knew." "I am, I am," said
the doctor. "From the crown of my head to the sole of my foot,
I'm alive, I'm alive!" Any one who ever saw him will imagine
the vivid relish he had in recognizing the fact. He could not be
with you a moment without shedding upon you the light of his
flashing wit, his radiant humor, and he shone equally upon the
rich and poor in mind. His gayety of heart could not withhold
itself from any chance of response, but he did wish always to be
fully understood, and to be liked by those he liked. He gave his
liking cautiously, though, for the affluence of his sympathies left
him without the reserves of colder natures, and he had to make
up for these with careful circumspection. He wished to know the
character of the person who made overtures to his acquaintance,
for he was aware that his friendship lay close to it; he wanted to
be sure that he was a nice person, and though I think he preferred
social quality in his fellow-man, he did not refuse himself to
those who had merely a sweet and wholesome humanity. He did
not like anything that tasted or smelt of bohemianism in the
personnel of literature, but he did not mind the scent of the new-
ploughed earth, or even of the barn-yard. I recall his telling me
once that after two younger brothers-in-letters had called upon
him in the odor of a habitual beeriness and smokiness, he opened
the window; and the very last time I saw him he remembered at
eighty-five the offence he had found on his first visit to New York,
when a metropolitan poet had asked him to lunch in a basement
restaurant.

III

He seemed not to mind, however, climbing to the little apartment we had in Boston when we came there in 1866, and he made
this call upon us in due form, bringing Mrs. Holmes with him as
if to accent the recognition socially. We were then incredibly
young, much younger than I find people ever are, nowadays, and
in the consciousness of our youth we felt, to the last exquisite
value of the fact, what it was to have the Autocrat come to see

us; and I believe he was not displeased to perceive this; he liked to know that you felt his quality in every way. That first winter, however, I did not see him often, and in the spring we went to live in Cambridge, and thereafter I met him chiefly at Longfellow's, or when I came in to dine at the Fieldses', in Boston. It was at certain meetings of the Dante Club, when Longfellow read aloud his translation for criticism, and there was supper later, that one saw the doctor; and his voice was heard at the supper rather than at the criticism, for he was no Italianate. He always seemed to like a certain turn of the talk toward the mystical, but with space for the feet on a firm ground of fact this side of the shadows; when it came to going over among them, and laying hold of them with the hand of faith, as if they were substance, he was not of the excursion. It is well known how fervent, I cannot say devout, a spiritualist Longfellow's brother-in-law, Appleton, was; and when he was at the table too, it took all the poet's delicate skill to keep him and the Autocrat from involving themselves in a cataclysmal controversy upon the matter of manifestations. With Dr. Holmes the inquiry was inquiry, to the last, I believe, and the burden of proof was left to the ghosts and their friends. His attitude was strictly scientific; he denied nothing, but he expected the supernatural to be at least as convincing as the natural.

There was a time in his history when the popular ignorance classed him with those who were once rudely called infidels; but the world has since gone so fast and so far that the mind he was of concerning religious belief would now be thought religious by a good half of the religious world. It is true that he had and always kept a grudge against the ancestral Calvinism which afflicted his youth; and he was through all rises and lapses of opinion essentially Unitarian; but of the honest belief of any one, I am sure he never felt or spoke otherwise than most tolerantly, most tenderly. As often as he spoke of religion, and his talk tended to it very often, I never heard an irreligious word from him, far less a scoff or sneer at religion; and I am certain that this was not merely because he would have thought it bad taste, though undoubtedly he would have thought it bad taste; I think it annoyed, it hurt him, to be counted among the iconoclasts, and he would have been profoundly grieved if he could have known how widely this false notion of him once prevailed. It can do no harm at this late day to impart from the secrets of the publishing house the fact that a supposed infidelity in the tone of his story The Guardian Angel cost the *Atlantic Monthly* many subscribers. Now, the tone of that story would not be thought even mildly agnostic, I fancy; and long before his death the author had outlived the error concerning him.

It was not the best of his stories, by any means, and it would not be too harsh to say that it was the poorest. His novels all belonged to an order of romance which was as distinctly his own as the form of dramatized essay which he invented in the Autocrat. If he did not think poorly of them, he certainly did not think too proudly, and I heard him quote with relish the phrase of a lady who had spoken of them to him as his "medicated novels." That, indeed, was perhaps what they were; a faint, faint odor of the pharmacopœia clung to their pages; their magic was scientific. He knew this better than any one else, of course, and if any one had said it in his turn he would hardly have minded it. But what he did mind was the persistent misinterpretation of his intention in certain quarters where he thought he had the right to respectful criticism instead of the succession of sneers that greeted the successive numbers of his story; and it was no secret that he felt the persecution keenly. Perhaps he thought that he had already reached that time in his literary life when he was a fact rather than a question, and when reasons and not feelings must have to do with his acceptance or rejection. But he had to live many years yet before he reached this state. When he did reach it, happily a good while before his death, I do not believe any man ever enjoyed the like condition more. He loved to feel himself out of the fight, with much work before him still, but with nothing that could provoke ill-will in his activities. He loved at all times to take himself objectively, if I may so express my sense of a mental attitude that misled many. As I have said before, he was universally interested, and he studied the universe from himself. I do not know how one is to study it otherwise; the impersonal has really no existence; but with all his subtlety and depth he was of a make so simple, of a spirit so naïve, that he could not practise the feints some use to conceal that interest in self which, after all, every one knows is only concealed. He frankly and joyously made himself the starting-point in all his inquest of the hearts and minds of other men, but so far from singling himself out in this, and standing apart in it, there never was any one who was more eagerly and gladly your fellow-being in the things of the soul.

IV

In the things of the world, he had fences, and looked at some people through palings and even over the broken bottles on the tops of walls; and I think he was the loser by this, as well as they. But then I think all fences are bad, and that God has made enough differences between men; we need not trouble ourselves to multiply them. Even behind his fences, however, Holmes had a heart kind for the outsiders, and I do not believe any one came into personal relations with him who did not experience this kindness. In that long and delightful talk I had with him on my return from Venice (I can praise the talk because it was mainly his), we spoke of the status of domestics in the Old World, and how fraternal the relation of high and low was in Italy, while in England, between master and man, it seemed without acknowledgment of their common humanity. "Yes," he said, "I always felt as if English servants expected to be trampled on; but I can't do that. If they want to be trampled on, they must get some one else." He thought that our American way was infinitely better; and I believe that in spite of the fences there was always an instinctive impulse with him to get upon common ground with his fellow-man. I used to notice in the neighborhood cabman who served our block on Beacon Street a sort of affectionate reverence for the Autocrat, which could have come from nothing but the kindly terms between them; if you went to him when he was engaged to Dr. Holmes, he told you so with a sort of implication in his manner that the thought of anything else for the time was profanation. The good fellow who took him his drives about the Beverly and Manchester shores seemed to be quite in the joke of the doctor's humor, and within the bounds of his personal modesty and his functional dignity permitted himself a smile at the doctor's sallies, when you stood talking with him, or listening to him at the carriage-side.

The civic and social circumstance that a man values himself on is commonly no part of his value, and certainly no part of his greatness. Rather, it is the very thing that limits him, and I think that Dr. Holmes appeared in the full measure of his generous personality to those who did not and could not appreciate his circumstance, and not to those who formed it, and who from life-long association were so dear and comfortable to him. Those who best knew how great a man he was were those who came from far to pay him their duty, or to thank him for some help they had got from his books, or to ask his counsel or seek his sympathy. With all such he was most winningly tender, most intelligently patient. I suppose no great author was ever more visited by letter and in person than he, or kept a faithfuler conscience for his guests. With those who appeared to him in the flesh he used a miraculous tact, and I fancy in his treatment of all the physician native in him bore a characteristic part. No one seemed to be denied access to him, but it was after a moment of preparation that one was admitted, and any one who was at all sensitive must have felt from the first moment in his presence that there could be no trespassing in point of time. If now and then some insensitive began to trespass, there was a sliding-scale of dismissal that never failed of its work, and that really saved the author from the effect of intrusion. He was not bored because he would not be.

I transfer at random the impressions of many years to my page, and I shall not try to observe a chronological order in these memories. Vivid among them is that of a visit which I paid him with Osgood the publisher, then newly the owner of the *Atlantic*

Monthly, when I had newly become the sole editor. We wished to signalize our accession to the control of the magazine by a stroke that should tell most in the public eye, and we thought of asking Dr. Holmes to do something again in the manner of the Autocrat and the Professor at the Breakfast Table. Some letters had passed between him and the management concerning our wish, and then Osgood thought that it would be right and fit for us to go to him in person. He proposed the visit, and Dr. Holmes received us with a mind in which he had evidently formulated all his thoughts upon the matter. His main question was whether at his age of sixty years a man was justified in seeking to recall a public of the past, or to create a new public in the present. He seemed to have looked the ground over not only with a personal interest in the question, but with a keen scientific zest for it as something which it was delightful to consider in its generic relations; and I fancy that the pleasure of this inquiry more than consoled him for such pangs of misgiving as he must have had in the personal question. As commonly happens in the solution of such problems, it was not solved; he was very willing to take our minds upon it, and to incur the risk, if we thought it well and were willing to share it.

We came away rejoicing, and the new series began with the new year following. It was by no means the popular success that we had hoped; not because the author had not a thousand new things to say, or failed to say them with the gust and freshness of his immortal youth, but because it was not well to disturb a form associated in the public mind with an achievement which had become classic. It is of the Autocrat of the Breakfast Table that people think, when they think of the peculiar species of dramatic essay which the author invented, and they think also of the Professor at the Breakfast Table, because he followed so soon; but the Poet at the Breakfast Table came so long after, that his advent alienated rather than conciliated liking. Very likely, if the Poet had come first he would have had no second place in the affections of his readers, for his talk was full of delightful matter; and at least one of the poems which graced each instalment was one of the finest and greatest that Dr. Holmes ever wrote. I mean Homesick in Heaven, which seems to me not only what I have said, but one of the most important, the most profoundly pathetic in the language. Indeed, I do not know any other that in the same direction goes so far with suggestion so penetrating.

The other poems were mainly of a cast which did not win; the metaphysics in them were too much for the human interest, and again there rose a foolish clamor of the creeds against him on account of them. The great talent, the beautiful and graceful fancy, the eager imagination of the Autocrat could not avail in this third attempt, and I suppose the Poet at the Breakfast Table must be confessed as near a failure as Dr. Holmes could come. It certainly was so in the magazine which the brilliant success of the first had availed to establish in the high place the periodical must always hold in the history of American literature. Lowell was never tired of saying, when he recurred to the first days of his editorship, that the magazine could never have gone at all without the Autocrat papers. He was proud of having insisted upon Holmes's doing something for the new venture, and he was fond of recalling the author's misgivings concerning his contributions, which later repeated themselves with too much reason, though not with the reason that was in his own mind.

V

He lived twenty-five years after that self-question at sixty, and after eighty he continued to prove that threescore was not the limit of a man's intellectual activity or literary charm. During all that time the work he did in mere quantity was the work that a man in the prime of life might well have been vain of doing, and it was of a quality not less surprising. If I asked him with any sort of fair notice I could rely upon him always for something for the January number, and throughout the year I could count upon him for those occasional pieces in which he so easily excelled all former writers of occasional verse, and which he liked to keep from the newspapers for the magazine. He had a pride in his promptness with copy, and you could always trust his promise.

The printer's toe never galled the author's kibe in his case; he wished to have an early proof, which he corrected fastidiously, but not overmuch, and he did not keep it long. He had really done all his work in the manuscript, which came print-perfect and beautifully clear from his pen, in that flowing, graceful hand which to the last kept a suggestion of the pleasure he must have had in it. Like all wise contributors he was not only patient, but very glad of all the queries and challenges that proof-reader and editor could accumulate on the margin of his proofs, and when they were both altogether wrong he was still grateful. In one of his poems there was some Latin Quarter French, which our collective purism questioned, and I remember how tender of us he was in maintaining that in his Parisian time, at least, some ladies beyond the Seine said "Eh, b'en," instead of "Eh, bien." He knew that we must be always on the lookout for such little matters, and he would not wound our ignorance.

I do not think any one enjoyed praise more than he. Of course he would not provoke it, but if it came of itself, he would not deny himself the pleasure, as long as a relish of it remained. He used humorously to recognize his delight in it, and to say of the lecture audiences which in earlier times hesitated applause, "Why don't they give me three times three? I can stand it!" He himself gave in the generous fulness he desired. He did not praise foolishly or dishonestly, though he would spare an open dislike; but when a thing pleased him he knew how to say so cordially and skilfully, so that it might help as well as delight. I suppose no great author has tried more sincerely and faithfully to befriend the beginner than he; and from time to time he would commend something to me that he thought worth looking at, but never insistently. In certain cases, where he had simply to ease a burden from his own to the editorial shoulders, he would ask that the aspirant might be delicately treated. There might be personal reasons for this, but usually his kindness of heart moved him. His tastes had their geographical limit, but his sympathies were boundless, and the hopeless creature for whom he interceded was oftener remote from Boston and New England than otherwise.

Oliver Wendell Holmes

It seems to me that he had a nature singularly affectionate, and that it was this which was at fault if he gave somewhat too much of himself to the celebration of the Class of '29, and all the multitude of Boston occasions, large and little, embalmed in the clear amber of his verse, somewhat to the disadvantage of the amber. If he were asked he could not deny the many friendships and fellowships which united in the asking; the immediate réclame from these things was sweet to him; but he loved to comply as much as he loved to be praised. In the pleasure he got he could feel himself a prophet in his own country, but the country which owned him prophet began perhaps to feel rather too much as if it owned him, and did not prize his vaticinations at all their worth. Some polite Bostonians knew him chiefly on this side, and judged him to their own detriment from it.

VI

After we went to live in Cambridge, my life and the delight in it were so wholly there that in ten years I had hardly been in as many Boston houses. As I have said, I met Dr. Holmes at the Fieldses', and at Longfellow's, when he came out to a Dante supper, which was not often, and somewhat later at the Saturday Club dinners. One parlous time at the publisher's I have already recalled, when Mrs. Harriet Beecher Stowe and the Autocrat clashed upon homœopathy, and it required all the tact of the host to lure them away from the dangerous theme. As it was, a battle waged in the courteous forms of Fontenoy, went on pretty well through the dinner, and it was only over the coffee that a truce was called. I need not say which was heterodox, or that each had a deep and strenuous conscience in the matter. I have always felt it a proof of his extreme leniency to me, unworthy, that the doctor was able to tolerate my own defection from the elder faith in medicine; and I could not feel his kindness less caressing because I knew it a concession to an infirmity. He said something like, After all a good physician was the great matter; and I eagerly turned his clemency to praise of our family doctor.

He was very constant at the Saturday Club, as long as his strength permitted, and few of its members missed fewer of its meetings. He continued to sit at its table until the ghosts of Hawthorne, of Agassiz, of Emerson, of Longfellow, of Lowell, out of others less famous, bore him company there among the younger men in the flesh. It must have been very melancholy, but nothing could deeply cloud his most cheerful spirit. His strenuous interest in life kept him alive to all the things of it, after so many of his friends were dead. The questions which he was wont to deal with so fondly, so wisely, the great problems of the soul, were all the more vital, perhaps, because the personal concern in them was increased by the translation to some other being of the men who had so often tried with him to fathom them here. The last time I was at that table he sat alone there among those great memories; but he was as gay as ever I saw him; his wit sparkled, his humor gleamed; the poetic touch was deft and firm as of old; the serious curiosity, the instant sympathy remained. To the witness he was pathetic, but to himself he could only have been interesting, as the figure of a man surviving, in an alien but not unfriendly present, the past which held so vast a part of all that had constituted him. If he had thought of himself in this way, it would have been without one emotion of self-pity, such as more maudlin souls indulge, but with a love of knowledge and wisdom as keenly alert as in his prime.

For three privileged years I lived all but next-door neighbor of Dr. Holmes in that part of Beacon Street whither he removed after he left his old home in Charles Street, and during these years I saw him rather often. We were both on the water side, which means so much more than the words say, and our library windows commanded the same general view of the Charles rippling out into the Cambridge marshes and the sunsets, and curving eastward under Long Bridge, through shipping that increased onward to the sea. He said that you could count fourteen towns and villages in the compass of that view, with the three conspicuous monuments accenting the different attractions of it: the tower of Memorial Hall at Harvard; the obelisk on Bunker Hill; and in the centre of the picture that bulk of Tufts College which he said he expected to greet his eyes the first thing when he opened them in the other world. But the prospect, though generally the same, had certain precious differences for each of us, which I have no doubt he valued himself as much upon as I did. I have a notion that he fancied these were to be enjoyed best in his library through two oval panes let into the bay there apart from the windows, for he was apt to make you come and look out of them if you got to talking of the view before you left. In this pleasant study he lived among the books, which seemed to multiply from case to case and shelf to shelf, and climb from floor to ceiling. Everything was in exquisite order, and the desk where he wrote was as scrupulously neat as if the sloven disarray of most authors' desks were impossible to him. He had a number of ingenious little contrivances for helping his work, which he liked to show you; for a time a revolving book-case at the corner of his desk seemed to be his pet; and after that came his fountain-pen, which he used with due observance of its fountain principle, though he was tolerant of me when I said I always dipped mine in the inkstand; it was a merit in his eyes to use a fountain-pen in anywise. After you had gone over these objects with him, and perhaps taken a peep at something he was examining through his microscope, he sat down at one corner of his hearth, and invited you to an easy-chair at the other. His talk was always considerate of your wish to be heard, but the person who wished to talk when he could listen to Dr. Holmes was his own victim, and always the loser. If you were well advised you kept yourself to the question and response which manifested your interest in what he was saying, and let him talk on, with his sweet smile, and that husky laugh he broke softly into at times. Perhaps he was not very well when you came in upon him; then he would name his trouble, with a scientific zest and accuracy, and pass quickly to other matters. As I have noted, he was interested in himself only on the universal side; and he liked to find his peculiarity in you better than to keep it his own; he suffered a visible disappointment if he could not make you think or say you were so and so too. The querulous note was not in his most cheerful register; he would not dwell

upon a specialized grief; though sometimes I have known him
touch very lightly and currently upon a slight annoyance, or
disrelish for this or that. As he grew older, he must have had, of
course, an old man's disposition to speak of his infirmities; but
it was fine to see him catch himself up in this, when he became
conscious of it, and stop short with an abrupt turn to something
else. With a real interest, which he gave humorous excess, he
would celebrate some little ingenious thing that had fallen in his
way, and I have heard him expatiate with childlike delight upon
the merits of a new razor he had got: a sort of mower, which he
could sweep recklessly over cheek and chin without the least
danger of cutting himself. The last time I saw him he asked me
if he had ever shown me that miraculous razor; and I doubt if
he quite liked my saying I had seen one of the same kind.

It seemed to me that he enjoyed sitting at his chimney-corner
rather as the type of a person having a good time than as such a
person; he would rather be up and about something, taking
down a book, making a note, going again to his little windows,
and asking you if you had seen the crows yet that sometimes
alighted on the shoals left bare by the ebb-tide behind the house.
The reader will recall his lovely poem, My Aviary, which deals
with the winged life of that pleasant prospect. I shared with him
in the flock of wild-ducks which used to come into our neighbor
waters in spring when the ice broke up, and staid as long as the
smallest space of brine remained unfrozen in the fall. He was
graciously willing I should share in them, and in the cloud of
gulls which drifted about in the currents of the sea and sky
there, almost the whole year round. I did not pretend an original
right to them, coming so late as I did to the place, and I think
my deference pleased him.

VII

As I have said, he liked his fences, or at least liked you to
respect them, or to be sensible of them. As often as I went to see
him I was made to wait in the little reception-room below, and
never shown at once to his study. My name would be carried

up, and I would hear him verifying my presence from the maid through the opened door; then there came a cheery cry of welcome: "Is that you? Come up, come up!" and I found him sometimes half-way down the stairs to meet me. He would make an excuse for having kept me below a moment, and say something about the rule he had to observe in all cases, as if he would not have me feel his fence a personal thing. I was aware how thoroughly his gentle spirit pervaded the whole house; the Irish maid who opened the door had the effect of being a neighbor too, and of being in the joke of the little formality; she apologized in her turn for the reception-room; there was certainly nothing trampled upon in her manner, but affection and reverence for him whose gate she guarded, with something like the sentiment she would have cherished for a dignitary of the Church, but nicely differenced and adjusted to the Autocrat's peculiar merits.

The last time I was in that place, a visitant who had lately knocked at my own door was about to enter. I met the master of the house on the landing of the stairs outside his study, and he led me in for the few moments we could spend together. He spoke of the shadow so near, and said he supposed there could be no hope, but he did not refuse the cheer I offered him from my ignorance against his knowledge, and at something that was thought or said he smiled, with even a breath of laughter, so potent is the wont of a lifetime, though his eyes were full of tears, and his voice broke with his words. Those who have sorrowed deepest will understand this best.

It was during the few years of our Beacon Street neighborhood that he spent those hundred days abroad in his last visit to England and France. He was full of their delight when he came back, and my propinquity gave me the advantage of hearing him speak of them at first hand. He whimsically pleased himself most with his Derby-day experiences, and enjoyed contrasting the crowd and occasion with that of forty or fifty years earlier, when he had seen some famous race of the Derby won; nothing else in England seemed to have moved him so much, though all that royalties, dignities, and celebrities could well do for him had been done. Of certain things that happened to him, characteristic of the English, and interesting to him in their relation to himself through his character of universally interested man, he spoke freely; but he has said what he chose to the public about them, and I have no right to say more. The thing that most vexed him during his sojourn apparently was to have been described in one of the London papers as quite deaf; and I could truly say to him that I had never imagined him at all deaf, or heard him accused of it before. "Oh, yes," he said, "I am a little hard of hearing on one side. But it isn't deafness."

He had, indeed, few or none of the infirmities of age that make themselves painfully or inconveniently evident. He carried his slight figure erect, and until his latest years his step was quick and sure. Once he spoke of the lessened height of old people, apropos of something that was said, and "They *will shrink*, you know," he added, as if he were not at all concerned in the fact himself. If you met him in the street, you encountered a spare, carefully dressed old gentleman, with a clean-shaven face and a friendly smile, qualified by the involuntary frown of his thick, senile brows; well coated, lustrously shod, well gloved, in a silk hat, latterly wound with a mourning-weed. Sometimes he did not know you when he knew you quite well, and at such times I think it was kind to spare his years the fatigue of recalling your identity; at any rate, I am glad of the times when I did so. In society he had the same vagueness, the same dimness; but after the moment he needed to make sure of you, he was as vivid as ever in his life. He made me think of a bed of embers on which the ashes have thinly gathered, and which, when these are breathed away, sparkles and tinkles keenly up with all the freshness of a newly kindled fire. He did not mind talking about his age, and I fancied rather enjoyed doing so. Its approaches interested him; if he was going, he liked to know just how and when he was going. Once he spoke of his lasting strength in terms of imaginative humor: he was still so intensely interested in nature, the universe, that it seemed to him he was not like an old man so much as a lusty infant which struggles against having the breast snatched from it. He laughed at the notion of this, with that impersonal relish, which seemed to me singularly characteristic of the self-consciousness so marked in him. I never heard one lugubrious word from him in regard to his years. He liked your sympathy on all grounds where he could have it self-respectfully, but he was a most manly spirit, and he would not have had it even as a type of the universal decay. Possibly he would have been interested to have you share in that analysis of himself which he was always making, if such a thing could have been.

He had not much patience with the unmanly craving for sympathy in others, and chiefly in our literary craft, which is somewhat ignobly given to it, though he was patient, after all. He used to say, and I believe he has said it in print, that unless a man could show a good reason for writing verse, it was rather against him, and a proof of weakness. I suppose this severe conclusion was something he had reached after dealing with innumerable small poets who sought the light in him with verses that no editor would admit to print. Yet of morbidness he was often very tender; he knew it to be disease, something that must be scientifically rather than ethically treated. He was in the same degree kind to any sensitiveness, for he was himself as sensitive as he was manly, and he was most delicately sensitive to any rightful social claim upon him. I was once at a dinner with him, where he was in some sort my host, in a company of people whom he had not seen me with before, and he made a point of acquainting me with each of them. It did not matter that I knew most of them already; the proof of his thoughtfulness was precious, and I was sorry when I had to disappoint it by confessing a previous knowledge.

VIII

I had three memorable meetings with him not very long before he died: one a year before, and the other two within a few months of the end. The first of these was at luncheon in the summer-house of a friend whose hospitality made it summer the year round, and we all went out to meet him, when he drove up in his open carriage, with the little sunshade in his hand, which he took with him for protection against the heat, and also, a little, I think, for the whim of it. He sat a moment after he arrived, as if to orient himself in respect to each of us. Beside the gifted hostess, there was the most charming of all the American essayists, and the Autocrat seemed at once to find himself singularly at home with the people who greeted him. There was no interval needed for fanning away the ashes; he tinkled up before he entered the house, and at the table he was as vivid and scintillant as I ever saw him, if indeed I ever saw him as much so. The talk began at once, and we had made him believe that there was nothing egotistic in his taking the word, or turning it in illustration from himself upon universal matters. I spoke among other things of some humble ruins on the road to Gloucester, which gave the way-side a very aged look; the tumbled foundation-stones of poor bits of houses, and "Ah," he said, "the cellar and the well?" He added, to the company generally, "Do you know what I think are the two lines of mine that go as deep as any others, in a certain direction?" and he began to repeat stragglingly certain verses from one of his earlier poems, until he came to the closing couplet. But I will give them in full, because in going to look them up I have found them so lovely, and because I can hear his voice again in every fondly accented syllable:

"Who sees unmoved, a ruin at his feet,
  The lowliest home where human hearts have beat?
  Its hearth-stone, shaded with the bistre stain,
  A century's showery torrents wash in vain;
  Its starving orchard where the thistle blows,
  And mossy trunks still mark the broken rows;
  Its chimney-loving poplar, oftenest seen
  Next an old roof, or where a roof has been;
  Its knot-grass, plantain,—all the social weeds,
  Man's mute companions following where he leads;
  Its dwarfed pale flowers, that show their straggling
      heads,
  Sown by the wind from grass-choked garden beds;
  Its woodbine creeping where it used to climb;

Its roses breathing of the olden time;
All the poor shows the curious idler sees,
As life's thin shadows waste by slow degrees,
Till naught remains, the saddening tale to tell,
Save home's last wrecks—the cellar and the well !"

The poet's chaunting voice rose with a triumphant swell in the climax, and "There," he said, "isn't it so? The cellar and the well—they can't be thrown down or burnt up; they are the human monuments that last longest, and defy decay." He rejoiced openly in the sympathy that recognized with him the divination of a most pathetic, most signal fact, and he repeated the last couplet again at our entreaty, glad to be entreated for it. I do not know whether all will agree with him concerning the relative importance of the lines, but I think all must feel the exquisite beauty of the picture to which they give the final touch.

He said a thousand witty and brilliant things that day, but his pleasure in this gave me the most pleasure, and I recall the passage distinctly out of the dimness that covers the rest. He chose to figure us younger men, in touching upon the literary circumstance of the past and present, as representative of modern feeling and thinking, and himself as no longer contemporary. We knew he did this to be contradicted, and we protested, affectionately, fervently, with all our hearts and minds; and indeed there were none of his generation who had lived more widely into ours. He was not a prophet like Emerson, nor ever a voice crying in the wilderness like Whittier or Lowell. His note was heard rather amid the sweet security of streets, but it was always for a finer and gentler civility. He imagined no new rule of life, and no philosophy or theory of life will be known by his name. He was not constructive; he was essentially observant, and in this he showed the scientific nature. He made his reader known to himself, first in the little, and then in the larger things. From first to last he was a censor, but a most winning and delightful censor, who could make us feel that our faults were other people's, and who was not wont

"To bait his homilies with his brother worms."

At one period he sat in the seat of the scorner, as far as Reform was concerned, or perhaps reformers, who are so often tedious and ridiculous; but he seemed to get a new heart with the new mind which came to him when he began to write the Autocrat papers, and the light mocker of former days became the serious and compassionate thinker, to whom most truly nothing that was human was alien. His readers trusted and loved him; few men have ever written so intimately with so much dignity, and perhaps none has so endeared himself by saying just the thing for his reader that his reader could not say for himself. He sought the universal through himself in others, and he found to his delight and theirs that the most universal thing was often, if not always, the most personal thing.

In my later meetings with him I was struck more and more by his gentleness. I believe that men are apt to grow gentler as they grow older, unless they are of the curmudgeon type, which rusts and crusts with age, but with Dr. Holmes the gentleness was peculiarly marked. He seemed to shrink from all things that could provoke controversy, or even difference; he waived what might be a matter of dispute, and rather sought the things that he could agree with you upon. In the last talk I had with him he appeared to have no grudge left, except for the puritanic orthodoxy in which he had been bred as a child. This he was not able to forgive, though its tradition was interwoven with what was tenderest and dearest in his recollections of childhood. We spoke of puritanism, and I said I sometimes wondered what could be the mind of a man toward life who had not been reared in its awful shadow, say an English Churchman, or a Continental Catholic; and he said he could not imagine, and that he did not believe such a man could at all enter into our feelings; puritanism, he seemed to think, made an essential and ineradicable difference. I do not believe he had any of that false sentiment which attributes virtue of character to severity of creed, while it owns the creed to be wrong.

He differed from Longfellow in often speaking of his contemporaries. He spoke of them frankly, but with an appreciative rather than a censorious criticism. Of Longfellow himself he said that day, when I told him I had been writing about him, and he seemed to me a man without error, that he could think of but one error in him, and that was an error of taste, of almost merely literary taste. It was at an earlier time that he talked of Lowell, after his death, and told me that Lowell once in the fever of his antislavery apostolate had written him, urging him strongly, as a matter of duty, to come out for the cause he had himself so much at heart. Afterwards Lowell wrote again, owning himself wrong in his appeal, which he had come to recognize as invasive. "He was ten years younger than I," said the doctor.

I found him that day I speak of in his house at Beverly Farms, where he had a pleasant study in a corner by the porch, and he met me with all the cheeriness of old. But he confessed that he had been greatly broken up by the labor of preparing something that might be read at some commemorative meeting, and had suffered from finding first that he could not write something specially for it. Even the copying and adapting an old poem had overtaxed him, and in this he showed the failing powers of age. But otherwise he was still young, intellectually; that is, there was no failure of interest in intellectual things, especially literary things. Some new book lay on the table at his elbow, and he asked me if I had seen it, and made some joke about his having had the good luck to read it, and have it lying by him a few days before when the author called. I do not know whether he schooled himself against an old man's tendency to revert to the past or not, but I know that he seldom did so. That morning, however, he made several excursions into it, and told me that his youthful satire of the Spectre Pig had been provoked by a poem of the elder Dana's, where a phantom horse had been seriously employed, with an effect of anticlimax which he had found irresistible. Another foray was to recall the oppression and depression of his early religious associations, and to speak with moving tenderness of his father, whose hard doctrine as a minister was without effect upon his own kindly nature.

In a letter written to me a few weeks after this time, upon an occasion when he divined that some word from him would be more than commonly dear, he recurred to the feeling he then expressed: "Fifty-six years ago—more than half a century—I lost my own father, his age being seventy-three years. As I have reached that period of life, passed it, and now left it far behind, my recollections seem to brighten and bring back my boyhood and early manhood in a clearer and fairer light than it came to me in my middle decades. I have often wished of late years that I could tell him how I cherished his memory; perhaps I may have the happiness of saying all I long to tell him on the other side of that thin partition which I love to think is all that divides us."

Men are never long together without speaking of women, and I said how inevitably men's lives ended where they began, in the keeping of women, and their strength failed at last and surrendered itself to their care. I had not finished before I was made to feel that I was poaching, and "Yes," said the owner of the preserve, "I have spoken of that," and he went on to tell me just where. He was not going to have me suppose I had invented those notions, and I could not do less than own that I must have found them in his book, and forgotten it.

He spoke of his pleasant summer life in the air, at once soft and fresh, of that lovely coast, and of his drives up and down the country roads. Sometimes this lady and sometimes that came for him, and one or two habitually, but he always had his own carriage ordered, if they failed, that he might not fail of his drive in any fair weather. His cottage was not immediately on the sea, but in full sight of it, and there was a sense of the sea about it, as there is in all that incomparable region, and I do not think he could have been at home anywhere beyond the reach of its salt breath.

I was anxious not to outstay his strength, and I kept my eye on the clock in frequent glances. I saw that he followed me in one of these, and I said that I knew what his hours were, and I was watching so that I might go away in time, and then he sweetly protested. Did I like that chair I was sitting in? It was a gift to him, and he said who gave it, with a pleasure in the fact that was very charming, as if he liked the association of the thing with his friend. He was disposed to excuse the formal look of his bookcases, which were filled with sets, and presented some phalanxes of fiction in rather severe array.

When I rose to go, he was concerned about my being able to find my way readily to the station, and he told me how to go, and what turns to take, as if he liked realizing the way to himself. I believe he did not walk much of late years, and I fancy he found much the same pleasure in letting his imagination make this excursion to the station with me that he would have found in actually going.

I saw him once more, but only once, when a day or two later he drove up by our hotel in Magnolia toward the cottage where his secretary was lodging. He saw us from his carriage, and called us gayly to him, to make us rejoice with him at having finally got that commemorative poem off his mind. He made a jest of the trouble it had cost him, even some sleeplessness, and said he felt now like a convalescent. He was all brightness, and friendliness, and eagerness to make us feel his mood, through what was common to us all; and I am glad that this last impression of him is so one with the first I ever had, and with that which every reader receives from his work.

That is bright, and friendly and eager too, for it is throughout the very expression of himself. I think it is a pity if an author disappoints even the unreasonable expectation of the reader, whom his art has invited to love him; but I do not believe that Dr. Holmes could inflict this disappointment. Certainly he could disappoint no reasonable expectation, no intelligent expectation. What he wrote, that he was, and every one felt this who met him. He has therefore not died, as some men die, the remote impersonal sort, but he is yet thrillingly alive in every page of his books. The quantity of his literature is not great, but the quality is very surprising, and surprising first of all as equality. From the beginning to the end he wrote one man, of course in his successive consciousnesses. Perhaps every one does this, but his work gives the impression of an uncommon continuity, in spite of its being the effect of a later and an earlier impulse so very marked as to have made the later an astonishing revelation to those who thought they knew him.

IX

It is not for me in such a paper as this to attempt any judgment of his work. I have loved it, as I loved him, with a sense of its limitations which is by no means a censure of its excellences. He was not a man who cared to transcend; he liked bounds, he liked horizons, the constancy of shores. If he put to sea, he kept in sight of land, like the ancient navigators. He did not discover new continents; and I will own that I, for my part, should not have liked to sail with Columbus. I think one can safely affirm that as great and as useful men staid behind, and found an America of the mind without stirring from their thresholds.

Part Sixth

THE WHITE MR. LONGFELLOW

WE HAD EXPECTED to stay in Boston only until we could find a house in Old Cambridge. This was not so simple a matter as it might seem; for the ancient town had not yet quickened its scholarly pace to the modern step. Indeed, in the spring of 1866 the impulse of expansion was not yet visibly felt anywhere; the enormous material growth that followed the civil war had not yet begun. In Cambridge the houses to be let were few, and such as there were, fell either below our pride, or rose above our purse. I wish I might tell how at last we bought a house; we had no money, but we were rich in friends, who are still alive to shrink from the story of their constant faith in a financial future which we sometimes doubted, and who backed their credulity with their credit. It is sufficient for the present record, which professes to be strictly literary, to notify the fact that on the first day of May, 1866, we went out to Cambridge and began to live in a house which we owned in fee if not in deed, and which was none the less valuable for being covered with mortgages. Physically, it was a carpenter's box, of a sort which is readily imagined by the Anglo-American genius for ugliness, but which it is not so easy to impart a just conception of. A trim hedge of arbor-vitæ tried to hide it from the world in front, and a tall board fence behind; the little lot was well planted (perhaps too well planted) with pears, grapes, and currants, and there was a small open space which I lost no time in digging up for a kitchen-garden. On one side of us were the open fields; on the other a brief line of neighbor-houses; across the street before us was a grove of

151

stately oaks, which I never could persuade Aldrich had painted leaves on them in the fall. We were really in a poor suburb of a suburb; but such is the fascination of ownership, even the ownership of a fully mortgaged property, that we calculated the latitude and longitude of the whole earth from the spot we called ours. In our walks about Cambridge we saw other places where we might have been willing to live; only, we said, they were too far off. We even prized the architecture of our little box, though we had but so lately lived in a Gothic palace on the Grand Canal in Venice, and were not uncritical of beauty in the possessions of others. Positive beauty we could not have honestly said we thought our cottage had as a whole, though we might have held out for something of the kind in the brackets of turned wood under its eaves. But we were richly content with it; and with life in Cambridge, as it began to open itself to us, we were infinitely more than content. This life, so refined, so intelligent, so gracefully simple, I do not suppose has anywhere else had its parallel.

I

It was the moment before the old American customs had been changed by European influences among people of easier circumstances; and in Cambridge society kept what was best of its village traditions, and chose to keep them in the full knowledge of different things. Nearly every one had been abroad; and nearly every one had acquired the taste for olives without losing a relish for native sauces; through the intellectual life there was an entire democracy, and I do not believe that since the capitalistic era began there was ever a community in which money counted for less. There was little show of what money could buy; I remember but one private carriage (naturally, a publisher's); and there was not one livery, except a livery in the larger sense kept by the stableman Pike, who made us pay now a quarter and now a half dollar for a seat in his carriages, according as he lost or gathered courage for the charge. We thought him extortionate, and we mostly walked through snow and mud of amazing depth and thickness.

The reader will imagine how acceptable this circumstance was to a young literary man beginning life with a fully mortgaged house and a salary of untried elasticity. If there were distinctions made in Cambridge they were not against literature, and we found ourselves in the midst of a charming society, indifferent, apparently, to all questions but those of the higher education which comes so largely by nature. That is to say, in the Cambridge of that day (and, I dare say, of this) a mind cultivated in some sort was essential, and after that came civil manners, and the willingness and ability to be agreeable and interesting; but the question of riches or poverty did not enter. Even the question of family, which is of so great concern in New England, was in abeyance. Perhaps it was taken for granted that every one in Old Cambridge society must be of good family, or he could not be there; perhaps his mere residence tacitly ennobled him; certainly his acceptance was an informal patent of gentility. To my mind, the structure of society was almost ideal, and until we have a perfectly socialized condition of things I do not believe we shall ever have a more perfect society. The instincts which governed it were not such as can arise from the sordid competition of interests; they flowed from a devotion to letters, and from a self-sacrifice in material things which I can give no better notion of than by saying that the outlay of the richest college magnate seemed to be graduated to the income of the poorest.

In those days, the men whose names have given splendor to Cambridge were still living there. I shall forget some of them in the alphabetical enumeration of Louis Agassiz, Francis J. Child, Richard Henry Dana, Jun., John Fiske, Dr. Asa Gray, the family of the Jameses, father and sons, Lowell, Longfellow, Charles Eliot Norton, Dr. John G. Palfrey, James Peirce, Dr. Peabody, Professor Parsons, Professor Sophocles. The variety of talents and of achievements was indeed so great that Mr. Bret Harte, when fresh from his Pacific slope, justly said, after listening to a partial rehearsal of them, "Why, you couldn't fire a revolver from your front porch anywhere without bringing down a two-volumer!" Everybody had written a book, or an article, or a poem; or was in the process or expectation of doing it, and doubtless those whose names escape me will have greater difficulty in eluding fame. These kindly, these gifted folk each came to see us and to make us at home among them; and my home is still among them, on this side and on that side of the line between the living and the dead, which invisibly passes through all the streets of the cities of men.

II

We had the whole summer for the exploration of Cambridge before society returned from the mountains and the seashore, and it was not till October that I saw Longfellow. I heard again, as I heard when I first came to Boston, that he was at Nahant, and though Nahant was no longer so far away, now, as it was then, I did not think of seeking him out even when we went for a day to explore that coast during the summer. It seems strange that I cannot recall just when and where I saw him, but early after his return to Cambridge I had a message from him asking me to come to a meeting of the Dante Club at Craigie House.

Longfellow was that winter (1866–7) revising his translation of the Paradiso, and the Dante Club was the circle of Italianate friends and scholars whom he invited to follow him and criticise his work from the original, while he read his version aloud. Those who were most constantly present were Lowell and Professor Norton, but from time to time others came in, and we seldom sat down at the nine-o'clock supper that followed the reading of the canto in less number than ten or twelve.

The criticism, especially from the accomplished Danteists I have named, was frank and frequent. I believe they neither of them quite agreed with Longfellow as to the form of version he had chosen, but waiving that, the question was how perfectly he had done his work upon the given lines. I myself, with whatever right, great or little, I may have to an opinion, believe thoroughly in Longfellow's plan. When I read his version my sense aches for the rhyme which he rejected, but my admiration for his fidelity to Dante otherwise is immeasurable. I remember with equal admiration the subtle and sympathetic scholarship of his critics, who scrutinized every shade of meaning in a word or phrase that gave them pause, and did not let it pass till all the reasons and facts had been considered. Sometimes, and even often, Longfellow yielded to their censure, but for the most part, when he was of another mind, he held to his mind, and the passage had to go as he said. I make a little haste to say that in all the meetings of the Club, during a whole winter of Wednesday evenings, I myself, though I faithfully followed in an Italian Dante with the rest, ventured upon one suggestion only. This was kindly, even seriously, considered by the poet, and gently rejected. He could not do anything otherwise than gently, and I was not suffered to feel that I had done a presumptuous thing. I can see him now, as he looked up from the proof-sheets on the round table before him, and over at me, growing consciously smaller and smaller, like something through a reversed opera-glass. He had a shaded drop-light in front of him, and in its glow his beautiful and benignly noble head had a dignity pecul-iar to him.

All the portraits of Longfellow are likenesses more or less bad and good, for there was something as simple in the physiognomy as in the nature of the man. His head, after he allowed his beard to grow and wore his hair long in the manner of elderly men, was leonine, but mildly leonine, as the old painters conceived the lion of St. Mark. Once Sophocles, the ex-monk of Mount Athos, so long a Greek professor at Harvard, came in for supper, after the reading was over, and he was leonine too, but of a fierceness that contrasted finely with Longfellow's mildness. I remember the poet's asking him something about the punishment of im-paling, in Turkey, and his answering, with an ironical gleam of his fiery eyes, "Unhappily, it is obsolete." I dare say he was not so leonine, either, as he looked.

When Longfellow read verse, it was with a hollow, with a mellow resonant murmur, like the note of some deep-throated horn. His voice was very lulling in quality, and at the Dante Club it used to have early effect with an old scholar who sat in a cavernous arm-chair at the corner of the fire, and who drowsed audibly in the soft tone and the gentle heat. The poet had a fat terrier who wished always to be present at the meetings of the Club, and he commonly fell asleep at the same moment with that dear old scholar, so that when they began to make themselves heard in concert, one could not tell which it was that most took our thoughts from the text of the Paradiso. When the duet opened, Longfellow would look up with an arch recognition of the fact, and then go gravely on to the end of the canto. At the close he would speak to his friend and lead him out to supper as if he had not seen or heard anything amiss.

III

In that elect company I was silent, partly because I was conscious of my youthful inadequacy, and partly because I preferred to listen. But Longfellow always behaved as if I were saying a succession of edifying and delightful things, and from time to time he addressed himself to me, so that I should not feel left out. He did not talk much himself, and I recall nothing that he said. But he always spoke both wisely and simply, without the least touch of pose, and with no intention of effect, but with something that I must call quality for want of a better word; so that at a table where Holmes sparkled, and Lowell glowed, and Agassiz beamed, he cast the light of a gentle gayety, which seemed to dim all those vivider luminaries. While he spoke you did not miss Fields's story or Tom Appleton's wit, or even the gracious amity of Mr. Norton, with his unequalled intuitions.

The supper was very plain: a cold turkey, which the host carved, or a haunch of venison, or some braces of grouse, or a platter of quails, with a deep bowl of salad, and the sympathetic companionship of those elect vintages which Longfellow loved, and which he chose with the inspiration of affection. We usually began with oysters, and when some one who was expected did not come promptly, Longfellow invited us to raid his plate, as a just punishment of his delay. One evening Lowell remarked, with the cayenne poised above his blue-points, "It's astonishing how fond these fellows are of pepper."

The old friend of the cavernous arm-chair was perhaps not wide enough awake to repress an "Ah?" of deep interest in this fact of natural history, and Lowell was provoked to go on. "Yes, I've dropped a red pepper pod into a barrel of them, before now, and then taken them out in a solid mass, clinging to it like a swarm of bees to their queen."

"Is it possible?" cried the old friend; and then Longfellow intervened to save him from worse, and turned the talk.

I reproach myself that I made no record of the talk, for I find that only a few fragments of it have caught in my memory, and that the sieve which should have kept the gold has let it wash away with the gravel. I remember once Dr. Holmes's talking of the physician as the true seer, whose awful gift it was to behold with the fatal second sight of science the shroud gathering to the throat of many a doomed man apparently in perfect health, and happy in the promise of unnumbered days. The thought may have been suggested by some of the toys of superstition which intellectual people like to play with.

I never could be quite sure at first that Longfellow's brother-in-law, Appleton, was seriously a spiritualist, even when he disputed the most strenuously with the unbelieving Autocrat. But he really was in earnest about it, though he relished a joke at the expense of his doctrine, like some clerics when they are in the safe company of other clerics. He told me once of having recounted to Agassiz the facts of a very remarkable séance, where the souls of the departed outdid themselves in the athletics and acrobatics they seem so fond of over there, throwing large stones across the room, moving pianos, and lifting dinner tables and setting them atwirl under the chandelier. "And now," he demanded, "what do you say to that?" "Well, Mr. Appleton," Agassiz answered, to Appleton's infinite delight, "*I say that it did not happen.*"

One night they began to speak at the Dante supper of the unhappy man whose crime is a red stain in the Cambridge annals, and one and another recalled their impressions of Professor Webster. It was possibly with a retroactive sense that they had all felt something uncanny in him, but, apropos of the deep salad-bowl in the centre of the table, Longfellow remembered a supper Webster was at, where he lighted some chemical in such a dish and held his head over it, with a handkerchief noosed about his throat and lifted above it with one hand, while his face, in the pale light, took on the livid ghastliness of that of a man hanged by the neck.

Another night the talk wandered to the visit which an English author (now with God) paid America at the height of a popularity long since toppled to the ground, with many another. He was in very good humor with our whole continent, and at Longfellow's table he found the champagne even surprisingly fine. "But," he said to his host, who now told the story, "it cawn't be *genuine*, you know!"

Many years afterwards this author revisited our shores, and I dined with him at Longfellow's, where he was anxious to constitute himself a guest during his sojourn in our neighborhood. Longfellow was equally anxious that he should not do so, and he took a harmless pleasure in outmanœuvring him. He seized a chance to speak with me alone, and plotted to deliver him over to me without apparent unkindness, when the latest horse-car should be going in to Boston, and begged me to walk him to Harvard Square and put him aboard. "Put him aboard, and don't leave him till the car starts, and then watch that he doesn't get off."

These instructions he accompanied with a lifting of the eyebrows, and a pursing of the mouth, in an anxiety not altogether burlesque. He knew himself the prey of any one who chose to batten on him, and his hospitality was subject to frightful abuse. Perhaps Mr. Norton has somewhere told how, when he asked if a certain person who had been outstaying his time was not a dreadful bore, Longfellow answered, with angelic patience, "Yes; but then you know I have been bored so often!"

There was one fatal Englishman whom I shared with him during the great part of a season: a poor soul, not without gifts, but always ready for more, especially if they took the form of meat and drink. He had brought letters from one of the best

Englishmen alive, who withdrew them too late to save his American friends from the sad consequences of welcoming him. So he established himself impregnably in a Boston club, and came out every day to dine with Longfellow in Cambridge, beginning with his return from Nahant in October and continuing far into December. That was the year of the great horse-distemper, when the plague disabled the transportation in Boston, and cut off all intercourse between the suburb and the city on the street railways. "I did think," Longfellow pathetically lamented, "that when the horse-cars stopped running, I should have a little respite from L., *but he walks out.*"

In the midst of his own suffering he was willing to advise with me concerning some poems L. had offered to the Atlantic Monthly, and after we had desperately read them together he said, with inspiration, "I think these things are more adapted to music than the magazine," and this seemed so good a notion that when L. came to know their fate from me, I answered, confidently, "I think they are rather more adapted to music."

He calmly asked, "Why?" and as this was an exigency which Longfellow had not forecast for me, I was caught in it without hope of escape. I really do not know what I said, but I know that I did not take the poems, such was my literary conscience in those days; I am afraid I should be weaker now.

IV

The suppers of the Dante Club were a relaxation from the severity of their toils on criticism, and I will not pretend that their table-talk was of that seriousness which duller wits might have given themselves up to. The passing stranger, especially if a light or jovial person, was always welcome, and I never knew of the enforcement of the rule I heard of, that if you came in without question on the Club nights, you were a guest; but if you rang or knocked, you could not get in.

Any sort of diversion was hailed, and once Appleton proposed that Longfellow should show us his wine-cellar. He took up the candle burning on the table for the cigars, and led the way into thc basement of the beautiful old Colonial mansion, doubly memorable as Washington's headquarters while he was in Cambridge, and as the home of Longfellow for so many years. The taper cast just the right gleams on the darkness, bringing into relief the massive piers of brick, and the solid walls of stone, which gave the cellar the effect of a casemate in some fortress, and leaving the corners and distances to a romantic gloom. This basement was a work of the days when men built more heavily if not more substantially than now, but I forget, if I ever knew, what date the wine-cellar was of. It was well stored with precious vintages, aptly cobwebbed and dusty; but I could not find that it had any more charm than the shelves of a library: it is the inside of bottles and of books that makes its appeal. The whole place witnessed a bygone state and luxury, which otherwise lingered in a dim legend or two. Longfellow once spoke of certain old love-letters which dropped down on the basement stairs from some place overhead; and there was the fable or the fact of a subterranean passage under the street from Craigie House to the old Batchelder House, which I relate to these letters with no authority I can allege. But in Craigie House dwelt the proud fair lady who was buried in the Cambridge churchyard with a slave at her head and a slave at her feet.

"Dust is in her beautiful eyes,"

and whether it was they that smiled or wept in their time over those love-letters, I will leave the reader to say. The fortunes of her Tory family fell with those of their party, and the last Vassal ended his days a prisoner from his creditors in his own house, with a weekly enlargement on Sundays, when the law could not reach him. It is known how the place took Longfellow's fancy when he first came to be professor in Harvard, and how he was a lodger of the last Mistress Craigie there, long before he became its owner. The house is square, with Longfellow's study where he read and wrote on the right of the door, and a statelier library behind it; on the left is the drawing-room, with the dining-room in its rear; from its square hall climbs a beautiful stairway with twisted banisters, and a tall clock in their angle.

The study where the Dante Club met, and where I mostly saw Longfellow, was a plain, pleasant room, with broad panelling in white painted pine; in the centre before the fireplace stood his round table, laden with books, papers, and proofs; in the furthest corner by the window was a high desk which he sometimes stood at to write. In this room Washington held his councils and transacted his business with all comers; in the chamber overhead he slept. I do not think Longfellow associated the place much with him, and I never heard him speak of Washington in relation to it except once, when he told me with peculiar relish what he called the true version of a pious story concerning the aide-de-camp who blundered in upon him while he knelt in prayer. The father of his country rose and rebuked the young man severely, and then resumed his devotions. "He rebuked him," said Longfellow, lifting his brows and making rings round the pupils of his eyes, "by throwing his scabbard at his head."

All the front windows of Craigie House look out over the open fields across the Charles, which is now the Longfellow Memorial Garden. The poet used to be amused with the popular superstition that he was holding this vacant ground with a view to a rise in the price of lots, while all he wanted was to keep a feature of his beloved landscape unchanged. Lofty elms drooped at the corners of the house; on the lawn billowed clumps of the lilac, which formed a thick hedge along the fence. There was a terrace part way down this lawn, and when a white-painted balustrade was set some fifteen years ago upon its brink, it seemed always to have been there. Long verandas stretched on either side of the mansion; and behind was an old-fashioned garden with beds primly edged with box after a design of the poet's own. Longfellow had a ghost story of this quaint plaisance, which he used to tell with an artful reserve of the catastrophe. He was coming home one winter night, and as he crossed the garden he was startled by a white figure swaying before him. But he knew that the only way was to advance upon it. He pushed boldly forward, and was suddenly caught under the throat—by the clothes-line with a long night-gown on it.

Perhaps it was at the end of a long night of the Dante Club

that I heard him tell this story. The evenings were sometimes mornings before the reluctant break-up came, but they were never half long enough for me. I have given no idea of the high reasoning of vital things which I must often have heard at that table, and that I have forgotten it is no proof that I did not hear it. The memory will not be ruled as to what it shall bind and what it shall loose, and I should entreat mine in vain for record of those meetings other than what I have given. Perhaps it would be well, in the interest of some popular conceptions of what the social intercourse of great wits must be, for me to invent some ennobling and elevating passages of conversation at Longfellow's; perhaps I ought to do it for the sake of my own repute as a serious and adequate witness. But I am rather helpless in the matter; I must set down what I remember, and surely if I can remember no phrase from Holmes that a reader could live or die by, it is something to recall how, when a certain potent cheese was passing, he leaned over to gaze at it, and asked: "Does it kick? Does it kick?" No strain of high poetic thinking remains to me from Lowell, but he made me laugh unforgettably with his passive adventure one night going home late, when a man suddenly leaped from the top of a high fence upon the sidewalk at his feet, and after giving him the worst fright of his life, disappeared peaceably into the darkness. To be sure, there was one most memorable supper, when he read the Biglow Paper he had finished that day, and enriched the meaning of his verse with the beauty of his voice. There lingers yet in my sense his very tone in giving the last line of the passage lamenting the waste of the heroic lives which in those dark hours of Johnson's time seemed to have been

> "Butchered to make a blind man's holiday."

The hush that followed upon his ceasing was of that finest quality which spoken praise always lacks; and I suppose that I could not give a just notion of these Dante Club evenings without imparting the effect of such silences. This I could not hopefully undertake to do; but I am tempted to some effort of the kind by my remembrance of Longfellow's old friend George Washington Greene, who often came up from his home in Rhode Island, to be at those sessions, and who was a most interesting and amiable fact of those delicate silences. A full half of his earlier life had been passed in Italy, where he and Longfellow met and loved each other in their youth with an affection which the poet was constant to in his age, after many vicissitudes, with the beautiful fidelity of his nature. Greene was like an old Italian house-priest in manner, gentle, suave, very suave, smooth as creamy curds, cultivated in the elegancies of literary taste, and with a certain meek abeyance. I think I never heard him speak, in all those evenings, except when Longfellow addressed him, though he must have had the Dante scholarship for an occasional criticism. It was at more recent dinners, where I met him with the Long-fellow family alone, that he broke now and then into a quotation from some of the modern Italian poets he knew by heart (prefer-ably Giusti), and syllabled their verse with an exquisite Roman accent and a bewitching Florentine rhythm. Now and then at these times he brought out a faded Italian anecdote, faintly smelling of civet, and threadbare in its ancient texture. He liked to speak of Goldoni and of Nota, of Niccolini and Manzoni, of Monti and Leopardi; and if you came to America, of the Revo-lution and his grandfather, the Quaker General Nathanael Greene, whose life he wrote (and I read) in three volumes. He worshipped Longfellow, and their friendship continued while they lived, but toward the last of his visits at Craigie House it had a pathos for the witness which I should grieve to wrong. Greene was then a quivering paralytic, and he clung tremulously to Longfellow's arm in going out to dinner, where even the modern Italian poets were silent upon his lips. When we rose from table, Longfellow lifted him out of his chair, and took him upon his arm again for their return to the study.

He was of lighter metal than most other members of the Dante Club, and he was not of their immediate intimacy, living away from Cambridge, as he did, and I shared his silence in their presence with full sympathy. I was by far the youngest of their number, and I cannot yet quite make out why I was of it at all. But at every moment I was as sensible of my good fortune as of my ill desert. They were the men whom of all men living I most honored, and it seemed to be impossible that I at my age should be so perfectly fulfilling the dream of my life in their company. Often the nights were very cold, and as I returned home from Craigie House to the carpenter's box on Sacramento Street, a mile or two away, I was as if soul-borne through the air by my pride and joy, while the frozen blocks of snow clinked and tinkled before my feet stumbling along the middle of the road. I still think that was the richest moment of my life, and I look back at it as the moment, in a life not unblessed by chance, which I would most like to live over again—if I must live any.

The next winter the sessions of the Dante Club were transferred to the house of Mr. Norton, who was then completing his version of the Vita Nuova. This has always seemed to me a work of not less graceful art than Longfellow's translation of the Commedia. In fact, it joins the effect of a sympathy almost mounting to divination with a patient scholarship and a delicate skill unknown to me elsewhere in such work. I do not know whether Mr. Norton has satisfied himself better in his prose version of the Commedia than in this of the Vita Nuova, but I do not believe he could have satisfied Dante better, unless he had rhymed his sonnets and canzonets. I am sure he might have done this if he had chosen. He has always pretended that it was impossible, but miracles are never impossible in the right hands.

v

After three or four years we sold the carpenter's box on Sacramento Street, and removed to a larger house near Harvard Square, and in the immediate neighborhood of Longfellow. He gave me an easement across that old garden behind his house, through an opening in the high board fence which enclosed it, and I saw him oftener than ever, though the meetings of the Dante Club had come to an end. At the last of them, Lowell had asked him, with fond regret in his jest, "Longfellow, why don't

you do that Indian poem in forty thousand verses?" The demand
but feebly expressed the reluctance in us all, though I suspect
the Indian poem existed only by the challenger's invention. Before I leave my faint and unworthy record of these great times
I am tempted to mention an incident poignant with tragical
associations. The first night after Christmas the holly and the
pine wreathed about the chandelier above the supper table took
fire from the gas, just as we came out from the reading, and
Longfellow ran forward and caught the burning garlands down
and bore them out. No one could speak for thinking what he
must be thinking of when the ineffable calamity of his home befell
it. Curtis once told me that a little while before Mrs. Longfellow's
death he was driving by Craigie House with Holmes, who said
he trembled to look at it, for those who lived there had their
happiness so perfect that no change, of all the changes which
must come to them, could fail to be for the worse.

I did not know Longfellow before that fatal time, and I shall
not say that his presence bore record of it except in my fancy. He
may always have had that look of one who had experienced the
utmost harm that fate can do, and henceforth could possess himself of what was left of life in peace. He could never have been a
man of the flowing ease that makes all comers at home; some
people complained of a certain *gêne* in him; and he had a reserve
with strangers, which never quite lost itself in the abandon of
friendship, as Lowell's did. He was the most perfectly modest
man I ever saw, ever imagined, but he had a gentle dignity
which I do not believe any one, the coarsest, the obtusest, could
trespass upon. In the years when I began to know him, his long
hair and the beautiful beard which mixed with it were of one
iron-gray, which I saw blanch to a perfect silver, while that
pearly tone of his complexion, which Appleton so admired, lost
itself in the wanness of age and pain. When he walked, he had a
kind of spring in his gait, as if now and again a buoyant thought
lifted him from the ground. It was fine to meet him coming
down a Cambridge street; you felt that the encounter made you
a part of literary history, and set you apart with him for the

moment from the poor and mean. When he appeared in Harvard Square, he beatified if not beautified the ugliest and vulgarest looking spot on the planet outside of New York. You could meet him sometimes at the market, if you were of the same provision-man as he; and Longfellow remained as constant to his trades-people as to any other friends. He rather liked to bring his proofs back to the printer's himself, and we often found ourselves to-gether at the University Press, where the Atlantic Monthly used to be printed. But outside of his own house Longfellow seemed to want a fit atmosphere, and I love best to think of him in his study, where he wrought at his lovely art with a serenity expressed in his smooth, regular, and scrupulously perfect hand-writing. It was quite vertical, and rounded, with a slope neither to the right nor left, and at the time I knew him first, he was fond of using a soft pencil on printing paper, though commonly he wrote with a quill. Each letter was distinct in shape, and between the verses was always the exact space of half an inch. I have a good many of his poems written in this fashion, but whether they were the first drafts or not I cannot say; very likely not. Towards the last he no longer sent his poems to the magazines in his own hand, but they were always signed in autograph.

I once asked him if he were not a great deal interrupted, and he said, with a faint sigh, Not more than was good for him, he fancied; if it were not for the interruptions, he might overwork. He was not a friend to stated exercise, I believe, nor fond of walking, as Lowell was; he had not, indeed, the childish as-sociations of the younger poet with the Cambridge neighbor-hoods; and I never saw him walking for pleasure except on the east veranda of his house, though I was told he loved walking in his youth. In this and in some other things Longfellow was more European than American, more Latin than Saxon. He once said quaintly that one got a great deal of exercise in putting on and off one's overcoat and overshoes.

I suppose no one who asked decently at his door was denied access to him, and there must have been times when he was overrun with volunteer visitors; but I never heard him complain of them. He was very charitable in the immediate sort which Christ seems to have meant; but he had his preferences, humorously owned, among beggars. He liked the German beggars least, and the Italian beggars most, as having most savoir-faire; in fact, we all loved the Italians in Cambridge. He was pleased with the accounts I could give him of the love and honor I had known for him in Italy, and one day there came a letter from an Italian admirer, addressed to "Mr. Greatest Poet Longfellow," which he said was the very most amusing superscription he had ever seen.

It is known that the King of Italy offered Longfellow the cross of San Lazzaro, which is the Italian literary decoration. It came through the good offices of my old acquaintance Professor Messadaglia, then a deputy in the Italian Parliament, whom, for some reason I cannot remember, I had put in correspondence with Longfellow. The honor was wholly unexpected, and it brought Longfellow a distress which was chiefly for the gentleman who had procured him the impossible distinction. He showed me the pretty collar and cross, not, I think, without a natural pleasure in it. No man was ever less a bigot in things civil or religious than he, but he said, firmly, "Of course, as a republican and a Protestant, I can't accept a decoration from a Catholic prince." His decision was from his conscience, and I think that all Americans who think duly about it will approve his decision.

VI

Such honors as he could fitly permit himself he did not refuse, and I recall what zest he had in his election to the Arcadian Academy, which had made him a shepherd of its Roman Fold, with the title, as he said, of "Olimipico something." But I fancy his sweetest pleasure in his vast renown came from his popular recognition everywhere. Few were the lands, few the languages he was unknown to: he showed me a version of the Psalm of Life in Chinese. Apparently even the poor lost autograph-seeker was

not denied by his universal kindness; I know that he kept a store
of autographs ready written on small squares of paper for all
who applied by letter or in person; he said it was no trouble; but
perhaps he was to be excused for refusing the request of a lady
for fifty autographs, which she wished to offer as a novel attrac-
tion to her guests at a lunch party.

Foreigners of all kinds thronged upon him at their pleasure,
apparently, and with perfect impunity. Sometimes he got a little
fun, very, very kindly, out of their excuses and reasons; and the
Englishman who came to see him because there were no ruins to
visit in America was no fable, as I can testify from the poet himself. But he had no prejudice against Englishmen, and even at a
certain time when the coarse-handed British criticism began to
blame his delicate art for the universal acceptance of his verse,
and to try to sneer him into the rank of inferior poets, he was
without rancor for the clumsy misliking that he felt. He could
not understand rudeness; he was too finely framed for that; he
could know it only as Swedenborg's most celestial angels perceived evil, as something distressful, angular. The ill-will that
seemed nearly always to go with adverse criticism made him
distrust criticism, and the discomfort which mistaken or blunder-
ing praise gives probably made him shy of all criticism. He said
that in his early life as an author he used to seek out and save
all the notices of his poems, but in his latter days he read only
those that happened to fall in his way; these he cut out and
amused his leisure by putting together in scrap-books. He was
reluctant to make any criticism of other poets; I do not remember
ever to have heard him make one; and his writings show no trace
of the literary dislikes or contempts which we so often mistake
in ourselves for righteous judgments. No doubt he had his resentments, but he hushed them in his heart, which he did not
suffer them to embitter. While Poe was writing of "Longfellow
and other Plagiarists," Longfellow was helping to keep Poe alive
by the loans which always made themselves gifts in Poe's case.
He very, very rarely spoke of himself at all, and almost never of
the grievances which he did not fail to share with all who live.

Henry Wadsworth Longfellow

He was patient, as I said, of all things, and gentle beyond all mere gentlemanliness. But it would have been a great mistake to mistake his mildness for softness. It was most manly and firm; and of course it was braced with the New England conscience he was born to. If he did not find it well to assert himself, he was prompt in behalf of his friends, and one of the fine things told of him was his resenting some censures of Sumner at a dinner in Boston during the old pro-slavery times: he said to the gentlemen present that Sumner was his friend, and he must leave their company if they continued to assail him.

But he spoke almost as rarely of his friends as of himself. He liked the large, impersonal topics which could be dealt with on their human side, and involved characters rather than individuals. This was rather strange in Cambridge, where we were apt to take our instances from the environment. It was not the only thing he was strange in there; he was not to that manner born; he lacked the final intimacies which can come only of birth and lifelong association, and which make the men of the Boston breed seem exclusive when they least feel so; he was Longfellow to the friends who were James, and Charles, and Wendell to one another. He and Hawthorne were classmates at college, but I never heard him mention Hawthorne; I never heard him mention Whittier or Emerson. I think his reticence about his contemporaries was largely due to his reluctance from criticism: he was the finest artist of them all, and if he praised he must have praised with the reservations of an honest man. Of younger writers he was willing enough to speak. No new contributor made his mark in the magazine unnoted by him, and sometimes I showed him verse in manuscript which gave me peculiar pleasure. I remember his liking for the first piece that Mr. Maurice Thompson sent me, and how he tasted the fresh flavor of it, and inhaled its wild new fragrance. He admired the skill of some of the young story-tellers; he praised the subtlety of one in working out an intricate character, and said modestly that he could never have done that sort of thing himself. It was entirely safe to invite his judgment when in doubt, for he never suffered it to become aggressive, or used it to urge upon me the manuscripts that must often have been urged upon him.

Longfellow had a house at Nahant where he went every summer for more than a quarter of a century. He found the slight transition change enough from Cambridge, and liked it perhaps because it did not take him beyond the range of the friends and strangers whose company he liked. Agassiz was there, and Appleton; Sumner came to sojourn with him; and the tourists of all nations found him there in half an hour after they reached Boston. His cottage was very plain and simple, but was rich in the sight of the illimitable sea, and it had a luxury of rocks at the foot of its garden, draped with sea-weed, and washed with the indefatigable tides. As he grew older and feebler he ceased to go to Nahant; he remained the whole year round at Cambridge; he professed to like the summer which he said warmed him through there, better than the cold spectacle of summer which had no such effect at Nahant.

The hospitality which was constant at either house was not merely of the worldly sort. Longfellow loved good cheer; he tasted history and poetry in a precious wine; and he liked people who were acquainted with manners and men, and brought the air of capitals with them. But often the man who dined with Longfellow was the man who needed a dinner; and from what I have seen of the sweet courtesy that governed at that board, I am sure that such a man could never have felt himself the least honored guest. The poet's heart was open to all the homelessness of the world; and I remember how once when we sat at his table and I spoke of his poem of The Challenge, then a new poem, and said how I had been touched by the fancy of

"The poverty-stricken millions
  Who challenge our wine and bread,
And impeach us all as traitors,
  Both the living and the dead,"

his voice sank in grave humility as he answered, "Yes, I often think of those things." He had thought of them in the days of the slave, when he had taken his place with the friends of the hopeless and hapless, and as long as he lived he continued of the party which had freed the slave. He did not often speak of politics, but when the movement of some of the best Republicans away from their party began, he said that he could not see the wisdom of their course. But this was said without censure or criticism of them, and so far as I know he never permitted himself anything like denunciation of those who in any wise differed from him. On a matter of yet deeper interest, I do not feel authorized to speak for him, but I think that as he grew older, his hold upon anything like a creed weakened, though he remained of the Unitarian philosophy concerning Christ. He did not latterly go to church, I believe; but then, very few of his circle were church-goers. Once he said something very vague and uncertain concerning the doctrine of another life when I affirmed my hope of it, to the effect that he wished he could be sure, with the sigh that so often clothed the expression of a misgiving with him.

VII

When my acquaintance with Longfellow began he had written the things that made his fame, and that it will probably rest upon: Evangeline, Hiawatha, and the Courtship of Miles Standish were by that time old stories. But during the eighteen years that I knew him he produced the best of his minor poems, the greatest of his sonnets, the sweetest of his lyrics. His art ripened to the last, it grew richer and finer, and it never knew decay. He rarely read anything of his own aloud, but in three or four cases he read to me poems he had just finished, as if to give himself the pleasure of hearing them with the sympathetic sense of another. The hexameter piece, Elizabeth, in the third part of Tales of a Wayside Inn, was one of these, and he liked my liking its rhythmical form, which I believed one of the measures best adapted to the English speech, and which he had used himself with so much pleasure and success.

About this time he was greatly interested in the slight experiments I was beginning to make in dramatic form, and he said that if he were himself a young man he should write altogether for the stage; he thought the drama had a greater future with us. He was pleased when a popular singer wished to produce his Masque of Pandora, with music, and he was patient when it failed of the effect hoped for it as an opera. When the late Lawrence Barrett, in the enthusiasm which was one of the fine traits of his generous character, had taken my play of A Counterfeit Presentment, and came to the Boston Museum with it, Longfellow could not apparently have been more zealous for its popular acceptance if it had been his own work. He invited himself to one of the rehearsals with me, and he sat with me on the stage through the four acts with a fortitude which I still wonder at, and with the keenest zest for all the details of the performance. No finer testimony to the love and honor which all kinds of people had for him could have been given than that shown by the actors and employees of the theatre, high and low. They thronged the scenery, those who were not upon the stage, and at the edge of every wing were faces peering round at the poet, who sat unconscious of their adoration, intent upon the play. He was intercepted at every step in going out, and made to put his name to the photographs of himself which his worshippers produced from their persons.

He came to the first night of the piece, and when it seemed to be finding favor with the public, he leaned forward out of his line to nod and smile at the author; when they had the author up, it was the sweetest flattery of the applause which abused his fondness that Longfellow clapped first and loudest.

Where once he had given his kindness he could not again withhold it, and he was anxious no act should be interpreted as withdrawal. When the Emperor Dom Pedro of Brazil, who was so great a lover of Longfellow, came to Boston, he asked himself out to dine with the poet, who had expected to offer him some such hospitality. Soon after, Longfellow met me, and as if eager to forestall a possible feeling in me, said, "I wanted to ask *you* to dinner with the Emperor, but he not only sent word he was coming, he named his fellow-guests!" I answered that though I should probably never come so near dining with an emperor again, I prized his wish to ask me much more than the chance I had missed; and with this my great and good friend seemed a little consoled. I believe that I do not speak too confidently of our relation. He was truly the friend of all men, but I had certainly the advantage of my propinquity. We were near neighbors, as the pleonasm has it, both when I lived on Berkeley Street and after I had built my own house on Concord Avenue; and I suppose he found my youthful informality convenient. He always asked me to dinner when his old friend Greene came to visit him, and then we had an Italian time together, with more or less repetition in our talk, of what we had said before of Italian poetry and Italian character. One day there came a note from him saying, in effect, "Salvini is coming out to dine with me tomorrow night, and I want you to come too. There will be no one else but Greene and myself, and we will have an Italian dinner."

Unhappily I had accepted a dinner in Boston for that night, and this invitation put me in great misery. I must keep my engagement, but how could I bear to miss meeting Salvini at Longfellow's table on terms like these? We consulted at home together and questioned whether I might not rush into Boston, seek out my host there, possess him of the facts, and frankly throw myself on his mercy. Then a sudden thought struck us: Go to Longfellow, and submit the case to him! I went, and he entered with delicate sympathy into the affair. But he decided that, taking the large view of it, I must keep my engagement, lest I should run even a remote risk of wounding my friend's susceptibilities. I obeyed, and I had a very good time, but I still feel that I missed the best time of my life, and that I ought to be rewarded for my sacrifice, somewhere.

Longfellow so rarely spoke of himself in any way that one heard from him few of those experiences of the distinguished man in contact with the undistinguished, which he must have had so abundantly. But he told, while it was fresh in his mind, an incident that happened to him one day in Boston at a tobacconist's, where a certain brand of cigars was recommended to him as the kind Longfellow smoked. "Ah, then I must have some of them; and I will ask you to send me a box," said Longfellow, and he wrote down his name and address. The cigar-dealer read it with the smile of a worsted champion, and said, "Well, I guess you *had* me, *that* time." At a funeral a mourner wished to open conversation, and by way of suggesting a theme of common interest, began, "*You've* buried, I believe?"

Sometimes people were shown by the poet through Craigie House who had no knowledge of it except that it had been Washington's headquarters. Of course Longfellow was known by sight to every one in Cambridge. He was daily in the streets, while his health endured, and as he kept no carriage, he was often to be met in the horse-cars, which were such common ground in Cambridge that they were often like small invited parties of friends when they left Harvard Square, so that you expected the gentlemen to jump up and ask the ladies whether they would have chicken salad. In civic and political matters he mingled so far as to vote regularly, and he voted with his party, trusting it for a general regard to the public welfare.

I fancy he was somewhat shy of his fellow-men, as the scholar seems always to be, from the sequestered habit of his life; but I think Longfellow was incapable of marking any difference between himself and them. I never heard from him anything that was *de haut en bas*, when he spoke of people, and in Cambridge, where there was a good deal of contempt for the less lettered, and we liked to smile though we did not like to sneer, and to analyze if we did not censure, Longfellow and Longfellow's house were free of all that. Whatever his feeling may have been towards other sorts and conditions of men, his effect was of an entire democracy. He was always the most unassuming person in any company, and at some large public dinners where I saw him I found him patient of the greater attention that more public men paid themselves and one another. He was not a speaker, and I never saw him on his feet at dinner, except once, when he read a poem for Whittier, who was absent. He disliked after-dinner speaking, and made conditions for his own exemption from it.

VIII

Once your friend, Longfellow was always your friend; he would not think evil of you, and if he knew evil of you, he would be the last of all that knew it to judge you for it. This may have been from the impersonal habit of his mind, but I believe it was also the effect of principle, for he would do what he could to arrest the delivery of judgment from others, and would soften the sentences passed in his presence. Naturally this brought him under some condemnation with those of a severer cast; and I have heard him criticised for his benevolence towards all, and his constancy to some who were not quite so true to themselves, perhaps. But this leniency of Longfellow's was what constituted him great as well as good, for it is not our wisdom that censures others. As for his goodness, I never saw a fault in him. I do not mean to say that he had no faults, or that there were no better men, but only to give the witness of my knowledge concerning him. I claim in no wise to have been his intimate; such a thing was not possible in my case for quite apparent reasons; and I doubt if Longfellow was capable of intimacy in the sense we mostly attach to the word. Something more of egotism than I ever found in him must go to the making of any intimacy which did not come from the tenderest affections of his heart. But as a man shows himself to those often with him, and in his noted re- lations with other men, he showed himself without blame. All men that I have known, besides, have had some foible (it often endeared them the more), or some meanness, or pettiness, or bitterness; but Longfellow had none, nor the suggestion of any. No breath of evil ever touched his name; he went in and out among his fellow-men without the reproach that follows wrong; the worst thing I ever heard said of him was that he had *gêne*, and this was said by one of those difficult Cambridge men who would have found *gêne* in a celestial angel. Something that Björnstjerne Björnson wrote to me when he was leaving America after a winter in Cambridge, comes nearer suggesting Longfellow than all my talk. The Norsemen, in the days of their stormy and reluctant conversion, used always to speak of Christ as the White Christ, and Björnson said in his letter, "Give my love to the White Mr. Longfellow."

A good many years before Longfellow's death he began to be sleepless, and he suffered greatly. He said to me once that he felt as if he were going about with his heart in a kind of mist. The whole night through he would not be aware of having slept. "But," he would add, with his heavenly patience, "I always get a good deal of rest from lying down so long." I cannot say whether these conditions persisted, or how much his insomnia had to do with his breaking health; three or four years before the end came, we left Cambridge for a house farther in the country, and I saw him less frequently than before. He did not allow our meetings to cease; he asked me to dinner from time to time, as if to keep them up, but it could not be with the old frequency. Once he made a point of coming to see us in our cottage on the hill west of Cambridge, but it was with an effort not visible in the days when he could end one of his brief walks at our house on Concord Avenue; he never came but he left our house more luminous for his having been there. Once he came to supper there to meet Garfield (an old family friend of mine in Ohio), and though he was suffering from a heavy cold, he would not scant us in his stay. I had some very bad sherry which he drank with the serenity of a martyr, and I shudder to this day to think what his kindness must have cost him. He told his story of the clothes-line ghost, and Garfield matched it with the story of an umbrella ghost who sheltered a friend of his through a midnight storm, but was not cheerful company to his beneficiary, who passed his hand through him at one point in the effort to take his arm.

After the end of four years I came to Cambridge to be treated for a long sickness, which had nearly been my last, and when I could get about I returned the visit Longfellow had not failed to pay me. But I did not find him, and I never saw him again in

life. I went into Boston to finish the winter of 1881–2, and from
time to time I heard that the poet was failing in health. As soon
as I felt able to bear the horse-car journey I went out to Cambridge to see him. I had knocked once at his door, the friendly
door that had so often opened to his welcome, and stood with
the knocker in my hand when the door was suddenly set ajar,
and a maid showed her face wet with tears. "How is Mr. Longfellow?" I palpitated, and with a burst of grief she answered,
"Oh, the poor gentleman has just departed!" I turned away as
if from a helpless intrusion at a death-bed.

At the services held in the house before the obsequies at the
cemetery, I saw the poet for the last time, where

"Dead he lay among his books,"

in the library behind his study. Death seldom fails to bring
serenity to all, and I will not pretend that there was a peculiar
peacefulness in Longfellow's noble mask, as I saw it then. It was
calm and benign as it had been in life; he could not have worn
a gentler aspect in going out of the world than he had always
worn in it; he had not to wait for death to dignify it with "the
peace of God." All who were left of his old Cambridge were
present, and among those who had come farther was Emerson.
He went up to the bier, and with his arms crossed on his breast,
and his elbows held in either hand, stood with his head pathetically fallen forward, looking down at the dead face. Those who
knew how his memory was a mere blank, with faint gleams of
recognition capriciously coming and going in it, must have felt
that he was struggling to remember who it was lay there before
him; and for me the electly simple words confessing his failure
will always be pathetic with his remembered aspect: "The
gentleman we have just been burying," he said, to the friend
who had come with him, "was a sweet and beautiful soul; but I
forget his name."

I had the privilege and honor of looking over the unprinted
poems Longfellow left behind him, and of helping to decide
which of them should be published. There were not many of

them, and some of these few were quite fragmentary. I gave my voice for the publication of all that had any sort of completeness, for in every one there was a touch of his exquisite art, the grace of his most lovely spirit. We have so far had two men only who felt the claim of their gift to the very best that the most patient skill could give its utterance: one was Hawthorne and the other was Longfellow. I shall not undertake to say which was the greater artist of these two; but I am sure that every one who has studied it must feel with me that the art of Longfellow held out to the end with no touch of decay in it, and that it equalled the art of any other poet of his time. It knew when to give itself, and more and more it knew when to withhold itself.

What Longfellow's place in literature will be, I shall not offer to say; that is Time's affair, not mine; but I am sure that with Tennyson and Browning he fully shared in the expression of an age which more completely than any former age got itself said by its poets.

STUDIES OF LOWELL

I HAVE already spoken of my earliest meetings with Lowell at Cambridge when I came to New England on a literary pilgrimage from the West in 1860. I saw him more and more after I went to live in Cambridge in 1866; and I now wish to record what I knew of him during the years that passed between this date and that of his death. If the portrait I shall try to paint does not seem a faithful likeness to others who knew him, I shall only claim that so he looked to me, at this moment and at that. If I do not keep myself quite out of the picture, what painter ever did?

I

It was in the summer of 1865 that I came home from my consular post at Venice; and two weeks after I landed in Boston, I went out to see Lowell at Elmwood, and give him an inkstand that I had brought him from Italy. The bronze lobster whose back opened and disclosed an inkpot and a sand-box was quite ugly; but I thought it beautiful then, and if Lowell thought otherwise he never did anything to let me know it. He put the thing in the middle of his writing table (he nearly always wrote on a pasteboard pad resting upon his knees) and there it remained as long as I knew the place—a matter of twenty-five years; but in all that time I suppose the inkpot continued as dry as the sand-box.

My visit was in the heat of August, which is as fervid in Cambridge as it can well be anywhere, and I still have a sense of his study windows lifted to the summer night, and the crickets and grasshoppers crying in at them from the lawns and the gardens outside. Other people went away from Cambridge in the summer to the sea and to the mountains, but Lowell always stayed at Elmwood, in an impassioned love for his home and for his town. I must have found him there in the afternoon, and he must have made me sup with him (dinner was at two o'clock) and then go with him for a long night of talk in his study. He liked to have some one help him idle the time away, and keep him as long as possible from his work; and no doubt I was impersonally serving his turn in this way, aside from any pleasure he might have had in my company as some one he had always been kind to, and as a fresh arrival from the Italy dear to us both.

He lighted his pipe, and from the depths of his easy chair, invited my shy youth to all the ease it was capable of in his presence. It was not much; I loved him, and he gave me reason to think that he was fond of me, but in Lowell I was always conscious of an older and closer and stricter civilization than my own, an unbroken tradition, a more authoritative status. His democracy was more of the head and mine more of the heart, and his denied the equality which mine affirmed. But his nature was so noble and his reason so tolerant that whenever in our long acquaintance I found it well to come to open rebellion, as I more than once did, he admitted my right of insurrection, and never resented the outbreak. I disliked to differ with him, and perhaps he subtly felt this so much that he would not dislike me for doing it. He even suffered being taxed with inconsistency, and where he saw that he had not been quite just, he would take punishment for his error, with a contrition that was sometimes humorous and always touching.

Just then it was the dark hour before the dawn, with Italy, and he was interested but not much encouraged by what I could tell him of the feeling in Venice against the Austrians. He seemed to reserve a like skepticism concerning the fine things I was hoping for the Italians in literature, and he confessed an interest in the facts treated which in the retrospect I am aware, was more tolerant than participant of my enthusiasm. That was always

Lowell's attitude towards the opinions of people he liked, when he could not go their lengths with them, and nothing was more characteristic of his affectionate nature and his just intelligence. He was a man of the most strenuous convictions, but he loved many sorts of people whose convictions he disagreed with, and he suffered even prejudices counter to his own if they were not ignoble. In the whimsicalities of others he delighted as much as in his own.

II

Our associations with Italy held over until the next day, when after breakfast he went with me toward Boston as far as "the village": for so he liked to speak of Cambridge in the custom of his younger days when wide tracts of meadow separated Harvard Square from his life-long home at Elmwood. We stood on the platform of the horsecar together, and when I objected to his paying my fare in the American fashion, he allowed that the Italian usage of each paying for himself was the politer way. He would not commit himself about my returning to Venice, (for I had not given up my place, yet, and was away on leave), but he intimated his distrust of the flattering conditions of life abroad. He said it was charming to be treated *da signore*, but he seemed to doubt whether it was well; and in this as in all other things he showed his final fealty to the American ideal.

It was that serious and great moment after the successful close of the Civil War when the republican consciousness was more robust in us than ever before or since; but I cannot recall any reference to the historical interest of the time in Lowell's talk. It had been all about literature and about travel; and now with the suggestion of the word village it began to be a little about his youth. I have said before how reluctant he was to let his youth go from him; and perhaps the touch with my juniority had made him realize how near he was to fifty, and set him thinking of the past which had sorrows in it to age him beyond his years. He would never speak of these, though he often spoke of the past. He told once of having been on a brief journey, when he was six years old, with his father, and of driving up to the gate of Elm-wood in the evening, and his father saying, "Ah, this is a pleasant place! I wonder who lives here—what little boy?" At another time he pointed out a certain window in his study, and said he could see himself standing by it when he could only get his chin on the window sill. His memories of the house, and of everything belonging to it were very tender; but he could laugh over an escapade of his youth when he helped his fellow-students pull down his father's fences, in the pure zeal of good comradeship.

III

My fortunes took me to New York, and I spent most of the winter of 1865–6 writing in the office of The Nation. I contributed several sketches of Italian travel to that paper; and one of these brought me a precious letter from Lowell. He praised my sketch, which he said he had read without the least notion who had written it, and he wanted me to feel the full value of such an impersonal pleasure in it. At the same time he did not fail to tell me that he disliked some pseudo-cynical verses of mine which he had read in another place; and I believe it was then that he bade me "sweat the Heine out of" me, "as men sweat the mercury out of their bones."

When I was asked to be assistant editor of the Atlantic Monthly, and came on to Boston to talk the matter over with the publishers, I went out to Cambridge and consulted Lowell. He strongly urged me to take the position, (I thought myself hopefully placed in New York on The Nation); and at the same time he seemed to have it on his heart to say that he had recommended some one else for it, never, he owned, having thought of me.

He was most cordial, but after I came to live in Cambridge, (where the magazine was printed, and I could more conveniently look over the proofs) he did not call on me for more than a month, and seemed quite to have forgotten me. We met one night at Mr. Norton's, for one of the Dante readings, and he took no special notice of me till I happened to say something that offered him a chance to give me a little humorous snub. I was speaking of a paper in the magazine on the Claudian Emissary, and I demanded (no doubt a little too airily) something like "Who in the world ever heard of the Claudian Emissary?" "*You are in Cambridge,* Mr. Howells," Lowell answered, and laughed at my confusion. Having put me down, he seemed to soften toward me, and at parting he said, with a light of half-mocking tenderness in his beautiful eyes, "Good-night, fellow-townsman." "I hardly knew we were fellow-townsmen," I returned. He liked that, apparently, and said he had been meaning to call upon me, and that he was coming very soon.

He was as good as his word, and after that hardly a week of any kind of weather passed but he mounted the steps to the door of the ugly little house in which I lived, two miles away from him, and asked me to walk. These walks continued, I suppose, until Lowell went abroad for a winter in the early seventies. They took us all over Cambridge, which he knew and loved every inch of, and led us afield through the straggling, unhandsome outskirts, bedrabbled with squalid Irish neighborhoods, and fraying off into marshes and salt meadows. He liked to indulge an excess of admiration for the local landscape, and though I never heard him profess a preference for the Charles River flats to the finest Alpine scenery, I could well believe he would do so under provocation of a fit listener's surprise. He had always so much of the boy in him that he liked to tease the over-serious or over-sincere. He liked to tease and he liked to mock, especially his juniors, if any touch of affectation, or any little exuberance of manner gave him the chance; when he once came to fetch me, and the young mistress of the house entered with a certain excessive elasticity, he sprang from his seat, and minced toward her with a burlesque of her buoyant carriage which made her laugh. When he had given us his heart in trust of ours, he used us like a younger brother and sister, or like his own children. He included our children in his affection, and he enjoyed our fondness for them as if it were something that had come back to him from his own youth. I think he had also a sort of artistic, a sort of ethical pleasure in it, as being of the good tradition, of the old honest, simple material, from which pleasing effects in literature and civilization were wrought. He liked giving the children books, and writing tricksy fancies in these where he masked as a fairy prince; and as long as he lived he remembered his early kindness for them.

IV

In those walks of ours I believe he did most of the talking, and from his talk then and at other times there remains to me an impression of his growing conservatism. I had in fact come into his life when it had spent its impulse towards positive reform, and I was to be witness of its increasing tendency toward the negative sort. He was quite past the storm and stress of his anti-slavery age; with the close of the war which had broken for him all his ideals of inviolable peace, he had reached the age of misgiving. I do not mean that I ever heard him express doubt of what he had helped to do, or regret for what he had done; but I know that he viewed with critical anxiety what other men were doing with the accomplished facts. His anxiety gave a cast of what one may call reluctance from the political situation, and turned him back toward those civic and social defences which he had once seemed willing to abandon. I do not mean that he lost faith in democracy; this faith he constantly then and signally afterwards affirmed; but he certainly had no longer any faith in insubordination as a means of grace. He preached a quite Socratic reverence for law, as law, and I remember that once when I had got back from Canada in the usual disgust for the American custom-house, and spoke lightly of smuggling as not an evil in itself, and perhaps even a right under our vexatious tariff, he would not have it, but held that the illegality of the act made it a moral offence. This was not the logic that would have justified the attitude of the anti-slavery men towards the fugitive slave act; but it was in accord with Lowell's feeling about John Brown, whom he honored while always condemning his violation of law; and it was in the line of all his later thinking.

James Russell Lowell

In this, he wished you to agree with him, or at least he wished to make you; but he did not wish you to be more of his mind than he was himself. In one of those squalid Irish neighborhoods I confessed a grudge (a mean and cruel grudge, I now think it) for the increasing presence of that race among us, but this did not please him; and I am sure that whatever misgiving he had as to the future of America, he would not have had it less than it had been the refuge and opportunity of the poor of any race or color. Yet he would not have had it this alone. There was a line in his poem on Agassiz which he left out of the printed version, at the fervent entreaty of his friends, as saying too bitterly his disappointment with his country. Writing at the distance of Europe, and with America in the perspective which the alien environment clouded, he spoke of her as "the Land of Broken Promise." It was a splendid reproach, but perhaps too dramatic to bear the full test of analysis, and yet it had the truth in it, and might, I think, have usefully stood, to the end of making people think. Undoubtedly it expressed his sense of the case, and in the same measure it would now express that of many who love their country most among us. It is well to hold one's country to her promises, and if there are any who think she is forgetting them it is their duty to say so, even to the point of bitter accusation. I do not suppose it was the "common man" of Lincoln's dream, that Lowell thought America was unfaithful to, though as I have suggested he could be tender of the common man's hopes in her; but he was impeaching in that blotted line her sincerity with the uncommon man: the man who had expected of her a constancy to the ideals of her youth and to the high martyr-moods of the war which had given an unguarded and bewildering freedom to a race of slaves. He was thinking of the shame of our municipal corruptions, the debased quality of our national statesmanship, the decadence of our whole civic tone, rather than of the increasing disabilities of the hardworking poor, though his heart when he thought of them was with them, too, as it was in "the times when the slave would not let him sleep."

He spoke very rarely of those times, perhaps because their

political and social associations were so knit up with the saddest
and tenderest personal memories, which it was still anguish to
touch. Not only was he

"not of the race
That hawk their sorrows in the market place,"

but so far as my witness went he shrank from mention of them.
I do not remember hearing him speak of the young wife who
influenced him so potently at the most vital moment, and turned
him from his whole scholarly and aristocratic tradition to an
impassioned championship of the oppressed; and he never spoke
of the children he had lost. I recall but one allusion to the days
when he was fighting the anti-slavery battle along the whole
line, and this was with a humorous relish of his Irish servant's
disgust in having to wait upon a negro whom he had asked to his
table.

He was rather severe in his notions of the subordination his
domestics owed him. They were "to do as they were bid," and
yet he had a tenderness for such as had been any time with him,
which was wounded when once a hired man long in his employ
greedily over reached him in a certain transaction. He complained of that with a simple grief for the man's indelicacy after
so many favors from him, rather than with any resentment. His
hauteur toward his dependents was theoretic; his actual behavior
was of the gentle consideration common among Americans of
good breeding; and that recreant hired man had no doubt never
been suffered to exceed him in shows of mutual politeness. Often
when the maid was about weightier matters, he came and
opened his door to me himself, welcoming me with the smile that
was like no other. Sometimes he said, "Siete il benvenuto," or
used some other Italian phrase, which put me at ease with him
in the region where we were most at home together.

Looking back I must confess that I do not see what it was he
found to make him wish for my company, which he presently
insisted upon having once a week at dinner. After the meal we
turned into his study where we sat before a wood fire in winter,
and he smoked and talked. He smoked a pipe which was always

needing tobacco, or going out, so that I have the figure of him before my eyes constantly getting out of his deep chair to rekindle it from the fire with a paper lighter. He was often out of his chair to get a book from the shelves that lined the walls, either for a passage which he wished to read, or for some disputed point which he wished to settle. If I had caused the dispute, he enjoyed putting me in the wrong; if he could not, he sometimes whimsically persisted in his error, in defiance of all authority; but mostly he had such reverence for the truth that he would not question it even in jest.

If I dropped in upon him in the afternoon I was apt to find him reading the old French poets, or the plays of Calderon, or the Divina Commedia, which he magnanimously supposed me much better acquainted with than I was because I knew some passages of it by heart. One day I came in quoting—

"Io son, cantava, io son dolce Sirena,
    Che i marinai in mezzo al mar dismago."

He stared at me in a rapture with the matchless music, and then uttered all his adoration and despair in one word. "Damn!" he said, and no more. I believe he instantly proposed a walk that day, as if his study walls with all their vistas into the great literatures cramped his soul liberated to a sense of ineffable beauty of the verse of the *sommo poeta*. But commonly he preferred to have me sit down with him there among the mute witnesses of the larger part of his life. As I have suggested in my own case, it did not matter much whether you brought anything to the feast or not. If he liked you he liked being with you, not for what he got, but for what he gave. He was fond of one man whom I recall as the most silent man I ever met. I never heard him say anything, not even a dull thing, but Lowell delighted in him, and would have you believe that he was full of quaint humor.

V

While Lowell lived there was a superstition which has perhaps survived him that he was an indolent man, wasting himself in barren studies and minor efforts instead of devoting his great powers to some monumental work worthy of them. If the robust body of literature, both poetry and prose, which lives after him does not yet correct this vain delusion, the time will come when it must; and in the meantime the delusion cannot vex him now. I think it did vex him, then, and that he even shared it, and tried at times to meet such shadowy claim as it had. One of the things that people urged upon him was to write some sort of story, and it is known how he attempted this in verse. It is less known that he attempted it in prose, and that he went so far as to write the first chapter of a novel. He read this to me, and though I praised it then, I have a feeling now that if he had finished the novel it would have been a failure. "But I shall never finish it," he sighed as if he felt irremediable defects in it, and laid the manuscript away, to turn and light his pipe. It was a rather old fashioned study of a whimsical character, and it did not arrive anywhere, so far as it went; but I believe that it might have been different with a Yankee story in verse such as we have fragmentarily in "The Nooning" and "FitzAdam's Story." Still, his gift was essentially lyrical and meditative, with the universal New England tendency to allegory. He was wholly undramatic in the actuation of the characters which he imagined so dramatically. He liked to deal with his subject at first hand, to indulge through himself all the whim and fancy which the more dramatic talent indulges through its personages.

He enjoyed writing such a poem as "The Cathedral," which is not of his best, but which is more immediately himself, in all his moods, than some better poems. He read it to me soon after it was written, and in the long walk which we went hard upon the reading (our way led us through the Port far toward East Cambridge, where he wished to show me a tupelo tree of his acquaintance, because I said I had never seen one,) his talk was still of the poem which he was greatly in conceit of. Later his satisfaction with it received a check from the reserves of other friends concerning some whimsical lines which seemed to them too great a drop from the higher moods of the piece. Their reluctance nettled him; perhaps he agreed with them; but he would not change the lines, and they stand as he first wrote them. In fact most of his lines stand as he first wrote them; he would often change them in revision, and then, in a second revision go back to the first version.

He was very sensitive to criticism, especially from those he valued through his head or heart. He would try to hide his hurt, and he would not let you speak of it, as though your sympathy unmanned him, but you could see that he suffered. This notably happened in my remembrance from a review in a journal which he greatly esteemed; and once when in a notice of my own I had put one little thorny point among the flowers, he confessed a puncture from it. He praised the criticism hardily, but I knew that he winced under my recognition of the didactic quality which he had not quite guarded himself against in the poetry otherwise praised. He liked your liking, and he openly rejoiced in it; and I suppose he made himself believe that in trying his verse with his friends he was testing it; but I do not believe that he was, and I do not think he ever corrected his judgment by theirs, however he suffered from it.

In any matter that concerned literary morals he was more than eager to profit by another eye. One summer he sent me for the magazine a poem which, when I read it, I trembled to find in motive almost exactly like one we had lately printed by another contributor. There was nothing for it but to call his attention to the resemblance, and I went over to Elmwood with the two poems. He was not at home, and I was obliged to leave the poems, I suppose with some sort of note, for the next morning's post brought me a delicious letter from him, all one cry of confession, the most complete, the most ample. He did not trouble himself to say that his poem was an unconscious repro-duction of the other; that was for every reason unnecessary, but he had at once rewritten it upon wholly different lines; and I do not think any reader was reminded of Mrs. Akers's "Among the Laurels" by Lowell's "Foot-path." He was not only much more sensitive of others' rights than his own, but in spite of a certain severity in him, he was most tenderly regardful of their sensibilities when he had imagined them: he did not always imagine them.

VI

At this period, between the years 1866 and 1874, when he unwillingly went abroad for a twelvemonth, Lowell was seen in very few Cambridge houses, and in still fewer Boston houses. He was not an unsocial man, but he was most distinctly not a society man. He loved chiefly the companionship of books, and of men who loved books; but of women generally he had an amusing diffidence; he revered them and honored them, but he would rather not have had them about. This is oversaying it, of course, but the truth is in what I say. There was never a more devoted husband, and he was content to let his devotion to the sex end with that. He especially could not abide difference of opinion in women; he valued their taste, their wit, their humor, but he would have none of their reason. I was by one day when he was arguing a point with one of his nieces, and after it had gone on for some time, and the impartial witness must have owned that she was getting the better of him he closed the controversy by giving her a great kiss, with the words, "You are a very good girl, my dear," and practically putting her out of the room. As to women of the flirtatious type, he did not dislike them; no man, perhaps, does; but he feared them, and he said that with them there was but one way, and that was to run.

I have a notion that at this period Lowell was more freely and fully himself than at any other. The passions and impulses of his younger manhood had mellowed, the sorrows of that time had softened; he could blamelessly live to himself in his affections and his sobered ideals. His was always a duteous life; but he had pretty well given up making man over in his own image, as we all wish some time to do, and then no longer wish it. He fulfilled his obligations to his fellow-men as these sought him out, but he had ceased to seek them. He loved his friends and their love, but he had apparently no desire to enlarge their circle. It was that hour of civic suspense, in which public men seemed still actuated by unselfish aims, and one not essentially a politician might contentedly wait to see what would come of their doing their best. At any rate, without occasionally withholding open criticism or acclaim Lowell waited among his books for the wounds of the war to heal themselves, and the nation to begin her healthfuller and nobler life. With slavery gone, what might not one expect of American democracy!

His life at Elmwood was of an entire simplicity. In the old colonial mansion in which he was born, he dwelt in the embowering leafage, amid the quiet of lawns and garden plots broken by few noises ruder than those from the elms and the syringas where

"The oriole clattered and the cat-bird sang."

From the tracks on Brattle street, came the drowsy tinkle of horsecar bells; and sometimes a funeral trailed its black length past the corner of his grounds, and lost itself from sight under the shadows of the willows that hid Mount Auburn from his study windows. In the winter the deep New England snows kept their purity in the stretch of meadow behind the house, which a double row of pines guarded in a domestic privacy. All was of a modest dignity within and without the house, which Lowell loved but did not imagine of a manorial presence; and he could not conceal his annoyance with an over-enthusiastic account of his home in which the simple chiseling of some panels was vaunted as rich wood-carving. There was a graceful staircase, and a good wide hall, from which the dining-room and drawing-room opened by opposite doors; behind the last, in the southwest corner of the house, was his study.

There, literally, he lived during the six or seven years in which I knew him after my coming to Cambridge. Summer and winter he sat there among his books, seldom stirring abroad by day except for a walk, and by night yet more rarely. He went to the monthly mid-day dinner of the Saturday Club in Boston; he was very constant at the fortnightly meetings of his whist-club, because he loved the old friends who formed it; he came always to the Dante suppers at Longfellow's, and he was familiarly in and out at Mr. Norton's, of course. But, otherwise, he kept to his study, except for some rare and almost unwilling absences upon university lecturing at Johns Hopkins or at Cornell.

For four years I did not take any summer outing from Cambridge myself, and my associations with Elmwood and with Lowell are more of summer than of winter weather meetings. But often we went our walks through the snows, trudging along between the horse-car tracks which enclosed the only well-broken-out paths in that simple old Cambridge. I date one memorable expression of his from such a walk, when, as we were passing Longfellow's house, in mid-street, he came as near the declaration of his religious faith as he ever did in my presence. He was speaking of the New Testament, and he said the truth was in it; but "they had covered it up with their hagiology." Though he had been bred a Unitarian, and had more and more liberated himself from all creeds, he humorously affected an abiding belief in hell, and similarly contended for the eternal punishment of the wicked. He was of a religious nature, and he was very reverent of other people's religious feelings; he expressed a special tolerance for my own inherited faith, no doubt because Mrs. Lowell was also a Swedenborgian; but I do not think he was interested in it, and I suspect that all religious formulations bored him. In his earlier poems are many intimations and affirmations of belief in an overruling providence, and especially in the God who declares vengeance His and will repay men for their evil deeds, and will right the weak against the strong. I think he never quite lost this, though when, in the last years of his life, I asked him if he believed there was a moral government of the universe, he answered gravely and with a sort of pain, The scale was so vast, and we saw such a little part of it.

As to the notion of a life after death, I never had any direct or indirect expression from him; but I incline to the opinion that his hold upon this weakened with his years, as it is sadly apt to do with men who have read much and thought much: they have apparently exhausted their potentialities of psychological life. Mystical Lowell was, as every poet must be, but I do not think he liked mystery. One morning he told me that when he came home the night before he had seen the Doppelgänger of one of his household: though, as he joked, he was not in a state to see double. He then said he used often to see people's Doppelgänger; at another time, as to ghosts, he said, He was like Coleridge: he had seen too many of 'em. Lest any weaker brethren should be caused to offend by the restricted oath which I have reported him using in a moment of transport it may be best to note here that I never heard him use any other imprecation, and this one seldom.

Any grossness of speech was inconceivable of him; now and then, but only very rarely, the human nature of some story "unmeet for ladies" was too much for his sense of humor, and overcame him with amusement which he was willing to impart, and did impart, but so that mainly the human nature of it reached you. In this he was like the other great Cambridge men, though he was opener than the others to contact with the commoner life. He keenly delighted in every native and novel turn of phrase, and he would not undervalue a vital word or a notion picked up out of the road even if it had some dirt sticking to it.

He kept as close to the common life as a man of his patrician instincts and cloistered habits could. I could go to him with any new find about it and be sure of delighting him; after I began making my involuntary and all but unconscious studies of Yankee character, especially in the country, he was always glad to talk them over with me. Still, when I had discovered a new accent or turn of speech in the fields he had cultivated, I was aware of a subtle grudge mingling with his pleasure; but this was after all less envy than a fine regret.

At the time I speak of there was certainly nothing in Lowell's dress or bearing that would have kept the common life aloof from him, if that life were not always too proud to make advances to any one. In this retrospect, I see him in the sack coat and rough suit which he wore upon all outdoor occasions, with heavy shoes, and a round hat. I never saw him with a high hat on till he came home after his diplomatic stay in London; then he had become rather rigorously correct in his costume, and as conventional as he had formerly been indifferent. In both epochs he was apt to be gloved, and the strong, broad hands, which left the sensation of their vigor for some time after they had clasped yours, were notably white. At the earlier period, he still wore his auburn hair somewhat long; it was darker than his beard, which was branching and full, and more straw-colored than auburn, as were his thick eyebrows; neither hair nor beard was then touched with gray, as I now remember. When he uncovered, his straight wide white forehead showed itself one of the most beautiful that could be; his eyes were gay with humor, and alert with all intelligence. He had an enchanting smile, a laugh that was full of friendly joyousness, and a voice that was exquisite music. Everything about him expressed his strenuous physical condition: he would not wear an overcoat in the coldest Cambridge weather; at all times he moved vigorously, and walked with a quick step, lifting his feet well from the ground.

VII

It gives me a pleasure which I am afraid I cannot impart, to linger in this effort to materialize his presence from the fading memories of the past. I am afraid I can as little impart a due sense of what he spiritually was to my knowledge. It avails nothing for me to say that I think no man of my years and desert had ever so true and constant a friend. He was both younger and older than I by insomuch as he was a poet through and through, and had been out of college before I was born. But he had already come to the age of self-distrust when a man likes to take counsel with his juniors as with his elders, and fancies he can correct his perspective by the test of their fresher vision. Besides, Lowell was most simply and pathetically reluctant to part with youth, and was willing to cling to it wherever he found it. He could not in any wise bear to be left out. When Mr. Bret Harte came to

Cambridge, and the talk was all of the brilliant character-poems with which he had then first dazzled the world, Lowell casually said, with a most touching, however ungrounded, sense of obsolescence, He could remember when the Biglow Papers were all the talk. I need not declare that there was nothing ungenerous in that. He was only too ready to hand down his laurels to a younger man; but he wished to do it himself. Through the modesty that is always a quality of such a nature, he was magnanimously sensitive to the appearance of fading interest; he could not take it otherwise than as a proof of his fading power. I had a curious hint of this when one year in making up the prospectus of the magazine for the next, I omitted his name because I had nothing special to promise from him, and because I was half ashamed to be always flourishing it in the eyes of the public. "I see that you have dropped me this year," he wrote, and I could see that it had hurt, and I knew that he was glad to believe the truth when I told him.

He did not care so much for popularity, as for the praise of his friends. If he liked you he wished you not only to like what he wrote, but to say so. He was himself most cordial in his recognition of the things that pleased him. What happened to me from him, happened to others, and I am only describing his common habit when I say that nothing I did to his liking failed to bring me a spoken or oftener a written acknowledgement. This continued to the latest years of his life when the effort even to give such pleasure must have cost him a physical pang.

He was of a very catholic taste; and he was apt to be carried away by a little touch of life or humor, and to overvalue the piece in which he found it; but mainly his judgments of letters and men were just. One of the dangers of scholarship was a peculiar danger in the Cambridge keeping, but Lowell was almost as averse as Longfellow from contempt. He could snub, and pitilessly, where he thought there was presumption and apparently sometimes merely because he was in the mood; but I cannot remember ever to have heard him sneer. He was often wonderfully patient of tiresome people, and sometimes celestially insensible to vulgarity. In spite of his reserve, he really wished people to like him; he was keenly alive to neighborly goodwill or illwill; and when there was a question of widening Elmwood avenue by taking part of his grounds, he was keenly hurt by hearing that some one who lived near him had said he hoped the city would cut down Lowell's elms: his English elms, which his father had planted, and with which he was himself almost one blood!

VIII

In the period of which I am speaking, Lowell was constantly writing and pretty constantly printing, though still the superstition held that he was an idle man. To this time belongs the publication of some of his finest poems, if not their inception: there were cases in which their inception dated far back, even to ten or twenty years. He wrote his poems at a heat, and the manuscript which came to me for the magazine was usually the first draft, very little corrected. But if the cold fit took him quickly it might hold him so fast that he would leave the poem in abeyance till he could slowly live back to a liking for it.

The most of his best prose belongs to the time between 1866 and 1874, and to this time we owe the several volumes of essays and criticisms called "Among My Books" and "My Study Windows." He wished to name these more soberly, but at the urgence of his publishers he gave them titles which they thought would be attractive to the public, though he felt that they took from the dignity of his work. He was not a good business man in a literary way, he submitted to others' judgment in all such matters. I doubt if he ever put a price upon anything he sold, and I dare say he was usually surprised at the largeness of the price paid him; but sometimes if his need was for a larger sum, he thought it too little, without reference to former payments. This happened with a long poem in the "Atlantic," which I had urged the counting-room authorities to deal handsomely with him for. I did not know how many hundred they gave him, and when I met him I ventured to express the hope that the publishers had done their part. He held up four fingers, "*Quattro*," he said in Italian, and then added with a disappointment which he tried to smile away, "I thought they might have made it *cinque*."

Between me and me I thought *quattro* very well, but probably Lowell had in mind some end which *cinque* would have fitted better. It was pretty sure to be an unselfish end, a pleasure to some one dear to him, a gift that he had wished to make. Long afterwards when I had been the means of getting him *cinque* for a poem one tenth the length, he spoke of the payment to me. "It came very handily; I had been wanting to give ——— a watch."

I do not believe at anytime Lowell was able to deal with money,

> "Like wealthy men, not knowing what they give."

More probably he felt a sacredness in the money got by literature, which the literary man never quite rids himself of, even when he is not a poet, and which made him wish to dedicate it to something finer than the everyday uses. He lived very quietly, but he had by no means more than he needed to live upon, and at that time he had pecuniary losses. He was writing hard, and was doing full work in his Harvard professorship, and he was so far dependent upon his salary, that he felt its absence for the year he went abroad. I do not know quite how to express my sense of something unworldly, of something almost womanlike in his relation to money.

He was not only generous of money, but he was generous of himself, when he thought he could be of use, or merely of encouragement. He came all the way into Boston to hear certain lectures of mine on the Italian poets, which he could not have found either edifying or amusing, that he might testify his interest in me, and show other people that they were worth coming to. He would go carefully over a poem with me, word by word, and criticise every turn of phrase, and after all be magnanimously tolerant of my sticking to phrasings that he disliked. In a certain line:

"The silvern chords of the piano trembled,"

he objected to *silvern*. Why not silver? I alleged leathern, golden, and like adjectives in defence of my word; but still he found an affectation in it, and suffered it to stand with extreme reluctance. Another line of another piece—

"And what she would, would rather that she would not"—

he would by no means suffer. He said that the stress falling on the last word made it "public school English," and he mocked it with the answer a maid had lately given him when he asked if the master of the house was at home. She said, "No, sir, he is *not*," when she ought to have said "No, sir, he *isn't*." He was appeased when I came back the next day with the stanza amended so that the verse could read—

"And what she would, would rather she would not so"—

but I fancy he never quite forgave my word *silvern*. Yet, he professed not to have prejudices in such matters, but to use any word that would serve his turn, without wincing; and he certainly did use and defend words, as *undisprivacied* and *disnatured*, that made others wince.

He was otherwise such a stickler for the best diction that he would not have had me use slovenly vernacular even in the dialogue in my stories: my characters must not say they *wanted* to do so and so, but *wished*, and the like. In a copy of one of my books which I found him reading, I saw he had corrected my erring Western *woulds* and *shoulds*; as he grew old he was less and less able to restrain himself from setting people right to their faces. Once, in the vast area of my ignorance, he specified my small acquaintance with a certain period of English poetry, saying, "You're rather shady, there, old fellow." But he would not have had me too learned, holding that he had himself been hurt for literature by his scholarship.

His patience in analyzing my work with me might have been the easy effort of his habit of teaching; and his willingness to give himself and his own was no doubt more signally attested in his asking a brother man of letters who wished to work up a subject in the college library, to stay a fortnight in his house, and to share his study, his beloved study, with him. This must truly have cost him dear, as any author of fixed habits will understand. Happily the man of letters was a good fellow, and knew how to prize the favor done him, but if he had been otherwise, it would have been the same to Lowell. He not only endured, but did many things for the weaker brethren, which were amusing enough to one in the secret of his inward revolt. Yet in these things he was considerate also of the editor whom he might have made the sharer of his self-sacrifice, and he seldom offered me manuscripts for others. The only real burden of the kind that he put upon me was the diary of a Virginian who had traveled in New England during the early thirties, and had set down his impressions of men and manners there. It began charmingly, and went on very well under Lowell's discreet pruning, but after a while he seemed to fall in love with the character of the diarist so much that he could not bear to cut anything.

IX

He had a great tenderness for the broken and ruined South, whose sins he felt that he had had his share in visiting upon her, and he was willing to do what he could to ease her sorrows in the case of any particular Southerner. He could not help looking askance upon the dramatic shows of retribution which some of the Northern politicians were working, but with all his misgivings he continued to act with the Republican party until after the election of Hayes; he was away from the country during the Garfield campaign. He was in fact one of the Massachusetts electors chosen by the Republican majority in 1876, and in that most painful hour when there was question of the policy and justice of counting Hayes in for the presidency, it was suggested by some of Lowell's friends that he should use the original right of the electors under the constitution, and vote for Tilden, whom one vote would have chosen president over Hayes. After he had cast his vote for Hayes, he quietly referred to the matter one day, in the moment of lighting his pipe, with perhaps the faintest trace of indignation in his tone. He said that whatever the first intent of the constitution was, usage had made the presidential electors strictly the instruments of the party which chose them, and that for him to have voted for Tilden when he had been chosen to vote for Hayes would have been an act of bad faith.

He would have resumed for me all the old kindness of our relations before the recent year of his absence, but this had inevitably worked a little estrangement. He had at least lost the habit of me, and that says much in such matters. He was not so perfectly at rest in the Cambridge environment; in certain indefinable ways it did not so entirely suffice him, though he would have been then and always the last to allow this. I imagine his friends realized more than he, that certain delicate but vital filaments of attachment had frayed and parted in alien air, and left him heart-loose as he had not been before.

I do not know whether it crossed his mind after the election of Hayes that he might be offered some place abroad, but it certainly crossed the minds of some of his friends, and I could not feel that I was acting for myself alone when I used a family connection with the President, very early in his term, to let him know that I believed Lowell would accept a diplomatic mission. I could assure him that I was writing wholly without Lowell's privity or authority, and I got back such a letter as I could wish in its delicate sense of the situation. The President said that he had already thought of offering Lowell something, and he gave me the pleasure, a pleasure beyond any other I could imagine, of asking Lowell whether he would accept the mission to Austria. I lost no time carrying his letter to Elmwood, where I found Lowell over his coffee at dinner. He saw me at the threshold, and called to me through the open door to come in, and I handed him the letter, and sat down at table while he ran it through. When he had read it, he gave a quick "Ah!" and threw it over the length of the table to Mrs. Lowell. She read it in a smiling and loyal reticence, as if she would not say one word of all she might wish to say in urging his acceptance, though I could see that she was intensely eager for it. The whole situation was of a perfect New England character in its tacit significance; after Lowell had taken his coffee we turned into his study without further allusion to the matter.

A day or two later he came to my house to say that he could not accept the Austrian mission, and to ask me to tell the President so for him, and make his acknowledgments, which he would also write himself. He remained talking a little while of other things, and when he rose to go, he said with a sigh of vague reluctance, "I *should* like to see a play of Calderon," as if it had nothing to do with any wish of his that could still be fulfilled. "Upon this hint I acted," and in due time it was found in Washington, that the gentleman who had been offered the Spanish mission would as lief go to Austria, and Lowell was sent to Madrid.

x

When we met in London, some years later, he came almost every afternoon to my lodging, and the story of our old-time Cambridge walks began again in London phrases. There were not the vacant lots and outlying fields of his native place, but we made shift with the vast, simple parks, and we walked on the grass as we could not have done in an American park, and were glad to feel the earth under our feet. I said how much it was like those earlier tramps; and that pleased him, for he wished, whenever a thing delighted him, to find a Cambridge quality in it.

But he was in love with everything English, and was determined I should be so too, beginning with the English weather, which in summer cannot be overpraised. He carried, of course, an umbrella, but he would not put it up in the light showers that caught us at times, saying that the English rain never wetted you. The thick short turf delighted him; he would scarcely allow that the trees were the worse for foliage blighted by a vile easterly storm in the spring of that year. The tender air, the delicate veils that the moisture in it cast about all objects at the least remove, the soft colors of the flowers, the dull blue of the low sky showing through the rifts of the dirty white clouds, the hovering pall of London smoke, were all dear to him, and he was anxious that I should not lose anything of their charm.

He was anxious that I should not miss the value of anything in England, and while he volunteered that the aristocracy had the corruptions of aristocracies every where, he insisted upon my respectful interest in it because it was so historical. Perhaps there was a touch of irony in this demand, but it is certain that he was very happy in England. He had come of the age when a man likes smooth, warm keeping, in which he need make no struggle for his comfort; disciplined and obsequious service; society, perfectly ascertained within the larger society which we call civilization; and in an alien environment, for which he was in nowise responsible, he could have these without a pang of the self-reproach which at home makes a man unhappy amidst his luxuries, when he considers their cost to others. He had a position which forbade thought of unfairness in the conditions; he must not wake because of the slave, it was his duty to sleep. Besides, at that time Lowell needed all the rest he could get, for he had lately passed through trials such as break the strength of men, and bow them with premature age. He was living alone in his little house in Lowndes Square, and Mrs. Lowell was in the country, slowly recovering from the effects of the terrible typhus which she had barely survived in Madrid. He was yet so near the anguish of that experience that he told me he had still in his nerves the expectation of a certain agonized cry from her which used to rend them. But he said he had adjusted himself to this, and he went on to speak with a patience which was more affecting in him than in men of more phlegmatic temperament, of how we were able to adjust ourselves to all our trials and to the constant presence of pain. He said he was never free of a certain distress, which was often a sharp pang, in one of his shoulders, but his physique had established such relations with it, that though he was never unconscious of it he was able to endure it without a recognition of it as suffering.

He seemed to me, however, very well, and at his age of sixty-three, I could not see that he was less alert and vigorous than he was when I first knew him in Cambridge. He had the same brisk, light step, and though his beard was well whitened and his auburn hair had grown ashen through the red, his face had the freshness and his eyes the clearness of a young man's. I suppose the novelty of his life kept him from thinking about his years; or perhaps in contact with those great, insenescent Englishmen, he could not feel himself old. At any rate he did not once speak of age, as he used to do ten years earlier, and I, then half through my forties, was still "You young dog" to him. It was a bright and cheerful renewal of the early kindliness between us, on which indeed there had never been a shadow, except such as distance throws. He wished apparently to do everything he could to assure us of his personal interest; and we were amused to find him nervously apprehensive of any purpose, such as was far from us, to profit by him officially. He betrayed a distinct relief when he found we were not going to come upon him even for admissions to the houses of parliament, which we were to see by means of an English acquaintance. He had not perhaps found some other fellow-citizens so considerate; he dreaded the half-duties of his place, like presentations to the queen, and complained of the cheap ambitions he had to gratify in that way.

He was so eager to have me like England in every way, and seemed so fond of the English, that I thought it best to ask him whether he minded my quoting, in a paper about Lexington, which I was just then going to print in a London magazine, some humorous lines of his expressing the mounting satisfaction of an imaginary Yankee story-teller who has the old fight terminate in Lord Percy's coming

"To hammer stone for life in Concord jail."

It had occurred to me that it might possibly embarrass him to have this patriotic picture presented to a public which could not take our Fourth of July pleasure in it, and I offered to suppress it, as I did afterwards quite for literary reasons. He said, No, let it stand, and let them make the worst of it; and I fancy that much of his success with a people who are not gingerly with other people's sensibilities came from the frankness with which he trampled on their prejudice when he chose. He said he always told them, when there was question of such things, that the best society he had ever known was in Cambridge, Massachusetts. He contended that the best English was spoken there; and so it was, when he spoke it.

We were in London out of the season, and he was sorry that he could not have me meet some titles who he declared had found pleasure in my books; when we returned from Italy in the following June, he was prompt to do me this honor. I dare say he wished me to feel it to its last implication, and I did my best, but there was nothing in the evening I enjoyed so much as his coming up to Mrs. Lowell, at the close, when there was only a title or two left, and saying to her as he would have said to her at Elmwood, where she would have personally planned it, "Fanny, that was a fine dinner you gave us." Of course, this was in a tender burlesque; but it remains the supreme impression of what seemed to me a cloudlessly happy period for Lowell. His wife was quite recovered of her long suffering, and was again at the head of his house, sharing in his pleasures, and enjoying his successes for his sake: successes so great that people spoke of him seriously, as "an addition to society" in London, where one man more or less seemed like a drop in the sea. She was a woman perfectly of the New England type and tradition: almost repellently shy at first, and almost glacially cold with new acquaintance, but afterwards very sweet and cordial. She was of a dark beauty with a regular face of the Spanish outline; Lowell was of an ideal manner toward her, and of an admiration which delicately travestied itself and which she knew how to receive with smiling irony. After her death, which occurred while he was still in England, he never spoke of her to me, though before that he used to be always bringing her name in, with a young lover-like fondness.

XI

In the hurry of the London season I did not see so much of Lowell on our second sojourn as on our first, but once when we were alone in his study there was a return to the terms of the old meetings in Cambridge. He smoked his pipe, and sat by his fire and philosophized; and but for the great London sea swirling outside and bursting through our shelter, and dashing him with notes that must be instantly answered, it was a very fair image of the past. He wanted to tell me about his coachman, whom he had got at on his human side with great liking and amusement, and there was a patient gentleness in his manner with the footman who had to keep coming in upon him with those notes which was like the echo of his young faith in the equality of men. But he always distinguished between the simple unconscious equality of the ordinary American and its assumption by a foreigner. He said he did not mind such an American's coming into his house with his hat on; but if a German or Englishman did it, he wanted to knock it off. He was apt to be rather punctilious in his shows of deference towards others, and at one time he practiced removing his own hat when he went into shops in Cambridge. It must have mystified the Cambridge salesmen, and I doubt if he kept it up.

With reference to the doctrine of his young poetry, the fierce and the tender humanity of his storm and stress period, I fancy a kind of baffle in Lowell, which I should not perhaps find it easy to prove. I never knew him by word or hint to renounce this doctrine, but he could not come to seventy years without having seen many high hopes fade, and known many inspired prophecies fail. When we have done our best to make the world over, we are apt to be dismayed by finding it in much the old shape. As he said of the moral government of the universe, the scale is so vast, and a little difference, a little change for the better, is scarcely perceptible to the eager consciousness of the wholesale reformer. But with whatever sense of disappointment, of doubt as to his own deeds for truer freedom and for better conditions I believe his sympathy was still with those who had some heart for hoping and striving. I am sure that though he did not agree with me in some of my own later notions for the redemption of the race, he did not like me the less but rather the more because (to my own great surprise I confess) I had now and then the courage of my convictions, both literary and social.

He was probably most at odds with me in regard to my theories of fiction, though he persisted in declaring his pleasure in my own fiction. He was in fact, by nature and tradition thoroughly romantic, and he could not or would not suffer realism in any but a friend. He steadfastly refused even to read the Russian masters, to his immense loss as I tried to persuade him, and even among the modern Spaniards, for whom he might have had a sort of personal kindness from his love of Cervantes, he chose one for his praise the least worthy of it, and bore me down with his heavier metal in argument when I opposed to Alarcon's factitiousness the delightful genuineness of Valdés. Ibsen, with all the Norwegians, he put far from him; he would no more know them than the Russians; the French naturalists he abhorred. I thought him all wrong, but you do not try improving your elders when they have come to three score and ten years, and I would rather have had his affection unbroken by our difference of opinion than a perfect agreement. Where he even imagined that this difference could work me harm, he was anxious to have me know that he meant me none; and he was at the trouble to write me a letter when a Boston paper had perverted its report of what he said in a public lecture to my disadvantage, and to assure me that he had not me in mind. When once he had given his liking, he could not bear that any shadow of change should seem to have come upon him. He had a most beautiful and endearing ideal of friendship; he desired to affirm it and to reaffirm it as often as occasion offered, and if occasion did not offer, he made occasion. It did not matter what you said or did that contraried him; if he thought he had essentially divined you, you were still the same: and on his part he was by no means exacting of equal demonstration, but seemed not even to wish it.

XII

After he was replaced at London by a minister more immediately representative of the Democratic administration, he came home. He made a brave show of not caring to have remained away, but in truth he had become very fond of England, where he had made so many friends, and where the distinction he had, in that comfortably padded environment, was so agreeable to him. It would have been like him to have secretly hoped that the new President might keep him in London, but he never betrayed any ignoble disappointment, and he would not join in any blame of him. At our first meeting after he came home he spoke of the movement which had made Mr. Cleveland president, and said he supposed that if he had been here, he should have been in it. All his friends were, he added, a little helplessly; but he seemed not to dislike my saying I knew one of his friends who was not: in fact, as I have told, he never disliked a plump difference—unless he disliked the differer.

For several years he went back to England every summer, and it was not until he took up his abode at Elmwood again that he spent a whole year at home. One winter he passed at his sister's home in Boston, but mostly he lived with his daughter at Southborough. I have heard a story of his going to Elmwood soon after his return in 1885, and sitting down in his old study, where he declared with tears that the place was full of ghosts. But four or five years later it was well for family reasons that he should live there; and about the same time it happened that I had taken a house for the summer in his neighborhood. He came to see me, and to assure me, in all tacit forms, of his sympathy in a sorrow for which there could be no help; but it was not possible that the old intimate relations should be resumed. The affection was there, as much on his side as on mine, I believe; but he was now an old man and I was an elderly man, and we could not without insincerity approach each other in the things that had drawn us together in earlier and happier years. His course was run; my own, in which he had taken such a generous pleasure, could scarcely move his jaded interest. His life, so far as it remained to him, had renewed itself in other air; the later friendships beyond seas sufficed him, and were without the pang, without the effort that must attend the knitting up of frayed ties here.

He could never have been anything but American, if he had

tried, and he certainly never tried; but he certainly did not return to the outward simplicities of his life as I first knew it. There
was no more round-hat-and-sack-coat business for him; he wore
a frock and a high hat, and whatever else was rather like London
than Cambridge; I do not know but drab gaiters sometimes
added to the effect of a gentleman of the old school which he now
produced upon the witness. Some fastidiousnesses showed themselves in him, which were not so surprising. He complained of
the American lower class manner; the conductor and cabman
would be kind to you but they would not be respectful, and he
could not see the fun of this in the old way. Early in our acquaintance he rather stupified me by saying, "I like you because
you don't put your hands on me," and I heard of his consenting
to some sort of reception in those last years, "Yes, if they won't
shake hands."

Ever since his visit to Rome in 1875 he had let his heavy
mustache grow long till it drooped below the corners of his beard,
which was now almost white; his face had lost the ruddy hue so
characteristic of him. I fancy he was then ailing with premoni-
tions of the disorder which a few years later proved mortal, but
he still bore himself with sufficient vigor, and he walked the distance between his house and mine, though once when I missed
his visit the family reported that after he came in he sat a long
time with scarcely a word, as if too weary to talk. That winter,
I went into Boston to live, and I saw him only at infrequent intervals, when I could go out to Elmwood. At such times I found him
sitting in the room which was formerly the drawing-room, but
which had been joined with his study by taking away the parti-
tions beside the heavy mass of the old colonial chimney. He told
me that when he was a new-born babe, the nurse had carried
him round this chimney, for luck, and now in front of the same
hearth, the white old man stretched himself in an easy chair,
with his writing pad on his knees and his books on the table at
his elbow, and was willing to be entreated not to rise. I remember
the sun used to come in at the eastern windows full pour, and
bathe the air in its warmth.

He always hailed me gaily, and if I found him with letters newly come from England, as I sometimes did, he glowed and sparkled with fresh life. He wanted to read passages from those letters, he wanted to talk about their writers, and to make me feel their worth and charm as he did. He still dreamed of going back to England the next summer, but that was not to be. One day he received me not less gaily than usual, but with a certain excitement, and began to tell me about an odd experience he had had, not at all painful, but which had very much mystified him. He had since seen the doctor, and the doctor had assured him that there was nothing alarming in what had happened, and in recalling this assurance, he began to look at the humorous aspects of the case, and to make some jokes about it. He wished to talk of it, as men do of their maladies, and very fully, and I gave him such proof of my interest as even inviting him to talk of it would convey. In spite of the doctor's assurance, and his joyful acceptance of it, I doubt if at the bottom of his heart there was not the stir of an uneasy misgiving; but he had not for a long time shown himself so cheerful.

It was the beginning of the end. He recovered and relapsed, and recovered again; but never for long. Late in the spring I came out, and he had me stay to dinner, which was somehow as it used to be at two o'clock; and after dinner we went out on his lawn. He got a long-handled spud, and tried to grub up some dandelions which he found in his turf, but after a moment or two he threw it down, and put his hand upon his back with a groan. I did not see him again till I came out to take leave of him before going away for the summer, and then I found him sitting on the little porch in a western corner of his house, with a volume of Scott closed upon his finger. There were some other people, and our meeting was with the constraint of their presence. It was natural in nothing so much as his saying very significantly to me, as if he knew of my heresies concerning Scott, and would have me know he did not approve of them, that there was nothing he now found so much pleasure in as Scott's novels. Another friend, equally heretical, was by, but neither of us attempted to gainsay him. Lowell talked very little, but he told of having been a walk to Beaver Brook, and of having wished to jump from one stone to another in the stream, and of having had to give it up. He said, without completing the sentence, If it had come to *that* with him! Then he fell silent again; and with some vain talk of seeing him when I came back in the fall, I went away sick at heart. I was not to see him again, and I shall not look upon his like.

I am aware that I have here shown him from this point and from that in a series of sketches which perhaps collectively impart, but do not assemble his personality in one impression. He did not, indeed, make one impression upon me, but a thousand impressions, which I should seek in vain to embody in a single presentment. What I have cloudily before me is the vision of a very lofty and simple soul, perplexed, and as it were surprised and even dismayed, at the complexity of the effects from motives so single in it, but escaping always to a clear expression of what was noblest and loveliest in itself at the supreme moments, in the divine exigencies. I believe neither in heroes nor in saints; but I believe in great and good men, for I have known them; and among such men Lowell was of the richest nature I have known. His nature was not always serene or pellucid; it was sometimes roiled by the currents that counter and cross in all of us; but it was without the least alloy of insincerity and it was never darkened by the shadow of a selfish fear. His genius was an instrument that responded in affluent harmony to the power that made him a humorist and that made him a poet, and appointed him rarely to be quite either alone.

CAMBRIDGE NEIGHBORS

BEING the wholly literary spirit I was when I went to make my home in Cambridge, I do not see how I could well have been more content if I had found myself in the Elysian Fields with an agreeable eternity before me. At twenty-nine, indeed, one is practically immortal, and at that age, time had for me the effect of an eternity in which I had nothing to do but to read books and dream of writing them, in the overflow of endless hours from my work with the manuscripts, critical notices, and proofs of the *Atlantic Monthly*. As for the social environment I should have been puzzled if given my choice among the elect of all the ages, to find poets and scholars more to my mind than those still in the flesh at Cambridge in the early afternoon of the nineteenth century. They are now nearly all dead, and I can speak of them in the freedom which is death's doubtful favor to the survivor; but if they were still alive I could say little to their offence, unless their modesty was hurt with my praise.

I

One of the first and truest of our Cambridge friends was that exquisite intelligence, who, in a world where so many people are grotesquely miscalled, was most fitly named; for no man ever kept here more perfectly and purely the heart of such as the kingdom of heaven is of than Francis J. Child. He was then in his prime, and I like to recall the outward image which expressed the inner man as happily as his name. He was of low stature and of an inclination which never became stoutness; but what you most saw when you saw him was his face of consummate refinement: very regular, with eyes always glassed by gold-rimmed spectacles, a straight, short, most sensitive nose, and a beautiful mouth with the sweetest smile mouth ever wore, and that was as wise and shrewd as it was sweet. In a time when every other man was more or less bearded he was clean shaven, and of a delightful freshness of coloring which his thick sunny hair, clustering upon his head in close rings, admirably set off. I believe he never became gray, and the last time I saw him, though he was broken then with years and pain, his face had still the brightness of his inextinguishable youth.

It is well known how great was Professor Child's scholarship in the branches of his Harvard work; and how especially, how uniquely, effective it was in the study of English and Scottish balladry to which he gave so many years of his life. He was a poet in his nature, and he wrought with passion as well as knowledge in the achievement of as monumental a task as any American has performed. But he might have been indefinitely less than he was in any intellectual wise, and yet been precious to those who knew him for the gentleness and the goodness which in him were protected from misconception by a final dignity as delicate and as inviolable as that of Longfellow himself.

We were still much less than a year from our life in Venice, when he came to see us in Cambridge, and in the Italian interest which then commended us to so many fine spirits among our neighbors we found ourselves at the beginning of a life-long friendship with him. I was known to him only by my letters from Venice, which afterwards became *Venetian Life*, and by a bit of devotional verse which he had asked to include in a collection he was making, but he immediately gave us the freedom of his heart, which afterwards was never withdrawn. In due time he imagined a home-school, to which our little one was asked, and she had her first lessons with his own daughter under his roof. These things drew us closer together, and he was willing to be still nearer to me in any time of trouble. At one such time when the shadow which must some time darken every door, hovered at ours, he had the strength to make me face it and try to realize, while it was still there, that it was not cruel and not evil. It passed, for that time, but the sense of his help remained; and in my own case I can testify of the potent tenderness which all who knew him must have known in him. But in bearing my witness I feel accused, almost as if he were present, by his fastidious reluctance from any recognition of his helpfulness. When this came in the form of gratitude taking credit to itself in a pose which reflected honor upon him as the architect of greatness, he was delightfully impatient of it, and he was most amusingly dramatic in reproducing the consciousness of certain ineffectual alumni who used to overwhelm him at Commencement solemnities with some such pompous acknowledgment as, "Professor Child, all that I have become, sir, I owe to your influence in my college career." He did, with delicious mockery, the old-fashioned intellectual *poseurs* among the students, who used to walk the groves of Harvard with bent head, and the left arm crossing the back, while the other lodged its hand in the breast of the high-buttoned frock-coat; and I could fancy that his classes in college did not form the sunniest exposure for young folly and vanity. I know that he was intolerant of any manner of insincerity, and no flattery could take him off his guard. I have seen him meet this with a cutting phrase of rejection, and no man was more apt at snubbing the patronage that offers itself at times to all men. But mostly he wished to do people pleasure, and he seemed always to be studying how to do it; as for need, I am sure that worthy and unworthy want had alike the way to his heart.

Children were always his friends, and they repaid with adoration the affection which he divided with them and with his flowers. I recall him in no moments so characteristic as those he spent in making the little ones laugh out of their hearts at his drolling, some festive evening in his house, and those he gave to sharing with you his joy in his gardening. This, I believe, began with violets, and it went on to roses, which he grew in a splendor and profusion impossible to any but a true lover with a genuine gift for them. Like Lowell, he spent his summers in Cambridge, and in the afternoon, you could find him digging or pruning among his roses with an ardor which few caprices of the weather could interrupt. He would lift himself from their ranks, which he scarcely over-topped, as you came up the footway to his door, and peer purblindly across at you. If he knew you at once, he traversed the nodding and swaying bushes, to give you the hand free of the trowel or knife; or if you got indoors unseen by him he would come in holding towards you some exquisite blossom that weighed down the tip of its long stem with a succession of hospitable obeisances.

He graced with unaffected poetry a life of as hard study, of as hard work, and as varied achievement as any I have known or read of; and he played with gifts and acquirements such as in no great measure have made reputations. He had a rare and lovely humor which could amuse itself both in English and Italian with such an airy burletta as "Il Pesceballo" (he wrote it in Metastasian Italian, and Lowell put it in libretto English); he had a critical sense as sound as it was subtle in all literature; and whatever he wrote he imbued with the charm of a style finely personal to himself. His learning in the line of his Harvard teaching included an early English scholarship unrivalled in his time, and his researches in ballad literature left no corner of it untouched. I fancy this part of his study was peculiarly pleasant to him; for he loved simple and natural things, and the beauty which he found nearest life. At least he scorned the pedantic affectations of literary superiority; and he used to quote with joyous laughter the swelling exclamation of an Italian critic who proposed to leave the summits of polite learning for a moment, with the cry, "*Scendiamo fra il popolo !*" (Let us go down among the people.)

II

Of course it was only so hard worked a man who could take thought and trouble for another. He once took thought for me at a time when it was very important to me, and when he took the trouble to secure for me an engagement to deliver that course of Lowell lectures in Boston, which I have said Lowell had the courage to go in town to hear. I do not remember whether Professor Child was equal to so much, but he would have been if it were necessary; and I rather rejoice now in the belief that he did not seek quite that martyrdom.

He had done more than enough for me, but he had done only what he was always willing to do for others. In the form of a favor to himself he brought into my life the great happiness of intimately knowing Hjalmar Hjorth Boyesen, whom he had found one summer day among the shelves in the Harvard library, and found to be a poet and an intending novelist. I do not remember now just how this fact imparted itself to the professor, but literature is of easily cultivated confidence in youth, and possibly the revelation was spontaneous. At any rate, as a susceptible young editor, I was asked to meet my potential contributor at the professor's two o'clock dinner, and when we came to coffee in the study, Boyesen took from the pocket nearest his heart a chapter of *Gunnar*, and read it to us.

Perhaps the good professor who brought us together had plotted to have both novel and novelist make their impression at once upon the youthful sub-editor; but at any rate they did not fail of an effect. I believe it was that chapter where Gunnar and Ragnhild dance and sing a *stev* together, for I associate with that far happy time the rich mellow tones of the poet's voice in the poet's verse. These were most characteristic of him, and it is as if I might put my ear against the ethereal wall beyond which he is rapt and hear them yet.

Our meeting was on a lovely afternoon of summer, and the odor of the professor's roses stole in at the open windows, and became part of the gentle event. Boyesen walked home with me, and for a fortnight after I think we parted only to dream of the literature which we poured out upon each other in every waking moment. I had just learned to know Björnson's stories, and Boyesen told me of his poetry and of his drama, which in even measure embodied the great Norse literary movement, and filled

me with the wonder and delight of that noble revolt against convention, that brave return to nature and the springs of poetry
in the heart and the speech of the common people. Literature
was Boyesen's religion more than the Swedenborgian philosophy
in which we had both been spiritually nurtured, and at every
step of our mounting friendship we found ourselves on common
ground in our worship of it. I was a decade his senior, but at
thirty-five I was not yet so stricken in years as not to be able fully
to rejoice in the ardor which fused his whole being in an incandescent poetic mass. I have known no man who loved poetry
more generously and passionately; and I think he was above all
things a poet. His work took the shape of scholarship, fiction,
criticism, but poetry gave it all a touch of grace and beauty. Some
years after this first meeting of ours I remember a pathetic
moment with him, when I asked him why he had not written
any verse of late, and he answered, as if still in sad astonishment
at the fact, that he had found life was not all poetry. In those
earlier days I believe he really thought it was!

Perhaps it really is, and certainly in the course of a life that
stretched almost to half a century Boyesen learned more and more
to see the poetry of the every-day world at least as the material of
art. He did battle valiantly for that belief in many polemics,
which I suppose gave people a sufficiently false notion of him;
and he showed his faith by works in fiction which better illustrated his motive. *Gunnar* stands at the beginning of these works,
and at the farthest remove from it in matter and method stands
The Mammon of Unrighteousness. The lovely idyl won him fame and
friendship, and the great novel added neither to him, though he
had put the experience and the observation of his ripened life
into it. Whether it is too late or too early for it to win the place in
literature which it merits I do not know; but it always seemed to
me the very spite of fate that it should have failed of popular
effect. Yet I must own that it has so failed, and I own this without
bitterness toward *Gunnar*, which embalmed the spirit of his
youth as *The Mammon of Unrighteousness* embodied the thought of
his manhood.

III

It was my pleasure, my privilege, to bring *Gunnar* before the public as editor of the *Atlantic Monthly,* and to second the author in many a struggle with the strange idiom he had cast the story in. The proofs went back and forth between us till the author had profited by every hint and suggestion of the editor. He was quick to profit by any hint, and he never made the same mistake twice. He lived his English as fast as he learned it; the right word became part of him; and he put away the wrong word with instant and final rejection. He had not learned American English without learning newspaper English, but if one touched a phrase of it in his work, he felt in his nerves, which are the ultimate arbiters in such matters, its difference from true American and true English. It was wonderful how apt and how elect his diction was in those days; it seemed as if his thought clothed itself in the fittest phrase without his choosing. In his poetry he had extraordinary good fortune from the first; his mind had an apparent affinity with what was most native, most racy in our speech; and I have just been looking over *Gunnar* and marvelling anew at the felicity and the beauty of his phrasing.

I do not know whether those who read his books stop much to consider how rare his achievement was in the mere means of expression. Our speech is rather more hospitable than most, and yet I can remember but five other writers born to different languages, who have handled English with anything like his mastery. Two Italians, Ruffini the novelist, and Gallenga the journalist; two Germans, Carl Schurz and Carl Hillebrand, and the Dutch novelist Maarten Maartens, have some of them equalled but none of them surpassed him. Yet he was a man grown when he began to speak and to write English, though I believe he studied it somewhat in Norway before he came to America. What English he knew he learned the use of here, and in the measure of its idiomatic vigor we may be proud of it as Americans.

He had least of his native grace, I think, in his criticism; and yet as a critic he had qualities of rare temperance, acuteness, and knowledge. He had very decided convictions in literary art; one kind of thing he believed was good and all other kinds less good down to what was bad; but he was not a bigot, and he made allowances for art in error. His hand fell heavy only upon those heretics who not merely denied the faith but pretended that artifice was better than nature, that decoration was more than structure, that make-believe was something you could live by as you live by truth. He was not strongest, however, in damnatory criticism. His spirit was too large, too generous to dwell in that, and it rose rather to its full height in his appreciations of the great authors whom he loved, and whom he commented from the plenitude of his scholarship as well as from his delighted sense of their grandeur. Here he was almost as fine as in his poetry, and only less fine than in his more fortunate essays in fiction.

After *Gunnar* he was a long while in striking another note so true. He did not strike it again till he wrote *The Mammon of Unrighteousness*, and after that he was sometimes of a wandering and uncertain touch. There are certain stories of his which I cannot read without a painful sense of their inequality not only to his talent, but to his knowledge of human nature, and of American character. He understood our character quite as well as he understood our language, but at times he seemed not to do so. I think these were the times when he was overworked, and ought to have been resting instead of writing. In such fatigue one loses command of alien words, alien situations; and in estimating Boyesen's achievements we must never forget that he was born strange to our language and to our life. In *Gunnar* he handled the one with grace and charm; in his great novel he handled both with masterly strength. I call *The Mammon of Unrighteousness* a great novel, and I am quite willing to say that I know few novels by born Americans that surpass it in dealing with American types and conditions. It has the vast horizon of the masterpieces of fictions; its meanings are not for its characters alone, but for every reader of it; when you close the book the story is not at an end.

I have a pang in praising it, for I remember that my praise cannot please him any more. But it was a book worthy the powers which could have given us yet greater things if they had not been spent on lesser things. Boyesen could "toil terribly," but for his fame he did not always toil wisely, though he gave himself as utterly in his unwise work as in his best; it was always the best he could do. Several years after our first meeting in Cambridge, he went to live in New York, a city where money counts for more and goes for less than in any other city of the world, and he could not resist the temptation to write more and more when he should have written less and less. He never wrote anything that was not worth reading, but he wrote too much for one who was giving himself with all his conscience to his academic work in the university honored by his gifts and his attainments, and was lecturing far and near in the vacations which should have been days and weeks and months of leisure. The wonder is that even such a stock of health as his could stand the strain so long, but he had no vices, and his only excesses were in the direction of the work which he loved so well. When a man adds to his achievements every year, we are apt to forget the things he has already done; and I think it well to remind the reader that Boyesen, who died at forty-eight, had written, besides articles, reviews, and lectures unnumbered, four volumes of scholarly criticism on German and Scandinavian literature, a volume of literary and social essays, a popular history of Norway, a volume of poems, twelve volumes of fiction, and four books for boys.

Boyesen's energies were inexhaustible. He was not content to be merely a scholar, merely an author; he wished to be an active citizen, to take his part in honest politics, and to live for his day in things that most men of letters shun. His experience in them helped him to know American life better and to appreciate it more justly, both in its good and its evil; and as a matter of fact he knew us very well. His acquaintance with us had been wide and varied beyond that of most of our literary men, and touched many aspects of our civilization which remain unknown to most Americans. When he died he had been a journalist in Chicago, and a teacher in Ohio; he had been a professor in Cornell University and a literary free lance in New York; and everywhere his eyes and ears had kept themselves open. As a teacher he learned to know the more fortunate or the more ambitious of our youth, and as a lecturer his knowledge was continually extending itself among all ages and classes of Americans.

He was through and through a Norseman, but he was none the less a very American. Between Norsk and Yankee there is an affinity of spirit more intimate than the ties of race. Both have the common-sense view of life; both are unsentimental. When Boyesen told me that among the Norwegians men never kissed each other, as the Germans, and the Frenchmen, and the Italians do, I perceived that we stood upon common ground. When he explained the democratic character of society in Norway, I could well understand how he should find us a little behind his own countrymen in the practice, if not the theory of equality, though they lived under a king and we under a president. But he was proud of his American citizenship; he knew all that it meant, at its best, for humanity. He divined that the true expression of America was not civic, not social, but domestic almost, and that the people in the simplest homes, or those who remained in the tradition of a simple home life, were the true Americans as yet, whatever the future Americans might be.

When I first knew him he was chafing with the impatience of youth and ambition at what he thought his exile in the West. There was, to be sure, a difference between Urbana, Ohio, and Cambridge, Massachusetts, and he realized the difference in the extreme and perhaps beyond it. I tried to make him believe that if a man had one or two friends anywhere who loved letters and sympathized with him in his literary attempts, it was incentive enough; but of course he wished to be in the centres of literature, as we all do; and he never was content until he had set his face and his foot Eastward. It was a great step for him from the Swedenborgian school at Urbana to the young university at Ithaca; and I remember his exultation in making it. But he could not rest there, and in a few years he resigned his professorship, and came to New York, where he entered high-heartedly upon the struggle with fortune which ended in his appointment in Columbia.

New York is a mart and not a capital, in literature as well as in other things, and doubtless he increasingly felt this. I know that there came a time when he no longer thought the West must be exile for a literary man; and his latest visits to its summer schools as a lecturer impressed him with the genuineness of the interest felt there in culture of all kinds. He spoke of this, with a due sense of what was pathetic as well as what was grotesque in some of its manifestations; and I think that in reconciling himself to our popular crudeness for the sake of our popular earnestness, he completed his naturalization, in the only sense in which our citizenship is worth having.

I do not wish to imply that he forgot his native land, or ceased to love it proudly and tenderly. He kept for Norway the fondness which the man sitting at his own hearth feels for the home of his boyhood. He was of good family; his people were people of substance and condition, and he could have had an easier life there than here. He could have won even wider fame, and doubtless if he had remained in Norway, he would have been one of that group of great Norwegians who have given their little land renown surpassed by that of no other in the modern republic of letters. The name of Boyesen would have been set with the names of Björnson, of Ibsen, of Kielland, and of Lie. But when once he had seen America (at the wish of his father, who had visited the United States before him), he thought only of becoming an American. When I first knew him he was full of the poetry of his mother-land; his talk was of fjords and glaciers, of firs and birches, of hulders and nixies, of housemen and gardsmen; but he was glad to be here, and I think he never regretted that he had cast his lot with us. Always, of course, he had the deepest interest in his country and countrymen. He stood the friend of every Norwegian who came to him in want or trouble, and they came to him freely and frequently. He sympathized strongly with Norway in her quarrel with Sweden, and her wish for equality as well as autonomy; and though he did not go all lengths with the national party, he was decided in his feeling that Sweden was unjust to her sister kingdom, and strenuous for the principles of the Norwegian leaders.

But, as I have said, poetry was what his ardent spirit mainly meditated in that hour when I first knew him in Cambridge, before we had either of us grown old and sad, if not wise. He overflowed with it, and he talked as little as he dreamed of anything else in the vast half-summer we spent together. He was constantly at my house, where in an absence of my family I was living bachelor, and where we sat indoors and talked, or sauntered outdoors and talked, with our heads in a cloud of fancies, not unmixed with the mosquitoes of Cambridge: if I could have back the fancies, I would be willing to have the mosquitoes with them. He looked the poetry he lived: his eyes were the blue of sunlit fjords; his brown silken hair was thick on the crown which it later abandoned to a scholarly baldness; his soft, red lips half hid a boyish pout in the youthful beard and mustache. He was short of stature, but of a stalwart breadth of frame, and his voice was of a peculiar and endearing quality, indescribably mellow and tender when he read his verse.

I have hardly the right to dwell so long upon him here, for he was only a sojourner in Cambridge, but the memory of that early intimacy is too much for my sense of proportion. As I have hinted, our intimacy was renewed afterwards, when I too came to live in New York, where as long as he was in this *dolce lome*, he hardly let a week go by without passing a long evening with me. Our talk was still of literature and life, but more of life than of literature, and we seldom spoke of those old times. I still found him true to the ideals which had clarified themselves to both of us as the duty of unswerving fealty to the real thing in whatever we did. This we felt, as we had felt it long before, to be the sole source of beauty and of art, and we warmed ourselves at each other's hearts in our devotion to it, amidst a misunderstanding environment which we did not characterize by so mild an epithet. Boyesen, indeed, out-realisted me, in the polemics of our æsthetics, and sometimes when an unbeliever was by, I willingly left to my friend the affirmation of our faith, not without some quaking at his unsparing strenuousness in disciplining the heretic. But now that ardent and active soul is Elsewhere, and I have ceased even to expect the ring, which, making itself heard at the late hour of his coming, I knew always to be his and not another's. That mechanical expectation of those who will come no more is something terrible, but when even that ceases, we know the irreparability of our loss, and begin to realize how much of ourselves they have taken with them.

IV

It was some years before the Boyesen summer, which was the fourth or fifth of our life in Cambridge, that I made the acquaintance of a man, very much my senior, who remains one of the vividest personalities in my recollection. I speak of him in this order perhaps because of an obscure association with Boyesen through their religious faith, which was also mine. But Henry James was incommensurably more Swedenborgian than either of us: he lived and thought and felt Swedenborg with an entirety and intensity far beyond the mere assent of other men. He did not do this in any stupidly exclusive way, but in the most luminously inclusive way, with a constant reference of these vain mundane shadows to the spiritual realities from which they project. His piety, which sometimes expressed itself in terms of alarming originality and freedom, was too large for any ecclesiastical limits, and one may learn from the books which record it, how absolutely individual his interpretations of Swedenborg were. Clarifications they cannot be called, and in that other world whose substantial verity was the inspiration of his life here, the two sages may by this time have met and agreed to differ as to some points in the doctrine of the Seer. In such a case, I cannot imagine the apostle giving way; and I do not say he would be wrong to insist, but I think he might now be willing to allow that the exegetic pages which sentence by sentence were so brilliantly suggestive, had sometimes a collective opacity which the most resolute vision could not penetrate. He put into this dark wisdom the most brilliant intelligence ever brought to the service of his mystical faith; he lighted it up with flashes of the keenest wit and bathed it in the glow of a lambent humor, so that it is truly wonderful to me how it should remain so unintelligible. But I have only tried to read certain of his books, and perhaps if I had persisted in the effort I might have found them all as clear at last as the one which seems to me the clearest, and is certainly most encouragingly suggestive: I mean the one called *Society the Redeemed Form of Man.*

He had his whole being in his belief; it had not only liberated him from the bonds of the Calvinistic theology in which his youth was trammelled, but it had secured him against the conscious ethicism of the prevailing Unitarian doctrine which supremely worshipped Conduct; and it had colored his vocabulary to such strange effects that he spoke of *moral men* with abhorrence, as more hopelessly lost than sinners. Any one whose sphere tempted him to recognition of the foibles of others, he called the Devil; but in spite of his perception of such diabolism, he was rather fond of yielding to it, for he had a most trenchant tongue. I myself once fell under his condemnation as the Devil, by having too plainly shared his joy in his characterization of certain fellow-men; perhaps a group of Bostonians from whom he had just parted and whose reciprocal pleasure of themselves he presented in the image of "simmering in their own fat and putting a nice brown on each other."

Swedenborg himself he did not spare as a man. He thought that very likely his life had those lapses in it which some of his followers deny; and he regarded him, on the æsthetical side, as essentially commonplace, and as probably chosen for his prophetic function just because of his imaginative nullity: his tremendous revelations could be the more distinctly and unmistakably inscribed upon an intelligence of that sort, which alone could render again a strictly literal report of them.

As to some other sorts of believers who thought they had a special apprehension of the truth, he had no mercy upon them if they betrayed, however innocently, any self-complacency in their possession. I went one evening to call upon him with a dear old Shaker elder, who had the misfortune to say that his people believed themselves to be living the angelic life. James fastened upon him with the suggestion that according to Swedenborg the most celestial angels were unconscious of their own perfection, and that if the Shakers felt they were of angelic condition they were probably the sport of the hells. I was very glad to get my poor old friend off alive, and to find that he was not even aware of being cut asunder: I did not invite him to shake himself.

With spiritualists James had little or no sympathy; he was not so impatient of them as the Swedenborgians commonly are, and he probably acknowledged a measure of verity in the spiritistic phenomena; but he seemed rather incurious concerning them, and he must have regarded them as superfluities of naughtiness, mostly; as emanations from the hells. His powerful and penetrating intellect interested itself with all social and civil facts through his religion. He was essentially religious, but he was very consciously a citizen, with most decided opinions upon political questions. My own darkness as to anything like social reform was then so dense that I cannot now be clear as to his feeling in such matters, but I have the impression that it was far more radical than I could understand. He was of a very merciful mind regarding things often held in pitiless condemnation, but of charity, as it is commonly understood, he had misgivings. He would never have turned away from him that asketh; but he spoke with regret of some of his benefactions in the past, large gifts of money to individuals, which he now thought had done more harm than good.

I never knew him to judge men by the society scale. He was most human in his relations with others, and was in correspondence with all sorts of people seeking light and help; he answered their letters and tried to instruct them, and no one was so low or weak but he or she could reach him on his or her own level, though he had his humorous perception of their foibles and disabilities; and he had that keen sense of the grotesque which often goes with the kindliest nature. He told of his dining, early in life, next a fellow-man from Cape Cod at the Astor House, where such a man could seldom have found himself. When they were served with meat this neighbor asked if he would mind his putting his fat on James's plate: he disliked fat. James said that he considered the request, and seeing no good reason against it, consented.

He could be cruel with his tongue when he fancied insincerity or pretence, and then cruelly sorry for the hurt he gave. He was indeed tremulously sensitive, not only for himself but for others, and would offer atonement far beyond the measure of the offence he supposed himself to have given.

At all times he thought originally in words of delightful originality, which painted a fact with the greatest vividness. Of a person who had a nervous twitching of the face, and who wished to call up a friend to them, he said, "He *spasmed* to the fellow across the room, and introduced him." His written style had traits of the same bold adventurousness, but it was his speech which was most captivating. As I write of him I see him before me: his white bearded face, with a kindly intensity which at first glance seemed fierce, the mouth humorously shaping the mustache, the eyes vague behind the glasses; his sensitive hand gripping the stick on which he rested his weight to ease it from the artificial limb he wore.

v

The Goethean face and figure of Louis Agassiz were in those days to be seen in the shady walks of Cambridge to which for me they lent a Weimarish quality, in the degree that in Weimar itself a few years ago, I felt a quality of Cambridge. Agassiz, of course, was Swiss and Latin, and not Teutonic, but he was of the Continental European civilization, and was widely different from the other Cambridge men in everything but love of the place. "He is always an *Europäer*," said Lowell one day, in distinguishing concerning him; and for any one who had tasted the flavor of the life beyond the ocean and the channel, this had its charm.

Yet he was extremely fond of his adoptive compatriots, and no alien born had a truer or tenderer sense of New England character. I have an idea that no one else of his day could have got so much money for science out of the General Court of Massachusetts; and I have heard him speak with the wisest and warmest appreciation of the hard material from which he was able to extract this treasure. The legislators who voted appropriations for his Museum and his other scientific objects were not usually lawyers or professional men, with the perspectives of a liberal education, but were hard-fisted farmers, who had a grip of the State's money as if it were their own, and yet gave it with intelligent munificence. They understood that he did not want it for himself, and had no interested aim in getting it; they knew that, as he once said, he had no time to make money, and wished to use it solely for the advancement of learning; and with this understanding they were ready to help him generously. He compared their liberality with that of kings and princes, when these patronized science, with a recognition of the superior plebeian generosity. It was on the veranda of his summer house at Nahant, while he lay in the hammock, talking of this, that I heard him refer also to the offer which Napoleon III. had made him, inviting him upon certain splendid conditions to come to Paris after he had established himself in Cambridge. He said that he had not come to America without going over every such possibility in his own mind, and deciding beforehand against it. He was a republican, by nationality and by preference, and was entirely satisfied with his position and environment in New England.

Outside of his scientific circle in Cambridge he was more friends with Longfellow than with any one else, I believe, and Longfellow told me how, after the doctors had condemned Agassiz to inaction, on account of his failing health, he had broken down in his friend's study, and wept like an Europäer, and lamented, "I shall never finish my work!" Some papers which he had begun to write for the magazine, in contravention of the Darwinian theory, or part of it, which it is known Agassiz did not accept, remained part of the work which he never finished. After his death, I wished Professor Jeffries Wyman to write of him in the *Atlantic*, but he excused himself on account of his many labors, and then he voluntarily spoke of Agassiz's methods, which he agreed with rather than his theories, being himself thoroughly Darwinian. I think he said Agassiz was the first to imagine establishing a fact not from a single example, but from examples indefinitely repeated. If it was a question of something about robins for instance, he would have a hundred robins examined before he would receive an appearance as a fact.

Of course no preconception or prepossession of his own was suffered to bar his way to the final truth he was seeking, and he joyously renounced even a conclusion if he found it mistaken. I do not know whether Mrs. Agassiz has put into her interesting life of him, a delightful story which she told me about him. He came to her beaming one day, and demanded, "You know I have always held such and such an opinion about a certain group of fossil fishes?" "Yes, yes!" "Well, I have just been reading ———'s new book, and he has shown me that there isn't the least truth in my theory"; and he burst into a laugh of unalloyed pleasure in relinquishing his error.

I could touch science at Cambridge only on its literary and social side, of course, and my meetings with Agassiz were not many. I recall a dinner at his house to Mr. Bret Harte, when the poet came on from California, and Agassiz approached him over the coffee through their mutual scientific interest in the last meeting of the geological "Society upon the Stanislow." He quoted to the author some passages from the poem recording the final proceedings of this body, which had particularly pleased him, and I think Mr. Harte was as much amused at finding himself thus in touch with the savant, as Agassiz could ever have been with that delicious poem.

Agassiz lived at one end of Quincy Street, and James almost at the other end, with an interval between them which but poorly typified their difference of temperament. The one was all philosophical and the other all scientific, and yet towards the close of his life, Agassiz may be said to have led that movement towards the new position of science in matters of mystery which is now characteristic of it. He was ancestrally of the Swiss "Brahminical caste," as so many of his friends in Cambridge were of the Brahminical caste of New England; and perhaps it was the line of ancestral *pasteurs* which at last drew him back, or on, to the affirmation of an unformulated faith of his own. At any rate, before most other savants would say that they had souls of their own he became, by opening a summer school of science with prayer, nearly as consolatory to the unscientific who wished to believe they had souls, as Mr. John Fiske himself, though Mr. Fiske, as the arch-apostle of Darwinism, had arrived at nearly the same point by such a very different road.

VI

Mr. Fiske had been our neighbor in our first Cambridge home, and when we went to live in Berkeley Street, he followed with his family and placed himself across the way in a house which I already knew as the home of Richard Henry Dana, the author of *Two Years Before the Mast*. Like nearly all the other Cambridge men of my acquaintance Dana was very much my senior, and like the rest he welcomed my literary promise as cordially as if it were performance, with no suggestion of the condescension which was said to be his attitude towards many of his fellow-men. I never saw anything of this, in fact, and I suppose he may have been a blend of those patrician qualities and democratic principles which made Lowell anomalous even to himself. He is part of the antislavery history of his time, and he gave to the oppressed his strenuous help both as a man and a politician; his gifts and learning in the law were freely at their service. He never lost his interest in those white slaves, whose brutal bondage he remembered as bound with them in his *Two Years Before the Mast*, and any luckless seaman with a case or cause might count upon his friendship as surely as the black slaves of the South. He was able to temper his indignation for their oppression with a humorous perception of what was droll in its agents and circumstances;

and I wish I could recall all that he said once about sea-etiquette on merchant vessels, where the chief mate might no more speak to the captain at table without being addressed by him than a subject might put a question to his sovereign. He was amusing in his stories of the Pacific trade in which he said it was very noble to deal in furs from the Northwest, and very ignoble to deal in hides along the Mexican and South American coasts. Every ship's master wished naturally to be in the fur-carrying trade, and in one of Dana's instances, two vessels encounter in mid-ocean, and exchange the usual parley as to their respective ports of departure and destination. The final demand comes through the trumpet, "What cargo?" and the captain so challenged yields to temptation and roars back *"Furs!"* A moment of hesitation elapses, and then the questioner pursues, "Here and there *a horn?"*

There were other distinctions, of which seafaring men of other days were keenly sensible, and Dana dramatized the meeting of a great, swelling East Indiaman, with a little Atlantic trader, which has hailed her. She shouts back through her captain's trumpet that she is from Calcutta, and laden with silks, spices, and other orient treasures, and in her turn she requires like answer from the sail which has presumed to enter into parley with her. "What cargo?" The trader confesses to a mixed cargo for Boston, and to the final question, her master replies in meek apology, *"Only from Liverpool, sir!"* and scuttles down the horizon as swiftly as possible.

Dana was not of the Cambridge men whose calling was in Cambridge. He was a lawyer in active practice, and he went every day to Boston. One was apt to meet him in those horse-cars which formerly tinkled back and forth between the two cities, and which were often so full of one's acquaintance that they had all the social elements of an afternoon tea. They were abusively overcrowded at times, of course, and one might easily see a prime literary celebrity swaying from a strap, or hanging uneasily by the hand-rail to the lower steps of the back platform. I do not mean that I ever happened to see the author of *Two Years Before the Mast* in either fact, but in his celebrity he had every qualification for the illustration of my point. His book probably carried the American name farther and wider than any American books except those of Irving and Cooper at a day when our writers were very little known, and our literature was the only infant industry not fostered against foreign ravage, but expressly left to harden and strengthen itself as it best might in a heartless neglect even at home. The book was delightful, and I remember it from a reading of thirty years ago, as of the stuff that classics are made of. I venture no conjecture as to its present popularity, but of all books relating to the sea I think it is the best. The author when I knew him was still Richard Henry Dana, Jr., his father, the aged poet, who first established the name in the public recognition, being alive, though past literary activity. It was distinctively a literary race, and in the actual generation it has given proofs of its continued literary vitality in the romance of *Espíritu Santo* by the youngest daughter of the Dana I knew.

VII

There could be no stronger contrast to him in origin, education, and character than a man who lived at the same time in Cambridge, and who produced a book which in its final fidelity to life is not unworthy to be named with *Two Years Before the Mast*. Ralph Keeler wrote the *Vagabond Adventures* which he had lived. I have it on my heart to name him in the presence of our great literary men not only because I had an affection for him, tenderer than I then knew, but because I believe his book is worthier of more remembrance than it seems to enjoy. I was reading it only the other day, and I found it delightful, and much better than I imagined when I accepted for the *Atlantic* the several papers which it is made up of. I am not sure but it belongs to the great literature in that fidelity to life which I have spoken of, and which the author brought himself to practise with such difficulty, and under so much stress from his editor. He really wanted to *fake* it at times, but he was docile at last and did it so honestly that it tells the history of his strange career in much better terms than it can be given again. He had been, as he claimed, "a cruel uncle's ward" in his early orphanhood, and while yet almost a child he had run away from home, to fulfil his heart's desire of becoming a clog-dancer in a troupe of negro minstrels. But it was first his fate to be cabin-boy and bootblack on a lake steamboat, and meet with many squalid adventures, scarcely to be matched outside of a Spanish picaresque novel. When he did become a dancer (and even a *danseuse*) of the sort he aspired to be, the fruition of his hopes was so little what he imagined that he was very willing to leave the Floating Palace on the Mississippi in which his troupe voyaged and exhibited, and enter the college of the Jesuit Fathers at Cape Girardeau in Missouri. They were very good to him, and in their charge he picked up a good deal more Latin, if not less Greek than another strolling player who also took to literature. From college Keeler went to Europe, and then to California, whence he wrote me that he was coming on to Boston with the manuscript of a novel which he wished me to read for the magazine. I reported against it to my chief, but nothing could shake Keeler's faith in it, until he had printed it at his own cost, and known it fail instantly and decisively. He had come to Cambridge to see it through the press, and he remained there four or five years, with certain brief absences. Then, during the Cuban insurrection of the early seventies, he accepted the invitation of a New York paper to go to Cuba as its correspondent.

"Don't go, Keeler," I entreated him, when he came to tell me of his intention. "They'll garrote you down there."

"Well," he said, with the air of being pleasantly interested by the coincidence, as he stood on my study hearth with his feet wide apart in a fashion he had, and gayly flirted his hand in the air, "that's what Aldrich says, and he's agreed to write my biography, on condition that I make a last dying speech when they bring me out on the plaza to do it, 'If I had taken the advice of my friend T. B. Aldrich, author of *Marjorie Daw and Other People*, I should not now be in this place.'"

He went, and he did not come back. He was not indeed

garroted as his friends had promised, but he was probably assassinated on the steamer by which he sailed from Santiago, for he never arrived in Havana, and was never heard of again.

I now realize that I loved him, though I did as little to show it as men commonly do. If I am to meet somewhere else the friends who are no longer here, I should like to meet Ralph Keeler, and I would take some chances of meeting in a happy place a soul which had by no means kept itself unspotted, but which in all its consciousness of error, cheerfully trusted that "the Almighty was not going to scoop any of us." The faith worded so grotesquely could not have been more simply or humbly affirmed, and no man I think could have been more helplessly sincere. He had nothing of that false self-respect which forbids a man to own himself wrong promptly and utterly when need is; and in fact he owned to some things in his checkered past which would hardly allow him any sort of self-respect. He had always an essential gayety not to be damped by any discipline, and a docility which expressed itself in cheerful compliance. "Why do you use *bias* for opinion?" I demanded, in going over a proof with him. "Oh, because I'm such an ass—such a bi-ass."

He had a philosophy which he liked to impress with a vivid touch on his listener's shoulder: "Put your finger on the present moment and enjoy it. It's the only one you've got, or ever will have." This light and joyous creature could not but be a Pariah among our Brahmins, and I need not say that I never met him in any of the great Cambridge houses. I am not sure that he was a *persona grata* to every one in my own, for Keeler was framed rather for men's liking, and Mr. Aldrich and I had our subtleties as to whether his mind about women was not so Chinese as somewhat to infect his manner. Keeler was too really modest to be of any rebellious mind towards the society which ignored him, and of too sweet a cheerfulness to be greatly vexed by it. He lived on in the house of a suave old actor, who oddly made his home in Cambridge, and he continued of a harmless bohemianism in his daily walk, which included lunches at Boston restaurants as often as he could get you to let him give them you, if you were of his acquaintance. On a Sunday he would appear coming out of the post-office usually at the hour when all cultivated Cambridge was coming for its letters, and wave a glad hand in air, and shout a blithe salutation to the friend he had marked for his companion in a morning stroll. The stroll was commonly over the flats towards Brighton (I do not know why, except perhaps that it was out of the beat of the better element) and the talk was mainly of literature, in which he was doing less than he meant to do, and which he seemed never able quite to feel was not a branch of the Show Business, and might not be legitimately worked by like advertising, though he truly loved and honored it.

I suppose it was not altogether a happy life, and Keeler had his moments of amusing depression, which showed their shadows in his smiling face. He was of a slight figure and low stature, with hands and feet of almost womanish littleness. He was very blonde, and his restless eyes were blue; he wore his yellow beard in whiskers only, which he pulled nervously but perhaps did not get to droop so much as he wished.

VIII

Keeler was a native of Ohio, and there lived at Cambridge when I first came there an Indianian, more accepted by literary society, who was of real quality as a poet. Forceythe Willson, whose poem of "The Old Sergeant" Doctor Holmes used to read publicly in the closing year of the civil war, was of a Western altitude of figure, and of an extraordinary beauty of face in an oriental sort. He had large, dark eyes with clouded whites; his full, silken beard was of a flashing Persian blackness. He was excessively nervous, to such an extreme that when I first met him at Longfellow's, he could not hold himself still in his chair. I think this was an effect of shyness in him, as well as physical, for afterwards when I went to find him in his own house he was much more at ease.

He preferred to receive me in the dim, large hall after opening his door to me himself, and we sat down there and talked, I remember, of supernatural things. He was much interested in spiritualism, and he had several stories to tell of his own experience in such matters. But none was so good as one which I had at second hand from Lowell, who thought it almost the best ghost story he had ever heard. The spirit of Willson's father appeared to him, and stood before him. Willson was accustomed to apparitions, and so he said simply, "Won't you sit down, father?" The phantom put out his hand to lay hold of a chair-back as some people do in taking a seat, and his shadowy arm passed through the frame-work. "Ah!" he said, "I forgot that I was not substance."

I do not know whether "The Old Sergeant" is ever read now; it has probably passed with other great memories of the great war; and I am afraid none of Willson's other verse is remembered. But he was then a distinct literary figure, and not to be left out of the count of our poets. I did not see him again. Shortly afterwards I heard that he had left Cambridge with signs of consumption, which must have run a rapid course, for a very little later came the news of his death.

IX

The most devoted Cantabrigian, after Lowell, whom I knew, would perhaps have contended that if he had stayed with us Willson might have lived; for John Holmes affirmed a faith in the virtues of the place which ascribed almost an aseptic character to its air, and when he once listened to my own complaints of an obstinate cold, he cheered himself, if not me, with the declaration, "Well, *one* thing, Mr. Howells, Cambridge never let a man keep a cold yet!"

If he had said it was better to live in Cambridge with a cold than elsewhere without one I should have believed him; as it was, Cambridge bore him out in his assertion, though she took her own time to do it.

Lowell had talked to me of him before I met him, celebrating his peculiar humor with that affection which was not always so discriminating, and Holmes was one of the first Cambridge men I knew. I knew him first in the charming old Colonial house in which his famous brother and he were born. It was demolished long before I left Cambridge, but in memory it still stands on the ground since occupied by the Hemenway Gymnasium, and shows for me through that bulk a phantom frame of Continental buff in the shadow of elms that are shadows themselves. The *genius loci* was limping about the pleasant mansion with the rheumatism which then expressed itself to his friends in a resolute smile, but which now insists upon being an essential trait of the full-length presence to my mind: a short stout figure, helped out with a cane, and a grizzled head with features formed to win the heart rather than the eye of the beholder. In one of his own eyes there was a cast of such winning humor and geniality that it took the liking more than any beauty could have done, and the sweetest, shy laugh in the world went with this cast.

I long wished to get him to write something for the magazine, and at last I prevailed with him to review a history of Cambridge which had come out. He did it charmingly of course, for he loved more to speak of Cambridge than anything else. He held his native town in an idolatry which was not blind, but which was none the less devoted because he was aware of her droll points and her weak points. He always celebrated these as so many virtues, and I think it was my own passion for her that first commended me to him. I was not her son, but he felt that this was my misfortune more than my fault, and he seemed more and more to forgive it. After we had got upon the terms of editor and contributor, we met oftener than before, though I do not now remember that I ever persuaded him to write again for me. Once he gave me something, and then took it back, with a self-distrust of it which I could not overcome.

When the Holmes house was taken down, he went to live with an old domestic in a small house on the street amusingly called Appian Way. He had certain rooms of her, and his own table, but he would not allow that he was ever anything but a lodger in the place, where he continued till he died. In the process of time he came so far to trust his experience of me, that he formed the habit of giving me an annual supper. Some days before this event, he would appear in my study, and with divers delicate and tentative approaches, nearly always of the same tenor, he would say that he should like to ask my family to an oyster supper with him. "But you know," he would explain, "I haven't a house of my own to ask you to, and I should like to give you the supper *here.*" When I had agreed to this suggestion with due gravity, he would inquire our engagements, and then say, as if a great load were off his mind, "Well, then, I will send up a few oysters to-morrow," or whatever day we had fixed on; and after a little more talk to take the strangeness out of the affair, would go his way. On the day appointed the fish-man would come with several gallons of oysters, which he reported Mr. Holmes had asked him to bring, and in the evening the giver of the feast would reappear, with a lank oil-cloth bag, sagged by some bottles of wine. There was always a bottle of red wine, and sometimes a bottle of champagne, and he had taken the precaution to send some crackers beforehand, so that the supper should be as entirely of his own giving as possible. He was forced to let us do the cooking and to supply the cold-slaw, and perhaps he indemnified himself for putting us to these charges and for the use of our linen and silver, by the vast superfluity of his oysters, with which we remained inundated for days. He did not care to eat many himself, but seemed content to fancy doing us a pleasure; and I have known few greater ones in life, than in the hospitality that so oddly played the host to us at our own table.

It must have seemed incomprehensible to such a Cantabrigian that we should ever have been willing to leave Cambridge, and in fact I do not well understand it myself. But if he resented it, he never showed his resentment. As often as I happened to meet him after our defection he used me with unabated kindness, and sparkled into some gayety too ethereal for remembrance. The last time I met him was at Lowell's funeral, when I drove home with him and Curtis and Child, and in the revulsion from the stress of that saddest event, had our laugh, as people do in the presence of death, at something droll we remembered of the friend we mourned.

X

My nearest literary neighbor, when we lived in Sacramento Street, was the Rev. Dr. John G. Palfrey, the historian of New England, whose chimney-tops amid the pine-tops I could see from my study window when the leaves were off the little grove of oaks between us. He was one of the first of my acquaintances, not suffering the great disparity of our ages to count against me, but tactfully and sweetly adjusting himself to my youth in the friendly intercourse which he invited. He was a most gentle and kindly old man, with still an interest in liberal things which lasted till the infirmities of age secluded him from the world and all its interests. As is known, he had been in his prime one of the foremost of the New England antislavery men, and he had fought the good fight with a heavy heart for a brother long settled in Louisiana who sided with the South, and who after the civil war found himself disfranchised. In this temporary disability he came North to visit Doctor Palfrey upon the doctor's insistence, though at first he would have nothing to do with him, and refused even to answer his letters. "Of course," the doctor said, "I was not going to stand that from my mother's son, and I simply kept on writing." So he prevailed, but the fiery old gentleman from Louisiana was reconciled to nothing in the North but his brother, and when he came to return my visit, he quickly touched upon his cause of quarrel with us. "I can't vote," he declared, "but my coachman can, and I don't know how I'm to get the suffrage, unless my physician paints me all over with the iodine he's using for my rheumatic side."

Doctor Palfrey was most distinctly of the Brahminical caste and was long an eminent Unitarian minister, but at the time I began to know him he had long quitted the pulpit. He was so far of civic or public character as to be postmaster at Boston, when we were first neighbors, but this officiality was probably so little in keeping with his nature that it was like a return to his truer self when he ceased to hold the place, and gave his time altogether to his history. It is a work which will hardly be superseded in the interest of those who value thorough research and temperate expression. It is very just, and without endeavor for picture or drama it is to me very attractive. Much that has to be recorded of New England lacks charm, but he gave form and dignity and presence to the memories of the past, and the finer moments of that great story, he gave with the simplicity that was their best setting. It seems to me such an apology (in the old sense) as New England might have written for herself, and in fact Doctor Palfrey was a personification of New England in one of the best and truest kinds. He was refined in the essential gentleness of his heart without being refined away; he kept the faith of her Puritan tradition though he no longer kept the Puritan faith, and his defence of the Puritan severity with the witches and Quakers was as impartial as it was efficient in positing the Puritans as of their time, and rather better and not worse than other people of the same time. He was himself a most tolerant man, and his tolerance was never weak or fond; it stopped well short of condoning error, which he condemned when he preferred to leave it to its own punishment. Personally he was without any flavor of harshness; his mind was as gentle as his manner, which was one of the gentlest I have ever known.

Of as gentle make but of more pensive temper, with unexpected bursts of lyrical gayety, was Christopher Pearce Cranch, the poet, whom I had known in New York long before he came to live in Cambridge. He could not only play and sing most amusing songs, but he wrote very good poems and painted pictures perhaps not so good. I always like his Venetian pictures, for their poetic, unsentimentalized veracity, and I printed as well as liked many of his poems. During the time that I knew him more than his due share of troubles and sorrows accumulated themselves on his fine head, which the years had whitened, and gave a droop to the beautiful, white-bearded face. But he had the artist soul and the poet heart, and no doubt he could take refuge in these from the cares that shadowed his visage. My acquaintance with him in Cambridge renewed itself upon the very terms of its beginning in New York. We met at Longfellow's table,

where he lifted up his voice in the Yankee folk-song, "On Springfield Mountain there did dwell," which he gave with a perfectly
killing mock-gravity.

XI

At Cambridge the best society was better, it seems to me, than
even that of the neighboring capital. It would be rather hard to
prove this, and I must ask the reader to take my word for it, if
he wishes to believe it. The great interests in that pleasant world,
which I think does not present itself to my memory in a false
iridiscence, were the intellectual interests, and all other interests
were lost in these to such as did not seek them too insistently.

People held themselves high; they held themselves personally
aloof from people not duly assayed; their civilization was still
Puritan though their belief had long ceased to be so. They had
weights and measures stamped in an earlier time, a time surer of
itself than ours, by which they rated the merit of all comers, and
rejected such as did not bear the test. These standards were their
own, and they were satisfied with them; most Americans have no
standards of their own, but these are not satisfied even with other
people's, and so our society is in a state of tolerant and tremulous
misgiving.

Family counted in Cambridge, without doubt, as it counts in
New England everywhere, but family alone did not mean position, and the want of family did not mean the want of it. Money
still less than family commanded; one could be openly poor in
Cambridge without open shame, or shame at all, for no one was
very rich there, and no one was proud of his riches.

I do not wonder that Tourguénief thought the conditions
ideal, as Boyesen portrayed them to him; and I look back at my
own life there with wonder at my good fortune. I was sensible,
and I still am sensible this had its alloys. I was young and unknown and was making my way, and I had to suffer some of the
penalties of these disadvantages; but I do not believe that anywhere else in this ill-contrived economy, where it is vainly
imagined that the material struggle forms a high incentive and

inspiration, would my penalties have been so light. On the other hand the good that was done me I could never repay if I lived all over again for others the life that I have so long lived for myself. At times, when I had experienced from those elect spirits with whom I was associated, some act of friendship, as signal as it was delicate, I used to ask myself, how I could ever do anything unhandsome or ungenerous toward any one again, and I had a bad conscience the next time I did it.

The air of the Cambridge that I knew was sufficiently cool to be bracing, but what was of good import in me flourished in it. The life of the place had its lateral limitations; sometimes its lights failed to detect excellent things that lay beyond it; but upward it opened illimitably. I speak of it frankly because that life as I witnessed it is now almost wholly of the past. Cambridge is still the home of much that is good and fine in our literature: one realizes this if one names Colonel Thomas Wentworth Higginson, Mr. John Fiske, Mr. William James, Mr. Horace E. Scudder, not to name any others, but the first had not yet come back to live in his birthplace at the time I have been writing of, and the rest had not yet their actual prominence. One, indeed among so many absent, is still present there, whom from time to time I have hitherto named without offering him the recognition which I should have known an infringement of his preferences. But the literary Cambridge of thirty years ago could not be clearly imagined or justly estimated without taking into account the creative sympathy of a man whose contributions to our literature only partially represent what he has constantly done for the humanities. I am sure that after the easy heroes of the day are long forgot, and the noisy fames of the strenuous life shall dwindle to their essential insignificance before these of the gentle life, we shall all see in Charles Eliot Norton the eminent scholar who left the quiet of his books to become our chief citizen at the moment when he warned his countrymen of the ignominy and disaster of doing wrong.

———————

A BELATED GUEST

IT IS DOUBTFUL whether the survivor of any order of things finds compensation in the privilege, however undisputed by his contemporaries, of recording his memories of it. This is, in the first two or three instances, a pleasure. It is sweet to sit down, in the shade or by the fire, and recall names, looks, and tones from the past; and if the Absences thus entreated to become Presences are those of famous people, they lend to the fond historian a little of their lustre, in which he basks for the time with an agreeable sense of celebrity. But another time comes, and comes very soon, when the pensive pleasure changes to the pain of duty, and the precious privilege converts itself into a grievous obligation. You are unable to choose your company among those immortal shades; if one, why not another, where all seem to have a right to such gleams of this *dolce lome* as your reminiscences can shed upon them? Then, they gather so rapidly, as the years pass, in these pale realms, that one, if one continues to survive, is in danger of wearing out such welcome, great or small, as met one's recollections in the first two or three instances, if one does one's duty by each. People begin to say, and not without reason, in a world so hurried and wearied as this, "Ah, here he is again with his recollections!" Well, but if the recollections by some magical good fortune chance to concern such a contemporary of his as, say, Bret Harte, shall not he be partially justified, or at least excused?

I

My recollections of Bret Harte begin with the arrest, on the Atlantic shore, of that progress of his from the Pacific slope, which, in the simple days of 1871, was like the progress of a prince, in the universal attention and interest which met and followed it. He was indeed a prince, a fairy prince in whom every lover of his novel and enchanting art felt a patriotic property, for his promise and performance in those earliest tales of "The Luck of Roaring Camp," and "Tennessee's Partner," and "Miggles," and "The Outcasts of Poker Flat," were the earnests of an American literature to come. If it is still to come, in great measure, that is not Harte's fault, for he kept on writing those stories, in one form or another, as long as he lived. He wrote them first and last in the spirit of Dickens, which no man of his time could quite help doing, but he wrote them from the life of Bret Harte, on the soil and in the air of the newest kind of new world, and their freshness took the soul of his fellow countrymen not only with joy, but with pride such as the Europeans, who adored him much longer, could never know in him.

When the adventurous young editor who had proposed being his host for Cambridge and the Boston neighborhood, while Harte was still in San Francisco, and had not yet begun his princely progress Eastward, read of the honors that attended his coming from point to point, his courage fell, as if he had perhaps committed himself in too great an enterprise. Who was he, indeed, that he should think of making this

Dear son of memory, great heir of fame,

his guest, especially when he heard that in Chicago Harte failed of attending a banquet of honor because the givers of it had not sent a carriage to fetch him to it, as the alleged use was in San Francisco? Whether true or not, and it was probably not true in just that form, it must have been this rumor which determined his host to drive into Boston for him with the handsomest hack which the livery of Cambridge afforded, and not trust to the horse-car and the local expressman to get him and his baggage out, as he would have done with a less portentous guest. However it was, he instantly lost all fear when they met at the station, and Harte pressed forward with his cordial hand-clasp, as if he were not even a fairy prince, and with that voice and laugh which were surely the most winning in the world. He was then, as always, a child of extreme fashion as to his clothes and the cut of his beard, which he wore in a mustache and the drooping side whiskers of the day, and his jovial physiognomy was as winning as his voice, with its straight nose, and fascinating thrust of the under lip, its fine eyes, and good forehead, then thickly crowned with the black hair which grew early white, while his mustache remained dark: the most enviable and consoling effect possible in the universal mortal necessity of either aging or dying. He was, as one could not help seeing, thickly pitted, but after the first glance one forgot this, so that a lady who met him for the first time could say to him, "Mr. Harte, aren't you afraid to go about in the cars so recklessly when there is this scare about smallpox?" "No, madam," he could answer in that rich note of his, with an irony touched by pseudo-pathos, "I bear a charmèd life."

The drive out from Boston was not too long for getting on terms of personal friendship with the family which just filled the hack, the two boys intensely interested in the novelties of a New England city and suburb, and the father and mother continually exchanging admiration of such aspects of nature as presented themselves in the leafless sidewalk trees, and patches of park and lawn. They found everything so fine, so refined, after the gigantic coarseness of California, where the natural forms were so vast that one could not get on companionable terms with them. Their host heard them without misgiving for the world of romance which Harte had built up among those huge forms, and with a subtle perception that this was no excursion of theirs to the East, but a lifelong exodus from the exile which he presently understood they must always have felt California to be. It is different now, when people are every day being born in California, and must begin to feel it home from the first breath, but it is notable that none of the Californians of that great early day have gone back to live amidst the scenes which inspired and prospered them.

Before they came in sight of the editor's humble roof he had mocked himself to his guest for his trepidations, and Harte with burlesque magnanimity had consented to be for that occasion only something less formidable than he had loomed afar. He accepted with joy the theory of passing a week in the home of virtuous poverty, and the week began as delightfully as it went on. From first to last Cambridge amused him as much as it charmed him by that air of academic distinction which was stranger to him even than the refined trees and grass. It has already been told how, after a list of the local celebrities had been recited to him, he said, "Why, you couldn't stand on your front porch and fire off your revolver without bringing down a two-volumer," and no doubt the pleasure he had in it was the effect of its contrast with the wild California he had known, and perhaps, when he had not altogether known it, had invented.

II

Cambridge began very promptly to show him those hospitalities which he could value, and continued the fable of his fairy princeliness in the curiosity of those humbler admirers who could not hope to be his hosts or his fellow guests at dinner or luncheon. Pretty presences in the tie-backs of the period were seen to flit before the home of virtuous poverty, hungering for any chance sight of him which his outgoings or incomings might give. The chances were better with the outgoings than with the incomings, for these were apt to be so hurried, in the final result of his constitutional delays, as to have the rapidity of the homing pigeon's flight, and to afford hardly a glimpse to the quickest eye. It cannot harm him, or any one now, to own that Harte was nearly always late for those luncheons and dinners which he was always going out to, and it needed the anxieties and energies of both families to get him into his clothes, and then into the carriage where a good deal of final buttoning must have been done, in order that he might not arrive so very late. He was the only one concerned who was quite unconcerned; his patience with his delays was inexhaustible; he arrived at the expected houses smiling, serenely jovial, radiating a bland gayety from his whole person, and ready to ignore any discomfort he might have occasioned.

Of course people were glad to have him on his own terms, and it may be truly said that it was worth while to have him on any terms. There never was a more charming companion, an easier or more delightful guest. It was not from what he said, for he was not much of a talker, and almost nothing of a story-teller; but he could now and then drop the fittest word, and with a glance or smile of friendly intelligence express the appreciation of another's fit word which goes far to establish for a man the character of boon humorist. It must be said of him that if he took the honors easily that were paid him he took them modestly, and never by word or look invited them, or implied that he expected them. It was fine to see him humorously accepting the humorous attribution of scientific sympathies from Agassiz, in compliment of his famous epic describing the incidents that "broke up the society upon the Stanislow." It was a little fearsome to hear him frankly owning to Lowell his dislike for something overliterary in the phrasing of certain verses of "The Cathedral." But Lowell could stand that sort of thing from a man who could say the sort of things that Harte said to him of that delicious line picturing the bobolink as he—

Runs down a brook of laughter in the air.

This, Harte told him, was the line he liked best of all his lines, and Lowell smoked well content with the praise. Yet they were not men to get on easily together, Lowell having limitations in directions where Harte had none. Afterwards in London they did not meet often or willingly. Lowell owned the brilliancy and uncommonness of Harte's gift, while he sumptuously surfeited his passion of finding everybody more or less a Jew by finding that Harte was at least half a Jew on his father's side; he had long contended for the Hebraicism of his name.

With all his appreciation of the literary eminencies whom Fields used to class together as "the old saints," Harte had a spice of irreverence that enabled him to take them more ironically than they might have liked, and to see the fun of a minor literary man's relation to them. Emerson's smoking amused him, as a Jovian self-indulgence divinely out of character with so supreme a god, and he shamelessly burlesqued it, telling how Emerson at Concord had proposed having a "wet night" with him over a glass of sherry, and had urged the scant wine upon his young friend with a hospitable gesture of his cigar. But this was long after the Cambridge episode, in which Longfellow alone escaped the corrosive touch of his subtle irreverence, or, more strictly speaking, had only the effect of his reverence. That gentle and exquisitely modest dignity of Longellow's he honored with as much veneration as it was in him to bestow, and he had that sense of Longfellow's beautiful and perfected art which is almost a test of a critic's own fineness.

III

As for Harte's talk, it was mostly ironical, not to the extreme of satire, but tempered to an agreeable coolness even for the things he admired. He did not apparently care to hear himself praised, but he could very accurately and perfectly mark his discernment of excellence in others. He was at times a keen observer of nature, and again not, apparently. Something was said before him and Lowell of the beauty of his description of a rabbit, startled with fear among the ferns, and lifting its head with the pulsation of its frightened heart visibly shaking it; then the talk turned on the graphic homeliness of Dante's noticing how the dog's skin moves upon it, and Harte spoke of the exquisite shudder with which a horse tries to rid itself of a fly. But once again, when an azalea was shown to him as the sort of bush that Sandy drunkenly slept under in "The Idyl of Red Gulch," he asked, "Why, is *that* an azalea?" To be sure, this might have been less from his ignorance or indifference concerning the quality of the bush he had sent Sandy to sleep under than from his willingness to make a mock of an azalea in a very small pot, so disproportionate to uses which an azalea of Californian size could easily lend itself to.

You never could be sure of Harte; he could only by chance be caught in earnest about anything or anybody. Except for those slight recognitions of literary traits in his talk with Lowell, nothing remained from his conversation but the general criticism he passed upon his brilliant fellow-Hebrew Heine, as "rather scorbutic." He preferred to talk about the little matters of common incident and experience. He amused himself with such things as the mystification of the postman of whom he asked his way to Phillips Avenue, where he adventurously supposed his host to be living. "Why," the postman said, "there *is* no Phillips Avenue in Cambridge. There's Phillips Place." "Well," Harte assented, "Phillips Place will *do*; but there *is* a Phillips Avenue." He entered eagerly into the canvass of the distinctions and celebrities asked to meet him at the reception made for him, but he had even a greater pleasure in compassionating his host for the vast disparity between the caterer's china and plated ware and the simplicities and humilities of the home of virtuous poverty; and he spluttered with delight at the sight of the lofty *epergnes* set up and down the supper table when he was brought in to note the preparations made in his honor. Those monumental structures were an inexhaustible joy to him; he walked round and round the room, and viewed them in different perspectives, so as to get the full effect of the towering forms that dwarfed it so.

He was a tease, as many a sweet and fine wit is apt to be, but his teasing was of the quality of a caress, so much kindness went with it. He lamented as an irreparable loss his having missed seeing that night an absent-minded brother in literature, who came in rubber shoes, and forgetfully wore them throughout the evening. That hospitable soul of Ralph Keeler, who had known him in California, but had trembled for their acquaintance when

Bret Harte

he read of all the honors that might well have spoiled Harte for the friends of his simpler days, rejoiced in the unchanged cordiality of his nature when they met, and presently gave him one of those restaurant lunches in Boston, which he was always sumptuously providing out of his destitution. Harte was the life of a time which was perhaps less a feast of reason than a flow of soul. The truth is, there was nothing but careless stories, carelessly told, and jokes and laughing, and a great deal of mere laughing without the jokes, the whole as unlike the ideal of a literary symposium as well might be; but there was present one who met with that pleasant Boston company for the first time, and to whom Harte attributed a superstition of Boston seriousness not realized then and there. "Look at him," he said, from time to time. "*This is the dream of his life*," and then shouted and choked with fun at the difference between the occasion and the expectation he would have imagined in his commensal's mind. At a dinner long after in London, where several of the commensals of that time met again, with other literary friends of a like age and stature, Harte laid his arms well along their shoulders as they formed in a half-circle before him, and screamed out in mocking mirth at the bulbous favor to which the slim shapes of the earlier date had come. The sight was not less a rapture to him that he was himself the prey of the same practical joke from the passing years. The hair which the years had wholly swept from some of those thoughtful brows, or left spindling autumnal spears, "or few or none," to "shake against the cold," had whitened to a wintry snow on his, while his mustache had kept its youthful black. "He looks," one of his friends said to another as they walked home together, "like a French marquis of the *ancien régime*." "Yes," the other assented, thoughtfully, "or like an American actor made up for the part."

The saying closely fitted the outward fact, but was of a subtle injustice in its implication of anything histrionic in Harte's nature. Never was any man less a poseur; he made simply and helplessly known what he was at any and every moment, and he would join the witness very cheerfully in enjoying whatever was amusing in the disadvantage to himself. In the course of events, which were in his case so very human, it came about on a subsequent visit of his to Boston that an impatient creditor decided to right himself out of the proceeds of the lecture which was to be given, and had the law corporeally present at the house of the friend where Harte dined, and in the anteroom at the lecture-hall, and on the platform, where the lecture was delivered with beautiful aplomb and untroubled charm. He was indeed the only one privy to the law's presence who was not the least affected by it, so that when his host of an earlier time ventured to suggest, "Well, Harte, this is the old literary tradition; this is the Fleet business over again," he joyously smote his thigh, and crowed out, "Yes, the Fleet!" No doubt he tasted all the delicate humor of the situation, and his pleasure in it was quite unaffected.

If his temperament was not adapted to the harsh conditions of the elder American world, it might very well be that his temperament was not altogether in the wrong. If it disabled him for certain experiences of life, it was the source of what was most delightful in his personality, and perhaps most beautiful in his talent. It enabled him to do such things as he did without being at all anguished for the things he did not do, and indeed could not. His talent was not a facile gift; he owned that he often went day after day to his desk, and sat down before that yellow post-office paper on which he liked to write his literature, in that exquisitely refined script of his, without being able to inscribe a line. It may be owned for him that though he came to the East at thirty-four, which ought to have been the very prime of his powers, he seemed to have arrived after the age of observation was past for him. He saw nothing aright, either in Newport, where he went to live, or in New York, where he sojourned, or on those lecturing tours which took him about the whole country; or if he saw it aright, he could not report it aright, or would not. After repeated and almost invariable failures to deal with the novel characters and circumstances which he encountered he left off trying, and frankly went back to the semimythical

California he had half discovered, half created, and wrote Bret Harte over and over as long as he lived. This, whether he did it from instinct or from reason, was the best thing he could do, and it went as nearly as might be to satisfy the insatiable English fancy for the wild America no longer to be found on our map.

It is imaginable of Harte that this temperament defended him from any bitterness in the disappointment he may have shared with that simple American public which in the early eighteen-seventies expected any and everything of him in fiction and drama. The long breath was not his; he could not write a novel, though he produced the like of one or two, and his plays were too bad for the stage, or else too good for it. At any rate they could not keep it even when they got it, and they denoted the fatigue or the indifference of their author in being dramatizations of his longer or shorter fictions, and not originally dramatic efforts. The direction in which his originality lasted longest, and most strikingly affirmed his power, was in the direction of his verse.

Whatever minds there may be about Harte's fiction, finally, there can hardly be more than one mind about his poetry. He was indeed a poet; whether he wrote what drolly called itself dialect, or wrote language, he was a poet of a fine and fresh touch. It must be allowed him that in prose as well he had the inventive gift, but he had it in verse far more importantly. There are lines, phrases, turns, in his poems, characterizations and pictures, which will remain as enduringly as anything American, if that is not saying altogether too little for them. In poetry he rose to all the occasions he made for himself, though he could not rise to the occasions made for him, and so far failed in the demands he acceded to for a Phi Beta Kappa poem, as to come to that august Harvard occasion with a jingle so trivial, so out of keeping, so inadequate that his enemies, if he ever truly had any, must have suffered from it almost as much as his friends. He himself did not suffer from his failure, from having read before the most elect assembly of the country a poem which would hardly have served the careless needs of an informal dinner after the speaking had begun; he took the whole disastrous business lightly, gayly, leniently, kindly, as that golden temperament of his enabled him to take all the good or bad of life.

The first year of his Eastern sojourn was salaried in a sum which took the souls of all his young contemporaries with wonder, if no baser passion, in the days when dollars were of so much farther flight than now, but its net result in a literary return to his publishers was one story and two or three poems. They had not profited much by his book, which, it will doubtless amaze a time of fifty-thousand editions selling before their publication, to learn had sold only thirty-five hundred in the sixth month of its career, as Harte himself,

> With sick and scornful looks averse,

confided to his Cambridge host after his first interview with the Boston counting-room. It was the volume which contained "The Luck of Roaring Camp," and the other early tales which made him a continental, and then an all but a world-wide fame. Stories that had been talked over, and laughed over, and cried over all up and down the land, that had been received with acclaim by criticism almost as boisterous as their popularity, and recognized as the promise of greater things than any done before in their kind, came to no more than this pitiful figure over the booksellers' counters. It argued much for the publishers that in spite of this stupefying result they were willing, they were eager, to pay him ten thousand dollars for whatever, however much or little, he chose to write in a year. Their offer was made in Boston, after some offers mortifyingly mean, and others insultingly vague, had been made in New York.

It was not his fault that their venture proved of such slight return in literary material. Harte was in the midst of new and alien conditions, and he had always his temperament against him, as well as the reluctant if not the niggard nature of his muse. He would no doubt have been only too glad to do more than he did for the money, but actually if not literally he could not do more. When it came to literature, all the gay improvidence of life forsook him, and he became a stern, rigorous, exacting self-

master, who spared himself nothing to achieve the perfection
at which he aimed. He was of the order of literary men like
Goldsmith and De Quincey, and Sterne and Steele, in his relations with the outer world, but in his relations with the inner
world he was one of the most duteous and exemplary citizens.
There was nothing of his easy-going hilarity in that world; there
he was of a Puritanic severity, and of a conscience that forgave
him no pang. Other California writers have testified to the
fidelity with which he did his work as editor. He made himself
not merely the arbiter but the inspiration of his contributors,
and in a region where literature had hardly yet replaced the
wild sage-brush of frontier journalism, he made the sand-lots of
San Francisco to blossom as the rose, and created a literary
periodical of the first class on the borders of civilization.

It is useless to wonder now what would have been his future
if the publisher of the *Overland Monthly* had been of imagination
or capital enough to meet the demand which Harte dimly intimated to his Cambridge host as the condition of his remaining
in California. Publishers, men with sufficient capital, are of a
greatly varying gift in the regions of prophecy, and he of the
Overland Monthly was not to be blamed if he could not foresee his
account in paying Harte ten thousand a year to continue editing
the magazine. He did according to his lights, and Harte came
to the East, and then went to England, where his last twenty-five
years were passed in cultivating the wild plant of his Pacific
slope discovery. It was always the same plant, leaf and flower
and fruit, but it perennially pleased the constant English world,
and thence the European world, though it presently failed of
much delighting these fastidious States. Probably he would have
done something else if he could; he did not keep on doing the
wild mining-camp thing because it was the easiest, but because
it was for him the only possible thing. Very likely he might have
preferred not doing anything.

IV

The joyous visit of a week, which has been here so poorly recovered from the past, came to an end, and the host went with

his guest to the station in as much vehicular magnificence as had marked his going to meet him there. Harte was no longer the alarming portent of the earlier time, but an experience of unalloyed delight. You must love a person whose worst troublegiving was made somehow a favor by his own unconsciousness of the trouble, and it was a most flattering triumph to have got him in time, or only a little late, to so many luncheons and dinners. If only now he could be got to the train in time the victory would be complete, the happiness of the visit without a flaw. Success seemed to crown the fondest hope in this respect. The train had not yet left the station; there stood the parlor-car which Harte had seats in; and he was followed aboard for those last words in which people try to linger out pleasures they have known together. In this case the sweetest of the pleasures had been sitting up late after those dinners, and talking them over, and then degenerating from that talk into the mere giggle and making giggle which Charles Lamb found the best thing in life. It had come to this as the host and guest sat together for those parting moments, when Harte suddenly started up in the discovery of having forgotten to get some cigars. They rushed out of the train together, and after a wild descent upon the cigar-counter of the restaurant, Harte rushed back to his car. But by this time the train was already moving with that deceitful slowness of the departing train, and Harte had to clamber up the steps of the rearmost platform. His host clambered after, to make sure that he was aboard, which done, he dropped to the ground, while Harte drew out of the station, blandly smiling, and waving his hand with a cigar in it, in picturesque farewell from the platform.

Then his host realized that he had dropped to the ground barely in time to escape being crushed against the side of the archway that sharply descended beside the steps of the train, and he went and sat down in that handsomest hack, and was for a moment deathly sick at the danger that had not realized itself to him in season. To be sure, he was able, long after, to adapt the incident to the exigencies of fiction, and to have a character, not otherwise to be conveniently disposed of, actually crushed to death between a moving train and such an archway.

Besides, he had then, and always afterwards, the immense supercompensation of the memories of that visit from one of the most charming personalities in the world,

> In life's morning march when his bosom was young,

and when infinitely less would have sated him. Now death has come to join its vague conjectures to the broken expectations of life, and that blithe spirit is elsewhere. But nothing can take from him who remains the witchery of that most winning presence. Still it looks smiling from the platform of the car, and casts a farewell of mock heart-break from it. Still a gay laugh comes across the abysm of the years that are now numbered, and out of somewhere the hearer's sense is rapt with the mellow cordial of a voice that was like no other.

_____

Part Ten

MY MARK TWAIN

I

IT WAS in the little office of James T. Fields, over the bookstore of Ticknor & Fields, at 124 Tremont Street, Boston, that I first met my friend of now forty-four years, Samuel L. Clemens. Mr. Fields was then the editor of *The Atlantic Monthly*, and I was his proud and glad assistant, with a pretty free hand as to manuscripts, and an unmanacled command of the book notices at the end of the magazine. I wrote nearly all of them myself, and in 1869 I had written rather a long notice of a book just winning its way to universal favor. In this review I had intimated my reservations concerning the *Innocents Abroad*, but I had the luck, if not the sense, to recognize that it was such fun as we had not had before. I forget just what I said in praise of it, and it does not matter; it is enough that I praised it enough to satisfy the author. He now signified as much, and he stamped his gratitude into my memory with a story wonderfully allegorizing the situation, which the mock modesty of print forbids my repeating here. Throughout my long acquaintance with him his graphic touch was always allowing itself a freedom which I cannot bring my fainter pencil to illustrate. He had the Southwestern, the Lincolnian, the Elizabethan breadth of parlance, which I suppose one ought not to call coarse without calling one's self prudish; and I was often hiding away in discreet holes and corners the letters in which he had loosed his bold fancy to stoop on rank suggestion; I could not bear to burn them, and I could not, after the first reading, quite bear to look at them. I shall best give my feeling on this point by saying that in it he was Shakespearian, or if his ghost will not suffer me the word, then he was Baconian.

At the time of our first meeting, which must have been well toward the winter, Clemens (as I must call him instead of Mark Twain, which seemed always somehow to mask him from my personal sense) was wearing a sealskin coat, with the fur out, in the satisfaction of a caprice, or the love of strong effect which he was apt to indulge through life. I do not know what droll comment was in Fields's mind with respect to this garment, but probably he felt that here was an original who was not to be brought to any Bostonian book in the judgment of his vivid qualities. With his crest of dense red hair, and the wide sweep of his flaming mustache, Clemens was not discordantly clothed in that sealskin coat, which afterward, in spite of his own warmth in it, sent the cold chills through me when I once accompanied it down Broadway, and shared the immense publicity it won him. He had always a relish for personal effect, which expressed itself in the white suit of complete serge which he wore in his last years, and in the Oxford gown which he put on for every possible occasion, and said he would like to wear all the time. That was not vanity in him, but a keen feeling for costume which the severity of our modern tailoring forbids men, though it flatters women to every excess in it; yet he also enjoyed the shock, the offence, the pang which it gave the sensibilities of others. Then there were times he played these pranks for pure fun, and for the pleasure of the witness. Once I remember seeing him come into his drawing-room at Hartford in a pair of white cowskin slippers, with the hair out, and do a crippled colored uncle to the joy of all beholders. Or, I must not say all, for I remember also the dismay of Mrs. Clemens, and her low, despairing cry of, "Oh, Youth!" That was her name for him among their friends, and it fitted him as no other would, though I fancied with her it was a shrinking from his baptismal Samuel, or the vernacular Sam of his earlier companionships. He was a youth to the end of his days, the heart of a boy with the head of a sage; the heart of a good boy, or a bad boy, but always a wilful boy, and wilfulest to show himself out at every time for just the boy he was.

II

There is a gap in my recollections of Clemens, which I think is of a year or two, for the next thing I remember of him is meeting him at a lunch in Boston given us by that genius of hospitality, the tragically destined Ralph Keeler, author of one of the most unjustly forgotten books, *Vagabond Adventures*, a true bit of picaresque autobiography. Keeler never had any money, to the general knowledge, and he never borrowed, and he could not have had credit at the restaurant where he invited us to feast at his expense. There was T. B. Aldrich, there was J. T. Fields, much the oldest of our company, who had just freed himself from the trammels of the publishing business, and was feeling his freedom in every word; there was Bret Harte, who had lately come East in his princely progress from California; and there was Clemens. Nothing remains to me of the happy time but a sense of idle and aimless and joyful talk-play, beginning and ending nowhere, of eager laughter, of countless good stories from Fields, of a heat lightning shimmer of wit from Aldrich, of an occasional concentration of our joint mockeries upon our host, who took it gladly; and amidst the discourse, so little improving, but so full of good fellowship, Bret Harte's fleering dramatization of Clemens's mental attitude toward a symposium of Boston illuminates. "Why, fellows," he spluttered, "this is the dream of Mark's life," and I remember the glance from under Clemens's feathery eyebrows which betrayed his enjoyment of the fun. We had beefsteak with mushrooms, which in recognition of their shape Aldrich hailed as shoe-pegs, and to crown the feast we had an omelette soufflé, which the waiter brought in as flat as a pancake, amidst our shouts of congratulations to poor Keeler, who took them with appreciative submission. It was in every way what a Boston literary lunch ought not to have been in the popular ideal which Harte attributed to Clemens.

Our next meeting was at Hartford, or rather at Springfield,

where Clemens greeted us on the way to Hartford. Aldrich was
going on to be his guest, and I was going to be Charles Dudley
Warner's, but Clemens had come part way to welcome us both.
In the good fellowship of that cordial neighborhood we had two
such days as the aging sun no longer shines on in his round.
There was constant running in and out of friendly houses where
the lively hosts and guests called one another by their Christian
names or nicknames, and no such vain ceremony as knocking
or ringing at doors. Clemens was then building the stately
mansion in which he satisfied his love of magnificence as if it had
been another sealskin coat, and he was at the crest of the prosperity which enabled him to humor every whim or extravagance.
The house was the design of that most original artist, Edward
Potter, who once, when hard pressed by incompetent curiosity
for the name of his style in a certain church, proposed that it
should be called the English violet order of architecture; and this
house was so absolutely suited to the owner's humor that I suppose there never was another house like it; but its character must
be for recognition farther along in these reminiscences. The
vividest impression which Clemens gave us two ravenous young
Boston authors was of the satisfying, the surfeiting nature of
subscription publication. An army of agents was overrunning the
country with the prospectuses of his books, and delivering them
by the scores of thousands in completed sale. Of the *Innocents
Abroad* he said, "It sells right along just like the Bible," and
Roughing It was swiftly following, without perhaps ever quite
overtaking it in popularity. But he lectured Aldrich and me on
the folly of that mode of publication in the trade which we had
thought it the highest success to achieve a chance in. "Anything
but subscription publication is printing for private circulation,"
he maintained, and he so won upon our greed and hope that on
the way back to Boston we planned the joint authorship of a
volume adapted to subscription publication. We got a very good
name for it, as we believed, in *Memorable Murders*, and we never
got farther with it, but by the time we reached Boston we were
rolling in wealth so deep that we could hardly walk home in the

frugal fashion by which we still thought it best to spare car fare; carriage fare we did not dream of even in that opulence.

III

The visits to Hartford which had begun with this affluence continued without actual increase of riches for me, but now I went alone, and in Warner's European and Egyptian absences I formed the habit of going to Clemens. By this time he was in his new house, where he used to give me a royal chamber on the ground floor, and come in at night after I had gone to bed to take off the burglar alarm so that the family should not be roused if anybody tried to get in at my window. This would be after we had sat up late, he smoking the last of his innumerable cigars, and soothing his tense nerves with a mild hot Scotch, while we both talked and talked and talked, of everything in the heavens and on the earth, and the waters under the earth. After two days of this talk I would come away hollow, realizing myself best in the image of one of those locust-shells which you find sticking to the bark of trees at the end of summer. Once, after some such bout of brains, we went down to New York together, and sat facing each other in the Pullman smoker without passing a syllable till we had occasion to say, "Well, we're there." Then, with our installation in a now vanished hotel (the old Brunswick, to be specific), the talk began again with the inspiration of the novel environment, and went on and on. We wished to be asleep, but we could not stop, and he lounged through the rooms in the long nightgown which he always wore in preference to the pajamas which he despised, and told the story of his life, the inexhaustible, the fairy, the Arabian Nights story, which I could never tire of even when it began to be told over again. Or at times he would reason high—

"Of Providence, foreknowledge, will and fate,
    Fixed fate, free will, foreknowledge absolute,"

walking up and down, and halting now and then, with a fine toss and slant of his shaggy head, as some bold thought or splendid joke struck him.

He was in those days a constant attendant at the church of his great friend, the Rev. Joseph H. Twichell, and at least tacitly far from the entire negation he came to at last. I should say he had hardly yet examined the grounds of his passive acceptance of his wife's belief, for it was hers and not his, and he held it unscanned in the beautiful and tender loyalty to her which was the most moving quality of his most faithful soul. I make bold to speak of the love between them, because without it I could not make him known to others as he was known to me. It was a greater part of him than the love of most men for their wives, and she merited all the worship he could give her, all the devotion, all the implicit obedience, by her surpassing force and beauty of character. She was in a way the loveliest person I have ever seen, the gentlest, the kindest, without a touch of weakness; she united wonderful tact with wonderful truth; and Clemens not only accepted her rule implicitly, but he rejoiced, he gloried in it. I am not sure that he noticed all her goodness in the actions that made it a heavenly vision to others, he so had the habit of her goodness; but if there was any forlorn and helpless creature in the room Mrs. Clemens was somehow promptly at his side or hers; she was always seeking occasion of kindness to those in her household or out of it; she loved to let her heart go beyond the reach of her hand, and imagined the whole hard and suffering world with compassion for its structural as well as incidental wrongs. I suppose she had her ladyhood limitations, her female fears of etiquette and convention, but she did not let them hamper the wild and splendid generosity with which Clemens rebelled against the social stupidities and cruelties. She had been a life-long invalid when he met her, and he liked to tell the beautiful story of their courtship to each new friend whom he found capable of feeling its beauty or worthy of hearing it. Naturally, her father had hesitated to give her into the keeping of the young strange Westerner, who had risen up out of the unknown with his giant reputation of burlesque humorist, and demanded guaranties, demanded proofs. "He asked me," Clemens would say, "if I couldn't give him the names of people who knew me in

California, and when it was time to hear from them, I heard from him. 'Well, Mr. Clemens,' he said, 'nobody seems to have a very good word for you.' I hadn't referred him to people that I thought were going to whitewash me. I thought it was all up with me, but I was disappointed. 'So I guess I shall have to back you myself.'"

Whether this made him faithfuler to the trust put in him I cannot say, but probably not; it was always in him to be faithful to any trust, and in proportion as a trust of his own was betrayed he was ruthlessly and implacably resentful. But I wish now to speak of the happiness of that household in Hartford which responded so perfectly to the ideals of the mother when the three daughters, so lovely and so gifted, were yet little children. There had been a boy, and "Yes, *I* killed him," Clemens once said, with the unsparing self-blame in which he would wreak an unavailing regret. He meant that he had taken the child out imprudently, and the child had taken the cold which he died of, but it was by no means certain this was through its father's imprudence. I never heard him speak of his son except that once, but no doubt in his deep heart his loss was irreparably present. He was a very tender father, and delighted in the minds of his children, but he was wise enough to leave their training altogether to the wisdom of their mother. He left them to that in everything, keeping for himself the pleasure of teaching them little scenes of drama, learning languages with them, and leading them in singing. They came to the table with their parents, and could have set him an example in behavior when, in moments of intense excitement, he used to leave his place, and walk up and down the room, flying his napkin, and talking and talking.

It was after his first English sojourn that I used to visit him, and he was then full of praise of everything English: the English personal independence and public spirit, and hospitality, and truth. He liked to tell stories in proof of their virtues, but he was not blind to the defects of their virtues: their submissive acceptance of caste, their callousness with strangers, their bluntness with one another. Mrs. Clemens had been in a way to suffer socially more than he, and she praised the English less. She had sat after dinner with ladies who snubbed and ignored one another, and left her to find her own amusement in the absence of the attention with which Americans perhaps cloy their guests, but which she could not help preferring. In their successive sojourns among them I believe he came to like the English less and she more; the fine delight of his first acceptance among them did not renew itself till his Oxford degree was given him; then it made his cup run over, and he was glad the whole world should see it.

His wife would not chill the ardor of his early Anglomania, and in this, as in everything, she wished to humor him to the utmost. No one could have realized more than she his essential fineness, his innate nobleness. Marriages are what the parties to them alone really know them to be, but from the outside I should say that this marriage was one of the most perfect. It lasted in his absolute devotion to the day of her death, that delayed long in cruel suffering, and that left one side of him in lasting night. From Florence there came to me heartbreaking letters from him about the torture she was undergoing, and at last a letter saying she was dead, with the simple-hearted cry, "I wish I was with Livy." I do not know why I have left saying till now that she was a very beautiful woman, classically regular in features, with black hair smooth over her forehead, and with tenderly peering, myopic eyes, always behind glasses, and a smile of angelic kindness. But this kindness went with a sense of humor which qualified her to appreciate the self-lawed genius of a man who will be remembered with the great humorists of all time, with Cervantes, with Swift, or with any others worthy his company; none of them was his equal in humanity.

IV

Clemens had appointed himself, with the architect's connivance, a luxurious study over the library in his new house, but as his children grew older this study, with its carved and cushioned armchairs, was given over to them for a school-room, and he took the room above his stable, which had been intended for his coachman. There we used to talk together, when we were not walking and talking together, until he discovered that he could make a more commodious use of the billiard-room at the top of his house, for the purposes of literature and friendship. It was pretty cold up there in the early spring and late fall weather, with which I chiefly associate the place, but by lighting up all the gas-burners and kindling a reluctant fire on the hearth, we could keep it well above freezing. Clemens could also push the balls about, and, without rivalry from me, who could no more play billiards than smoke, could win endless games of pool, while he carried points of argument against imaginable differers in opinion. Here he wrote many of his tales and sketches, and for anything I know, some of his books. I particularly remember his reading me here his first rough sketch of "Captain Stormfield's Visit to Heaven," with the real name of the captain, whom I knew already from his many stories about him.

We had a peculiar pleasure in looking off from the high windows on the pretty Hartford landscape, and down from them into the tops of the trees clothing the hillside by which his house stood. We agreed that there was a novel charm in trees seen from such a vantage, far surpassing that of the farther scenery. He had not been a country boy for nothing; rather he had been a country boy, or, still better, a village boy, for everything that Nature can offer the young of our species, and no aspect of her was lost on him. We were natives of the same vast Mississippi Valley; and Missouri was not so far from Ohio but that we were akin in our first knowledges of woods and fields, as we were in our early parlance. I had outgrown the use of mine through my greater bookishness, but I gladly recognized the phrases which he employed for their lasting juiciness and the long-remembered savor they had on his mental palate.

I have elsewhere sufficiently spoken of his unsophisticated use of words, of the diction which forms the backbone of his manly style. If I mention my own greater bookishness, by which I mean his less quantitative reading, it is to give myself better occasion to note that he was always reading some vital book. It might be some out-of-the-way book, but it had the root of the human

Mark Twain

matter in it: a volume of great trials; one of the supreme autobiographies; a signal passage of history, a narrative of travel, a
story of captivity, which gave him life at first hand. As I remember, he did not care much for fiction, and in that sort he had
certain distinct loathings; there were certain authors whose
names he seemed not so much to pronounce as to spew out of his
mouth. Goldsmith was one of these, but his prime abhorrence
was my dear and honored prime favorite, Jane Austen. He once
said to me, I suppose after he had been reading some of my
unsparing praises of her—I am always praising her: "*You* seem
to think that woman could write," and he forbore withering me
with his scorn, apparently because we had been friends so long,
and he more pitied than hated me for my bad taste. He seemed
not to have any preferences among novelists; or at least I never
heard him express any. He used to read the modern novels I
praised, in or out of print; but I do not think he much liked
reading fiction. As for plays, he detested the theatre, and said
he would as lief do a sum as follow a plot on the stage. He could
not, or did not, give any reasons for his literary abhorrences, and
perhaps he really had none. But he could have said very distinctly, if he had needed, why he liked the books he did. I was away
at the time of his great Browning passion, and I know of it
chiefly from hearsay; but at the time Tolstoy was doing what
could be done to make me over, Clemens wrote, "That man
seems to have been to you what Browning was to me." I do not
know that he had other favorites among the poets, but he had
favorite poems which he liked to read to you, and he read, of
course, splendidly. I have forgotten what piece of John Hay's it
was that he liked so much, but I remembered how he fiercely
revelled in the vengefulness of William Morris's *Sir Guy of the
Dolorous Blast*, and how he especially exulted in the lines which
tell of the supposed speaker's joy in slaying the murderer of his
brother:

> "I am threescore years and ten,
>   And my hair is nigh turned gray,
> But I am glad to think of the moment when
>   I took his life away."

Generally, I fancy his pleasure in poetry was not great, and I do not believe he cared much for the conventionally accepted masterpieces of literature. He liked to find out good things and great things for himself; sometimes he would discover these in a masterpiece new to him alone, and then, if you brought his ignorance home to him, he enjoyed it, and enjoyed it the more the more you rubbed it in.

Of all the literary men I have known he was the most un-literary in his make and manner. I do not know whether he had any acquaintance with Latin, but I believe not the least; German he knew pretty well, and Italian enough late in life to have fun with it; but he used English in all its alien derivations as if it were native to his own air, as if it had come up out of American, out of Missourian ground. His style was what we know, for good and for bad, but his manner, if I may difference the two, was as entirely his own as if no one had ever written before. I have noted before this how he was not enslaved to the consecutiveness in writing which the rest of us try to keep chained to. That is, he wrote as he thought, and as all men think, without sequence, without an eye to what went before or should come after. If something beyond or beside what he was saying occurred to him, he invited it into his page, and made it as much at home there as the nature of it would suffer him. Then, when he was through with the welcoming of this casual and unexpected guest, he would go back to the company he was entertaining, and keep on with what he had been talking about. He observed this manner in the construction of his sentences, and the arrangement of his chapters, and the ordering or disordering of his compilations. I helped him with a Library of Humor, which he once edited, and when I had done my work according to tradition, with authors, times, and topics carefully studied in due sequence, he tore it all apart, and "chucked" the pieces in wherever the fancy for them took him at the moment. He was right: we were not making a text-book, but a book for the pleasure rather than the instruction of the reader, and he did not see why the principle on which he built his travels and reminiscences and tales and novels should not apply to it; and I do not, now, see, either, though at the time it confounded me. On minor points he was, beyond any author I have known, without favorite phrases or pet words. He utterly despised the avoidance of repetitions out of fear of tautology. If a word served his turn better than a substitute, he would use it as many times in a page as he chose.

v

At that time I had become editor of *The Atlantic Monthly*, and I had allegiances belonging to the conduct of what was and still remains the most scrupulously cultivated of our periodicals. When Clemens began to write for it he came willingly under its rules, for with all his wilfulness there never was a more biddable man in things you could show him a reason for. He never made the least of that trouble which so abounds for the hapless editor from narrower-minded contributors. If you wanted a thing changed, very good, he changed it; if you suggested that a word or a sentence or a paragraph had better be struck out, very good, he struck it out. His proof-sheets came back each a veritable "mush of concession," as Emerson says. Now and then he would try a little stronger language than *The Atlantic* had stomach for, and once when I sent him a proof I made him observe that I had left out the profanity. He wrote back: "Mrs. Clemens opened that proof, and lit into the room with danger in her eye. What profanity? You see, when I read the manuscript to her I skipped that." It was part of his joke to pretend a violence in that gentlest creature which the more amusingly realized the situation to their friends.

I was always very glad of him, and proud of him as a contributor, but I must not claim the whole merit, or the first merit of having him write for us. It was the publisher, the late H. O. Houghton, who felt the incongruity of his absence from the leading periodical of the country, and was always urging me to get him to write. I will take the credit of being eager for him, but it is to the publisher's credit that he tried, so far as the modest traditions of *The Atlantic* would permit, to meet the expectations in pay which the colossal profits of Clemens's books might naturally have bred in him. Whether he was really able to do this he never knew from Clemens himself, but probably twenty dollars a page did not surfeit the author of books that "sold right along just like the Bible."

We had several short contributions from Clemens first, all of capital quality, and then we had the series of papers which went mainly to the making of his great book, *Life on the Mississippi*. Upon the whole I have the notion that Clemens thought this his greatest book, and he was supported in his opinion by that of the *portière* in his hotel at Vienna, and that of the German Emperor, who, as he told me with equal respect for the preference of each, united in thinking it his best; with such far-sundered social poles approaching in its favor, he apparently found himself without standing for opposition. At any rate, the papers won instant appreciation from his editor and publisher, and from the readers of their periodical, which they expected to prosper beyond precedent in its circulation. But those were days of simpler acceptance of the popular rights of newspapers than these are, when magazines strictly guard their vested interests against them. The New York *Times* and the St. Louis *Democrat* profited by the advance copies of the magazine sent them to reprint the papers month by month. Together they covered nearly the whole reading territory of the Union, and the terms of their daily publication enabled them to anticipate the magazine in its own restricted field. Its subscription list was not enlarged in the slightest measure, and *The Atlantic Monthly* languished on the news stands as undesired as ever.

VI

It was among my later visits to Hartford that we began to talk up the notion of collaborating a play, but we did not arrive at any clear intention, and it was a telegram out of the clear sky that one day summoned me from Boston to help with a continuation of *Colonel Sellers*. I had been a witness of the high joy of Clemens in the prodigious triumph of the first *Colonel Sellers*, which had been dramatized from the novel of *The Gilded Age*. This was the joint work of Clemens and Charles Dudley Warner, and the story had been put upon the stage by some one in Utah, whom Clemens first brought to book in the courts for violation of his copyright, and then indemnified for such rights as his adaptation of the book had given him. The structure of the play as John T. Raymond gave it was substantially the work of this unknown dramatist. Clemens never pretended, to me at any rate, that he had the least hand in it; he frankly owned that he was incapable of dramatization; yet the vital part was his, for the characters in the play were his as the book embodied them, and the success which it won with the public was justly his. This he shared equally with the actor, following the company with an agent, who counted out the author's share of the gate money, and sent him a note of the amount every day by postal card. The postals used to come about dinner-time, and Clemens would read them aloud to us in wild triumph. $150—$200—$300 were the gay figures which they bore, and which he flaunted in the air before he sat down at table, or rose from it to brandish, and then flinging his napkin into his chair, walked up and down to exult in.

By and by the popularity of the play waned, and the time came when he sickened of the whole affair, and withdrew his agent, and took whatever gain from it the actor apportioned him. He was apt to have these sudden surceases, following upon the intensities of his earlier interest; though he seemed always to have the notion of making something more of *Colonel Sellers*. But when I arrived in Hartford in answer to his summons, I found him with no definite idea of what he wanted to do with him. I represented that we must have some sort of plan, and he agreed that we should both jot down a scenario, overnight, and compare our respective schemes the next morning. As the author of a large number of little plays which have been privately presented throughout the United States and in parts of the United Kingdom, without ever getting upon the public stage except for the noble ends of charity, and then promptly getting off it, I felt authorized to make him observe that his scheme was as nearly nothing as chaos could be. He agreed hilariously with me, and was willing to let it stand in proof of his entire dramatic inability. At the same time he liked my plot very much, which ultimated Sellers, according to Clemens's intention, as a man crazed by his own inventions and by his superstition that he was the rightful heir to an English earldom. The exuberant nature of Sellers and the vast range of his imagination served our purpose in other ways. Clemens made him a spiritualist, whose specialty in the occult was materialization; he became on impulse an ardent temperance-reformer, and he headed a procession of temperance ladies after disinterestedly testing the deleterious effects of liquor upon himself, until he could not walk straight; always he wore a marvellous fire-extinguisher strapped on his back, to give proof in any emergency of the effectiveness of his invention in that way.

We had a jubilant fortnight in working the particulars of these things out. It was not possible for Clemens to write like anybody else, but I could very easily write like Clemens, and we took the play scene and scene about, quite secure of coming out in temperamental agreement. The characters remained for the most part his, and I varied them only to make them more like his than, if possible, he could. Several years after, when I looked over a copy of the play, I could not always tell my work from his; I only knew that I had done certain scenes. We would work all day long at our several tasks, and then at night, before dinner, read them over to each other. No dramatists ever got greater joy out of their creations, and when I reflect that the public never had the chance of sharing our joy I pity the public from a full heart. I still believe that the play was immensely funny; I still believe that if it could once have got behind the footlights it would have continued to pack the house before them for an indefinite succession of nights. But this may be my fondness.

At any rate, it was not to be. Raymond had identified himself with Sellers in the play-going imagination, and whether consciously or unconsciously we constantly worked with Raymond in our minds. But before this time bitter displeasures had risen between Clemens and Raymond, and Clemens was determined that Raymond should never have the play. He first offered it to several other actors, who eagerly caught at it, only to give it back with the despairing renunciation, "That is a Raymond play." We tried managers with it, but their only question was whether they could get Raymond to do it. In the mean time Raymond had provided himself with a play for the winter—a very good play, by Demarest Lloyd; and he was in no hurry for ours. Perhaps he did not really care for it; perhaps he knew when he heard of it that it must come to him in the end. In the end it did, from my hand, for Clemens would not meet him. I found him in a mood of sweet reasonableness, perhaps the more softened by one of those lunches which our publisher, the hospitable James R. Osgood, was always bringing people together over in Boston. He said that he could not do the play that winter, but he was sure that he should like it, and he had no doubt he would do it the next winter. So I gave him the manuscript, in spite of Clemens's charges, for his suspicions and rancors were such that he would not have had me leave it for a moment in the actor's hands. But it seemed a conclusion that involved success and fortune for us. In due time, but I do not remember how long after, Raymond declared himself delighted with the piece; he entered into a satisfactory agreement for it, and at the beginning of the next season he started with it to Buffalo, where he was to give a first production. At Rochester he paused long enough to return it, with the explanation that a friend had noted to him the fact that Colonel Sellers in the play was a lunatic, and insanity was so serious a thing that it could not be represented on the stage without outraging the sensibilities of the audience; or words to that effect. We were too far off to allege Hamlet to the contrary, or King Lear, or to instance the delight which generations of readers throughout the world had taken in the mad freaks of Don Quixote.

Whatever were the real reasons of Raymond for rejecting the play, we had to be content with those he gave, and to set about getting it into other hands. In this effort we failed even more signally than before, if that were possible. At last a clever and charming elocutionist, who had long wished to get himself on the stage, heard of it and asked to see it. We would have shown it to any one by this time, and we very willingly showed it to him. He came to Hartford, and did some scenes from it for us. I must say he did them very well, quite as well as Raymond could have done them, in whose manner he did them. But now, late toward spring, the question was where he could get an engagement with the play, and we ended by hiring a theatre in New York for a week of trial performances.

Clemens came on with me to Boston, where we were going to make some changes in the piece, and where we made them to our satisfaction, but not to the effect of that high rapture which we had in the first draft. He went back to Hartford, and then the cold fit came upon me, and "in visions of the night, in slumberings upon the bed," ghastly forms of failure appalled me, and when I rose in the morning I wrote him: "Here is a play which every manager has put out-of-doors, and which every actor known to us has refused, and now we go and give it to an elocutioner. We are fools." Whether Clemens agreed with me or not in my conclusion, he agreed with me in my premises, and we promptly bought our play off the stage at a cost of $700, which we shared between us. But Clemens was never a man to give up. I relinquished gratis all right and title I had in the play, and he paid its entire expenses for a week of one-night stands in the country. It never came to New York; and yet I think now that if it had come, it would have succeeded. So hard does the faith of the unsuccessful dramatist in his work die!

VII

There is an incident of this time so characteristic of both men that I will yield to the temptation of giving it here. After I had gone to Hartford in response to Clemens's telegram, Matthew Arnold arrived in Boston, and one of my family called on his, to explain why I was not at home to receive his introduction: I had gone to see Mark Twain. "Oh, but he doesn't like *that* sort of thing, does he?" "He likes Mr. Clemens very much," my representative answered, "and he thinks him one of the greatest men he ever knew." I was still Clemens's guest at Hartford when Arnold came there to lecture, and one night we went to meet him at a reception. While his hand laxly held mine in greeting, I saw his eyes fixed intensely on the other side of the room. "Who—who in the world is that?" I looked and said, "Oh, that is Mark Twain." I do not remember just how their instant encounter was contrived by Arnold's wish, but I have the impression that they were not parted for long during the evening, and the next night Arnold, as if still under the glamour of that potent presence, was at Clemens's house. I cannot say how they got on, or what they made of each other; if Clemens ever spoke of Arnold, I do not recall what he said, but Arnold had shown a sense of him from which the incredulous sniff of the polite world, now so universally exploded, had already perished. It might well have done so with his first dramatic vision of that prodigious head. Clemens was then hard upon fifty, and he had kept, as he did to the end, the slender figure of his youth, but the ashes of the burnt-out years were beginning to gray the fires of that splendid shock of red hair which he held to the height of a stature apparently greater than it was, and tilted from side to side in his undulating walk. He glimmered at you from the narrow slits of fine blue-greenish eyes, under branching brows, which with age grew more and more like a sort of plumage, and he was apt to smile into your face, with a subtle but amiable perception, and yet with a sort of remote absence; you were all there for him, but he was not all there for you.

VIII

I shall not try to give chronological order to my recollections of him, but since I am just now with him in Hartford, I will speak of him in association with the place. Once when I came on from Cambridge, he followed me to my room, to see that the water was not frozen in my bath, or something of the kind, for it was very cold weather, and then hospitably lingered. Not to lose time in banalities I began at once from the thread of thought in my mind. "I wonder why we hate the past so," and he responded from the depths of his own consciousness, "It's so damned humiliating," which is what any man would say of his past, if he were honest; but honest men are few when it comes to themselves. Clemens was one of the few, and the first of them among all the people I have known. I have known, I suppose, men as truthful, but not so promptly, so absolutely, so positively, so almost aggressively truthful. He could lie, of course, and did to save others from grief or harm; he was not stupidly truthful; but his first impulse was to say out the thing and everything that was in him. To those who can understand it will not be contradictory of his sense of humiliation from the past, that he was not ashamed for anything he ever did, to the point of wishing to hide it. He could be, and he was, bitterly sorry for his errors, which he had enough of in his life, but he was not ashamed in that mean way. What he had done, he owned to, good, bad, or indifferent, and if it was bad he was rather amused than troubled as to the effect in your mind. He would not obtrude the fact upon you, but if it were in the way of personal history, he would not dream of withholding it, far less of hiding it.

He was the readiest of men to allow an error, if he were found in it. In one of our walks about Hartford, when he was in the first fine flush of his agnosticism, he declared that Christianity had done nothing to improve morals and conditions, and that the world under the highest pagan civilization was as well off as it was under the highest Christian influences. I happened to be fresh from the reading of Charles Loring Brace's *Gesta Christi, or History of Humane Progress*, and I could offer him abundant proofs that he was wrong. He did not like that, evidently, but he instantly gave way, saying he had not known those things. Later he was more tolerant in his denials of Christianity, but just then he was feeling his freedom from it, and rejoicing in having broken what he felt to have been the shackles of belief worn so long. He greatly admired Robert Ingersoll, whom he called an angelic orator, and regarded as an evangel of a new gospel, the gospel of free thought. He took the warmest interest in the newspaper controversy raging at the time as to the existence of a hell; when the noes carried the day, I suppose that no enemy of perdition was more pleased. He still loved his old friend and pastor, Mr. Twichell, but he no longer went to hear him preach his sane and beautiful sermons, and was, I think, thereby the greater loser. Long before that, I had asked him if he went regularly to church, and he groaned out: "Oh, yes, I go. It 'most kills me, but I go," and I did not need his telling me to understand that he went because his wife wished it. He did tell me, after they both ceased to go, that it had finally come to her saying, "Well, if you are to be lost, I want to be lost with you." He could accept that willingness for supreme sacrifice, and exult in it, because of the supreme truth as he saw it. After they had both ceased to be formal Christians, she was still grieved by his denial of immortality, so grieved that he resolved upon one of those heroic lies, which for love's sake he held above even the truth, and he went to her, saying that he had been thinking the whole matter over, and now he was convinced that the soul did live after death. It was too late. Her keen vision pierced through his ruse, as it did when he brought the doctor who had diagnosticated her case as organic disease of the heart, and after making him go over the facts of it again with her, made him declare it merely functional.

To make an end of these records as to Clemens's beliefs, so far as I knew them, I should say that he never went back to anything like faith in the Christian theology, or in the notion of life after death, or in a conscious divinity. It is best to be honest in this matter; he would have hated anything else, and I do not believe that the truth in it can hurt any one. At one period he argued that there must have been a cause, a conscious source of things; that the universe could not have come by chance. I have heard, also, that in his last hours or moments he said, or his dearest ones hoped he had said, something about meeting again. But the expression, of which they could not be certain, was of the vaguest, and it was perhaps addressed to their tenderness out of his tenderness. All his expressions to me were of a courageous re-

nunciation of any hope of living again, or elsewhere seeing those
he had lost. He suffered terribly in their loss, and he was not fool
enough to try ignoring his grief. He knew that for this there were
but two medicines; that it would wear itself out with the years,
and that meanwhile there was nothing for it but those respites in
which the mourner forgets himself in slumber. I remember that
in a black hour of my own when I was called down to see him,
as he thought from sleep, he said, with an infinite, an exquisite
compassion, "Oh, did I wake you, did I *wake* you?" Nothing
more, but the look, the voice, were everything; and while I live
they cannot pass from my sense.

IX

He was the most caressing of men in his pity, but he had the
fine instinct, which would have pleased Lowell, of never putting
his hands on you—fine, delicate hands, with taper fingers, and
pink nails, like a girl's, and sensitively quivering in moments of
emotion; he did not paw you with them, to show his affection,
as so many of us Americans are apt to do. Among the half-dozen,
or half-hundred, personalities that each of us becomes, I should
say that Clemens's central and final personality was something
exquisite. His casual acquaintance might know him, perhaps,
from his fierce intensity, his wild pleasure in shocking people
with his ribaldries and profanities, or from the mere need of
loosing his rebellious spirit in that way, as anything but exquisite,
and yet that was what in the last analysis he was. They might
come away loathing or hating him, but one could not know him
well without realizing him the most serious, the most humane,
the most conscientious of men. He was Southwestern, and born
amidst the oppression of a race that had no rights as against ours,
but I never saw a man more regardful of negroes. He had a yellow
butler when I first began to know him, because he said he could
not bear to order a white man about, but the terms of his ordering
George were those of the softest entreaty which command ever
wore. He loved to rely upon George, who was such a broken reed
in some things, though so stanch in others, and the fervent Re-

publican in politics that Clemens then liked him to be. He could interpret Clemens's meaning to the public without conveying his mood, and could render his roughest answer smooth to the person denied his presence. His general instructions were that this presence was to be denied all but personal friends, but the soft heart of George was sometimes touched by importunity, and once he came up into the billiard-room saying that Mr. Smith wished to see Clemens. Upon inquiry, Mr. Smith developed no ties of friendship, and Clemens said, "You go and tell Mr. Smith that I wouldn't come down to see the Twelve Apostles." George turned from the threshold where he had kept himself, and framed a paraphrase of this message which apparently sent Mr. Smith away content with himself and all the rest of the world.

The part of him that was Western in his Southwestern origin Clemens kept to the end, but he was the most desouthernized Southerner I ever knew. No man more perfectly sensed, and more entirely abhorred, slavery, and no one has ever poured such scorn upon the second-hand, Walter-Scotticised, pseudo-chivalry of the Southern ideal. He held himself responsible for the wrong which the white race had done the black race in slavery, and he explained, in paying the way of a negro student through Yale, that he was doing it as his part of the reparation due from every white to every black man. He said he had never seen this student, nor ever wished to see him, or know his name; it was quite enough that he was a negro. About that time a colored cadet was expelled from West Point for some point of conduct "unbecoming an officer and gentleman," and there was the usual shabby philosophy in a portion of the press to the effect that a negro could never feel the claim of honor. The man was fifteen parts white, but, "Oh, yes," Clemens said, with bitter irony, "it was that one part black that undid him." It made him a "nigger" and incapable of being a gentleman. It was to blame for the whole thing. The fifteen parts white were guiltless.

Clemens was entirely satisfied with the result of the Civil War, and he was eager to have its facts and meanings brought out at once in history. He ridiculed the notion, held by many, that "it was not yet time" to philosophize the events of the great struggle; that we must "wait till its passions had cooled," and "the clouds of strife had cleared away." He maintained that the time would never come when we should see its motives and men and deeds more clearly, and that now, now, was the hour to ascertain them in lasting verity. Picturesquely and dramatically, he portrayed the imbecility of deferring the inquiry at any point to the distance of future years when inevitably the facts would begin to put on fable.

He had powers of sarcasm and a relentless rancor in his contempt which those who knew him best appreciated most. The late Noah Brooks, who had been in California at the beginning of Clemens's career, and had witnessed the effect of his ridicule before he had learned to temper it, once said to me that he would rather have any one else in the world down on him than Mark Twain. But as Clemens grew older he grew more merciful, not to the wrong, but to the men who were in it. The wrong was often the source of his wildest drolling. He considered it in such hopelessness of ever doing it justice that his despair broke in laughter.

X

I go back to that house in Hartford, where I was so often a happy guest, with tenderness for each of its endearing aspects. Over the chimney in the library, which had been cured of smoking by so much art and science, Clemens had written in perennial brass the words of Emerson, "The ornament of a house is the friends who frequent it," and he gave his guests a welcome of the simplest and sweetest cordiality. But I must not go aside to them from my recollections of him, which will be of sufficient garrulity, if I give them as fully as I wish. The windows of the library looked northward from the hillside above which the house stood, and over the little valley with the stream in it, and they showed the leaves of the trees that almost brushed them as in a Claude Lorrain glass. To the eastward the dining-room opened amply, and to the south there was a wide hall, where the voices of friends made themselves heard as they entered without ceremony, and answered his joyous hail. At the west was a little semicircular conservatory of a pattern invented by Mrs. Harriet Beecher Stowe, and adopted in most of the houses of her kindly neighborhood. The plants were set in the ground, and the flowering vines climbed up the sides and overhung the roof above the silent spray of a fountain companied by callas and other water-loving lilies. There, while we breakfasted, Patrick came in from the barn, and sprinkled the pretty bower, which poured out its responsive perfume in the delicate accents of its varied blossoms. Breakfast was Clemens's best meal, and he sat longer at his steak and coffee than at the courses of his dinner; luncheon was nothing to him, unless, as might happen, he made it his dinner, and reserved the later repast as the occasion of walking up and down the room, and discoursing at large on anything that came into his head. Like most good talkers, he liked other people to have their say; he did not talk them down; he stopped instantly at another's remark, and gladly or politely heard him through; he even made believe to find suggestion or inspiration in what was said. His children came to the table, as I have told, and after dinner he was apt to join his fine tenor to their trebles in singing.

Fully half our meetings were at my house in Cambridge, where he made himself as much at home as in Hartford. He would come ostensibly to stay at the Parker House, in Boston, and take a room, where he would light the gas and leave it burning, after dressing, while he drove out to Cambridge, and stayed two or three days with us. Once, I suppose it was after a lecture, he came in evening dress, and passed twenty-four hours with us in that guise, wearing an overcoat to hide it when we went for a walk. Sometimes he wore the slippers which he preferred to shoes at home, and if it was muddy, as it was wont to be in Cambridge, he would put a pair of rubbers over them for our rambles. He liked the lawlessness, and our delight in allowing it, and he rejoiced in the confession of his hostess, after we had once almost worn ourselves out in our pleasure with the intense talk, with the stories and the laughing, that his coming almost killed her, but it was worth it.

In those days he was troubled with sleeplessness, or rather with reluctant sleepiness, and he had various specifics for promoting it. At first it had been champagne just before going to bed, and we provided that, but later he appeared from Boston with four bottles of lager-beer under his arms; lager-beer, he said, now, was the only thing to make you go to sleep, and we provided that. Still later, on a visit I paid him at Hartford, I learned that hot Scotch was the only soporific worth considering, and Scotch whiskey duly found its place on our sideboard. One day, very long afterward, I asked him if he were still taking hot Scotch to make him sleep. He said he was not taking anything. For a while he had found going to bed on the bath-room floor a soporific; then one night he went to rest in his own bed at ten o'clock, and had gone promptly to sleep without anything. He had done the like with the like effect ever since. Of course it amused him; there were few experiences of life, grave or gay, which did not amuse him, even when they wronged him.

He came on to Cambridge in April, 1875, to go with me to the centennial ceremonies at Concord in celebration of the battle of the Minute Men with the British troops a hundred years before. We both had special invitations, including passage from Boston; but I said, Why bother to go into Boston, when we could just as well take the train for Concord at the Cambridge station? He equally decided that it would be absurd; so we breakfasted deliberately, and then walked to the station, reasoning of many things, as usual. When the train stopped, we found it packed inside and out. People stood dense on the platforms of the cars; to our startled eyes they seemed to project from the windows, and unless memory betrays me they lay strewn upon the roofs like brakemen slain at the post of duty. Whether this was really so or not, it is certain that the train presented an impenetrable front even to our imagination, and we left it to go its way without the slightest effort to board. We remounted the fame-worn steps of Porter's station, and began exploring North Cambridge for some means of transportation overland to Concord, for we were that far on the road by which the British went and came on the day of the battle. The liverymen whom we appealed to received us, some with compassion, some with derision, but in either mood convinced us that we could not have hired a cat to attempt our conveyance, much less a horse, or vehicle of any description. It was a raw, windy day, very unlike the exceptionally hot April day when the routed redcoats, pursued by the Colonials, fled panting back to Boston, with "their tongues hanging out like dogs," but we could not take due comfort in the vision of their discomfiture; we could almost envy them, for they had at least got to Concord. A swift procession of coaches, carriages, and buggies, all going to Concord, passed us, inert and helpless, on the sidewalk in the peculiarly cold mud of North Cambridge. We began to wonder if we might not stop one of them, and bribe it to take us, but we had not the courage to try, and Clemens seized the opportunity to begin suffering with an acute indigestion, which gave his humor a very dismal cast. I felt keenly the shame of defeat, and the guilt of responsibility for our failure, and when a gay party of students came toward us on the top of a tally-ho, luxuriously empty inside, we felt that our chance had come, and our last chance. He said that if I would stop them and tell them who I was, they would gladly, perhaps proudly, give us passage; I contended that if with his far vaster renown he would approach them, our success would be assured. While we stood, lost in this "contest of civilities," the coach passed us, with gay notes blown from the horns of the students, and then Clemens started in pursuit, encouraged with shouts from the merry party, who could not imagine who was trying to run them down, to a rivalry in speed. The unequal match could end only in one way, and I am glad I cannot recall what he said when he came back to me. Since then I have often wondered at the grief which would have wrung those blithe young hearts, if they could have known that they might have had the company of Mark Twain to Concord that day and did not.

We hung about, unavailingly, in the bitter wind a while longer, and then slowly, very slowly, made our way home. We wished to pass as much time as possible, in order to give probability to the deceit we intended to practise, for we could not bear to own ourselves baffled in our boasted wisdom of taking the train at Porter's station, and had agreed to say that we had been to Concord and got back. Even after coming home to my house, we felt that our statement would be wanting in verisimilitude without further delay, and we crept quietly into my library, and made up a roaring fire on the hearth, and thawed ourselves out in the heat of it, before we regained our courage for the undertaking. With all these precautions, we failed, for when our statement was imparted to the proposed victim, she instantly pronounced it unreliable, and we were left with it on our hands intact. I think the humor of this situation was finally a greater pleasure to Clemens than an actual visit to Concord would have been; only a few weeks before his death, he laughed our defeat over with one of my family in Bermuda, and exulted in our prompt detection.

XI

From our joint experience in failing I argue that Clemens's affection for me must have been great to enable him to condone in me the final defection which was apt to be the end of our enterprises. I have fancied that I presented to him a surface of such entire trustworthiness that he could not imagine the depths of unreliability beneath it; and that never realizing it, he always broke through with fresh surprise but unimpaired faith. He liked beyond all things to push an affair to the bitter end, and the end was never too bitter unless it brought grief or harm to another. Once in a telegraph-office at a railway station he was treated with such insolent neglect by the young lady in charge, who was preoccupied in a flirtation with a "gentleman friend," that, emulous of the public spirit which he admired in the English, he told her he should report her to her superiors, and (probably to her astonishment) he did so. He went back to Hartford and in due time the poor girl came to me in terror and in tears; for I had abetted Clemens in his action, and had joined my name to his in his appeal to the authorities. She was threatened with dismissal unless she made full apology to him and brought back assurance of its acceptance. I felt able to give this, and of course he eagerly approved; I think he telegraphed his approval. Another time, some years afterward, we sat down together in places near the end of a car, and a brakeman came in looking for his official note-book. Clemens found that he had sat down upon it, and handed it to him; the man scolded him very abusively, and came back again and again, still scolding him for having no more sense than to sit down on a note-book. The patience of Clemens in bearing it was so angelic that I saw fit to comment, "I suppose you will report this fellow." "Yes," he answered, slowly and sadly. "That's what I should have done once. But now I remember that he gets twenty dollars a month."

Nothing could have been wiser, nothing tenderer, and his humanity was not for humanity alone. He abhorred the dull and savage joy of the sportsman in a lucky shot, an unerring aim, and once when I met him in the country he had just been sickened by the success of a gunner in bringing down a blackbird, and he described the poor, stricken, glossy thing, how it lay throbbing its life out on the grass, with such pity as he might have given a wounded child. I find this a fit place to say that his mind and soul were with those who do the hard work of the world, in fear of those who give them a chance for their livelihoods and underpay them all they can. He never went so far in socialism as I have gone, if he went that way at all, but he was fascinated with *Looking Backward* and had Bellamy to visit him; and from the first he had a luminous vision of organized labor as the only present help for working-men. He would show that side with such clearness and such force that you could not say anything in hopeful contradiction; he saw with that relentless insight of his that in the Unions was the working-man's only present hope of standing up like a man against money and the power of it. There was a time when I was afraid that his eyes were a little holden from the truth; but in the very last talk I heard from him I found that I was wrong, and that this great humorist was as great a humanist as ever. I wish that all the work-folk could know this, and could know him their friend in life as he was in literature; as he was in such a glorious gospel of equality as the *Connecticut Yankee in King Arthur's Court.*

XII

Whether I will or no I must let things come into my story thoughtwise, as he would have let them, for I cannot remember them in their order. One night, while we were giving a party, he suddenly stormed in with a friend of his and mine, Mr. Twichell, and immediately began to eat and drink of our supper, for they had come straight to our house from walking to Boston, or so great a part of the way as to be ahungered and athirst. I can see him now as he stood up in the midst of our friends, with his head thrown back, and in his hand a dish of those escalloped oysters without which no party in Cambridge was really a party, exulting in the tale of his adventure, which had abounded in the most original characters and amusing incidents at every mile of their progress. They had broken their journey with a night's rest, and they had helped themselves lavishly out by rail in the last half; but still it had been a mighty walk to do in two days. Clemens was a great walker in those years, and was always telling of his tramps with Mr. Twichell to Talcott's Tower, ten miles out of Hartford. As he walked, of course he talked, and of course he smoked. Whenever he had been a few days with us, the whole house had to be aired, for he smoked all over it from breakfast to bedtime. He always went to bed with a cigar in his mouth, and sometimes, mindful of my fire insurance, I went up and took it away, still burning, after he had fallen asleep. I do not know how much a man may smoke and live, but apparently he smoked as much as a man could, for he smoked incessantly.

He did not care much to meet people, as I fancied, and we were greedy of him for ourselves; he was precious to us; and I would not have exposed him to the critical edge of that Cambridge acquaintance which might not have appreciated him at, say, his transatlantic value. In America his popularity was as instant as it was vast. But it must be acknowledged that for a much longer time here than in England polite learning hesitated his praise. In England rank, fashion, and culture rejoiced in him. Lord Mayors, Lord Chief Justices, and magnates of many kinds were his hosts; he was desired in country houses, and his bold genius captivated the favor of periodicals which spurned the rest of our nation. But in his own country it was different. In proportion as people thought themselves refined they questioned that quality which all recognize in him now, but which was then the inspired knowledge of the simple-hearted multitude. I went with him to see Longfellow, but I do not think Longfellow made much of him, and Lowell made less. He stopped as if with the long Semitic curve of Clemens's nose, which in the indulgence of his passion for finding every one more or less a Jew he pronounced unmistakably racial. It was two of my most fastidious Cambridge friends who accepted him with the English, the European entirety—namely, Charles Eliot Norton and Professor Francis J. Child. Norton was then newly back from a long sojourn abroad, and his judgments were delocalized. He met Clemens as if they had both been in England, and rejoiced in his bold freedom from environment, and in the rich variety and boundless reach of his talk. Child was of a personal liberty as great in its fastidious way as that of Clemens himself, and though he knew him only at second hand, he exulted in the most audacious instance of his grotesquery, as I shall have to tell by and by, almost solely. I cannot say just why Clemens seemed not to hit the favor of our community of scribes and scholars, as Bret Harte had done, when he came on from California, and swept them before him, disrupting their dinners and delaying their lunches with impunity; but it is certain he did not, and I had better say so.

I am surprised to find from the bibliographical authorities that it was so late as 1875 when he came with the manuscript of *Tom Sawyer*, and asked me to read it, as a friend and critic, and not as an editor. I have an impression that this was at Mrs. Clemens's instance in his own uncertainty about printing it. She trusted me, I can say with a satisfaction few things now give me, to be her husband's true and cordial adviser, and I was so. I believe I never failed him in this part, though in so many of our enterprises and projects I was false as water through my temperamental love of backing out of any undertaking. I believe this never ceased to astonish him, and it has always astonished me; it appears to me quite out of character; though it is certain that an undertaking, when I have entered upon it, holds me rather than I it. But however this immaterial matter may be, I am glad to remember that I thoroughly liked *Tom Sawyer*, and said so with every possible amplification. Very likely, I also made my suggestions for its improvement; I could not have been a real critic without that; and I have no doubt they were gratefully accepted, and I hope never acted upon. I went with him to the horse-car station in Harvard Square, as my frequent wont was, and put him aboard a car with his MS. in his hand, stayed and reassured, so far as I counted, concerning it. I do not know what his misgivings were; perhaps they were his wife's misgivings, for she wished him to be known not only for the wild and boundless humor that was in him, but for the beauty and tenderness and "natural piety"; and she would not have had him judged by a too close fidelity to the rude conditions of Tom Sawyer's life. This is the meaning that I read into the fact of his coming to me with those doubts.

XIII

Clemens had then and for many years the habit of writing to me about what he was doing, and still more of what he was experiencing. Nothing struck his imagination, in or out of the daily routine, but he wished to write me of it, and he wrote with the greatest fulness and a lavish dramatization, sometimes to the length of twenty or forty pages, so that I have now perhaps fifteen hundred pages of his letters. They will no doubt some day be published, but I am not even referring to them in these records, which I think had best come to the reader with an old man's falterings and uncertainties. With his frequent absences and my own abroad, and the intrusion of calamitous cares, the rich tide of his letters was more and more interrupted. At times it almost ceased, and then it would come again, a torrent. In the very last weeks of his life, he burst forth, and though too weak himself to write, he dictated his rage with me for recommending to him a certain author whose truthfulness he could not deny, but whom he hated for his truthfulness to sordid and ugly conditions. At heart Clemens was romantic, and he would have had the world of fiction stately and handsome and whatever the real world was not, but he was not romanticistic, and he was too helplessly an artist not to wish his own work to show life as he had seen it. I was preparing to rap him back for these letters when I read that he had got home to die; he would have liked the rapping back.

He liked coming to Boston, especially for those luncheons and dinners in which the fertile hospitality of our publisher, Osgood, abounded. He dwelt equidistant from Boston and New York, and he had special friends in New York, but he said he much preferred coming to Boston; of late years he never went there, and he had lost the habit of it long before he came home from Europe to live in New York. At these feasts, which were often of after-dinner-speaking measure, he could always be trusted for something of amazing delightfulness. Once, when Osgood could think of no other occasion for a dinner, he gave himself a birthday dinner, and asked his friends and authors. The beautiful and splendid trooper-like Waring was there, and I recall how in the long, rambling speech in which Clemens went round the table hitting every head at it, and especially visiting Osgood with thanks for his ingenious pretext for our entertainment, he congratulated Waring upon his engineering genius, and his hypnotic control of municipal governments. He said that if there was a plan for draining a city at a cost of a million, by seeking the level of the water in the down-hill course of the sewers, Waring would come with a plan to drain that town up-hill at twice the cost and carry it through the Common Council without opposition. It is hard to say whether the time was gladder at these dinners, or at the small lunches at which Osgood and Aldrich and I foregathered with him, and talked the afternoon away till well toward the winter twilight.

He was a great figure, and the principal figure, at one of the first of the now worn-out Authors' Readings, which was held in the Boston Museum to aid a Longfellow memorial. It was the late George Parsons Lathrop (everybody seems to be late in these sad days) who imagined the reading, but when it came to a price for seats I can always claim the glory of fixing it at five dollars. The price if not the occasion proved irresistible, and the Museum was packed from the floor to the topmost gallery. Norton presided, and when it came Clemens's turn to read he introduced him with such exquisite praises as he best knew how to give, but before he closed he fell a prey to one of those lapses of tact which are the peculiar peril of people of the greatest tact. He was reminded of Darwin's delight in Mark Twain, and how when he came from his long day's exhausting study, and sank into bed at midnight, he took up a volume of Mark Twain, whose books he always kept on a table beside him, and whatever had been his tormenting problem, or excess of toil, he felt secure of a good night's rest from it. A sort of blank ensued which Clemens filled in the only possible way. He said he should always be glad that he had contributed to the repose of that great man, whom science owed so much, and then without waiting for the joy in every breast to burst forth, he began to read. It was curious to watch his triumph with the house. His carefully studied effects would reach the first rows in the orchestra first, and ripple in laughter back to the standees against the wall, and then with a fine resurgence come again to the rear orchestra seats, and so rise from gallery to gallery, till it fell back a cataract of applause from the topmost rows of seats. He was such a practised speaker that he knew all the stops of that simple instrument man, and there is no doubt that these results were accurately intended from his unerring knowledge. He was the most consummate public performer I ever saw, and it was an incomparable pleasure to hear him lecture; on the platform he was the great and finished actor which he probably would not have been on the stage. He was fond of private theatricals, and liked to play in them with his children and their friends, in dramatizations of such stories of his as *The Prince and the Pauper*; but I never saw him in any of these scenes. When he read his manuscript to you, it was with a thorough, however involuntary, recognition of its dramatic qualities; he held that an actor added fully half to the character the author created. With my own hurried and half-hearted reading of passages which I wished to try on him from unprinted chapters (say, out of *The Undiscovered Country*, or *A Modern Instance*) he said frankly that my reading could spoil anything. He was realistic, but he was essentially histrionic, and he was rightly so. What we have strongly conceived we ought to make others strongly imagine, and we ought to use every genuine art to that end.

XIV

There came a time when the lecturing which had been the joy of his prime became his loathing, loathing unutterable, and when he renounced it with indescribable violence. Yet he was always hankering for those fleshpots, whose savor lingered on his palate and filled his nostrils after his withdrawal from the platform. The Authors' Readings when they had won their brief popularity abounded in suggestion for him. Reading from one's book was not so bad as giving a lecture written for a lecture's purpose, and he was willing at last to compromise. He had a magnificent scheme for touring the country with Aldrich and Mr. G. W. Cable and myself, in a private car, with a cook of our own, and every facility for living on the fat of the land. We should read only four times a week, in an entertainment that should not last more than an hour and a half. He would be the impresario, and would guarantee us others at least seventy-five dollars a day, and pay every expense of the enterprise, which he provisionally called the Circus, himself. But Aldrich and I were now no longer in those earlier thirties when we so cheerfully imagined *Memorable Murders* for subscription publication; we both abhorred public appearances, and at any rate I was going to Europe for a year. So the plan fell through except as regarded Mr. Cable, who, in his way, was as fine a performer as Clemens, and could both read and sing the matter of his books. On a far less stupendous scale they two made the rounds of the great lecturing circuit together. But I believe a famous lecture-manager had charge of them, and travelled with them.

He was a most sanguine man, a most amiable person, and such a believer in fortune that Clemens used to say of him, as he said of one of his early publishers, that you could rely upon fifty per cent. of everything he promised. I myself many years later became a follower of this hopeful prophet, and I can testify that in my case at least he was able to keep ninety-nine, and even a hundred, per cent. of his word. It was I who was much nearer failing of mine, for I promptly began to lose sleep from the nervous stress of my lecturing and from the gratifying but killing receptions afterward, and I was truly in that state from insomnia which Clemens recognized in the brief letter I got from him in the Western city, after half a dozen wakeful nights. He sardonically congratulated me on having gone into "the lecture field," and then he said: "I know where you are *now*. You are in hell."

It was this perdition which he re-entered when he undertook that round-the-world lecturing tour for the payment of the debts left to him by the bankruptcy of his firm in the publishing business. It was not purely perdition for him, or rather it was perdition for only one-half of him, the author-half; for the actor-half it was paradise. The author who takes up lecturing without the ability to give histrionic support to the literary reputation which he brings to the crude test of his reader's eyes and ears, invokes a peril and a misery unknown to the lecturer who has made his first public from the platform. Clemens was victorious on the platform from the beginning, and it would be folly to pretend that he did not exult in his triumphs there. But I suppose, with the wearing nerves of middle life, he hated more and more the personal swarming of interest upon him, and all the inevitable clatter of the thing. Yet he faced it, and he labored round our tiresome globe that he might pay the uttermost farthing of debts which he had not knowingly contracted, the debts of his partners who had meant well and done ill, not because they were evil, but because they were unwise, and as unfit for their work as he was. "Pay what thou owest." That is right, even when thou owest it by the error of others, and even when thou owest it to a bank, which had not lent it from love of thee, but in the hard line of business and thy need.

Clemens's behavior in this matter redounded to his glory among the nations of the whole earth, and especially in this nation, so wrapped in commerce, and so little used to honor among its many thieves. He had behaved like Walter Scott, as millions rejoiced to know, who had not known how Walter Scott had behaved till they knew it was like Clemens. No doubt it will be put to his credit in the books of the Recording Angel, but what the Judge of all the Earth will say of it at the Last Day, there is no telling. I should not be surprised if He accounted it of less merit than some other things that Clemens did and was: less than his abhorrence of the Spanish War, and the destruction of the South-African republics, and our deceit of the Filipinos, and his hate of slavery, and his payment of his portion of our race's debt to the race of the colored student whom he saw through college, and his support of a poor artist for three years in Paris, and his loan of opportunity to the youth who became the most brilliant of our actor-dramatists, and his eager pardon of the thoughtless girl who was near paying the penalty of her impertinence with the loss of her place, and his remembering that the insolent brakeman got so few dollars a month, and his sympathy for working-men standing up to money in their unions, and even his pity for the wounded bird throbbing out its little life on the grass for the pleasure of the cruel fool who shot it. These and the thousand other charities and beneficences in which he abounded, openly or secretly, may avail him more than the discharge of his firm's liabilities with the Judge of all the Earth, who surely will do right, but whose measures and criterions no man knows, and I least of all men.

He made no great show of sympathy with people in their anxieties, but it never failed, and at a time when I lay sick for many weeks his letters were of comfort to those who feared I might not rise again. His hand was out in help for those who needed help, and in kindness for those who needed kindness. There remains in my mind the dreary sense of a long, long drive to the uttermost bounds of the South End at Boston, where he went to call upon some obscure person whose claim stretched in a lengthening chain from his early days in Missouri—a most inadequate person, in whose vacuity the gloom of the dull day deepened till it was almost too deep for tears. He bore the ordeal with grim heroism, and silently smoked away the sense of it, as we drove back to Cambridge, in his slippered feet, sombrely musing, sombrely swearing. But he knew he had done the right, the kind thing, and he was content. He came the whole way from Hartford to go with me to a friendless play of mine, which Alessandro Salvini was giving in a series of matinées, to houses never enlarging themselves beyond the count of the brave two hundred who sat it through, and he stayed my fainting spirit with a cheer beyond flagons, joining me in my joke at the misery of it, and carrying the fun farther.

Before that he had come to witness the æsthetic suicide of Anna Dickinson, who had been a flaming light of the political platform in the war days, and had been left by them consuming in a hapless ambition for the theatre. The poor girl had had a play written especially for her, and, as Anne Boleyn, she ranted and exhorted through the five acts, drawing ever nearer the utter defeat of the anti-climax. We could hardly look at each other for pity, Clemens sitting there in the box he had taken, with his shaggy head out over the corner, and his slippered feet curled under him: he either went to a place in his slippers or he carried them with him, and put them on as soon as he could put off his boots. When it was so that we could not longer follow her failure and live, he began to talk of the absolute close of her career which the thing was, and how probably she had no conception that it was the end. He philosophized the mercifulness of the fact, and of the ignorance of most of us, when mortally sick or fatally wounded. We think it is not the end, because we have never ended before, and we do not see how we can end. Some can push by the awful hour, and live again, but for Anna Dickinson there could be, and was, no such palingenesis. Of course, we got that solemn joy out of reading her fate aright which is the compensation of the wise spectator in witnessing the inexorable doom of others.

XV

When Messrs. Houghton & Mifflin became owner of *The Atlantic Monthly,* Mr. Houghton fancied having some breakfasts and dinners, which should bring the publisher and the editor face to face with the contributors, who were bidden from far and near. Of course, the subtle fiend of advertising, who has now grown so unblushing bold, lurked under the covers at these banquets, and the junior partner and the young editor had their joint and separate fine anguishes of misgiving as to the taste and the principle of them; but they were really very simple-hearted and honestly meant hospitalities, and they prospered as they ought, and gave great pleasure and no pain. I forget some of the "emergent occasions," but I am sure of a birthday dinner most unexpectedly accepted by Whittier, and a birthday luncheon to Mrs. Stowe, and I think a birthday dinner to Longfellow; but the passing years have left me in the dark as to the pretext of that supper at which Clemens made his awful speech, and came so near being the death of us all. At the breakfasts and luncheons, we had the pleasure of our lady-contributors' company, but that night there were only men, and because of our great strength we survived.

I suppose the year was about 1879, but here the almanac is unimportant, and I can only say that it was after Clemens had become a very valued contributor of the magazine, where he found himself to his own great explicit satisfaction. He had jubilantly accepted our invitation, and had promised a speech, which it appeared afterward he had prepared with unusual care and confidence. It was his custom always to think out his speeches, mentally wording them, and then memorizing them by a peculiar system of mnemonics which he had invented. On the dinner table a certain succession of knife, spoon, saltcellar, and butter-plate symbolized a train of ideas, and on the billiard-table a ball, a cue, and a piece of chalk served the same purpose. With a diagram of these printed on the brain he had full command of the phrases which his excogitation had attached to them, and which embodied the ideas in perfect form. He believed he had been particularly fortunate in his notion for the speech of that evening, and he had worked it out in joyous self-reliance. It was the notion of three tramps, three deadbeats, visiting a California mining-camp, and imposing themselves upon the innocent miners as respectively Ralph Waldo Emerson, Henry Wadsworth Longfellow, and Oliver Wendell Holmes. The humor of the conception must prosper or must fail according to the mood of the hearer, but Clemens felt sure of compelling this to sympathy, and he looked forward to an unparalleled triumph.

But there were two things that he had not taken into account. One was the species of religious veneration in which these men were held by those nearest them, a thing that I should not be able to realize to people remote from them in time and place. They were men of extraordinary dignity, of the thing called *presence*, for want of some clearer word, so that no one could well approach them in a personally light or trifling spirit. I do not suppose that anybody more truly valued them, or more piously loved them, than Clemens himself, but the intoxication of his fancy carried him beyond the bounds of that regard, and emboldened him to the other thing which he had not taken into account, namely, the immense hazard of working his fancy out before their faces, and expecting them to enter into the delight of it. If neither Emerson, nor Longfellow, nor Holmes had been there, the scheme might possibly have carried, but even this is doubtful, for those who so devoutly honored them would have overcome their horror with difficulty, and perhaps would not have overcome it at all.

The publisher, with a modesty very ungrateful to me, had abdicated his office of host, and I was the hapless president, fulfilling the abhorred function of calling people to their feet and making them speak. When I came to Clemens I introduced him with the cordial admiring I had for him as one of my greatest contributors and dearest friends. Here, I said, in sum, was a humorist who never left you hanging your head for having enjoyed his joke; and then the amazing mistake, the bewildering blunder, the cruel catastrophe was upon us. I believe that after the scope of the burlesque made itself clear, there was no one there, including the burlesquer himself, who was not smitten with a desolating dismay. There fell a silence, weighing many tons to the square inch, which deepened from moment to moment, and was broken only by the hysterical and blood-curdling laughter of a single guest, whose name shall not be handed down to infamy. Nobody knew whether to look at the speaker, or down at his plate. I chose my plate as the least affliction, and so I do not know how Clemens looked, except when I stole a glance at him, and saw him standing solitary amid his appalled and appalling listeners, with his joke dead on his hands. From a first glance at the great three whom his jest had made its theme, I was aware of Longfellow sitting upright, and regarding the humorist with an air of pensive puzzle, of Holmes busily writing on his menu, with a well-feigned effect of preoccupation, and of Emerson, holding his elbows, and listening with a sort of Jovian oblivion of this nether world in that lapse of memory which saved him in those later years from so much bother. Clemens must have dragged his joke to the climax, and left it there, but I cannot say this from any sense of the fact. Of what happened afterward at the table where the immense, the wholly innocent, the truly unimagined affront was offered, I have no longer the least remembrance. I next remember being in a room of the hotel, where Clemens was not to sleep, but to toss in despair, and Charles Dudley Warner's saying, in the gloom, "Well, Mark! *You're* a funny fellow." It was as well as anything else he could have said, but Clemens seemed unable to accept the tribute.

I stayed the night with him, and the next morning, after a

haggard breakfast, we drove about and he made some purchases of bric-à-brac for his house in Hartford, with a soul as far away from bric-à-brac as ever the soul of man was. He went home by an early train, and he lost no time in writing back to the three divine personalities which he had so involuntarily seemed to flout. They all wrote back to him, making it as light for him as they could. I have heard that Emerson was a good deal mystified, and in his sublime forgetfulness asked, Who was this gentleman who appeared to think he had offered him some sort of annoyance? But I am not sure that this is accurate. What I am sure of is that Longfellow, a few days after, in my study, stopped before a photograph of Clemens, and said, "Ah! He is a *wag*," and nothing more. Holmes told me, with deep emotion, such as a brother humorist might well feel, that he had not lost an instant in replying to Clemens's letter, and assuring him that there had not been the least offence, and entreating him never to think of the matter again. "He said that he was a fool, but he was God's fool." Holmes quoted from the letter with a true sense of the pathos and the humor of the self-abasement.

To me, Clemens wrote a week later, "It doesn't get any better; it burns like fire." But now I understand that it was not shame that burnt, but rage for a blunder which he had so incredibly committed. That to have conceived of those men, the most dignified in our literature, our civilization, as impersonable by three hoboes, and then to have imagined that he could ask them personally to enjoy the monstrous travesty, was a break, he saw too late, for which there was no repair. Yet the time came, and not so very long afterward, when some mention was made of the incident as a mistake, and he said, with all his fierceness, "But I don't admit that it *was* a mistake," and it was not so in the minds of all witnesses at second hand. The morning after the dreadful dinner, there came a glowing note from Professor Child, who had read the newspaper report of it, praising Clemens's burlesque as the richest piece of humor in the world, and betraying no sense of incongruity in its perpetration in the presence of its victims. I think it must always have ground in Clemens's soul, that he was the prey of circumstances, and that if he had some more favoring occasion he could retrieve his loss in it, by giving the thing the right setting. Not more than two or three years ago, he came to try me as to trying it again at a meeting of newspaper men in Washington. I had to own my fears, while I alleged Child's note on the other hand, but in the end he did not try it with the newspaper men. I do not know whether he has ever printed it or not, but since the thing happened, I have often wondered how much offence there really was in it. I am not sure but the horror of the spectators read more indignation into the subjects of the hapless drolling than they felt. But it must have been difficult for them to bear it with equanimity. To be sure they were not themselves mocked; the joke was, of course, beside them; nevertheless their personality was trifled with, and I could only end by reflecting that if I had been in their place I should not have liked it myself. Clemens would have liked it himself, for he had the heart for that sort of wild play, and he so loved a joke that even if it took the form of a liberty, and was yet a good joke, he would have loved it. But perhaps this burlesque was not a good joke.

XVI

Clemens was oftenest at my house in Cambridge, but he was also sometimes at my house in Belmont; when, after a year in Europe, we went to live in Boston he was more rarely with us. We could never be long together without something out of the common happening, and one day something far out of the common happened, which fortunately refused the nature of absolute tragedy, while remaining rather the saddest sort of comedy. We were looking out of my library window on that view of the Charles which I was so proud of sharing with my all-but-next-door neighbor, Doctor Holmes, when another friend who was with us called out with curiously impersonal interest, "Oh, see that woman getting into the water!" This would have excited curiosity and alarmed anxiety far less lively than ours, and Clemens and I rushed down-stairs and out through my basement and back gate. At the same time a coachman came out of a stable next door, and grappled by the shoulders a woman who was somewhat deliberately getting down the steps to the water over the face of the embankment. Before we could reach them he had pulled her up to the driveway, and stood holding her there while she crazily grieved at her rescue. As soon as he saw us he went back into his stable, and left us with the poor, wild creature on our hands. She was not very young and not very pretty, and we could not have flattered ourselves with the notion of anything romantic in her suicidal mania, but we could take her on the broad human level, and on this we proposed to escort her up Beacon Street till we could give her into the keeping of one of those kindly policemen whom our neighborhood knew. Naturally there was no policeman, known to us or unknown, the whole way to the Public Garden. We had to circumvent our charge in her present design of drowning herself, and walk her past the streets crossing Beacon to the river. At these points it needed considerable reasoning to overcome her wish and some active manœuvring in both of us to enforce our arguments. Nobody else appeared to be interested, and though we did not court publicity in the performance of the duty so strangely laid upon us, still it was rather disappointing to be so entirely ignored.

There are some four or five crossings to the river between 302 Beacon Street and the Public Garden, and the suggestions at our command were pretty well exhausted by the time we reached it. Still the expected policeman was nowhere in sight; but a brilliant thought occurred to Clemens. He asked me where the nearest police station was, and when I told him, he started off at his highest speed, leaving me in sole charge of our hapless ward. All my powers of suasion were now taxed to the utmost, and I began attracting attention as a short, stout gentleman in early middle life endeavoring to distrain a respectable female of her personal liberty, when his accomplice had abandoned him to his wicked design. After a much longer time than I thought *I* should have taken to get a policeman from the station Clemens reappeared in easy conversation with an officer, who had probably realized that he was in the company of Mark Twain, and was in no hurry to end the interview. He took possession of our captive and we saw her no more. I now wonder that with our joint instinct for failure we ever got rid of her; but I am sure we did, and few things in life have given me greater relief. When we got back to my house we found the friend we had left there quite unruffled and not much concerned to know the facts of our adventure. My impression is that he had been taking a nap on my lounge; he appeared refreshed and even gay; but if I am inexact in these details he is alive to refute me.

XVII

A little after this Clemens went abroad with his family and lived several years in Germany. His letters still came, but at longer intervals, and the thread of our intimate relations was inevitably broken. He would write me when something I had written pleased him, or when something signal occurred to him, or some political or social outrage stirred him to wrath, and he wished to free his mind in pious profanity. During this sojourn he came near dying of pneumonia in Berlin, and he had slight relapses from it after coming home. In Berlin also he had the honor of dining with the German Emperor at the table of a cousin married to a high officer of the court. Clemens was a man to enjoy such a distinction; he knew how to take it as a delegated recognition from the German people; but as coming from a rather cockahoop sovereign who had as yet only his sovereignty to value himself upon, he was not very proud of it. He expressed a quiet disdain of the event as between the imperiality and himself, on whom it was supposed to confer such glory, crowning his life with the topmost leaf of laurel. He was in the same mood in his account of an English dinner many years before, where there was a "little Scotch lord" present, to whom the English tacitly referred Clemens's talk, and laughed when the lord laughed, and were grave when he failed to smile. Of all the men I have known he was the farthest from a snob, though he valued recognition, and liked the flattery of the fashionable fair when it came in his way. He would not go out of his way for it, but like most able and brilliant men he loved the minds of women, their wit, their agile cleverness, their sensitive perception, their humorous appreciation, the saucy things they would say, and their pretty, temerarious defiances. He had of course the keenest sense of what was truly dignified and truly undignified in people; but he was not really interested in what we call society affairs; they scarcely existed for him; though his books witness how he abhorred the dreadful fools who through some chance of birth or wealth hold themselves different from other men.

Commonly he did not keep things to himself, especially dislikes and condemnations. Upon most current events he had strong opinions, and he uttered them strongly. After a while he was silent in them, but if you tried him you found him in them still. He was tremendously worked up by a certain famous trial, as most of us were who lived in the time of it. He believed the accused guilty, but when we met some months after it was over, and I tempted him to speak his mind upon it, he would only say, The man had suffered enough; as if the man had expiated his wrong, and he was not going to do anything to renew his penalty. I found that very curious, very delicate. His continued blame could not come to the sufferer's knowledge, but he felt it his duty to forbear it.

He was apt to wear himself out in the vehemence of his resentments; or, he had so spent himself in uttering them that he had literally nothing more to say. You could offer Clemens offences that would anger other men and he did not mind; he would account for them from human nature; but if he thought you had in any way played him false you were anathema and maranatha forever. Yet not forever, perhaps, for by and by, after years, he would be silent. There were two men, half a generation apart in their succession, whom he thought equally atrocious in their treason to him, and of whom he used to talk terrifyingly, even after they were out of the world. He went farther than Heine, who said that he forgave his enemies, but not till they were dead.

Clemens did not forgive his dead enemies; their death seemed to deepen their crimes, like a base evasion, or a cowardly attempt to escape; he pursued them to the grave; he would like to dig them up and take vengeance upon their clay. So he said, but no doubt he would not have hurt them if he had had them living before him. He was generous without stint; he trusted without measure, but where his generosity was abused, or his trust betrayed, he was a fire of vengeance, a consuming flame of suspicion that no sprinkling of cool patience from others could quench; it had to burn itself out. He was eagerly and lavishly hospitable, but if a man seemed willing to batten on him, or in any way to lie down upon him, Clemens despised him unutterably. In his frenzies of resentment or suspicion he would not, and doubtless could not, listen to reason. But if between the paroxysms he were confronted with the facts he would own them, no matter how much they told against him. At one period he fancied that a certain newspaper was hounding him with biting censure and poisonous paragraphs, and he was filling himself up with wrath to be duly discharged on the editor's head. Later, he wrote me with a humorous joy in his mistake that Warner had advised him to have the paper watched for these injuries. He had done so, and how many mentions of him did I reckon he had found in three months? Just two, and they were rather indifferent than unfriendly. So the paper was acquitted, and the editor's life was spared. The wretch never knew how near he was to losing it, with incredible preliminaries of obloquy, and a subsequent devotion to lasting infamy.

XVIII

His memory for favors was as good as for injuries, and he liked to return your friendliness with as loud a band of music as could be bought or bribed for the occasion. All that you had to do was to signify that you wanted his help. When my father was consul at Toronto during Arthur's administration, he fancied that his place was in danger, and he appealed to me. In turn I appealed to Clemens, bethinking myself of his friendship with

Grant, and Grant's friendship with Arthur. I asked him to write to Grant in my father's behalf, but No, he answered me, I must come to Hartford, and we would go on to New York together and see Grant personally. This was before, and long before, Clemens became Grant's publisher and splendid benefactor, but the men liked each other as such men could not help doing. Clemens made the appointment, and we went to find Grant in his business office, that place where his business innocence was afterward so betrayed. He was very simple and very cordial, and I was instantly the more at home with him, because his voice was the soft, rounded, Ohio River accent to which my years were earliest used from my steamboating uncles, my earliest heroes. When I stated my business, he merely said, Oh, no; that must not be; he would write to Mr. Arthur; and he did so that day—and my father lived to lay down his office when he tired of it, with no urgence from above.

It is not irrelevant to Clemens to say that Grant seemed to like finding himself in company with two literary men, one of whom at least he could make sure of, and unlike that silent man he was reputed, he talked constantly, and so far as he might he talked literature. At least he talked of John Phœnix, that delightfulest of the early Pacific Slope humorists, whom he had known under his real name of George H. Derby, when they were fellow cadets at West Point. It was mighty pretty, as Pepys would say, to see the delicate deference Clemens paid our plain hero, and the manly respect with which he listened. While Grant talked, his luncheon was brought in from some unassuming restaurant near by, and he asked us to join him in the baked beans and coffee which were served us in a little room out of the office with about the same circumstance as at a railroad refreshment-counter. The baked beans and coffee were of about the railroad-refreshment quality; but eating them with Grant was like sitting down to baked beans and coffee with Julius Cæsar, or Alexander, or some other great Plutarchan captain.

One of the highest satisfactions of Clemens's often supremely satisfactory life was his relation to Grant. It was his proud joy to tell how he found Grant about to sign a contract for his book on certainly very good terms, and said to him that he would himself publish the book, and give him a percentage three times as large. He said Grant seemed to doubt whether he could honorably withdraw from the negotiation at that point, but Clemens overbore his scruples, and it was his unparalleled privilege, his princely pleasure to pay the author a far larger check for his work than had ever been paid to an author before. He valued even more than this splendid opportunity the sacred moments in which their business brought him into the presence of the slowly dying, heroically living man whom he was so befriending; and he told me in words which surely lost none of their simple pathos through his report how Grant described his suffering.

The prosperity of this venture was the beginning of Clemens's adversity, for it led to excesses of enterprise which were forms of dissipation. The young sculptor who had come back to him from Paris modelled a small bust of Grant, which Clemens multiplied in great numbers to his great loss, and the success of Grant's book tempted him to launch on publishing seas where his bark presently foundered. The first and greatest of his disasters was the Life of Pope Leo XIII., which he came to tell me of, when he had imagined it, in a sort of delirious exultation. He had no words in which to paint the magnificence of the project, or to forecast its colossal success. It would have a currency bounded only by the number of Catholics in Christendom. It would be translated into every language which was anywhere written or printed; it would be circulated literally in every country of the globe, and Clemens's book-agents would carry the prospectuses and then the bound copies of the work to the ends of the whole earth. Not only would every Catholic buy it, but every Catholic must, as he was a good Catholic, as he hoped to be saved. It was a magnificent scheme, and it captivated me, as it had captivated Clemens; it dazzled us both, and neither of us saw the fatal defect in it. We did not consider how often Catholics could not read, how often when they could, they might not wish to read. The event proved that whether they could read or not the immeasurable majority did not wish to read the life of the Pope, though it was written by a dignitary of the Church and issued to the world with every sanction from the Vatican. The failure was incredible to Clemens; his sanguine soul was utterly confounded, and soon a silence fell upon it where it had been so exuberantly jubilant.

XIX

The occasions which brought us to New York together were not nearly so frequent as those which united us in Boston, but there was a dinner given him by a friend which remains memorable from the fatuity of two men present, so different in everything but their fatuity. One was the sweet old comedian Billy Florence, who was urging the unsuccessful dramatist across the table to write him a play about Oliver Cromwell, and giving the reasons why he thought himself peculiarly fitted to portray the character of Cromwell. The other was a modestly millioned rich man who was then only beginning to amass the moneys afterward heaped so high, and was still in the condition to be flattered by the condescension of a yet greater millionaire. His contribution to our gayety was the verbatim report of a call he had made upon William H. Vanderbilt, whom he had found just about starting out of town, with his trunks actually in the front hall, but who had stayed to receive the narrator. He had, in fact, sat down on one of the trunks, and talked with the easiest friendliness, and quite, we were given to infer, like an ordinary human being. Clemens often kept on with some thread of the talk when we came away from a dinner, but now he was silent, as if "high sorrowful and cloyed"; and it was not till well afterward that I found he had noted the facts from the bitterness with which he mocked the rich man, and the pity he expressed for the actor.

He had begun before that to amass those evidences against mankind which eventuated with him in his theory of what he called "the damned human race." This was not an expression of piety, but of the kind contempt to which he was driven by our follies and iniquities as he had observed them in himself as well as in others. It was as mild a misanthropy, probably, as ever caressed the objects of its malediction. But I believe it was about the year 1900 that his sense of our perdition became insupportable and broke out in a mixed abhorrence and amusement which spared no occasion; so that I could quite understand why Mrs. Clemens should have found some compensation, when kept to her room by sickness, in the reflection that now she should not hear so much about the "damned human race." He told of that with the same wild joy that he told of overhearing her repetition of one of his most inclusive profanities, and her explanation that she meant him to hear it so that he might know how it sounded. The contrast of the lurid blasphemy with her heavenly whiteness should have been enough to cure any one less grounded than he in what must be owned was as fixed a habit as smoking with him. When I first knew him he rarely vented his fury in that sort, and I fancy he was under a promise to her which he kept sacred till the wear and tear of his nerves with advancing years disabled him. Then it would be like him to struggle with himself till he could struggle no longer and to ask his promise back, and it would be like her to give it back. His profanity was the heritage of his boyhood and young manhood in social conditions and under the duress of exigencies in which everybody swore about as impersonally as he smoked. It is best to recognize the fact of it, and I do so the more readily because I cannot suppose the Recording Angel really minded it much more than that Guardian Angel of his. It probably grieved them about equally, but they could equally forgive it. Nothing came of his pose regarding the damned human race except his invention of the Human Race Luncheon Club. This was confined to four persons who were never all got together, and it soon perished of their indifference.

In the earlier days that I have more specially in mind one of the questions that we used to debate a good deal was whether every human motive was not selfish. We inquired as to every impulse, the noblest, the holiest in effect, and he found them in the last analysis of selfish origin. Pretty nearly the whole time of a certain railroad run from New York to Hartford was taken up with the scrutiny of the self-sacrifice of a mother for her child, of the abandon of the lover who dies in saving his mistress from fire or flood, of the hero's courage in the field and the martyr's at the stake. Each he found springing from the unconscious love of self and the dread of the greater pain which the self-sacrificer would suffer in forbearing the sacrifice. If we had any time left from this inquiry that day, he must have devoted it to a high regret that Napoleon did not carry out his purpose of invading England, for then he would have destroyed the feudal aristocracy, or "reformed the lords," as it might be called now. He thought that would have been an incalculable blessing to the English people and the world. Clemens was always beautifully and unfalteringly a republican. None of his occasional misgivings for America implicated a return to monarchy. Yet he felt passionately the splendor of the English monarchy, and there was a time when he gloried in that figurative poetry by which the king was phrased as "the Majesty of England." He rolled the words deep-throatedly out, and exulted in their beauty as if it were beyond any other glory of the world. He read, or read *at*, English history a great deal, and one of the by-products of his restless invention was a game of English Kings (like the game of Authors) for children. I do not know whether he ever perfected this; but I am quite sure it was not put upon the market. Very likely he brought it to a practicable stage, and then tired of it, as he was apt to do in the ultimation of his vehement undertakings.

XX

He satisfied the impassioned demand of his nature for incessant activities of every kind by taking a personal as well as a pecuniary interest in the inventions of others. At one moment the damned human race was almost to be redeemed by a process of founding brass without air bubbles in it; if this could once be accomplished, as I understood, or misunderstood, brass could be used in art-printing to a degree hitherto impossible. I dare say I have got it wrong, but I am not mistaken as to Clemens's enthusiasm for the process, and his heavy losses in paying its way to ultimate failure. He was simultaneously absorbed in the perfection of a type-setting machine, which he was paying the inventor a salary to bring to a perfection so expensive that it was practically impracticable. We were both printers by trade, and I could take the same interest in this wonderful piece of mechanism that he could; and it was so truly wonderful that it did everything but walk and talk. Its ingenious creator was so bent upon realizing the highest ideal in it that he produced a machine of quite unimpeachable efficiency. But it was so costly, when finished, that it could not be made for less than twenty thousand dollars, if the parts were made by hand. This sum was prohibitive of its introduction, unless the requisite capital could be found for making the parts by machinery, and Clemens spent many months in vainly trying to get this money together. In the mean time simpler machines had been invented and the market filled, and his investment of three hundred thousand dollars in the beautiful miracle remained permanent but not profitable. I once went with him to witness its performance, and it did seem to me the last word in its way, but it had been spoken too exquisitely, too fastidiously. I never heard him devote the inventor to the infernal gods, as he was apt to do with the geniuses he lost money by, and so I think he did not regard him as a traitor.

In these things, and in his other schemes for the *subiti guadagni* of the speculator and the "sudden making of splendid names" for the benefactors of our species, Clemens satisfied the Colonel Sellers nature in himself (from which he drew the picture of that wild and lovable figure), and perhaps made as good use of his money as he could. He did not care much for money in itself, but he luxuriated in the lavish use of it, and he was as generous with it as ever a man was. He liked giving it, but he commonly wearied of giving it himself, and wherever he lived he established an almoner, whom he fully trusted to keep his left hand ignorant of what his right hand was doing. I believe he felt no finality in charity, but did it because in its provisional way it was the only thing a man could do. I never heard him go really into any sociological inquiry, and I have a feeling that that sort of thing baffled and dispirited him. No one can read *The Connecticut Yankee* and not be aware of the length and breadth of his sympathies with poverty, but apparently he had not thought out any scheme for righting the economic wrongs we abound in. I cannot remember our ever getting quite down to a discussion of the matter; we came very near it once in the day of the vast wave of emotion sent over the world by *Looking Backward*, and again when we were all so troubled by the great coal strike in Pennsylvania; in considering that he seemed to be for the time doubtful of the justice of the working-man's cause. At all other times he seemed to know that whatever wrongs the working-man committed work was always in the right.

When Clemens returned to America with his family, after lecturing round the world, I again saw him in New York, where I so often saw him while he was shaping himself for that heroic enterprise. He would come to me, and talk sorrowfully over his financial ruin, and picture it to himself as the stuff of some unhappy dream, which, after long prosperity, had culminated the wrong way. It was very melancholy, very touching, but the sorrow to which he had come home from his long journey had not that forlorn bewilderment in it. He was looking wonderfully well, and when I wanted the name of his elixir, he said it was plasmon. He was apt, for a man who had put faith so decidedly away from him, to take it back and pin it to some superstition, usually of a hygienic sort. Once, when he was well on in years, he came to New York without glasses, and announced that he and all his family, so astigmatic and myopic and old-sighted, had, so to speak, burned their spectacles behind them, upon the instruction of some sage who had found out that they were a delusion. The next time he came he wore spectacles freely, almost ostentatiously, and I heard from others that the whole Clemens family had been near losing their eyesight by the miracle worked in their behalf. Now, I was not surprised to learn that the damned human race was to be saved by plasmon, if anything, and that my first duty was to visit the plasmon agency with him, and procure enough plasmon to secure my family against the ills it was heir to for evermore. I did not immediately understand that plasmon was one of the investments which he had made from "the substance of things hoped for," and in the destiny of a disastrous disappointment. But after paying off the creditors of his late publishing firm, he had to do something with his money, and it was not his fault if he did not make a fortune out of plasmon.

XXI

For a time it was a question whether he should not go back with his family to their old home in Hartford. Perhaps the father's and mother's hearts drew them there all the more strongly because of the grief written ineffaceably over it, but for the younger ones, it was no longer the measure of the world. It was easier for all to stay on indefinitely in New York, which is a sojourn without circumstance, and equally the home of exile and of indecision. The Clemenses took a pleasant, spacious house at Riverdale on the Hudson, and there I began to see them again on something like the sweet old terms. They lived far more unpretentiously than they used, and I think with a notion of economy, which they had never very successfully practised. I recall that at the end of a certain year in Hartford when they had been saving, and paying cash for everything, Clemens wrote, reminding me of their avowed experiment, and asking me to guess how many bills they had at New-Year's; he hastened to say that a horse-car would not have held them. At Riverdale they kept no carriage, and there was a snowy night when I drove up to their handsome old mansion in the station carryall, which was crusted with mud as from the going down of the Deluge after transporting Noah and his family from the Ark to whatever point they decided to settle at provisionally. But the good talk, the rich talk, the talk that could never suffer poverty of mind or soul, was there, and we jubilantly found ourselves again in our middle youth. It was the mighty moment when Clemens was building his engines of war for the destruction of Christian Science, which superstition nobody, and he least of all, expected to destroy. It would not be easy to say whether in his talk of it his disgust for the illiterate twaddle of Mrs. Eddy's book, or his admiration of her genius for organization was the greater. He believed that as a religious machine the Christian Science Church was as perfect as the Roman Church and destined to be more formidable in its control of the minds of men. He looked for its spread over the whole of Christendom; and throughout the winter he spent at Riverdale he was ready to meet all listeners more than half-way with his convictions of its powerful grasp of the average human desire to get something for nothing. The vacuous vulgarity of its texts was a perpetual joy to him, while he bowed with serious respect to the sagacity which built so securely upon the everlasting rock of human credulity and folly.

An interesting phase of his psychology in this business was not only his admiration for the masterly policy of the Christian Science hierarchy, but his willingness to allow the miracles of its healers to be tried on his friends and family, if they wished it. He had a tender heart for the whole generation of empirics, as well as the newer sorts of scientians, but he seemed to base his faith in them largely upon the failure of the regulars rather than upon their own successes, which also he believed in. He was recurrently, but not insistently, desirous that you should try their strange magics when your were going to try the familiar medicines.

XXII

The order of my acquaintance, or call it intimacy, with Clemens was this: our first meeting in Boston, my visits to him in Hartford, his visits to me in Cambridge, in Belmont, and in Boston, our briefer and less frequent meetings in Paris and New York, all with repeated interruptions through my absences in Europe, and his sojourns in London, Berlin, Vienna, and Florence, and his flights to the many ends, and odds and ends, of the earth. I will not try to follow the events, if they were not rather the subjective experiences, of those different periods and points of time, which I must not fail to make include his summer at York Harbor, and his divers residences in New York, on Tenth Street and on Fifth Avenue, at Riverdale, and at Stormfield, which his daughter has told me he loved best of all his houses and hoped to make his home for long years.

Not much remains to me of the week or so that we had together in Paris early in the summer of 1894. The first thing I got at my bankers was a cable message announcing that my father was stricken with paralysis, but urging my stay for further intelligence, and I went about till the final summons came with my head in a mist of care and dread. Clemens was very kind and brotherly through it all. He was living greatly to his mind in one of those arcaded little hotels in the Rue de Rivoli, and he was free from all household duties to range with me. We drove together to make calls of digestion at many houses where he had got indigestion through his reluctance from their hospitality, for he hated dining out. But, as he explained, his wife wanted him to make these visits, and he did it, as he did everything she wanted. At one place, some suburban villa, he could get no answer to his ring, and he "hove" his cards over the gate just as it opened, and he had the shame of explaining in his unexplanatory French to the man picking them up. He was excruciatingly helpless with his cabmen, but by very cordially smiling and casting himself on the drivers' mercy he always managed to get where he wanted. The family was on the verge of their many moves, and he was doing some small errands; he said that the others did the main things, and left him to do what the cat might.

It was with that return upon the buoyant billow of plasmon, renewed in look and limb, that Clemens's universally pervasive popularity began in his own country. He had hitherto been more intelligently accepted, or more largely imagined, in Europe, and I suppose it was my sense of this that inspired the stupidity of my saying to him when we came to consider "the state of polite learning" among us, "You mustn't expect people to keep it up here as they do in England." But it appeared that his countrymen were only wanting the chance, and they kept it up in honor of him past all precedent. One does not go into a catalogue of dinners, receptions, meetings, speeches, and the like when there are more vital things to speak of. He loved these obvious joys, and he eagerly strove with the occasions they gave him for the brilliancy which seemed so exhaustless and was so exhausting. His friends saw that he was wearing himself out, and it was not because of Mrs. Clemens's health alone that they were glad to have him take refuge at Riverdale. The family lived there two happy, hopeless years, and then it was ordered that they should change for his wife's sake to some less exacting climate. Clemens was not eager to go to Florence, but his imagination was taken as it would have been in the old-young days by the notion of packing his furniture into flexible steel cages from his house in Hartford and unpacking it from them untouched at his villa in Fiesole. He got what pleasure any man could out of that triumph of mind over matter, but the shadow was creeping up his life. One sunny afternoon we sat on the grass before the mansion, after his wife had begun to get well enough for removal, and we looked up toward a balcony where by and by that lovely presence made itself visible, as if it had stooped there from a cloud. A hand frailly waved a handkerchief; Clemens ran over the lawn toward it, calling tenderly: "What? What?" as if it might be an asking for him instead of the greeting it really was for me. It was the last time I saw her, if indeed I can be said to have seen her then, and long afterward when I said how beautiful we all thought her, how good, how wise, how wonderfully perfect in every relation of life, he cried out in a breaking voice: "Oh, why didn't you ever tell her? She thought you didn't like her." What a pang it was then not to have told her, but how could we have told her? His unreason endeared him to me more than all his widom.

To that Riverdale sojourn belong my impressions of his most violent anti-Christian Science rages, which began with the postponement of his book, and softened into acceptance of the delay till he had well-nigh forgotten his wrath when it come out. There was also one of those joint episodes of ours, which, strangely enough, did not eventuate in entire failure, as most of our joint episodes did. He wrote furiously to me of a wrong which had been done to one of the most helpless and one of the most helped of our literary brethren, asking me to join with him in recovering the money paid over by that brother's publisher to a false friend who had withheld it and would not give any account of it. Our hapless brother had appealed to Clemens, as he had to me with the facts, but not asking our help, probably because he knew he need not ask; and Clemens enclosed to me a very taking-by-the-throat message which he proposed sending to the false friend. For once, I had some sense, and answered that this would never do, for we had really no power in the matter, and I contrived a letter to the recreant so softly diplomatic that I shall always think of it with pride when my honesties no longer give me satisfaction, saying that this incident had come to our knowledge, and suggesting that we felt sure he would not finally wish to withhold the money. Nothing more, practically, than that, but that was enough; there came promptly back a letter of justification, covering a very substantial check, which we hilariously forwarded to our beneficiary. But the helpless man who was so used to being helped did not answer with the gladness I, at least, expected of him. He acknowledged the check as he would any ordinary payment, and then he made us observe that there was still a large sum due him out of the moneys withheld. At this point I proposed to Clemens that we should let the nonchalant victim collect the remnant himself. Clouds of sorrow had gathered about the bowed head of the delinquent since we began on him, and my fickle sympathies were turning his way from the victim, who was really to blame for leaving his affairs so unguardedly to him in the first place. Clemens made some sort of grim assent, and we dropped the matter. He was more used to ingratitude from those he helped than I was, who found being lain down upon not so amusing as he found my revolt. He reckoned I was right, he said, and after that I think we never recurred to the incident. It was not ingratitude that he ever minded; it was treachery that really maddened him past forgiveness.

XXIII

During the summer he spent at York Harbor I was only forty minutes away at Kittery Point, and we saw each other often;

but this was before the last time at Riverdale. He had a wide, low cottage in a pine grove overlooking York River, and we used to sit at a corner of the veranda farthest away from Mrs. Clemens's window, where we could read our manuscripts to each other, and tell our stories, and laugh our hearts out without disturbing her. At first she had been about the house, and there was one gentle afternoon when she made tea for us in the parlor, but that was the last time I spoke with her. After that it was really a question of how soonest and easiest she could be got back to Riverdale; but of course there were specious delays in which she seemed no worse and seemed a little better, and Clemens could work at a novel he had begun. He had taken a room in the house of a friend and neighbor, a fisherman and boatman; there was a table where he could write, and a bed where he could lie down and read; and there, unless my memory has played me one of those constructive tricks that people's memories indulge in, he read me the first chapters of an admirable story. The scene was laid in a Missouri town, and the characters such as he had known in boyhood; but as often as I tried to make him own it, he denied having written any such story; it is possible that I dreamed it, but I hope the MS. will yet be found. Upon reflection I cannot believe that I dreamed it, and I cannot believe that it was an effect of that sort of pseudo-mnemonics which I have mentioned. The characters in the novel are too clearly outlined in my recollection, together with some critical reservations of my own concerning them. Not only does he seem to have read me those first chapters, but to have talked them over with me and outlined the whole story.

I cannot say whether or not he believed that his wife would recover; he fought the fear of her death to the end; for her life was far more largely his than the lives of most men's wives are theirs. For his own life I believe he would never have much cared, if I may trust a saying of one who was so absolutely without pose as he was. He said that he never saw a dead man whom he did not envy for having had it over, and being done with it. Life had always amused him, and in the resurgence of its interests after his sorrow had ebbed away he was again deeply interested in the world, and in the human race, which, though damned, abounded in subjects of curious inquiry. When the time came for his wife's removal from York Harbor, I went with him to Boston, where he wished to look up the best means of her conveyance to New York. The inquiry absorbed him: the sort of invalid-car he could get; how she could be carried to the village station; how the car could be detached from the eastern train at Boston and carried round to the southern train on the other side of the city, and then how it could be attached to the Hudson River train at New York and left at Riverdale. There was no particular of the business which he did not scrutinize and master, not only with his poignant concern for her welfare, but with his strong curiosity as to how these unusual things were done with the usual means. With the inertness that grows upon an ageing man, he had been used to delegating more and more things, but of that thing I perceived that he would not delegate the least detail.

He had meant never to go abroad again, but when it came time to go he did not look forward to returning; he expected to live in Florence always after that; they were used to the life and they had been happy there some years earlier before he went with his wife for the cure of Nauheim. But when he came home again it was for good and all. It was natural that he should wish to live in New York, where they had already had a pleasant year in Tenth Street. I used to see him there in an upper room, looking south over a quiet open space of back yards where we fought our battles in behalf of the Filipinos and the Boers, and he carried on his campaign against the missionaries in China. He had not yet formed his habit of lying for whole days in bed, and reading and writing there, yet he was a good deal in bed, from weakness, I suppose, and for the mere comfort of it.

My perspectives are not very clear, and in the foreshortening of events which always takes place in our review of the past I may not always time things aright. But I believe it was not until he had taken his house at 21 Fifth Avenue that he began to talk to me of writing his autobiography. He meant that it should be a perfectly veracious record of his life and period; for the first time in literature there should be a true history of a man and a true presentation of the men the man had known. As we talked it over the scheme enlarged itself in our riotous fancy. We said it should be not only a book, it should be a library, not only a library but a literature. It should make good the world's loss through Omar's barbarity at Alexandria; there was no image so grotesque, so extravagant that we did not play with it; and the work so far as he carried it was really done on a colossal scale. But one day he said that as to veracity it was a failure; he had begun to lie, and that if no man ever yet told the truth about himself it was because no man ever could. How far he had carried his autobiography I cannot say; he dictated the matter several hours each day; and the public has already seen long passages from it, and can judge, probably, of the make and matter of the whole from these. It is immensely inclusive, and it observes no order or sequence. Whether now, after his death, it will be published soon or late, I have no means of knowing. Once or twice he said in a vague way that it was not to be published for twenty years, so that the discomfort of publicity might be minimized for all the survivors. Suddenly he told me he was not working at it; but I did not understand whether he had finished it, or merely dropped it; I never asked.

We lived in the same city, but, for old men, rather far apart, he at Tenth Street and I at Seventieth, and with our colds and other disabilities we did not see each other often. He expected me to come to him, and I would not, without some return of my visits, but we never ceased to be friends, and good friends, so far as I know. I joked him once as to how I was going to come out in his autobiography, and he gave me some sort of joking reassurance. There was one incident, however, that brought us very frequently and actively together. He came one Sunday afternoon to have me call with him on Maxim Gorky, who was staying at a hotel a few streets above mine. We were both interested in Gorky, Clemens rather more as a revolutionist and I as a realist, though I too wished the Russian Czar ill, and the novelist well in his mission to the Russian sympathizers in this republic. But I had lived through the episode of Kossuth's visit to us and his vain endeavor to raise funds for the Hungarian cause in 1851, when we were a younger and nobler nation than now, with hearts if not hands opener to the "oppressed of Europe"; the oppressed of America, the four or five millions of slaves, we did not count. I did not believe that Gorky could get the money for the cause of freedom in Russia which he had come to get; as I told a valued friend of his and mine, I did not believe he could get $2,500, and I think now I set the figure too high. I had already refused to sign the sort of general appeal his friends were making to our principles and pockets because I felt it so wholly idle, and when the paper was produced in Gorky's presence, and Clemens put his name to it, I still refused. The next day Gorky was expelled from his hotel with the woman who was not his wife, but who, I am bound to say, did not look as if she were not, at least to me, who am, however, not versed in those aspects of human nature.

I might have escaped unnoted, but Clemens's familiar head gave us away to the reporters waiting at the elevator's mouth for all who went to see Gorky. As it was, a hunt of interviewers ensued for us severally and jointly. I could remain aloof in my hotel apartment, returning answer to such guardians of the public right to know everything that I had nothing to say of Gorky's domestic affairs; for the public interest had now strayed far from the revolution, and centred entirely upon these. But with Clemens it was different; he lived in a house with a street door kept by a single butler, and he was constantly rung for. I forget how long the siege lasted, but long enough for us to have fun with it. That was the moment of the great Vesuvian eruption, and we figured ourselves in easy reach of a volcano which was every now and then "blowing a cone off," as the telegraphic phrase was. The roof of the great market in Naples had just broken in under its load of ashes and cinders, and crushed hundreds of people; and we asked each other if we were not sorry we had not been there, where the pressure would have been far less terrific than it was with us in Fifth Avenue. The forbidden butler came up with a message that there were some gentlemen below who wanted to see Clemens.

"How many?" he demanded.

"Five," the butler faltered.

"Reporters?"

The butler feigned uncertainty.

"What would you do?" he asked me.

"I wouldn't see them," I said, and then Clemens went directly down to them. How or by what means he appeased their voracity, I cannot say, but I fancy it was by the confession of the exact truth, which was harmless enough. They went away joyfully, and he came back in radiant satisfaction with having seen them. Of course he was right and I wrong, and he was right as to the point at issue between Gorky and those who had helplessly treated him with such cruel ignominy. In America it is not the convention for men to live openly in hotels with women who are not their wives. Gorky had violated this convention and he had to pay the penalty; and concerning the destruction of his efficiency as an emissary of the revolution, his blunder was worse than a crime.

XXIV

To the period of Clemens's residence in Fifth Avenue belongs his efflorescence in white serge. He was always rather aggressively indifferent about dress, and at a very early date in our acquaintance Aldrich and I attempted his reform by clubbing to buy him a cravat. But he would not put away his stiff little black bow, and until he imagined the suit of white serge, he wore always a suit of black serge, truly deplorable in the cut of the sagging frock. After his measure had once been taken he refused to make his clothes the occasion of personal interviews with his tailor; he sent the stuff by the kind elderly woman who had been in the service of the family from the earliest days of his marriage, and accepted the result without criticism. But the white serge was an inspiration which few men would have had the courage to act upon. The first time I saw him wear it was at the authors' hearing before the Congressional Committee on Copyright in Washington. Nothing could have been more dramatic than the gesture with which he flung off his long loose overcoat, and stood forth in white from his feet to the crown of his silvery head. It was a magnificent *coup*, and he dearly loved a *coup*; but the magnificent speech which he made, tearing to shreds the venerable farrago of nonsense about non-property in ideas which had formed the basis of all copyright legislation, made you forget even his spectacularity.

It is well known how proud he was of his Oxford gown, not merely because it symbolized the honor in which he was held by the highest literary body in the world, but because it was so rich and so beautiful. The red and the lavender of the cloth flattered his eyes as the silken black of the same degree of Doctor of Letters, given him years before at Yale, could not do. His frank, defiant happiness in it, mixed with a due sense of burlesque, was something that those lacking his poet-soul could never imagine; they accounted it vain, weak; but that would not have mattered to him if he had known it. In his London sojourn he had formed the top-hat habit, and for a while he lounged splendidly up and down Fifth Avenue in that society emblem; but he seemed to tire of it, and to return kindly to the soft hat of his Southwestern tradition.

He disliked clubs; I don't know whether he belonged to any in New York, but I never met him in one. As I have told, he himself had formed the Human Race Club, but as he never could get it together it hardly counted. There was to have been a meeting of it the time of my only visit to Stormfield in April of last year; but of three who were to have come, I alone came. We got on very well without the absentees, after finding them in the wrong, as usual, and the visit was like those I used to have with him so many years before in Hartford, but there was not the old ferment of subjects. Many things had been discussed and put away for good, but we had our old fondness for nature and for each other, who were so differently parts of it. He showed his absolute content with his house, and that was the greater pleasure for me because it was my son who designed it. The architect had been so fortunate as to be able to plan it where a natural avenue of savins, the close-knit, slender, cypress-like cedars of New England, led away from the rear of the villa to the little level of a pergola, meant some day to be wreathed and roofed with vines. But in the early spring days all the landscape was in the beautiful nakedness of the northern winter. It opened in the surpassing loveliness of wooded and meadowed uplands, under skies that were the first days blue, and the last gray over a rainy and then a snowy floor. We walked up and down, up and down, between the villa terrace and the pergola, and talked with the melancholy amusement, the sad tolerance of age for the sort of men and things that used to excite us or enrage us; now we were far past turbulence or anger. Once we took a walk together across the yellow pastures to a chasmal creek on his grounds, where the ice still knit the clayey banks together like crystal mosses; and the stream far down clashed through and over the stones and the shards of ice. Clemens pointed out the scenery he had bought to give himself elbow-room, and showed me the lot he was going to have me build on. The next day we came again with the geologist he had asked up to Stormfield to analyze its rocks. Truly he loved the place, though he had been so weary of change and so indifferent to it, that he never saw it till he came to live in it. He left it all to the architect whom he had known from a child in the intimacy which bound our families together, though we bodily lived far enough apart. I loved his little ones and he was sweet to mine and was their delighted-in and wondered-at friend. Once and once again, and yet again and again, the black shadow that shall never be lifted where it falls, fell in his house and in mine, during the forty years and more that we were friends, and endeared us the more to each other.

XXV

My visit at Stormfield came to an end with tender relucting on his part and on mine. Every morning before I dressed I heard him sounding my name through the house, for the fun of it and I know for the fondness; and if I looked out of my door, there he was in his long nightgown swaying up and down the corridor, and wagging his great white head like a boy that leaves his bed and comes out in the hope of frolic with some one. The last morning a soft sugar-snow had fallen and was falling, and I drove through it down to the station in the carriage which had been given him by his wife's father when they were first married, and been kept all those intervening years in honorable retirement for this final use. Its springs had not grown yielding with time; it had rather the stiffness and severity of age; but for him it must have swung low like the sweet chariot of the negro "spiritual" which I heard him sing with such fervor when those wonderful hymns of the slaves began to make their way northward. *Go down, Daniel,* was one in which I can hear his quavering tenor now. He was a lover of the things he liked, and full of a passion for them which satisfied itself in reading them matchlessly aloud. No one could read *Uncle Remus* like him; his voice echoed the voices of the negro nurses who told his childhood the wonderful tales. I remember especially his rapture with Mr. Cable's *Old Creole Days,* and the thrilling force with which he gave the forbidding of the leper's brother when the city's survey ran the course of an avenue through the cottage where the leper lived in hiding: "Strit must not pass!"

Out of a nature rich and fertile beyond any I have known, the material given him by the Mystery that makes a man and then leaves him to make himself over, he wrought a character of high nobility upon a foundation of clear and solid truth. At the last day he will not have to confess anything, for all his life was the free knowledge of any one who would ask him of it. The Searcher of hearts will not bring him to shame at that day, for he did not try to hide any of the things for which he was often so bitterly sorry. He knew where the Responsibility lay, and he took a man's share of it bravely; but not the less fearlessly he left the rest of the answer to the God who had imagined men.

It is in vain that I try to give a notion of the intensity with which he pierced to the heart of life, and the breadth of vision with which he compassed the whole world, and tried for the reason of things, and then left trying. We had other meetings, insignificantly sad and brief; but the last time I saw him alive was made memorable to me by the kind, clear judicial sense with which he explained and justified the labor-unions as the sole present help of the weak against the strong.

Next I saw him dead, lying in his coffin amidst those flowers with which we garland our despair in that pitiless hour. After the voice of his old friend Twichell had been lifted in the prayer, which it wailed through in broken-hearted supplication, I looked a moment at the face I knew so well; and it was patient with the patience I had so often seen in it: something of puzzle, a great silent dignity, an assent to what must be, from the depths of a nature whose tragical seriousness broke in the laughter which the unwise took for the whole of him. Emerson, Longfellow, Lowell, Holmes—I knew them all and all the rest of our sages, poets, seers, critics, humorists; they were like one another and like other literary men; but Clemens was sole, incomparable, the Lincoln of our literature.

Notes to the Text

Annotation is provided only where the information is unavailable in standard, one-volume reference works.

7.16–17   little volume of very unknown verse: *Poems of Two Friends*, 1860.

8.30   visiting young lady: Elinor Gertrude Mead, of Brattleboro, Vermont, who became Mrs. W. D. Howells on 24 December 1862.

8.34   my roommate: A. T. Fullerton, perhaps Artemus Thomas Fullerton (1835?–1914?).

9.14   "I too was born in Arcadia," Friedrich Schiller, "Resignation," l. 1.

18.9ff.   Cf. Longfellow, "My Lost Youth."

21.15   The last line of Heinrich Heine, "Ein Fichtenbaum steht einsam"; literally rendered, the line means, "On a burning precipice." Longfellow translated the poem as "The Fir-Tree and the Palm":

> A lonely fir-tree standeth
>   On a height where north winds blow;
> It sleepeth, with whitened garment,
>   Enshrouded by ice and snow.
>
> It dreameth of a palm-tree,
>   That far in the Eastern land,
> Lonely and silent, mourneth
>   On its burning shelf of sand.

24.15–16   "Old Harvard's scholar factories red": James Russell Lowell, "An Invitation," l. 33.

25.34–35   Tennyson, "The Poet," ll. 3–4.

27.2   Page's portrait: William Page (1811–1885), portraitist and friend to whom Lowell dedicated *Poems*, 1844, painted this in 1843.

28.7   Goldsmith, "The Deserted Village," l. 206.

28.23–24   "it was not for me to bandy words with my sovereign": Boswell, *Life of Samuel Johnson*, reads: "It was not for me to bandy civilities with my Sovereign."

36.36   Mutual Admiration Society: in *The Autocrat of the Breakfast Table*, first essay, Holmes said, "All generous companies of artists, authors, philanthropists, men of science, are, or ought to be, Societies of Mutual Admiration."

39.3   "beard as broad as ony spade": Chaucer, *The Canterbury Tales*, "Prologue," l. 553 reads, "And therto brood, as though it were a spade."

40.4   gracious spirit: Mrs. Annie Fields (1834–1915) kept the famous house and atmosphere intact for more than thirty years after her husband's death in 1881.

44.13–14   a Harvard Senior: the son who would become Justice Oliver Wendell Holmes.

45.7   The tomb of Cæcilia Metella, wife of Crassus the Younger, has stood on the Appian Way since the rule of Augustus.

45.12ff.   I am not able to say how . . . : since Lowell's note to Hawthorne was dated Sunday, 5 August, and delivered on Monday, and Thoreau was not in Concord until 10 August, how did this famous week go? It appears that the Parker House dinner occurred on Friday, 3 August; Howells left Boston on Monday for a first visit with the Meads at Brattleboro and stayed in Lowell, Massachusetts, on the night of 7 August, arriving in Concord

8 August. Thursday afternoon was devoted to Hawthorne. On Friday Howells saw Thoreau in the morning, had dinner at noon and after-dinner conversation with Emerson. On Saturday, 11 August, he returned to Boston, having spent three nights and two days in Concord.

45.24   Tennyson, "A Dream of Fair Women," l. 101.

53.26–27   the riddle of the painful earth: Tennyson, "The Palace of Art," l. 213.

54.10   the John Brown raid: Howells' father in Jefferson, Ohio, had been active in support of John Brown's associates, especially in shielding fugitives from Federal pursuit; and Howells in Columbus had been a passionate political and poetic advocate of Brown.

57.24ff.   a literary periodical . . . in Cincinnati: Moncure D. Conway, ed., *The Dial: A Monthly Magazine for Literature, Philosophy and Religion,* published two Howells poems in June 1860.

58.2   "pleached garden": Emerson, "Days," l. 7.

62.31   editor: Henry Clapp.

64.8   Henry Giles (1809–1882), American Unitarian clergyman, reformer, essayist, was also an Irish wit.

65.6–7   queen of Bohemia: Ada Clare.

69.26   Mr. Butler's poem: William Allen Butler, *Nothing to Wear: An Episode of City Life,* 1857.

71.19   the May number of the Knickerbocker: the *Knickerbocker* published "A Dream" by Howells in August 1861.

74.21   the young Boston publisher: Charles W. Eldridge (1811–1883).

74.28   a friend's house: John J. Piatt, then rooming with Stedman.

75.36   former editor: Alfred H. Guernsey (1825–1902) edited
          Harper's Monthly from 1856 to 1869.

76.5   a friend: Conway.

77.7   Franklin Square: location of Harper & Brothers.

77.35–36 Cf. Cowper, "The Task," II, ll. 3–4.

78.35   Stillman's place: William James Stillman (1828–1901),
          one of Howells' many friends among painters, attended
          this dinner.

79.16   the book I have written myself: *Venetian Life*, 1866.

81.18   Forceythe Willson (1837–1867), *The Old Sergeant, and
          Other Poems*, 1867.

91.24–25 Bartley Hubbard's: cf. Howells, *A Modern Instance*, 1882.

91.34   editor-in-chief: Henry J. Raymond.

92.5–6   a literary paper: *The Round Table*.

93.17   Huntington: William H. (1820–1885).

94.24   great speech on the Kansas question in 1855: the speech
          in question seems to have been "The Duty of the Ameri-
          can Scholar to Politics and the Times," delivered at
          Wesleyan University, 5 August 1856.

97.11   Mr. Osgood: James Ripley (1836–1892). A close friend,
          Osgood became a partner in the publishing firms which
          owned the *Atlantic* and employed Howells from 1866 to
          1881. Between 1881 and 1885, he was in a sense Howells'
          business manager.

104.20–21 Tennyson, "A Dream of Fair Women," ll. 43–44.

110.18   Artemus Ward: this last meeting took place early in March 1866. Ward actually sailed on his triumphant, fatal English visit in June 1866.

112.20   George Stillman Hillard (1808–1879) was best known for speeches like "The Relation of the Poet to His Age" (1843).

114.2   Stepniak: pseudonym of Sergei Michailovich Kravchinskii (1852–1895), Russian democrat and revolutionary. He and Howells became warm friends.

114.25–27 Tennyson, "The Two Voices," ll. 304–306.

118.29   *Othello*, V, ii, 145.

122.1   a book of mine describing boy-life: *A Boy's Town*, 1890.

123.7   a new light: Tolstoy.

127.30–31 my Bostonian: Miles Arbuton, *A Chance Acquaintance*, 1873.

134.1   sole editor: beginning 1 July 1871.

137.20–21 Saturday Club: Howells joined the Saturday Club in 1874.

138.23   three privileged years: Howells bought his house at 302 Beacon St. in August 1884.

141.16   a visitant: Howells' daughter Winifred died 3 March 1889; Holmes' daughter Amelia Sargent died 4 April 1889.

144.24ff. "The Exile's Secret," first published in *Songs in Many Keys*, 1862, as "The Island Ruin."

145.36   Holmes, "The Moral Bully," l. 56.

147.29   Spectre Pig: cf. R. H. Dana, "The Buccaneer," *Poems*, 1827.

148.1   occasion: William Cooper Howells died 28 August 1894.

153.30–31 John Gorham Palfrey (1796–1881), theologian, historian; James Mills Peirce (1834–1906), astronomer, mathematician, brother of Charles Sanders Peirce; Andrew Preston Peabody (1811–1893), theologian, ed. *North American Review*, 1853–1863; Evangelinus Apostolides Sophocles (*c.* 1805–1883), Harvard classicist.

154.20   Dante Club: Howells probably first attended about 28 January 1866.

157.35–36 John White Webster (1793–1850), Harvard professor of chemistry and mineralogy, committed the most notorious murder in American academic annals. Heavily in debt, Webster borrowed money from Robert Gould Shaw, Sr., offering as security a mineral collection previously pledged on money owed to Dr. George Parkman. Called to account, Webster invited Parkman to a conference in his laboratory, murdered him, and attempted to dispose of the body. When a suspicious janitor discovered human bones in the vault, Webster was arrested. The trial became famous for Chief Justice Lemuel Shaw's groundbreaking treatment of circumstantial evidence and because expert testimony, identifying as Parkman's the false teeth found in Webster's furnace, in effect hanged Professor Webster.

160.23   Longfellow, "In the Churchyard at Cambridge," l. 2.

162.30   Lowell's line in the penultimate stanza of "No. XI. Mr. Hosea Biglow's Speech in March Meeting," *Biglow Papers, Second Series*, reads "To flaunt it in a Blind Man's Holiday." Perhaps Howells was also remembering Byron's "Butcher'd to make a Roman holiday," *Childe Harold*, IV, cxli.

170.28   The Challenge: written 1873.

172.8–9   A Counterfeit Presentment: staged 1878.

176.1   winter: Björnson's Cambridge winter was 1880–1881.

176.23   Garfield: James A. Garfield, President-to-be.

177.13   Longfellow, "Bayard Taylor," l. 1.

182.14   a precious letter: Howells' memory conflated two letters. The one referred to was dated Elmwood, 2 November 1865; but Lowell's advice to "sweat the Heine out" appears in that letter of 28 July 1864, written to accept "Recent Italian Comedy" for *The North American Review*, which served as the "turning point" in Howells' life.

185.10   poem on Agassiz: published 1874.

186.4–5   Lowell, "A Winter-Evening Hymn to my Fire," ll. 175–176.

187.16–17   Cf. Dante, "Purgatorio," XIX, ll. 19–20. In Longfellow's translation:

> "I am," she sang, "I am the Siren sweet
> Who mariners amid the main unman . . ."

187.23   *sommo poeta*: total poet.

189.12   one little thorny point: Howells, reviewing Lowell's *Poetical Works*, 1876 (*Atlantic*, XXXIX, January 1877, 94), noted as a negative characteristic "the lofty psalm that loses itself in the echoes of the sounding-board," and in the proof of this essay recalled, but later cancelled the line, that Lowell had picked him up, saying: "That was a clever skit of yours about the echoes of the sounding board."

191.14   Lowell, "The Cathedral," l. 78, reads: "An oriole clattered and the robins shrilled."

192.6   four years: 1866–1869.

197.14   Tennyson, "Tithonus," l. 17, reads: "Like wealthy men
           who care not how they give."

198.1ff.   The first quotation is from "Forlorn," *Nation*, III (1866),
           134–135, reprinted *Poems*, 1873; the second is from "Be-
           fore the Gate," *Atlantic*, XXIV (1869), 176, reprinted
           Poems, 1873, where the last line of the third stanza reads:
           "And what they would, would rather they would not so."

199.13   diary of a Virginian: Lucian Minor, "A Virginian in
           New England Thirty-five Years Ago," *Atlantic*, XXVI
           (August–October, December, 1870).

200.20–21 family connection with the President: Elinor Mead
           Howells was a cousin of Hayes.

201.12   "Upon this hint I acted": *Othello*, I, iii, 166, reads: "Upon
           this hint I spake."

201.17   London: Howells went to London in July 1882.

203.30   *Biglow Papers, First Series*, "Introduction," reads "Had
           hammered stone . . ."

204.31   her death: Mrs. Lowell died 19 February 1885.

207.20–21 four or five years later: Lowell returned to Elmwood in
           1889.

208.24   That winter: 1889–1890.

212.29–30 a bit of devotional verse: "Thanksgiving" was included
           in Child's *Poems of Religious Sorrow, Comfort, Counsel, and
           Aspiration*, 1866.

219.1–2   my praise cannot please him any more: Boyesen died
           4 October 1895.

228.2   Jeffries Wyman (1814–1874): professor of anatomy, then
           curator of the Peabody Museum of archaeology and eth-

nology at Harvard. Like Agassiz a devout believer, he sided against Agassiz and on the Darwinian side in the evolution controversy.

242.14   *dolce lome*: Dante, "Inferno," X, l. 69. The speaker is Cavalcante, in whose Bolognese dialect "lume" becomes "lome." Longfellow's translation reads: "Does not the sweet light strike upon his eyes?" Cf. Eccles., XI, 7: "Truly the light is sweet, and a pleasant thing it is for the eyes to behold the sun."

243.27   Milton, "Epitaph on Shakespeare," l. 5.

246.28   Cf. *Biglow Papers, Second Series*, "No. VI. Sunthin' in the Pastoral Line," l. 108.

249.14   "*This is the dream of his life*": Mark Twain, cf. p. 258.

249.26   "or few or none," to "shake against the cold": cf. Shakespeare, Sonnet LXXIII, ll. 2–3.

252.13   Tennyson, "A Dream of Fair Women," l. 101; cf. p. 45.

253.16   publisher of the *Overland Monthly*: John H. Carmany.

254.35–36   adapt the incident to the exigencies of fiction: the death of Nevil, *The Shadow of a Dream*, 1890.

255.6   Cf. Thomas Campbell, "The Soldier's Dream," l. 14.

256.9   a long notice of a book: in the *Atlantic* for December 1869, available in mid-November.

258.6   a lunch in Boston: Keeler's lunches began in 1871.

258.35   Our next meeting: 6 March 1874.

260.31–32   *Paradise Lost*, II, ll. 559–560.

262.13–14   There had been a boy: Langdon Clemens died 2 June 1872.

262.30   his first English sojourn: Clemens sailed 21 August 1872, returning 26 November.

263.19–20   she was dead: Olivia Langdon Clemens died 5 June 1904.

265.34–37   Cf. William Morris, "Shameful Death," ll. 31–36.

268.34   *Sellers*: The "Ur" *Colonel Sellers* opened at the California Theatre on 22 April 1874. Clemens stopped the production and re-wrote the play, entering it for copyright in July 1874. It opened at the Park Theatre, New York, 16 September 1874, where it ran 119 nights. The "unknown dramatist" was Gilbert B. Densmore, drama critic for the San Francisco *Golden Era*.

271.8   Demarest Lloyd: Raymond was playing in David Demarest Lloyd's *For Congress*, which opened 10 January 1884.

272.19–20   an elocutioner: Alfred P. Burbank (1846–1894).

273.4   Arnold came there to lecture: the reception in Hartford fell on 14 November 1883.

278.11–12   The late Noah Brooks: Brooks (1830–1903) was a California journalist who finished his career in the East.

284.6   a party: 13 November 1874.

287.3   a certain author: Will Harben.

288.2   Authors' Readings: 31 March 1887.

290.3–4   a famous lecture-manager: James Burton Pond (1838–1903).

290.13   my lecturing: spring 1897.

291.21   a poor artist: the sculptor Karl Gerhardt (1853–1915).

291.22–23   the most brilliant of our actor-dramatists: William Gillette (1855–1937).

292.1–2   I might not rise again: Howells was seriously ill in November–December 1881.

292.14   a friendless play of mine: *A Foregone Conclusion*, 12 November 1889.

293.23   his awful speech: at the Whittier Birthday dinner, 17 December 1877.

297.7–8   ever printed it: the famous speech was published in *Mark Twain's Speeches* (1910), with an introduction by Howells.

297.26   one day: probably in March 1885.

300.16   a certain famous trial: the adultery trial of Henry Ward Beecher, January–July 1875.

301.16–17   a certain newspaper: the New York *Tribune* published four notices, all legitimately newsworthy, of Clemens in the fall of 1881.

303.21–22   Life of Pope Leo XIII.: Bernard O'Reilly, *Life of Pope Leo XIII*, 1887.

304.27–28   "high sorrowful and cloyed": Keats, "Ode on a Grecian Urn," l. 29.

307.23   *subiti guadagni*: "unexpected gain."

308.13–14   after lecturing round the world: Clemens returned to the United States 15 October 1900.

308.34   plasmon: a German patented food supplement.

309.16   Riverdale: in the fall of 1901, Clemens rented the Morris-Appleton mansion.

313.3   Our hapless brother: Charles Warren Stoddard.

313.35   the summer he spent at York Harbor: 1902.

315.23   the cure of Nauheim: 1892.

315.25–26   a pleasant year in Tenth Street: 1900.

315.36   21 Fifth Avenue: autumn 1904.

317.18   those aspects of human nature: Gorky, with the Russian
             actress Maria Andreyeva, arrived in New York 10 April
             1906. On Saturday, 14 April, the New York *World*, piqued
             because Gorky signed a contract to write for the *American*,
             proclaimed that Gorky and Andreyeva were not legally
             man and wife.

319.1–2   authors' hearing: Clemens and Howells testified on 7
             December 1906.

319.15–16   Doctor of Letters: Howells and Clemens both received
             honorary Doctor of Letters degrees from Yale on 23
             October 1901. Clemens' Oxford degree was conferred
             26 June 1907, three years after Howells'.

320.2   my son. . . . The architect: John Mead Howells.

TEXTUAL APPARATUS

Textual Commentary

Of the eight essays which comprise the first edition of *Literary Friends and Acquaintance: A Personal Retrospect of American Authorship* (BAL 9736), seven were initially published between 1894 and 1900 in *Harper's Monthly*; the other, "Studies of Lowell," appeared originally in *Scribner's* as "A Personal Retrospect of James Russell Lowell" in September 1900. "A Belated Guest," first published as an "Editor's Easy Chair" piece in *Harper's Monthly* for December 1903, and "My Mark Twain," published in three parts as "My Memories of Mark Twain" in the same magazine for July–September 1910 and later that year as the first part of *My Mark Twain: Reminiscences and Criticisms* (BAL 9803), were added to for an edition of *Literary Friends and Acquaintance* which appeared first in 1910.[1]

Although there are only these two editions of *Literary Friends and Acquaintance*, this composite text poses many editorial problems. Indeed, since for the several items different kinds of documentary evidence survive, since the history of textual transmission varies in degree of complexity from item to item, and since the measure of Howells' control over their publication also differs considerably, it is difficult to offer editorial generalizations that would apply to all of these items. Discussion of the special textual problems of each, therefore, has been reserved for the summary of textual information at the end of this commentary. It should be said at the outset, however, that the basic editorial decision affecting their publication in this volume was to consider each item as a separate editorial unit. That is, no attempt has been made to impose regularity or consistency among the parts, each of which has its own textual history.

As the "Bibliographical" note to the edition of 1910 makes clear,

---

1. This 1910 edition is not listed in either the *Bibliography of American Literature* or the Gibson and Arms Howells bibliography. Though the sheets of the first part of the book seem to have been printed from the same plates as those used for the original edition, the added material justifies designating it as a new edition. The "Library Edition" (BAL 9811) differs only in title-page and binding.

Howells had thought seriously of writing his literary reminiscences long before Harper & Brothers agreed to publish them in *Harper's Monthly*. When, in the spring of 1900, he contracted with Harper & Brothers for book publication, he characteristically took the occasion to revise in varying degrees the titles and contents of the several papers.[2] The trade "edition" of *Literary Friends and Acquaintance* (BAL 9736) was deposited for copyright on 17 November 1900. An "Autograph Edition," "limited to 150 copies," was prepared at the same time, using the same sheets but omitting the two pages of advertising matter; this impression also corrected the nonsense line at 26.20. Other impressions appeared late in 1900 and in 1901; a fifth impression in 1902 added an index. The new edition, adding a bibliographical note and the pieces on Bret Harte and Mark Twain, was published first in 1910 and then as part of the abortive thirty-two volume Harper's "Library Edition" on 26 July 1911, though the latter was not deposited for copyright until 30 January 1913.[3] Unfortunately, neither detailed printing and publishing information nor sales records are known to survive for any of these printings.

Throughout this volume, required but missing pointing has been supplied silently and merely visual appurtenances have been ignored. All other emendations, corrections, and variants are listed in the appropriate lists or accounted for in textual notes. It is our hope that by applying established editorial principles and procedures to each item separately we have produced as far as possible texts which reflect in each case Howells' final intentions with respect both to his words and to such elements of texture as spelling, capitalization, word-division, and punctuation.[4]

Following is the complete list of printed materials and manuscripts used in preparing this group of critically edited texts:

Printed items collated: copies of *Harper's Monthly*, *Harper's Weekly*, and *Scribner's*, in the Indiana University Library and the Carroll

---

2. The contract called for payment of 15% royalty up to 5,000 copies, 20% thereafter. Contract, 21 April 1900, Houghton Library.

3. For an account of this project see Robert W. Walts, "William Dean Howells and His Library Edition," *PBSA*, LII (1958), 283–294.

4. See, for example, Center for Editions of American Authors, *Statement of Editorial Principles: A Working Manual for Editing Nineteenth Century American Texts*, July 1967; Fredson Bowers, "The Centenary Texts: Editorial Principles," printed in volumes of The Centenary Edition of Nathaniel Hawthorne, concisely spells out these principles and procedures and illustrates their application.

College Library; a copy of *Harper's Bazar,* in the Public Library of Cincinnati and Hamilton County; copies of the first impression of the first edition of *Literary Friends and Acquaintance* in the Lilly Library (PS2029.L3) and the Howells Edition Center (HE9736.1.1, HE9736.1.2, HE9736.1.3, HE9736.1.5); a copy of the second impression of *Literary Friends and Acquaintance,* the "Autograph Edition," in the Houghton Library, Harvard University (AC85.H8395 900la); a copy of the third 1900 impression of *Literary Friends and Acquaintance* in the Howells Edition Center (HE9736.3.1); a copy of the 1902 impression of *Literary Friends and Acquaintance* in the Howells Edition Center (HE9736.4.1); a copy of the 1910 enlarged edition of *Literary Friends and Acquaintance* in the Haverford College Library (PS2033.A5 1910); a copy of the 1911 "Library Edition" of *Literary Friends and Acquaintance* (BAL 9811) in the Lilly Library (PS2029.L3 1911); copies of the 1910 first impression of *My Mark Twain* (BAL 9803) in the Lilly Library (PS2029.M88) and in the Howells Edition Center (HE9803.1.1); other copies of *My Mark Twain* in the Carroll College Library (PS1331.H65) and in the Indiana University Library (PS1330.H8).

Manuscripts and proofs collated: "First Impressions of Literary New York," in George Arms' collection; "Studies of Lowell," in Charles E. Feinberg's collection; "Cambridge Neighbors," in the Library of the Western Reserve Historical Society, Cleveland, Ohio, in the Houghton Library, Harvard University, and in the Rutherford B. Hayes Memorial Library, Fremont, Ohio.

Summary of Textual Information

BIBLIOGRAPHICAL

Printed only in the second edition of *Literary Friends and Acquaintance.* Neither manuscript nor proof has been located; the 1910 publication serves as copy-text.

MY FIRST VISIT TO NEW ENGLAND

First published in *Harper's Monthly,* LXXXVIII–LXXXIX (May–August 1894); reprinted in 1900 and 1910 editions of *Literary Friends and Acquaintance.* Neither manuscript nor proof has been located; the serial publication serves as copy-text.

First Impressions of Literary New York

First published in *Harper's Monthly*, XCI (June 1895); reprinted in 1900 and 1910 editions of *Literary Friends and Acquaintance*. A manuscript fragment survives, consisting of a single leaf, numbered 14, in regular typescript, mostly cancelled, and two autograph leaves, numbered A-14 and B-14, with a few revisions by Howells; the typescript leaf measures 7⅝ in. x 9⅝ in., the autograph leaves 7⅝ in. x 4⅞ in. The material on these leaves is similar in content but not in wording to pages 71–73; they did not serve as setting-copy for the serial text. The serial publication serves as copy-text.

Roundabout to Boston

First published in *Harper's Monthly*, XCI (August 1895); reprinted in 1900 and 1910 editions of *Literary Friends and Acquaintance*, with section V, 93.33–96.30, added. Section V was first published in *Harper's Weekly*, XXXVI (10 September 1892), as "George William Curtis." Neither manuscript nor proof has been located; the serial publications serve as copy-text: *Harper's Monthly* for 80.1–93.32, 96.31–97.31; *Harper's Weekly* for 93.33–96.30.

Literary Boston as I Knew It

First published as "Literary Boston Thirty Years Ago," in *Harper's Monthly*, XCI (November 1895). When reprinted in 1900 and 1910 editions of *Literary Friends and Acquaintance* as "Literary Boston as I Knew It," sections VIII–XI were added. Part of section XI derives from a typescript prepared for "Cambridge Neighbors" (for description of typescript see below). The periodical publication serves as copy-text for the first seven sections (98.1–114.5); the first book publication serves as copy-text for the four added sections (114.6–124.29), except for that part of section XI which exists in typescript (120.20–123.12).

Oliver Wendell Holmes

First published in *Harper's Monthly*, XCIV (December 1896); reprinted in 1900 and 1910 editions of *Literary Friends and Acquaintance*. Neither manuscript nor proof has been located; the serial publication serves as copy-text.

THE WHITE MR. LONGFELLOW

First published in *Harper's Monthly*, XCIII (August 1896); reprinted in 1900 and 1910 editions of *Literary Friends and Acquaintance*. Neither manuscript nor proof has been located; the serial publication serves as copy-text.

STUDIES OF LOWELL

First published as "A Personal Retrospect of James Russell Lowell" in *Scribner's*, XXVIII (September 1900); reprinted in 1900 and 1910 editions of *Literary Friends and Acquaintance*. The typescript and proof together consist of eighty leaves. Seventy-eight of these are author's or trial proof on buff, wove, watermarked paper measuring approximately 5½ in. x 8½ in., numbered [1] 2–78. Two leaves of blue, italic-face typescript are on buff, wove, watermarked paper measuring approximately 5½ in. x 8½ in., numbered 79–80. Both proof and typescript sheets were made by cutting or tearing 8½ in. x 11 in. sheets. The proof and typescript are revised frequently in black ink and black pencil in Howells' hand. The proof and typescript serve as copy-text. Because evidence suggests that book and serial were set from independently revised sets of proof (a third set, now in the Charles E. Feinberg Collection, was sent to Norton, 4 March 1900), when serial readings are variant they are listed in the Rejected Substantives.

CAMBRIDGE NEIGHBORS

First published as "Some Literary Memories of Cambridge" in *Harper's Monthly*, CI (November 1900). In reprinting it in 1900 and 1910 editions of *Literary Friends and Acquaintance* Howells added the greater part of an earlier essay, "Hjalmar Hjorth Boyesen," first published in *Harper's Bazar*, XXIX (25 January 1896). There are both manuscript-typescript and proof fragments for this chapter. The manuscript-typescript consists of seventeen leaves: fourteen leaves of blue, italic-face typescript, on gray, watermarked wove paper, measuring approximately 4⅞ in. x 8 in., numbered 121–134, with frequent revision by Howells in now faded black or brown ink. Written in pencil, not in Howells' hand, at the end of the third line of leaf 121: "To here / Feb 16" and at the bottom of leaf 121: "Feb 17." Three leaves of holograph manuscript are in now faded black or brown ink; the paper, which is of the same size and color as the typescript leaves, carries no watermark, but like the typescript sheets consists of larger sheets torn in half. These leaves are numbered 135, 136, 139, and show some revision by Howells. Most of the typescript was either cancelled or used for "Literary Boston as I Knew It" when it was reprinted in *Literary Friends and Acquaintance* (see above). In addition there is a single sheet of proof on cream-colored, watermarked wove paper, measuring 5½ in. x 8½ in.; the printed number "62" changed in Howells' hand to "63"; this and Howells' occasional revisions are in black ink. The proof sheet partly overlaps with leaf 139 of the manuscript. The manuscript-typescript serves as copy-text for the part of the text which drew on it (240.5–241.9, 241.26–241.32). The proof sheet serves as copy-text for the part of the text corresponding to it (241.20–241.34), except for the few lines (241.26–241.32) which exist in manuscript (presumably the copy for the proof).

The choice of copy-text for those portions of the text for which neither manuscript nor proof is available, however, was not so easily made. The choice is difficult because there is no evidence that the revised proof which (putatively) served as printer's copy for the serial represented more nearly Howells' final intentions (or that if it did was followed more faithfully) than the revised proofs from which *Literary Friends and Acquaintance* was (putatively) set. The independent descent of two almost simultaneously printed texts from missing documents with primary authority makes the choice of copy-text indifferent. There is no direct evidence that makes it possible to tell whether the accidentals of the serial or of the book have greater authority.

It would be tempting in these circumstances to argue by analogy with "Studies of Lowell," for which trial proof is also extant. But even though for the piece on Lowell the variations in accidentals between proof and serial and proof and book suggest that the book followed the proof more faithfully than the serial, the serial in that case was *Scribner's* and not one prepared by Harper. More reliable grounds for a choice would seem to lie in the extensiveness of revision which marks the book text. Since Howells seems to have had a good many second thoughts about his title, what to restore concerning Norton (he had cancelled a passage in proof prepared for the serial version) and what to add to the section on Boyesen, we decided to use the book version of "Cambridge Neighbors" as copy-text. For the Boyesen material added, the *Harper's Bazar* printing is copy-text (215.20–222.4).

A Belated Guest

First published as an "Editor's Easy Chair" piece in *Harper's Monthly*, CVIII (December 1903); reprinted in 1910 edition of *Literary Friends and Acquaintance*. Neither manuscript nor proof has been located; the serial publication serves as copy-text.

My Mark Twain

First published as "My Memories of Mark Twain" in *Harper's Monthly*, CXXI (July–September 1910); reprinted as "Part First. Memories. My Mark Twain" in *My Mark Twain: Reminiscences and Criticisms*, Harper, 1910; reprinted in 1910 edition of *Literary Friends and Acquaintance*. Neither manuscript nor proof has been located; the serial publication serves as copy-text.

R. G.

Textual Notes

7.1–2　　The first paragraph of the serial publication was reprinted as "Note" preceding table of contents in 1900 *Literary Friends and Acquaintance* (A1), with minor revision (see three word-changes in brackets). In the 1910 edition (B1) the "Note" was dropped.

41.2–3　　Civil War, uncapitalized in A1, is made consistent with S1, copy-text (see 44.5).

94.5　　This title and those at 94.28 and 94.29, italic in S4, have been emended to roman type to conform with S3, copy-text for the greater portion of this part.

102.25　　It is clear that Howells intended to list Flaubert's *Madame Bovary*, but it is surprising that such an obvious error remained uncorrected.

120.33–34　　Here and at 120.34 (twice) and 121.24 in the present text the titles are printed without the quotation marks of the copy-text. Howells styles titles inconsistently in the copy-text (TS2) for this portion, which is part of one of four sections added to the serial version for book publication in 1900. We have therefore normalized the styling of titles to make them conform with S5, the copy-text for the greatest portion of the final text. On the same principle, italic titles in copy-text A1 are printed in roman type.

120.34　　Howells wrote the title inaccurately in typescript and it remained uncorrected.

131.7　　Since this was the only title of a Holmes work set off by quotation marks in the serial, it has been made consistent with the other Holmes titles.

153.30   James Pierce should be James Peirce; see Notes to the Text, page 328.

182.12   Since this is the only instance of a title in italics in the proof, it has been made consistent with the other titles, which appear in roman.

198.14   A1 follows the punctuation of Howells' poem, "Before the Gate," as printed in *Poems*, 1873.

210.14   "Perplexed" is not cancelled in typescript; the first two words are written in above, the last two below the line. The five words are bracketed and followed by a question mark.

216.25   The roman titles of *Harper's Bazar* (S10), copy-text for 215.20–222.4, have been italicized to make them consistent with A1, the copy-text for the greatest portion of this part.

240.5–6   The manuscript-typescript fragment, prepared originally for "Cambridge Neighbors," was partially incorporated in the revision of "Literary Boston as I Knew It" for book publication (see above, pages 340–341). Two segments of the typescript, however, did not appear in either part. On the first leaf of the typescript (numbered 121) are three lines which precede the section printed in "Literary Boston as I Knew It" (120.20–123.12). The sentence fragment reads: "out any flavor of harshness; his mind was as gentle as his manner, which was one of the gentlest I have ever known, and he was of a modesty as fine in its way as Longfellow's modesty, and as little to trespassed upon." Following the "Literary Boston as I Knew It" passage in the typescript, before it becomes copy-text for "Cambridge Neighbors," is the following passage:

XII. ¶ Parton, again, was not of the Cambridge of which these reminiscences profess solely to be, and yet was so, by a devious way of association, both personal and editorial. While I lived there he was writing his life of Jefferson, and printing it in detachable chapters in the Atlantic monthly which I was editing there; and one day there came out to me an old gentleman from Boston, who conceived that some statements in the biography were injurious to his family past. He stated his points, and it seemed to me that he was justly aggrieved, but I could only say that as to the magazine publication it was now too late to do anything. I would, however, write to Mr. Parton, and lay the matter before him; I said I felt sure that whatever he could do he would do to correct the errors he had fallen into when he should prepare the biography for book publication. With this my visitor went away content, and I soon had the pleasure of sending him a letter from Mr. Parton which in its generous regret and good will was apparently everything he could wish. At anyrate I heard afterwards of his expressing his sense of our joint behavior as gentlemanly, with a certain measure of surprise which to this day I cannot understand why he need have felt. But the perspectives of the higher Boston were not always such as to allow the alien at the vanishing point to enjoy the proportions of the beholder at the point of view.

297.9   The footnote to which the asterisk in the serial calls attention appears at the bottom of the page and reads: See "Mark Twain's Speeches."

311.4   1904 appears to be a simple error for 1894.

312.17   The hyphens in C have been dropped here to make the form consistent with 269.21, 285.23, and 300.31.

Emendations

The following list records all substantive and accidental changes introduced into copy-text for each of the parts, except for required but missing punctuation, which has been supplied silently. The reading of the present edition appears to the left of the bracket; the authority for that reading, followed by a semicolon, the copy-text reading, and the copy-text symbol appear to the right of the bracket. The curved dash ∼ represents the same word that appears before the bracket and is used in recording punctuation variants. The abbreviation HE indicates emendation made on the authority of the Howells Edition. Occasionally changes in accidentals have been made on Howells Edition authority, with the first or later editions cited as their source, though these editions of course have no authority for accidentals; that is, an edition is cited because it is the first to incorporate a change and not because the change is thought to have resulted from Howells' intervention. An asterisk indicates that the reading is discussed in the Textual Notes. *Om.* means that the reading to the left of the bracket did not appear in the text cited to the right of the bracket.

The following texts are referred to:

MS 3 leaves of holograph manuscript, "Cambridge Neighbors" (Western Reserve Historical Society)

TS1 2 leaves of typescript, "Studies of Lowell" (Charles E. Feinberg)

TS2 14 leaves of typescript, "Literary Boston as I Knew It" and "Cambridge Neighbors" (Hayes Memorial Library)

P1 78 leaves of proof, "Studies of Lowell" (Charles E. Feinberg)

P2 1 leaf of proof, "Cambridge Neighbors" (Houghton Library)

S1   "My First Visit to New England," *Harper's Monthly*, LXXXVIII–LXXXIX (May–August 1894)

S2   "First Impressions of Literary New York," *Harper's Monthly*, XCI (June 1895)

S3   "Roundabout to Boston," *Harper's Monthly*, XCI (August 1895)

S4   "George William Curtis," *Harper's Weekly*, XXXVI (10 September 1892)

S5   "Literary Boston Thirty Years Ago," *Harper's Monthly*, XCI (November 1895)

S6   "Oliver Wendell Holmes," *Harper's Monthly*, XCIV (December 1896)

S7   "The White Mr. Longfellow," *Harper's Monthly*, XCIII (August 1896)

S8   "A Personal Retrospect of James Russell Lowell," *Scribner's*, XXVIII (September 1900)

S9   "Some Literary Memories of Cambridge," *Harper's Monthly*, CI (November 1900)

S10   "Hjalmar Hjorth Boyesen," *Harper's Bazar*, XXIX (25 January 1896)

S11   "Editor's Easy Chair," *Harper's Monthly*, CVIII (December 1903)

S12   "My Memories of Mark Twain," *Harper's Monthly*, CXXI (July–September 1910)

A1   *Literary Friends and Acquaintance*, Harper, 1900

A2   Harper, 1900: "Autograph Edition"

A3   Harper, 1900

A4   Harper, 1901

A5   Harper, 1902

B1   *Literary Friends and Acquaintance*, Harper, 1910

B2   Harper, 1911: "Library Edition"

C   *My Mark Twain*, Harper, 1910

MY FIRST VISIT TO NEW ENGLAND

*7.1–2   I ¶ If] A1; It seems to me that if one is to write such a paper [book] as this at all, one cannot profitably do so without a frankness concerning one's self as well as others which might be misunderstood. But I wish to make of my own personality merely a background which certain [divers] important figures are projected against, and I am willing even [*om.*] to sacrifice myself a little in giving them relief. I will try to show them as they seemed to me, and I shall not blame any one who says that they are not truly represented; I shall only claim that I have truly represented their appearance, and I shall not claim that I could fully conceive of them in their reality./I. ¶ If S1 [A1–A5]

7.5–6	than I then was] A1; *om.* S1
8.2	rather than blood] A1; *om.* S1
9.11	had] A1; had ever S1
10.11	of] A1; *om.* S1
10.13	seventies] A1; sixties S1
11.19	rich] A1; priceless S1
12.20	In] A1; Many times in S1
12.23	days] A1; years S1
13.28	letters] A1; letters, better than any other S1
13.36	sad] A1; funereal S1
14.32	expectations] A1; expectation S1
15.13	Edward Everett] A1; *om.* S1
16.2	kindle] A1; allume S1
16.3	chastise] A1; chasten S1
16.22	author, so that if] A1; author. If S1
16.24	fame] A1; fame, with some others, whose names would surprise the public S1
17.11	woodland] A1; woods S1
17.22	the feelings of] A1; his feelings as S1
20.8	for him] A1; honor for him in his own country S1
20.10	any] A1; too S1
23.12	Salem] A1; Boston S1
24.11	and] A1; and even S1
25.4	my purpose and pretended] A1; *om.* S1
26.8	tender] A1; tender and lofty S1
26.36	with] A1; by S1
26.36	by] A1; with S1
27.10	this] A1; his S1
28.30	suffer] A1; resent S1
30.24	now who he was] A1; who he was now S1
31.25	such] A1; of such quality S1

33.32	character] A1; quality S1
35.16	Holmes] A1; The Autocrat is with us still, and I shall have to ask his sufferance in saying that I felt myself then, as always when I met him, in the vividest intellectual presence I have ever known. He S1
35.22	The] A1; His renown has since steadily grown, but that, I fancy, may have been its most charming moment for him, when the S1
36.16	glimmered] A1; shone S1
38.18	flavor] A1; quality S1
39.13	suggest to] A1; give S1
*41.2–3	during our Civil War] A1; *om.* S1
41.4	a] A1; another S1
42.29	take] A1; mistake S1
45.7	afterwards] A1; *om.* S1
47.4	lives] A1; lived S1
49.24	about] A1; as to S1
51.16	me] A1; him S1
52.23	As I have said, we] A1; We S1
53.15	sensibilities] A1; senses and sensibilities S1
53.25	is] A1; was S1
55.29	must] A1; would S1
58.7	Ellery] B1; Henry S1
59.8	in my approaches that merited withholding] A1; that merited withholding in my approaches S1
59.18	forty] A1; thirty-four S1

First Impressions of Literary New York

61.1	It] A1; I. ¶ It S2
61.3	1900] A1; 1894 S2
61.15	trains] A1; trains, the ear-slitting bells of the horse-cars, S2
61.22	I] A1; II. S2
62.23	prevailed till very lately] A1; still prevails S2
62.24	thought] A1; think S2
62.24	gave] A1; gives S2
62.35	sort] A1; quality S2
63.24	II] A1; III. S2

65.15	forward] A1; backward S2
68.18	III] A1; IV. S2
69.20	but] A1; but not so much dirt, not so much squalor, and S2
70.33	IV] A1; V. S2
72.28	fifth] A1; third S2
73.30	V] A1; VI. S2
75.14	that] A1; *om.* S2
75.23	his] A1; his large S2
75.25	many,] A1; ~ S2
75.36–76.1	Harper's Monthly] B1; this Magazine S2
77.9	talks] A1; talk S2
77.18	merits] A1; merits, and which will be hers when Time begins to look about him for work worth remembering S2
78.14	for long afterwards] A1; now S2
78.27	VI] A1; VII. S2

ROUNDABOUT TO BOSTON

80.1	During] A1; I. ¶ During S3
81.1	I] A1; II. S3
81.27	war] A1; war, with an increasing tendency to the realism that now prevails, S3
82.8	an ardent] A1; a devoted S3
83.28–29	Mr. Motley] A1; him S3
85.6	II] A1; III. S3
85.14	Archy Moore] A1; Archie More S3
85.18	a] A1; a most S3
86.20	touch] A1; trade S3
87.8	massive] A1; massed S3
87.13	many] A1; *om.* S3
87.17	III] A1; IV. S3
87.29	and usually] A1; or S3
88.9	Brattleboro, Vermont] A1; Brattleboro S3
89.26	when] A1; and when S3
91.17	IV] A1; V. S3
92.10	joyfully] A1; gleefully S3
92.15	could] A1; could put on S3
93.33	V] A1; *om.* S4

93.34–94.21 It was one . . . was not reasonable. Yet he] A1; We
             involuntarily measure the greatness of a man by the
             things he has done for us, and I shall hardly be blamed
             by those who have lived through the time since George
             William Curtis became a fame, if I begin to speak of him
             by owning the debt which I have so long gladly owed
             him. It gives me such right as I have to the pang of
             personal grief which all acquainted with his work must
             share with those nearest him. [¶] He S4

*94.5   My Last Duchess] B1; *My Lost Duchess* A1

94.23   had become] A1; became S4

94.24   in 1855] A1; *om.* S4

94.32   had] A1; *om.* S4

95.2   love] A1; love, and all the glow of that happy moment
             comes back to me, with the gratitude and the new hope
             that filled me S4

95.8–9   him.] A1; him. ¶ When, indeed, he left the party
             which he helped then to establish and to glorify for me,
             I could not go with him, or think with him, but I believe
             that in this sad hour when all Americans mourn him,
             the old Republicans, who were young Republicans in
             those distant days, will gladly recognize that he was
             always the truest of Republicans. S4

95.15   it] A1; it, so that he had no enemies but those of his
             cause S4

95.15   so] A1; so wisely tolerant and so S4

95.18   In] A1; It is hard to realize that in S4

95.19   then] A4; that S4

95.23   He] A1; It is harder still to realize that he S4

95.25   him.] A1; him. Even when he turned from the Republi-
             can party because he thought it grown untrue to itself,
             the obloquy which followed him was faint-hearted and
             perfunctory. S4

96.14   He] A1; These columns have borne such abundant wit-
             ness to the sincerity and fidelity and the unsurpassed
             ability with which he urged his civic ideals, that it would
             hardly be the place here to lament that his gifts were not
             employed in another field. Neither would the multitudes
             who have listened to him on the platform or the stump

consent that such an orator should have been lost to
them in a writer of fiction, however great or fine. In
fact, he S4

96.17   purblind.] A1; purblind. It is marvellous to remember
that in these years, covering now almost a generation,
that have passed since his life was so largely given to the
practical activities of politics and journalism, he has
been constantly contributing to the stock of harmless
gayety, and refining while he instructed his readers by
the sweet civility of his criticisms of life, and manners,
and all the arts, in the Easy Chair. ¶ Now that he is
gone, we can see not only how great he was, but how
many-sided was his greatness. The great white light of
death, in which the qualities appear with such vivid
force, illumines his talents and his gifts, and we can
perceive in him the universality which the succession of
events and efforts obscured. S4

96.21   he was] A1; he was, and I return to this aspect of his life
with a despair of rendering it justice by any other word
S4

96.21   others] A1; other men S4
96.30   not] A1; never S4
96.32   those] A1; the S3
96.32   in New York,] A1; *om.* S3
97.3   eve] A1; *om.* S3

Literary Boston as I Knew It

98   LITERARY BOSTON AS I KNEW IT] A1; LITER-
ARY BOSTON THIRTY YEARS AGO. S5
98.1   Among] A1; I. ¶ Among S5
98.19   I] A1; *om.* S5
98.23   quality] A1; quantity S5
99.32   all] A1; *om.* S5
100.26   chief of the] A1; *om.* S5
101.20   shades] A1; shades and colors S5
102.2   they left] A1; they had left S5
102.13   supremacy] A1; perfection S5
102.17   in fiction] A1; *om.* S5

102.20	almost] A1; by far S5
*102.25	Madame Bovary] HE; Madame Flaubert S5
103.31	Mr. Aldrich] A1; He S5
103.33	nearly the same age] A1; the same age, with a shifting semester between us which neither cares now to claim S5
104.9	several] A1; many S5
106.23	which] A1; which always S5
107.8	race] A1; birth S5
107.9	town] A1; place S5
107.12	author.] A1; author. Celia Thaxter is so lately dead that one must speak of her with something of the hush of the house of mourning, even when one has nothing but praise to speak. S5
107.12	Celia Thaxter] A1; her S5
107.22	be] A1; be very S5
107.23	work] A1; work, which had qualities of keenest pathos, vivid fancy, humorous reality, and constant beauty S5
107.28	narrower] A1; narrow S5
110.10	way] A1; habit S5
110.11	way] A1; habit S5
110.12	had] A1; has S5
110.18	when] B1; before S5
110.34	sad] A1; pathetic S5
112.28	civil] A1; *om.* S5
113.1	that] A1; that pathetically S5
114.1	at the latest] A1; not long ago S5
114.25	chasms] B1; chasm A1
116.31	In the] A2; In th A1
118.29	chrysolite] HE; crysolite A1
120.15	*sérieux*] A5; *serieux* A1
120.20	In] A1; Later in my Cambridge life, another historian used now and then to look in upon me, and in TS2
120.20	much later than in some others] A1; *om.* TS2
120.22	like so many other Boston men of letters] A1; too TS2
120.24	paid] A1; compensated TS2
120.31	told] A1; said to TS2
*120.33–34	The Jesuits in North America,] A1; "The Jesuits in North America," TS2

120.34	Régime] A1; Regime TS2
*120.34	Montcalm and Wolfe] HE; Wolfe and Montcalm TS2
121.2	expressing] A1; expressing in TS2
121.7	first] A1; *om.* TS2
121.7	had] A1; always TS2
121.8	Cambridge, where I then lived,] A1; Cambridge TS2
121.12	experience] A1; experiences TS2
121.13	in] A1; in in TS2
121.14	him to] A1; him to to TS2
121.14	ideals] A1; idels TS2
121.15	remained] A1; remained as TS2
121.26	or me for it] A1; *om.* TS2
121.28	his] A1; his open TS2
121.33	displeasures] A1; displeasures apparently TS2
121.34	historian] A1; historien TS2
121.36	final] A1; latest TS2
121.36	apparently] A1; *om.* TS2
122.6	a] A1; the a TS2
122.13	I] A1; I always TS2
122.14	earlier] A1; *om.* TS2
122.15	cannot say] A1; do not know TS2
122.16	known] A1; read TS2
122.16	their] A1; their increasing TS2
122.17	have not read] A1; cannot indeed speak of TS2
122.17	last] A1; last, for I have not read it TS2
122.18	American] A1; *om.* TS2
122.19–20	could not say] A1; should not know TS2
122.29	outlived] A1; oulived TS2
122.30	man] A1; one TS2
122.32	gentle] A1; quiet TS2
122.34	endeared. I] A1; endeared the more. I suppose that I must have met him first in at the publisher's office, for he was then a frequent and welcome contributor the North American Review, and soon became a constant writer for the Atlantic, and I TS2
122.35	seldom] A1; never TS2

OLIVER WENDELL HOLMES

| 125.14 | I] A1; *om.* S6 |

126.11–12   humanities. ¶ Holmes] A1; humanities. He S6
126.15   by] A1; by all S6
127.4   II] A1; *om.* S6
127.9   near] A1; in S6
128.13   Street. "And if] A1; Street, and "if S6
129.24   him] A1; him, which was summer before last, S6
129.28   III] A1; *om.* S6
*131.7   The Guardian Angel] HE; "The Guardian Angel" S6
132.12   IV] A1; *om.* S6
132.18   Holmes] A1; he S6
135.23   V] A1; *om.* S6
137.8   réclame] B1; reclame S6
137.15   VI] A1; *om.* S6
137.16–17   delight in] A1; delight of S6
137.21–22   have already recalled] A1; recall S6
140.25   unfrozen] A1; unfettered S6
140.31   VII] A1; *om.* S6
142.11   make] A1; made S6
142.15   *will*] A1; will S6
142.16   added] A1; said S6
143.30   VIII] A1; *om.* S6
144.10   we] A1; we left it mostly to him, after we S6
144.26   Its] A5; The S6
145.5   *home's last*] A5; *last life's* S6
147.2   him I] A1; him that I S6
147.2   and] A1; and that S6
147.30   elder] B1; eldest S6
150.4   him.] A1; him. I remember Emerson's saying to me that
             every one had supposed Holmes had fully said him-
             self, or at least given the compass of his powers, when
             the Autocrat papers came to confound and amaze even
             his friends. S6
150.5   IX] A1; *om.* S6

THE WHITE MR. LONGFELLOW

151.1   We] A1; I. ¶ We S7
151.6   civil] A1; *om.* S7
152.17   anywhere else had] A1; had anywhere else S7
152.17–19   parallel./I ¶ It] A1; parallel. It S7

*153.30   Peirce] HE; Pierce S7
  156.34   of] A1; for S7
  158.5   of that] A1; *om.* S7
  159.19   asked] A1; asked me S7
  160.16   certain] A1; some S7
  160.16   which] A1; which were S7
  161.25   when] A1; where S7
  161.29   the poet's] A1; his S7
  162.15   Holmes] A1; the Autocrat S7
  163.9   smooth] A4; sooth S7
  163.36   sympathy] A1; intelligence S7
  164.19   with] A1; to S7
  166.5   he; and] A1; he, for S7
  169.7   censures] A1; things said S7
  170.4   than a] A4; than S7
  172.26   when] A1; and when S7
  175.17   were no] A1; were not S7
  176.8   heart] A1; head S7
  177.11   in] A1; at S7
  178.5   to] A1; of S7
  178.6   its] A1; their S7

Studies of Lowell

179   STUDIES OF LOWELL] A1; A RETROSPECT OF
            LOWELL. P1
179.1   I have already spoken] A1; In some former papers
            printed here, I spoke P1
179.4–6   1866; and I now wish to record what I knew of him
            during the years that passed between this date and that]
            A1; 1866, until the time P1
179.6   death.] A1; ~; P1
179.6   portrait] A1; portrait of him P1
179.6   paint] A1; ~, P1
179.13   I went] A1; I returned to that city and went P1
179.13   Elmwood, and] A1; Elmwood. I wished to P1
179.18   nearly always] A1; commonly P1
179.24   I still have a sense] A1; my recollection is P1
180.1   in at them] A1; *om.* P1
180.7   then] A1; *om.* P1

180.7	talk] A1; it P1
180.9	work] A1; work which he then got through at a burst P1
180.11	some one] A1; a youth P1
180.12–13	both. ¶ He] A1; both. He P1
180.14	my shy youth] A1; me P1
180.14	it] A1; I P1
180.14–15	his presence. It was not much;] A1; mine. But I must own that I was not wholly at my ease in Lowell's presence. P1
180.16	in Lowell] A1; I felt myself under correction of his better judgment, his greater knowledge, his more instructed opinions. No doubt his own essential shyness had something to do with my discomfort; but P1
180.16	always conscious] A1; aware P1
180.17	and closer] A1; *om.* P1
180.24	subtly] A1; *om.* P1
180.35	treated] A1; *om.* P1
181.13	meadow] A1; meadows P1
181.14	life-long] A1; *om.* P1
181.30	before] A1; before here P1
181.35	on] A4; *om.* P1
182.7	could] A1; liked to P1
182.10	III] A1; II P1
*182.12	The Nation] HE; *The Nation* P1
182.14	letter] A1; letter of recognition P1
182.17	pleasure in] A1; liking for P1
182.26	in New York on The Nation] A1; on The Nation in New York P1
182.29	me.] A1; me. He said that I would find Fields easy to work with, though he advised me to work in entire subordination, even (I remember his word) to *écraser* myself if necessary. P1
182.33	We] A1; Then we P1
183.3	airily] A1; cockily P1
183.9	-townsmen] A1; -townsman P1
183.14	ugly] A1; *om.* P1
183.19	bedrabbled] A1; bebrabbled P1
183.19	neighborhoods] A1; neighborhood P1
183.21	an] A1; a whimsical P1

183.31	burlesque] A1 ; mimicry P1
184.7	IV] A1 ; III. P1
184.35–185.1	thinking. In this, he] A1 ; thinking. ¶ He P1
185.13	in the] A1 ; in a P1
185.19	would] A1 ; would even P1
185.26	in that blotted line] A1 ; *om.* P1
186.7	hearing] A1 ; ever having heard P1
186.30	which] A1 ; meant to P1
186.31–32	together. ¶ Looking] A1 ; together./IV. ¶ I had a great and almost suffocating shyness in my early visits to Lowell, which was perhaps not wholly displeasing to him. I used to walk down the lane (which Elmwood Avenue then was) in the shelter of the lilac bushes which overhung the picket fence, wagering myself that he would not be at home, and up the path from the gate under the English elms, on the gravel or on the snow to his door, between the great syringa bushes, which flanked it, with my heart beating in my throat. ¶ I try to give the notion of his character by its effect upon me, and I shall not greatly mind the misconstruction of my own which this may occasion. Looking P1
187.12	poets,] A1 ; poets, or the Elizabethan dramatists P1
187.15	passages] A1 ; parts P1
187.16	cantava] A1 ; contava P1
187.18	then] A1 ; *om.* P1
187.20	said, and no more] A1 ; said P1
187.23	beauty of] A1 ; beauty by P1
188.3	prose,] A1 ; ~ P1
188.23	hand, to] A1 ; hands and P1
188.25	its] A1 ; its fictitious P1
189.2	would] A1 ; could P1
189.13	the criticism hardily] A1 ; it P1
189.17	that in] A1 ; when P1
189.18	friends] A1 ; friends that P1
189.19	think] A1 ; think that P1
189.23–24	in motive] A1 ; *om.* P1
189.25	contributor] A1 ; writer in motive P1
189.27	poems.] A1 ; ~ , P1

189.35   -path." He] A1; -path." ¶ He P1
190.2   had] A1; *om.* P1
190.3   them.] A1; them. ¶ Sometimes he was unable to
                  keep himself from wounding, and this was rather apt
                  to happen from him with women. I had gone with a
                  lady to one of his post-graduate lectures at Harvard
                  and had stayed with her after the close, that she
                  might be presented to him, and have a chance to say
                  her poor little say of pleasure in meeting him. He
                  received her compliment in freezing silence, and as
                  if he could not or would not do anything to put her
                  at ease, left us to leave him with scarcely a word. At
                  other times I have seen him use people as if forbid-
                  ding them to hope further acquaintance with him
                  from this or that encounter. He had moments when
                  the toryism of his nerves, as he called it, was too much
                  for his head and his heart; and possibly he had also
                  the involuntary cruelty of persons who have them-
                  selves suffered cruelly in some other sort. At any rate
                  I am not afraid to leave these conjectures with those
                  who realize that all natures, even the best, are mys-
                  teriously crossed with perverse and alien impulses. P1
190.10   but] A1; *om.* P1
191.10   mansion] A1; house P1
191.23   presence; and he] A1; presence. He P1
191.32   there] A1; *om.* P1
192.12   such] A1; *om.* P1
192.14   did in my presence] A1; to my knowledge P1
192.21   other] A1; *om.* P1
192.22   tolerance] A1; tolorance P1
192.22   faith] A1; belief P1
192.27   vengeance] A1; vengence P1
192.36–193.1   much: they have apparently exhausted their po-
                  tentialities of psychological life] A1; much P1
193.4   he] A1; and P1
193.17   mainly] A1; chiefly P1
193.21   or a] A1; or P1
193.26   and be] A1; *om.* P1
193.31   after all] A1; *om.* P1

193.36	rough] A1; rough tweed P1
194.9	darker] A1; rather darker P1
194.10	straw-colored] A1; yellowish P1
194.29	been] A1; been two years P1
195.4	Biglow] A1; Bigelow P1
195.14	of the] A1; of our P1
195.16	knew] A1; know P1
195.25–26	effort even to give such pleasure] A1; pleasure he imparted P1
195.31	Lowell] A1; ~, P1
195.32	as Longfellow from contempt] A1; from contempt as Longfellow P1
196.6	English] A1; elm English P1
196.10	of which I am speaking] A1; I am speaking of P1
196.12	held] A1; *om.* P1
196.12	man] A1; man held its own P1
196.14	their inception] A1; this P1
196.22	Among My] A1; Among my P1
197.22	dependent] A1; dependant P1
198.6	And] A1; Aud P1
198.10	home. She said,] A1; home: P1
*198.14	she would,] A1; ~ ~ P1
198.14	so"—] A1; ~—" P1
198.15	Yet,] A3; Yet, as I have noted in a former paper P1
198.17	would serve] A3; served P1
199.1	brother] A1; needy P1
199.16	a] A1; *om.* P1
200.7	He] A1; If he P1
200.8	but] A1; *om.* P1
200.18	some] A1; a P1
200.28	Lowell] A1; him P1
200.33	over] A1; across P1
201.15	Madrid.] A1; Madrid. Some years later when the English mission had become vacant, one of our household remembered that he had said, before he saw me about the Austrian mission, that he thought he "could do some good in England," and again we did our little most to be his friends at court, where he really needed no friends. P1

201.17	some years later, he] A1; he said, the first thing, with humorous exaggeration, "Well, how do you like your minister?" as if I had made him so. He P1
201.34	the moisture in it] A1; its moisture P1
202.5	volunteered] A1; admitted P1
202.7	in] A1; in in P1
202.22–23	in the country,] A1; *om.* P1
203.10	"You young] A1; a "young P1
203.14	and] A1; but P1
203.28	old] A1; *om.* P1
204.3	prejudice] A1; prejudices P1
204.19	period] A1; time P1
204.20	suffering] A1; sickness P1
204.25	repellently] HE; repellantly P1
204.32	before that] A1; *om.* P1
205.26	apt] A1; *om.* P1
205.37	social.] A1; social. He told me he had defended me in some inimical presences where I had been assailed for venturing to think injustice had been done the Chicago Anarchists, and in a letter he shortly afterwards wrote me, he said that though he thought them well hanged, he honored me for saying what I did about them. P1
206.1	most] A1; still more P1
206.6–7	tried to persuade him,] A1; think: P1
206.18	harm] A1; harm, at a time when the whole cry of petty critics was upon me from every side P1
206.24–27	He had a . . . . he made occasion.] A1; *om.* P1
208.5	drab gaiters sometimes] A1; some drab gaiters P1
208.14	won't] A1; wont P1
208.30	a] A1; *om.* P1
209.9	had had] A1; had lately had P1
210.1	Lowell] A1; He P1
210.9	series] A1; succession TS1
210.10	but] A1; but which TS1
210.10	personality] A1; character TS1
210.12	single] A1; single distinct TS1
*210.14	perplexed] A1; baffled harassed perplexed bewildered mystified TS1
210.14	as] A1; as as TS1

210.15–16 the effects from motives so single in it] A1; its effects, since all its motives were so single TS1

210.16 always] A1; always from the confusion TS1

210.20 of] A1; *om.* TS1

210.26 rarely] A1; not TS1

CAMBRIDGE NEIGHBORS

212.5 mouth ever wore] B1; that I ever beheld A1

215.20 Perhaps] A1; When we think of the dead we wish first to speak of ourselves, because we instinctively feel that they who are gone have really less to do with death than we who remain. There is a buoyant sense of their escape, of their release to the unknown, the untried. If they are at all, they are in the gracious presence of new conditions, new chances, new deeds. The miracle of creation has been wrought afresh for them; they have entered upon immortal youth; they have parted with age; they have turned their faces from death forever. Death, their own death, abides with us who call ourselves alive. ¶ We cannot pity them, even if we believe they are not, for then they are but as we all were before the beginning. It is ourselves we pity, and, if we are honest, it is of ourselves that we speak, our bereavement, our loneliness, our loss./I. ¶ I remember, with this self-compassion, how it was more than once on my tongue, in the first days after I got back to town, in the fall, to say, "Now I suppose Boyesen will be coming again," and how I recognized that the chief pleasure of my winters had been his coming every week for a full evening of such talk as only old friends, long agreed about life and art, can have. Then, before those first few days were past, before ever I got the words of affectionate expectation uttered, came the bewildering news of his sudden death. It was incredible, as death always is, but not so much in his case from its suddenness as from the void it made where so much power, so much will, so much vitality had lately been. It is still very hard to realize that he has ceased to be; he continues in the sense of his friend a living presence, as he will continue a lasting presence in the story of the alien literature in which he made himself citizen. ¶ I do not know . . . . it as Americans. [Printed in present text, 217.21–34] ¶ It was when he was just beginning to feel his power in it that I first knew him, a blond, comely, ardent youth, whom I met at luncheon, in a friendly house at Cambridge, nearly twenty-five years ago. He had his sweet young romance of Gunnar already in manuscript then, and, like the fond young author he was, he had it with him. Perhaps S2

215.22–23   rate they did not fail of an effect] B1; rate, after coffee, the author had the boyish-hearted courage to read a chapter of the story aloud S10

216.4   Boyesen's] A1; his S10

*216.25   *Gunnar*] A1; Gunnar S10

217.1   III] A1; II. S10

217.19–35   phrasing. ¶ I do not know . . . it as Americans. ¶ He had] A1; phrasing. Take this stanza from the *stev*:

> *Gunnar*: "A maiden I know as fair as the day,
> *Ragnhild*: As fair as the day;
> *Gunnar*: She shines like the birch in the sunlight's play,
> *Ragnhild*: In the sunlight's play;
> *Both*: She shines like the birch in the sunlight's play."

Here are exquisite grace and tender music won from the very sources of English, but there is no effort for the purity of origin of the diction, which is as sheer Saxon throughout the poem. Or take a passage of prose from the book, a passage that I have opened upon at random:

¶ "Not far from the court-hall, down toward the fjord, stood two huge fir-trees. They both had tall, naked trunks, and thick, bushy heads, and they looked so much alike that people called them the twin-firs. It was the saying, also, that lovers often met there. Between the trees was nailed a rough piece of plank to sit on. Here they stopped and sat down. He laid his arm round her waist, and drew her close up to him; she leaned her head on his breast. Then he turned his eyes upward to the dark crowns of the trees, and seemed lost in a stream of thought. The moonlight only shimmered through, for the foliage was very thick. Neither spoke; they felt no need of words. *Silence is the truest language of bliss.* And she also looked up into the heavy, moon-fretted trees overhead, wondering what his thoughts could be."

¶ It is the artless soul of youth and love that is uttered here, and the lovers are only peasant folk. But the absolute simplicity of the utterance and the perfect sufficiency of the means are not the less marvellous on that account. There is but one false note in the whole passage, and that is the sentence I have italicized: an unconscious echo of Shakespeare's line—

"Silence is the perfectest herald of joy."

¶ All that is Boyesen's own is fine, and firm, and true./ III. ¶ I must own that he did not always write so well; I suppose I must own that much of his later work bore the fatal marks of overwork, the defect of the hurried and the wearied hand. Yet the power never left him, and in the very last lines he is known to have written he keeps, brokenly, indeed, but faithfully, the promise of poetry which he gave in his youth. These lines were sent to The Bachelor of Arts three weeks before he died; he meant to have added a final stanza, the editor of the magazine tells us, but he did not even see a proof.

POLLEN.

Mounted on zephyrs the amorous host
   Rise from their warm, translucent bowers;
Lured by the fragrance that each loves most
   Into the hearts of the flowers.

Nestling now close to the gentian's breast;
   Now in the rose's bosom hidden;
Now by the lily coyly caressed,
   Whisper sweet things, forbidden.

What do they whisper? Delicious things!
   Secrets too shy for the sense to capture—
Vague like the breath to the poppy that clings,
   Murmurs that swoon with rapture!

Heavy with incense the golden dusk;
   Flushed are the virgin pulses chilly;
Richly exhales the rose's musk,
   Blent with the balm of the lily.

¶ It was in things so richly felt, so exquisitely said, that he spoke in his truest self; it was in the voice of a poet that Boyesen spoke as a master. Yet he was so excellent in so many kinds that the praise which limited itself to his work in verse would be far from justice. He had S10

217.21   stop] A1; stopped S10

217.24   remember] A1; notice S10

217.26   Ruffini] A1; Ruffine S10

218.14   their] A1; their beauty and S10

218.15   fiction.] A1; fiction. / IV. S10

219.2   more.] A1; more, and that I am at last his friend in vain, so far as that goes. S10

219.7–8   Several years after . . . in New York,] A1; He lived in S10

219.16   leisure.] A1; leisure. Often, on those evenings he spent with me, he had stopped in the walk which he must continue for hours after he left me, if he could hope to win as many hours of sleep, and sometimes he lost, and slept only with the help of drugs. S10

219.19   well. When] A1; well. ¶ When S10

219.26   boys.] A1; boys. In the beginning he must always have written with a consciousness of the strange speech in which he was thinking; and to the last, I suppose, when he was fagged, the English he had so wonderfully mastered must have been a serious part of this unconscious strain, and just so much beyond the effort that a writer native to it must make. His popular and social lecturing was also very exhausting, for he was deeply interested in it, and imparted himself with all possible fulness not only in the lecture itself (he sometimes discarded his manuscript and spoke freshly on the subject from an impulse of the moment), but in the wasting and wearing after-talk with those who came to confer with him about it. ¶ His work as professor in Columbia University I cannot measure, or very well imagine; but I know how greatly it was valued there, and I cannot suppose him to have done it with less thoroughness than he did whatever else he put his hand to. I suppose that it was indeed always first with him, and that it was not until he had most amply fulfilled his

duty to it that he turned to the other things that another man would have found sufficient employment for
his utmost energies. / V. ¶ But S10

219.30   shun.] A1; shun. He did not shrink from them, and
though I could not follow him in these paths of reform
which seemed to lead to no changed conditions, but
only from one political camp to another, I honored him
for the conscience and the public spirit which impelled
him. S10

219.36   When he died he] A1; He S10

220.10   view] A1; vices S10

221.27   thought only] A1; had no thought but S10

221.36   quarrel] A1; present quarrel S10

222.4   leaders.] A1; leaders. ¶ He was a most manful spirit,
and he wished to be a fully rounded man. He had his
errors and his faults; he had foibles that endeared him
the more to those who knew how to value his virtues;
he did unwise things that he never thought were wise.
He had great sense, great courage, great dignity, great
goodness. Those who mourn him as a friend may well
be proud that they had such a friend to mourn. S10

222.35   characterize] A3; characterize it A1

223.23   they project] A3; project them A1

224.29   side,] HE; ~ A1

227.32   health,] HE; ~ A1

228.2   Jeffries] B1; Jeffreys A1

231.17   *Espíritu*] B1; *Espíritú* A1

235.23   aseptic] A5; asceptic A1

236.35   came] A4; come A1

239.23   Pearce] A3; Pease A1

*240.5-6 At Cambridge the . . . than even that] A1; I take leave
to think it was rather different in Cambridge, which in
its best society was without the limitations TS2

240.11-22 insistently. ¶ People held . . . tremulous misgivings. ¶
Family] A1; insistently. Family TS2

240.22   in Cambridge] A1; *om.* TS2

240.23   alone] A1; *om.* TS2

240.26   without] A1; without being TS2

240.27   riches. ¶ I] A1; ~. ~ MS

240.29   ideal, as Boyesen portrayed them to him] A1; as
            Boyesen portrayed them ideal MS
240.31   alloys] A1; alloys of adversity MS
240.33   these] A1; those MS
241.1   my] A1; these MS
241.6   I could] A1; could I MS
241.21–22   from time to time] A1; *om.* P2
241.22   offering him the] A1; the fuller P2
241.23   I should have known] A1; might seem P2
241.28   humanities.] A1; humanities. If I began to speak of the
            debt which I myself owe him in every high sort that a
            man can be bound to another, I should never have done;
            and again his delicacy could not suffer this. But MS
241.28   day] A1; hour MS
241.29   noisy] A1; trumpery MS
241.30   these] A1; those MS
241.32   our chief citizen at] A1; the greatest citizen of P2
241.33   and disaster] A1; *om.* P2
241.34   wrong.] A1; wrong. The Cambridge spirit has risen to
            no greater heights. P2

A Belated Guest

242.24   excused?] B1; excused? ¶ At least, the listener will own
            that the garruler (if we may make a noun which is
            simply crying out for creation) has most tempting oc-
            casion for his garrulity, if he has read Mr. Charles War-
            ren Stoddard's book of "Exits and Entrances," which
            has been lying before the actual garruler the whole
            summer past, and softly beguiling, gently reproaching
            him to some recognition of its rare virtues of whimsical
            humor, frank confidence, capricious reserve, graphic
            portraiture of persons and places, and a heart of poetry
            pulsing through all. Mr. Stoddard, as we were never
            tired of testifying whenever we spoke of his "South Sea
            Idyls," is one of the most original talents of that vanished
            California of which Mark Twain and Bret Harte were
            the chief exemplars, and no one is better qualified to
            speak of them and the others of the California school,
            dead or alive. He speaks of these two, of Harte where he

knew him in San Francisco, and of Mark Twain where he knew him again in London, with that airy grace which is altogether personal to him: as he speaks of a score of other men and matters, in Italy, in Jerusalem, in Stratford-on-Avon, in Hawaii, in the Sierras, and wherever else a genius not so lucky as it is winning has made him an unarriving pilgrim and a votary at the shrines of the grotesque and the beautiful. But above all we believe we prefer among the desultory sketches of his latest book his "Early Recollections of Bret Harte," or, if we do not, we at any rate find it the most convenient for positing our own recollections of that charming personality. S11

243.2   My] B1; Our S11

243.13   another] B1; other S11

243.21   Cambridge and the Boston neighborhood] B1; Boston S11

244.1   local expressman] B1; express S11

244.10   fascinating] B1; fascinating forward S11

244.19   could answer] B1; said, S11

244.31   without] B1; with S11

245.21   those] B1; these S11

245.24   or his] B1; or S11

246.4   at the expected houses] B1; *om.* S11

246.9   truly] B1; *om.* S11

246.29   This] B1; That S11

246.31   easily] B1; well S11

246.34   surfeited] B1; satisfied S11

246.35   by] B1; in S11

247.2   his] B1; the S11

247.10   had] B1; *om.* S11

247.11   had] B1; *om.* S11

247.11   scant] B1; *om.* S11

247.33   shown to] B1; shown S11

247.34   drunkenly slept] B1; fell into a drunken sleep S11

247.34   he] B1; he only ingenuously S11

248.4   to] B1; to those S11

248.27   and round] B1; and about S11

248.30   many a] B1; every S11

249.16   have] B1; have had S11
249.21   at] B1; for all comment on S11
249.24   the years] B1; these S11
249.28   youthful] B1; youth S11
249.28   looks] B1; looked S11
250.15–16   unaffected. ¶ If] B1; unaffected./IV ¶ If S11
251.6   this] B1; his S11
251.21   called] B1; calls S11
251.29–30   demands] B1; demand S11
252.17   but a] B1; but S11
252.33   would no doubt] B1; must S11
252.36   and] B1; and as Mr. Stoddard has witnessed in his
              charming recollections, S11
253.8   pang. Other California writers have testified] B1; pang.
              ¶ Mr. Stoddard has testified also S11
253.34   IV] B1; V S11
254.17   found] B1; found about S11
254.34   at] B1; with S11
255.12   a gay laugh comes] B1; comes a gay laugh S11
255.14   the hearer's] B1; his S11

MY MARK TWAIN

256.1   I] C; *om.* S12
256.4   fourty-four] C; forty-five S12
256.11   *Abroad*,] C; *Abroad.* I had hinted that six hundred
              pages of fun was perhaps a good deal of fun, S12
256.13   and] C; but S12
258.3   II] C; *om.* S12
258.7   destined] C; destinied S12
258.19   countless] C; endless S12
258.21   mockeries] C; mockery S12
259.7   one another] C; each other S12
259.26   following] C; following it S12
260.3   III] C; *om.* S12
261.21   occasion] C; occasions S12
261.26   but] C; but she did not let them appear, and S12
261.32   into] C; to S12
263.1   had] C; had doubtless S12
263.30   IV] C; *om.* S12

264.16   about] C; of S12
264.26   that] C; *om.* S12
265.9–10   of my unsparing praises of her] C; unsparing praises of
            her from me S12
265.17   detested] C; loathed S12
266.14   we] C; we all S12
267.7   V] C; *om.* S12
267.26   which] C; which all S12
268.29   VI] C; *om.* S12
271.13–14   our publisher, the hospitable James R. Osgood,] C; the
            hospitable Osgood S12
272.10–11   performances. ¶ Clemens] C; performances. Clemens S12
272.28   die!] C; ~. S12
272.29   VII] C; *om.* S12
273.2   answered] C; responded S12
273.21   apparently] C; apparently far S12
273.29   VIII] C; *om.* S12
276.3   this] C; that S12
276.12   IX] C; *om.* S12
276.33   those of] C; *om.* S12
277.5   to be denied] C; denied to S12
277.34   Clemens] C; He S12
278.19   in] C; in convulsing S12
278.20   X] C; *om.* S12
281.19   luxuriously] C; luxuriantly S12
282.16   XI] C; *om.* S12
283.12   twenty] C; fifteen S12
284.2   *in*] C; *at* S12
284.3   XII] C; *om.* S12
285.4   spurned] C; spurned all S12
285.15   entirety—namely, Charles Eliot Norton] C; entirety:
            Charles Eliot Norton, namely, S12
286.14   counted] C; could S12
286.22   XIII] C; *om.* S12
287.12   He] C; Clemens S12
287.19   trusted] C; relied upon S12
287.31   at twice the cost] C; *om.* S12
287.35–36   till well toward the winter twilight] C; *om.* S12
288.10   such] C; those S12

288.10   as] C; which S12
289.1   *the*] C; *om.* S12
289.13   XIV] C; *om.* S12
291.22   loan] C; gift S12
291.26   so few] C; fifteen S12
292.7   Missouri] C; Hannibal S12
292.16   never enlarging] C; that never enlarged S12
293.7   XV] C; *om.* S12
293.30   very] C; most S12
296.19   and the] C; and S12
296.36   ground in] C; ground S12
297.1   prey] C; victim S12
297.9   it.] C; it. S12
297.13–14   the joke was, of course, beside them;] C; *om.* S12
297.19–20   But perhaps this burlesque was not a good joke.] C; *om.*
            S12
297.21   XVI] C; *om.* S12
297.22   Clemens] C; He S12
298.34   longer] C; long S12
299.11   XVII] C; *om.* S12
299.25   rather cockahoop] C; *om.* S12
299.33   the lord] C; he S12
300.2   most] C; all S12
300.16–25   still. He was tremendously . . . to forbear it. ¶ He was
            apt] C; still. He was apt S12
301.28   XVIII] C; *om.* S12
302.14   Mr.] C; President S12
303.2   would] C; could S12
303.6   overbore his] C; overbore such S12
303.23   delirious exultation] C; glorious intoxication S12
303.35–36   We did not . . . wish to read.] C; *om.* S12
304.1   whether they could read or not] C; *om.* S12
304.7   XIX] C; *om.* S12
304.24   with the] C; with S12
306.26   XX] C; *om.* S12
309.7   XXI] C; *om.* S12
310.12   folly.] C; folly. One Sunday afternoon we went together
            to hear an able judge from Kansas, a clever lawyer and
            a politician of note, deliver a Christian Science discourse

which was intellectually so much chopped food for
cattle, to a congregation of three thousand prosperous
persons mainly in sealskin sacks and frock coats. I suppose that this extraordinary spectacle afforded Clemens
a satisfaction which could have been matched for him
only by the claim of Shakespeare to be Shakespeare,
when he had come to the full perception that Bacon was
Shakespeare. S12

310.23   XXII] C; *om.* S12
*311.4   1894] HE; 1904 S12
311.13   through] C; in S12
*312.17   by and by] C; presently S12
312.26   her.''] C; her.'' How incredible, how impossible is ex-
              perience! S12
312.27   then] C; *om.* S12
312.29–33   his most . . . . There was also] C; *om.* S12
313.8   and] C; and we had better use the delicacy of Agag than
              the truculence of Samuel. S12
313.9   to the recreant] C; *om.* S12
313.22   remnant] C; balance S12
313.32   past] C; past all S12
313.34   XXIII] C; *om.* S12
314.19   but as] B1; but S12
314.21–29   found. Upon reflection I . . . the whole story. ¶ I] B1;
              found. ¶ I S12
317.26   and] C; and now S12
318.22   XXIV] B1; *om.* S12
319.15   eyes] C; eye S12
319.17   frank, defiant] C; simple-hearted S12
319.35   each other] C; one another S12
320.33   XXV] B1; *om.* S12
322.1   life] C; things S12
322.16   him. Emerson] C; him. ¶ Emerson S12
322.17   all and all the rest of our] C; all: S12
322.18   one another] C; each other S12

Rejected Substantives

The following list records all substantive variants in editions published after or independently of copy-text and rejected as non-authorial in the present text. The reading of the present edition appears to the left of the bracket; the authority for that reading, followed by a semicolon, the variant reading, and the source of that reading appear to the right of the bracket. The reading of any unlisted edition, other than copy-text, may be presumed to agree with the reading to the left of the bracket. If the authority of the present reading is other than the copy-text, the copy-text reading is recorded in Emendations.

The following texts are referred to:

MS   3 leaves of holograph manuscript, "Cambridge Neighbors" (Western Reserve Historical Society)

TS1 2 leaves of typescript, "Studies of Lowell" (Charles E. Feinberg)

TS2 14 leaves of typescript, "Literary Boston as I Knew It" and "Cambridge Neighbors" (Hayes Memorial Library)

P1   78 leaves of proof, "Studies of Lowell" (Charles E. Feinberg)

P2   1 leaf of proof, "Cambridge Neighbors" (Houghton Library)

S1   "My First Visit to New England," *Harper's Monthly*, LXXXVIII–LXXXIX (May–August 1894)

S2   "First Impressions of Literary New York," *Harper's Monthly*, XCI (June 1895)

S3   "Roundabout to Boston," *Harper's Monthly*, XCI (August 1895)

S4   "George William Curtis," *Harper's Weekly*, XXXVI (10 September 1892)

S5   "Literary Boston Thirty Years Ago," *Harper's Monthly*, XCI (November 1895)

S6   "Oliver Wendell Holmes," *Harper's Monthly*, XCIV (December 1896)

S7   "The White Mr. Longfellow," *Harper's Monthly*, XCIII (August 1896)

S8   "A Personal Retrospect of James Russell Lowell," *Scribner's*, XXVIII (September 1900)

S9   "Some Literary Memories of Cambridge," *Harper's Monthly*, CI (November 1900)

S10 "Hjalmar Hjorth Boyesen," *Harper's Bazar*, XXIX (25 January 1896)

S11 "Editor's Easy Chair," *Harper's Monthly*, CVIII (December 1903)

S12 "My Memories of Mark Twain," *Harper's Monthly*, CXXI (July–September 1910)

A1   *Literary Friends and Acquaintance*, Harper, 1900

A2   Harper, 1900: "Autograph Edition"

A3   Harper, 1900

A4   Harper, 1901

A5   Harper, 1902

B1   *Literary Friends and Acquaintance*, Harper, 1910

B2   Harper, 1911: "Library Edition"

C   *My Mark Twain*, Harper, 1910

My First Visit to New England

26.20   notably to men who have done something in the] S1 ; the effect was from him as well as in me; I dare A1

52.24   Hawthornes] S1 ; Hawthorne's A1–A5

First Impressions of Literary New York

70.12   who] S2 ; *om.* A1–A4

Roundabout to Boston

84.9   a] S3 ; an B1–B2

88.22   2.80] S3 ; $2.80 B1–B2

90.10   her] S3 ; its A4–B2

The White Mr. Longfellow

172.30   act] S7 ; fact A1–B2

Studies of Lowell

179   STUDIES OF LOWELL] A1 ; A PERSONAL

RETROSPECT OF JAMES RUSSELL LOWELL
S8

179.1	I have already] A1; In some former papers printed elsewhere I have S8
179.12–13	Venice; and two weeks after I landed in Boston, I went out] A1; Venice, and went out from Boston S8
180.7	long] P1; *om.* S8
180.15	gave] P1; had given S8
180.16	in Lowell] A1; *om.* S8
180.16	conscious] A1; aware in him S8
180.17	than my own] P1; *om.* S8
180.24–25	I disliked to . . . for doing it.] P1; *om.* S8
181.6	own] P1; *om.* S8
181.13	meadow] A1; meadows S8
181.14	life-long] A1; *om.* S8
183.14	ugly] A1; *om.* S8
185.34	times] P1; time A1–B2
186.7	remember] A1; remember ever S8
186.31–32	together. ¶ Looking] A1; together. Looking S8
187.17–18	dismago." He] P1; dismago." ¶ He A1–B2
187.19	all] P1; *om.* S8
187.23	beauty of] A1; beauty by S8
188.23	hand, to indulge] A1; hands and to indulge, S8
188.25	its] A1; its fictitious S8
188.35	whimsical] P1; humorous S8
189.2	would] A1; could S8
189.2	the] P1; his S8
189.19	think] A1; think that S8
189.25	contributor] A1; writer S8
190.2	had] A1; *om.* S8
191.23	presence; and] A1; presence; S8
192.1	came always] P1; always came S8
192.2	familiarly] P1; familiar S8
192.36–193.1	much: they have . . . of psychological life] A1; much S8
193.4	before he] A1; before and S8
193.21	or a] A1; or S8
193.22	dirt] P1; mud S8

193.26	and be] A1; *om.* S8
193.31	after all] A1; *om.* S8
195.14	of the] P1; of our S8
195.25–26	even to give such] A1; to give S8
196.4	keenly] A1; deeply S8
198.10	home. She said,] A1; home: S8
198.15	Yet,] A3; Yet, as I have noted in a former paper S8, A1–A2
198.17	would serve] A3; served S8, A1–A2
199.16–17	a while] A1; awhile S8
200.15	in] P1; in the S8
200.29	time] P1; time in S8
200.30	coffee at] P1; coffee after S8
201.17	some] A1; seven S8
202.5	volunteered] A1; admitted S8
202.22–23	in the country,] A1; *om.* S8
203.10	"You young] A1; a "young S8
204.3	prejudice] A1; prejudices S8
204.19	period] A1; time S8
204.29	travestied] P1; burlesqued S8
204.32	before that] A1; *om.* P1
208.17	drooped] P1; dropped A1–B2
208.36	in] P1; with S8
209.28	sitting] P1; *om.* S8
210.1	Lowell] A1; He S8
210.5	him] P1; him again S8
210.9	from] TS1; *om.* S8
210.9	collectively] TS1; successively S8
210.10	but] A1; but which S8
210.10	personality] A1; character S8
210.15–16	of the effects from motives so single in it] A1; effects from motives so single S8
210.19	for I have known them;] TS1; *om.* S8
210.20	of] A1; *om.* S8
210.21	or] TS1; and S8

Cambridge Neighbors

211	CAMBRIDGE NEIGHBORS] A1; SOME LITERARY MEMORIES OF CAMBRIDGE S9

211.18	and truest of our Cambridge] A1 ; of these S9
212.2	consummate] A1 ; winning S9
212.5	mouth ever wore] B1 ; that I ever beheld S9, A1–A5
212.18	knowledge] A1 ; consummate knowledge S9
212.25	us in] A1 ; us at S9
212.36	in] A1 ; at S9
213.5	tenderness] A1 ; tenderness in him S9
213.6	in him] A1 ; *om.* S9
213.12	consciousness] A1 ; pompous consciousness S9
213.14	pompous] A1 ; an S9
213.32	of] A1 ; *om.* S9
213.34	gardening] A1 ; garden S9
214.10–11	with a succession of hospitable obeisances] A1 ; like the finial of Adam Krafft's tabernacle S9
214.12	hard study, of as] A1 ; *om.* S9
214.14	and acquirements] A1 ; *om.* S9
214.15	great] A1 ; greater S9
214.16	both in English and Italian] A1 ; in Italian verse S9
214.17–18	(he wrote it in Metastasian Italian, and Lowell put it in libretto English)] A1 ; *om.* S9
214.28	the swelling exclamation of] A1 ; *om.* S9
214.30	cry] A1 ; swelling exclamation S9
214.33	take] A1 ; take so much S9
215.6	quite] A1 ; *om.* S9
215.7	more than enough for me, but he had] A1 ; for me, but he had more than enough S9
215.15	possibly the revelation was] A1 ; probably the confession was almost S9
215.18	study] A1 ; study looking out upon the garden S9
215.20–222.4	us. ¶ Perhaps the good . . . . Norwegian leaders.] S10 ; us. A chapter? It may have been two or three, with a judicious selection of passages from yet other chapters; but it does not matter. To be again in those dear presences, I would gladly listen to the whole novel! ¶ That young romance still remains the most beautiful thing that Boyesen wrote, though he wrote so much and so well in verse, in fiction, and in criticism. He had then already laid the wide foundations of his future scholarship in the Northern

European languages and literatures, but his soul was steeped in the aromas of his native poetry and romance, which all his talk breathed out again. ¶ For the rest of this summer I must have had nearly all his talk to myself; of course I wanted "Gunnar" for the magazine, and this brought us constantly and exclusively together. Boyesen afterwards came to know all Cambridge, and when he went back to Europe he celebrated our literary society with such effect that he inspired Tourguénief with the wish to witness it at first hands. The great Russian of course never visited Cambridge, but he affirmed to Boyesen his belief in it as an ideal situation, which could not be matched in his experience of literary centres elsewhere. I do not know whether it was Boyesen's enthusiasm that brought his great compatriot Björnstjerne Jjörnson actually among us; but if it was, it did not suffice, I believe, to realize Tourguénief's ideal to him. He ascertained the Cambridge limitations a little too quickly, a little too keenly, and felt himself cramped in a world where the expansions were upward rather than outward. ¶ However, no alien born more clearly conceived, not only Cambridge, but America, than Boyesen did. His mastery of our character was as extraordinary, as almost miraculous, as his mastery of our language. For full proof of his proficiency in both, he has left his great novel, *The Mammon of Unrighteousness*, which comes within one or two of being the great American novel we shall never have from any single hand. He left other stories of our life which showed how wonderfully well he had conceived it, and he left a volume of poems which testify of the beauty and truth with which he imagined the immeasurable life beyond the nationalities. S9

215.23   effect] B1; effort A1–A5
222.5   But, as I have said, poetry] A1; Poetry, indeed, S9
222.6   that] A1; that happy S9

222.15   them.] A1; them. He read me his things, and I read
                him mine, and he told me about the Hulder, and the
                Nixy, and the Midnight Sun, and the Fjords, and
                the Saeters; and that great movement toward
                nature and the speech of nature, then beginning
                among the Norwegian novelists and poets, which
                has since made their nation great while some other
                nations have grown big. S9
222.19   a stalwart] A1; stalwart S9
222.24   As I have hinted, our] A1; Our S9
222.25   too] A1; *om.* S9
222.28   and] A1; and of S9
223.2   my friend] A1; him S9
223.11   IV] A1; III S9
223.15   personalities in] A1; personalities of S9
223.18   incommensurably] A1; incomparably S9
223.23   from] A1; *om.* S9
223.23   they project] A3; project them S9, A2
223.27   absolutely individual] A1; personal S9
223.28   Clarifications they cannot be called, and] A1; Per-
                haps S9
224.1   He] A1; Yet he S9
224.2–3   the most brilliant . . . his mystical faith;] A1; a
                profound and comprehensive faith, and S9
224.6   perhaps] A1; possibly S9
224.11   He] A1; James S9
224.25   presented] A1; dramatically presented S9
224.34   report] A1; account S9
224.36   special] A1; mystical S9
225.8   sport] A1; mock S9
225.14   seemed] A1; was S9
225.14–15   concerning them] A1; concerning these S9
225.17   with] A1; in S9
225.23   He] A1; James S9
225.33   no one was] A1; none were S9
225.34   he or she] A1; they S9
225.34   his or her] A1; their S9
225.35–226.1   their foibles and . . . the kindliest nature] A1; limits
                S9

226.3	could] A1; could then S9
226.14	greatest vividness] A1; most graphic vividness, especially a grotesque fact S9
226.25	V] A1; IV S9
227.1-3	Yet he was ... New England character.] A1; He was of a bland politeness in manner, which he made go far in his encounters with New England character. ¶ It was by his real love for that character, also, that he succeeded so well with it. S9
227.9	usually] A1; mostly S9
227.18	with a recognition of] A1; and recognized S9
227.20	that] A1; when S9
227.21	which] A1; that S9
227.23	in Cambridge. He] A1; at Cambridge. But he S9
227.26	and was] A1; and I was S9
227.36–228.1	theory, or part ... did not accept,] A1; theory (it is well known that Agassiz did not accept this) S9
228.2	Jeffries] B1; *om.* S9
228.20	my theory] A1; it S9
228.20–21	unalloyed pleasure in relinquishing his] A1; pleasure, wholly unvexed by having found himself convicted of an S9
228.22	touch] A1; come in contact with S9
228.36	philosophical] A1; religious S9
229.3	ancestrally] A1; *om.* S9
229.8	say] A1; consent S9
229.8–9	had souls of their own he] A1; might have souls, he S9
229.10	nearly] A1; *om.* S9
229.12–13	at nearly the same point] A1; *om.* S9
229.13	road] A1; road at a trust which with Agassiz was intuitive S9
229.14	VI] A1; V S9
229.16	in] A1; at S9
229.21	welcomed] A1; recognized S9
229.23	be] A1; be sometimes S9
229.23	towards many of] A1; toward S9
229.24	fact] A1; fact, but I heard much S9
229.28	and a] A1; and as a S9

229.29	gifts] A1 ; great gifts S9
229.30	interest] A1 ; interest, either, S9
230.1	I wish I . . . he said once] A1 ; nothing could be more delightful than his talk S9
230.8	wished naturally] A1 ; naturally wished S9
230.20	and laden] A1 ; laden S9
230.32	all] A1 ; *om.* S9
230.32	were] A1 ; were often S9
230.33	at times] A1 ; *om.* S9
231.5	known] A1 ; known, even at home S9
231.7	harden and strengthen] A1 ; strengthen and harden S9
231.7–8	a heartless neglect even] A1 ; neglect S9
231.8	remember] A1 ; strongly remember S9
231.18	VII] A1 ; VI S9
231.33	and] A1 ; and some times S9
232.1	given again] A1 ; reported S9
232.2	"a cruel uncle's ward" in his early orphanhood,] A1 ; in his early orphanhood "a cruel uncle's ward," S9
232.10	imagined] A1 ; had imagined S9
232.13	good] A1 ; kind S9
232.33	on] A1 ; in S9
233.9	error, cheerfully trusted] A1 ; error relied cheerfully on the trust S9
233.12	affirmed, and no man] A1 ; affirmed; few men S9
233.17	any] A1 ; *om.* S9
233.21	philosophy] A1 ; philosophy of life, S9
233.21	impress] A1 ; express S9
234.8	of] A1 ; on S9
234.10	like] A1 ; *om.* S9
234.17–18	but perhaps did . . . as he wished] A1 ; from time to time S9
234.19	VIII] A1 ; VII S9
234.23	poem of] A1 ; poem S9
235.6	said simply] A1 ; simply said S9
235.9	forgot] A1 ; really forgot S9
235.18	little] A1 ; little while S9
235.19	IX] A1 ; VIII S9
235.32	talked to] A1 ; told S9

236.9	presence] A1 ; present S9
236.12	humor and] A1 ; *om.* S9
236.21	her weak] A1 ; weak S9
236.22	own] A1 ; *om.* S9
236.28–29	self-distrust] A1 ; distrust S9
237.1–2	and tentative] A1 ; *om.* S9
237.3	should] A1 ; would S9
237.17	should] A1 ; would S9
237.19	to supply] A1 ; supply S9
238.1	X] A1 ; IX S9
238.12–13	foremost] A1 ; most strenuous S9
238.30–31	so far of] A1 ; then so far a S9
238.31–32	when we were first neighbors,] A1 ; *om.* S9
238.32	this] A1 ; his S9
239.20–240.3	known. ¶ Of as . . . . perfectly killing mock-gravity.] A1 ; known./X ¶ Of like gentleness, but of a more pensive temper, with bursts of surprising lyrical gayety, was the poet Christopher Pearse Cranch, who came to live in Cambridge rather late in my own life there. I had already met him in New York at a house of literary sympathies and affiliations, where he had astonished me by breaking from his rather melancholy quiet and singing comic character songs; but again it was with a mixed emotion, for which I was not prepared by my former experience, that I heard him at Longfellow's supper table sing the old Yankee ballad, "On Springfield Mountain there did dwell." The tragical fate of the "young man" who was bitten by a rattlesnake on his native hill took a quality from the pathetic gravity of the singer which still affects me as heart-breakingly funny. It was a delightful piece of art in its way, and Cranch could not only sing and play most amusing songs, but was as much painter as he was poet. I especially liked his pictures of Venice for their simple, unconventionalized, unsentimentalized reality, and I liked and printed many of his poems. ¶ Troubles and sorrows accumulated themselves upon his fine head, which the years had whitened, and gave a

droop to the beautiful face which had once been merry. I recall his presence with a tender regard, and I would fain do my part to keep his memory alive, for I think he did things that merit remembrance. S9

240.5–6   At Cambridge the . . . the neighboring capital. It] A1; Cambridge, as separable from Boston, was, I think, socially of a wider mind and finer spirit than Boston. ¶ It S9

240.11   too] A1; *om.* S9

240.16   all comers] A1; new-comers S9

240.29   ideal, as Boyesen portrayed them to him] A1; as Boyesen portrayed them ideal S9

241.5   was associated] MS; associated S9

241.6   I could] A1; could I S9

241.9–34   The air . . . . of doing wrong.] A1; *om.* S9

241.28   humanities.] A1; humanities. If I began to speak of the debt which I myself owe him in every high sort that a man can be bound to another, I should never have done; and again his delicacy would suffer. But P2

241.28   day] A1; hour P2

241.29   long] MS; *om.* P2

241.29   noisy] A1; trumpery P2

241.30   these] A1; those P2

My Mark Twain

318.22   XXIV] B1; XXV C

320.33   XXV] B1; XXVI C

Word-Division

List A records compounds or possible compounds hyphenated at the end of the line in copy-text and resolved as hyphenated or one word as listed below. If Howells' manuscripts of this period fairly consistently followed one practice respecting the particular compound or possible compound, the resolution was made on that basis. Otherwise his *Harper's* or other periodical texts of this period were used as guides. List B is a guide to transcription of compounds or possible compounds hyphenated at the end of the line in the present text: compounds recorded here should be transcribed as given; words divided at the end of the line and not listed should be transcribed as one word.

LIST A

		50.35	half-filled
		54.5	prevision
5.4	pleasure-pain	58.15	*jingle-man*
12.33	single-hearted	59.3	shortcoming
14.21	world-wide	59.4	shorter-coming
16.34–35	elm-dotted	64.8–9	snapping-turtle
17.9	landscape	65.21	pancake
20.1	undercurrent	69.6–7	horse-cars
20.13	birthplaces	70.16	boarding-house
22.15	ironmongery	83.14	post-office
22.19	coal-oil	83.20	newspapers
22.26	shoe-making	84.22–23	commonwealth
25.24	antislavery	84.27	simple-hearted
26.23	subaltern	88.8	savings-bank
30.5	man-of-	96.12	well-nigh
31.8	Commonwealth	97.16	book-notices
33.11	Book-Store	98.8	newspaper
43.33	New-Englanders	98.21	newspaper
44.9	fire-eating	103.13	mother-country
44.32	Burying-ground	109.36	neckcloth
45.6	sixteen-thirties	112.26	Silver-gray
46.14	haycocks	113.33	hardships
46.20	hill-sides	120.27	headaches

14.10	New-Englanders	166.4	provision-man
16.5	New-Yorkish	173.15	to-morrow
16.34	elm-dotted	179.21	sand-box
25.15	old-fashioned	183.7	half-mocking
26.15	forty-one	183.8	fellow-townsman
26.28	high-sunned	184.13	anti-slavery
35.1	proof-reader	191.27	drawing-room
38.11	dinner-bell	192.10	well-broken-
47.4	fellow-passenger	202.36	sixty-three
54.34	air-drawn	203.20	half-duties
62.3	office-boy	213.19	frock-coat
62.4	by-and-by	229.23	fellow-men
64.8	snapping-turtle	230.9	mid-ocean
65.9	out-tragedies	236.28	self-distrust
69.6	horse-cars	237.8	to-morrow
78.5	Custom-house	245.16	two-volumer
83.32	Lombardo-	250.24	post-office
	Venetian	251.8	eighteen-seventies
96.13	pure-minded	252.36	self-master
96.16	self-limited	254.4	trouble-giving
101.26	conscience-stricken	254.21	cigar-counter
110.16	well-meaning	264.30	long-remembered
111.14	first-rate	283.4	note-book
113.15	clean-shaven	290.3	lecture-manager
115.11	self-criticism	294.3	billiard-table
119.31	proof-reading	295.12	blood-curdling
129.20	new-ploughed	297.30	-next-door
130.15	brother-in-law	302.30	refreshment-
143.4	self-respectfully		counter
144.14	foundation-stones	302.31	railroad-
155.16	opera-glass		refreshment
157.19	brother-in-law		

Index to Text and Notes to the Text

THIS EDITION OF

LITERARY FRIENDS AND ACQUAINTANCE

has been set in English Monotype Baskerville,

printed on Warren's Olde Style by Clarke & Way

and bound by The C. J. Krehbiel Company.

The format is by Bert Clarke.